DISABLING CRIMINAL JUSTICE

This book considers the governance of autistic defendants in the UK courts. Utilising the social model of disability, it considers the dominant strategies of governance, including 'vulnerability', which the author argues obscures the rights of disabled people in the criminal justice system. In doing so it sheds light on how this group should be governed.

Drawing on rigorously-researched case studies of autistic adult defendants through the court process, the book brings together relevant legal and policy literature, criminological and criminal justice theory and disability studies to provide insight into the 'dividing practices' that affect the governance of disabled defendants' conduct.

Using interviews with elites and practitioners, textual analysis, and court observation of eight autistic adult defendants through their court process, the book investigates why the status of autistic defendants as disabled under the Equality Act 2010 has been overlooked in criminal justice policy and criminal court decision-making.

It explores the impact of the 'collateral' effects and 'symbiotic harm' of the criminal justice process on family members who support these defendants through the criminal justice process.

Disabling Criminal Justice

The Governance of Autistic Adult Defendants in the English Criminal Justice System

Marie Tidball

•HART•
OXFORD • LONDON • NEW YORK • NEW DELHI • SYDNEY

HART PUBLISHING

Bloomsbury Publishing Plc

Kemp House, Chawley Park, Cumnor Hill, Oxford, OX2 9PH, UK

1385 Broadway, New York, NY 10018, USA

29 Earlsfort Terrace, Dublin 2, Ireland

HART PUBLISHING, the Hart/Stag logo, BLOOMSBURY and the Diana logo are trademarks of Bloomsbury Publishing Plc

First published in Great Britain 2024

A catalogue record for this book is available from the British Library.

A catalogue record for this book is available from the Library of Congress.

Library of Congress Control Number: 2023949482

ISBN: HB: 978-1-50995-694-4
ePDF: 978-1-50995-696-8
ePub: 978-1-50995-695-1

Typeset by Compuscript Ltd, Shannon

Disabling Criminal Justice

The Governance of Autistic Adult Defendants in the English Criminal Justice System

Marie Tidball

•HART•
OXFORD • LONDON • NEW YORK • NEW DELHI • SYDNEY

HART PUBLISHING

Bloomsbury Publishing Plc

Kemp House, Chawley Park, Cumnor Hill, Oxford, OX2 9PH, UK

1385 Broadway, New York, NY 10018, USA

29 Earlsfort Terrace, Dublin 2, Ireland

First published in Great Britain 2024

A catalogue record for this book is available from the British Library.

A catalogue record for this book is available from the Library of Congress.

Library of Congress Control Number: 2023949482

ISBN: HB: 978-1-50995-694-4
ePDF: 978-1-50995-696-8
ePub: 978-1-50995-695-1

Typeset by Compuscript Ltd, Shannon

In Memory of MK

For my grandmothers Mary Tidball (1910–1992) and Maurine Dorothy Herbert (1922–2014); the intelligent fighter and the elegant writer. A generation or so later and you two would have dreamed beneath the spires too.

FOREWORD

LUCIA ZEDNER

The criminal justice system holds individuals responsible for wrongdoing. To do this it assumes a hypothetical 'reasonable person' who can justly be held to account. The system does not deal well or fairly with diverse populations in general and disabled people in particular. Marie Tidball's *Disabling Criminal Justice* makes an important and original contribution to our understanding of how criminal processes and courts do, or more often do *not* do, justice to defendants with autism. Tidball prefers the term 'autistic defendants', which she explains better conveys the structural disablement they experience, and yet also 'reclaims the term to allow people to positively identify as disabled'. Her groundbreaking book reveals the importance of language, how disability is conceptualised, and how the 'ableist' assumptions of the CJS stereotype and do injustice to neurodiverse defendants.

Tidball's enquiry starts with the striking finding that while autistic people offend at the same or a lower rate than other people, they are overrepresented in the CJS. Her powerful analysis and painstaking research explain why. They expose the multiple obstacles that autistic defendants face in navigating their way through the system. And they evidence the many ways in which criminal justice officials fail to respond appropriately or adapt their conduct and language when interviewing, cross-examining and interacting with autistic defendants.

The book benefits from a sophisticated theoretical framework that draws on the social model of disability to understand the disjuncture between the laws on disability and criminal justice decision-making in practice. It adopts a Foucauldian 'history of the present' to trace changes in the governance of autistic adult offenders in England over 15 years of policy development. In so doing, it explores how the category of autism impacts the rationalities and technologies of defendants' treatment, the objectives set, and the outcomes sought.

The core question the book seeks to address is 'how are autistic adult defendants governed through English criminal justice policy and criminal court practice?' To set about answering this ambitious question, Tidball has undertaken impressive empirical research, which triangulates textual analysis of policy documents, legislation, elite interviews with decision-makers, and court observation.

Perhaps the richest and most thought-provoking contributions are to be found in her extensive accounts of court cases involving autistic defendants – an undertaking pursued with commendable sensitivity to the needs and interests of her research subjects. The central chapters of the book are replete with poignant illustrations of how persistent failures of understanding impact defendants and how criminal justice decision-makers struggle to respond appropriately to ensure a coherent approach to decision-making. These findings graphically illustrate the difficulties autistic defendants face. More positively, Tidball's pioneering research offers vitally important insights that inform the book's larger normative project of seeking to articulate ways of doing justice to difference and disability.

Marie Tidball's *Disabling Criminal Justice* makes a unique contribution to our understanding of how the CJS governs and misgoverns autistic defendants. Importantly, it shows how this better understanding might allow us to meet their needs and protect their rights.

Professor Lucia Zedner
Senior Research Fellow in Law, All Souls College
Professor, Faculty of Law, University of Oxford

FOREWORD

ANNA LAWSON

Disabling Criminal Justice, by Marie Tidball, is an important and engaging book which deserves to have long-lasting and far-reaching influence on scholarship and practice.

The book's particular focus is the interaction between the English criminal justice system and autistic defendants. Through the richness of the qualitative data it presents, readers are provided with powerful insights into the lives of autistic defendants and their families, whose experiences are thereby centred in the analysis. The data also sheds new light on the workings of professionals and structures in the criminal justice system. This original research is itself a valuable addition to existing knowledge and literature – but that is only part of what the book contributes to both criminological and disability studies scholarship.

Drawing on her cross-method qualitative research, as well as a wealth of interdisciplinary literature, Tidball crafts a compelling argument for a normative reorientation of the premises underpinning how the criminal justice system 'governs' autistic defendants. She argues that there is an urgent need to move away from approaches based on the mad/bad dichotomy. She also demonstrates how the concept of 'vulnerability' currently operates, in relation to autistic defendants, as a 'dividing practice' – an approach which, for various reasons, fails to achieve just outcomes for those individuals and risks obfuscating the rights of disabled defendants more generally. Tidball argues that, instead of relying on the concept of vulnerability to 'govern' autistic defendants, there should be a shift to an approach rooted in the recognition of autistic defendants as 'disabled' citizens – with 'disabled' here being understood in line with thinking based on a social model of disability.

For people working on issues of criminal justice and autistic people, the significance of Tidball's book is obvious. The book, however, also has much that will be of interest to a broader readership. As an example of excellent, but still all too rare, interdisciplinary scholarship sitting at the intersection of socio-legal studies and disability studies, it is a must-read for all scholars working in this space.

A particularly striking and commendable feature of the book is its willingness to recognise and engage with legal, as well as real-life, complexity. Tidball's probing and highly thoughtful analysis extends beyond law conventionally addressed in discussions of the criminal justice system, to embrace issues such as the potential and actual impact of the Equality Act 2010 and the Care Act 2014. These insightful discussions will undoubtedly be of value and interest to legal scholars and practitioners working on issues of equality and care in contexts other than the criminal justice system.

Finally, the book will be of interest and value to scholars using analogous methodological and theoretical approaches regardless of their jurisdictional or geographical location. The meticulousness of Tidball's research, when combined with the clarity and elegance of her writing, create a piece of work destined to become a reference-point and guide for the criminology, disability studies and disability law scholars of today and tomorrow. *Disabling Criminal Justice* has the rare quality amongst academic books of being a gripping read as well as a very impressive piece of scholarship.

Professor Anna Lawson FBA, FAcSS
Professor of Law and former Joint Director of the Centre for Disability Studies, University of Leeds

PREFACE

'Jack', aged 42, received a diagnosis of Asperger syndrome while on a section 2 Hospital Order, following an attempted overdose. A year later, he assaulted his mother. This followed a string of minor offences and the police advised his parents to press charges as the best route to get professional medical help and access support from social services. At sentencing for the assault, the Magistrates' Court ordered a section 37 Hospital Order under the 1983 Mental Health Act. Jack was remanded in custody for three weeks before being moved to a forensic hospital specifically for autistic adults in another part of the country. Over the next five years, he was subject to a series of sectioning orders.

In 2011, Jack was given a section 3 Hospital Order, after his domiciliary local authority had failed to fulfil their section 117 Mental Health Act duty to provide aftercare in the course of discharging him from the original section 37 issued by the court. Consequently, instead of discharging Jack from the court's original Hospital Order, he was made an informal patient and advised to stay in hospital because the local authority would not fund a care package for him to move into supported living accommodation. Frustrated by his continuing institutionalisation, and without any prospect of being able to build a life outside hospital, he consumed a considerable amount of alcohol during unescorted leave. A violent episode ensued and the police were called; he was taken back into hospital and placed on a section 3 Order.

Nevertheless, once discharge proceedings from this section 3 arose, his local authority conducted a community care assessment and the social worker concluded that he did not meet the authority's eligibility threshold for supported living accommodation. This was startling, considering that he had not lived independently in the community for five years. His parents – both in their mid-seventies – were unable to care for him at home. He did not meet the eligibility criteria because the local authority in question had raised its threshold for care and support needs from 'substantial' to 'critical', under its new adult social care policy (BCC, November 2010). At this time, judicial proceedings were being brought against the council on this very issue. The council subsequently lost these proceedings and were compelled by the Administrative Court to restore the previous threshold (*(W, M, G, H) v Birmingham City Council* [2011] EWHC 1147 (Admin)). However, social workers were still being told by the council to apply a higher threshold within this banding. Jack remained in hospital, informally, until June 2012 when he moved into independent living accommodation. In August 2012, Jack died of a heart attack.

Foucault's 'governmentality approach' developed the notion of 'dividing practices' which recognises that how groups are categorised determines how their conduct is governed (Foucault, 1991; see Seddon, 2007). Jack's case came to my attention when working with his parents as Policy and Legal Officer at Autism West Midlands. This work[1] revealed to me the complex interplay between health and social care systems for autistic adults who come into contact with the English Criminal Justice System (CJS). It motivated the present research and the need to better understand how 'dividing practices' are applied to autistic adult defendants in the CJS, which is an underdeveloped area of criminological expertise.

Research that brings autistic defendants more sharply into focus, within the discipline of criminology, is especially relevant given the developments in the wider legal and policy context through the Autism Act 2009 and accompanying Statutory Guidance (DOH, 2010d; 2015a).

The way certain sections of society are governed is an issue brought to the fore in criminological debate by Jonathan Simon's work *Governing Through Crime* (2007). Jack's case reflects the findings of the NAO (2009) and the Department of Health (DOH) (2009a) that autistic adults were falling through the gaps in health and social care provision. Mental Health and Learning Disability Services were not providing support to autistic adults where these individuals did not have a co-occurring mental health problem or did not come under medical definitions of 'learning disability', which use an intelligence quotient (IQ) of <70 (*ibid*). These 'dividing practices' (see Foucault, 1991) existed despite the inception of the Autism Act 2009 and accompanying Statutory Guidance. These statutory instruments use the 'umbrella term' 'autism' to cover all 'autistic spectrum conditions, including Asperger syndrome' (DOH, 2010c: 10) and 'adults with autism' coming under the statutory definition of disability in section 6 of the Equality Act 2010 (see NAO, 2009; DOH, 2010a: 16). Further, conduct prohibited by this Act, and the duty to provide a reasonable adjustment applies to criminal justice organisations (E&HRC, 2015: 13; 44–56). Yet, at this time, rather than being considered under the statutory definition of disability, autistic defendants were characterised as 'vulnerable', 'risky' or 'dangerous'.

I wanted to investigate why the Equality Act 2010 was overlooked in criminal justice policy and decision-making, to gain an understanding of why there appeared to be a fracture in the nexus between the conceptualisation of this group as disabled under equalities law and national and local government policies on defendants with mental health problems and learning disabilities. There was also a disconnect between equality law, along with autism-specific policies, and its implementation by decision-makers in the CJS. Therefore, I also wanted to examine to what extent these criminal justice decision-makers considered the defendant's autism in their decision-making and the impact that these alternative characterisations have on the treatment of their case through the court process.

[1] I am grateful to Jack and his family for giving me permission to relate their story and to his solicitor for allowing me to use case records to produce this account.

The contribution of the book to the existing literature relating to autistic defendants and criminal justice policy is made clear. This book records a 'history of the present' (Seddon; 2007; Foucault, 1984), using the Autism Act 2009's journey through parliament as the temporal starting point, covering developing policy and practice towards autistic defendants over the subsequent 15 years.

All the more pertinent as during this period data has recorded increased institutionalisation of autistic people, with stories like Jack's, in inpatient care. As of June 2021, the number of autistic people in inpatient mental health settings remained stubbornly at 1,200 (NHS Digital, 2021). Research has shown that the inequalities autistic people already face were exacerbated by the impact of the COVID-19 pandemic (Pais and Knapp, 2021; National Autistic Society, 2020). The pandemic led to far reaching changes to law and policy affecting disabled people in the UK, impacting upon every aspect of daily life. From reducing the number of professionals needed to make a hospital order under the Mental Health Act 1983 to 'easements' of the requirements on local authorities to provide care for disabled people under the Care Act 2014, the Coronavirus Act 2020 had wide ranging and damaging implications for the rights and freedoms of disabled people in the United Kingdom (see Joint Committee on Human Rights, 2020). The pandemic also saw the 2020 lockdown result in numerous courts having to shut down; leaving a backlog of 41,000 trials by June that year (Mulcahy, 2021). Consequently, a shift to remote or virtual courts sped up the process of using digital justice and the potential for further exclusion of disabled defendants in the court process, without the right reasonable adjustments and inclusive technology. Rooted in this context, the actions and focus of the *2021–26 Autism Strategy* were further shaped by the findings from the APPGA inquiry into the Autism Act, along with the review of *Think Autism* and call for evidence which were published in 2019 (DHSC & Dfe, 2021). Towards the end of this period, we have seen an acknowledgement that too 'many autistic people and people with learning disabilities are being detained in inappropriate mental health facilities' for too long (Joint Committee on the Draft Mental Health Bill, 2023: 6). It is hoped that the ongoing revisions to the Draft Mental Health Bill 2022 will help to effectively secure 'implementation of community care improvements and stronger safeguards against inappropriate detention' including by implementing 'stronger duties on health and care bodies to proactively identify those in need of community care and provide it' (*ibid*).

Unravelling the interconnected pathways between the CJS, health and social care, and illustrating why embedding this change is so important, is a golden thread running throughout this book. Thus, the product of this book's research is a contemporary account of the governance of autistic adult defendants in England through criminal justice policy and criminal court practice conceptualised through a disability lens which draws on the social model of disability. Disabling Criminal Justice requires attention to structural disablement experienced by disabled people, including autistic defendants, and to understand how articulating a disability perspective in our discipline can lead to more coherent law, policy and practice.

ACKNOWLEDGEMENTS

No book's journey could be completed without the support, advice and guidance of a number of people. I am indebted to my insightful supervisor, Professor Carolyn Hoyle, for encouraging me to take risks, to be ambitious about its content and for the endless patience she showed in reading the multi-coloured early versions of the original doctoral thesis. Thank you also to the ESRC for awarding me the financial scholarship which enabled me to undertake this piece of work. The quality and content have also benefited enormously from the input of my internal examiners at the Centre for Criminology, University of Oxford, Professor Lucia Zedner and Professor Mary Bosworth, along with the care taken by my external examiner, Professor Jill Peay at LSE. I am grateful too to Dr Rachel Condry for our conversations and – mid-pandemic – for the Zoom meeting which gave me the push I needed to send my book proposal to a publisher.

On that, Hart Publishing was top of my list. I am indebted to Kate Whetter for making the whole process more accessible and enjoyable than I ever expected. Her enthusiasm for this work gave me the confidence I needed. She was ably assisted by Verity Stuart.

I am so thankful to the autistic people and their families who were part of this research and for letting me tell their stories. Without them, this book would not exist. I am exceedingly grateful to my friends, colleagues and experts in autism who helped to keep the research grounded – John Simpson, John Lish, Dave Sandy and Natasha Muirhead. My sincere thanks to my friend and amanuensis, Helen Neill, who transcribed the interviews contained within this research.

To my inimitable parents, Frances Tidball and John Tidball, my deepest thanks for engendering the belief in social justice which drove the conception and motivation to complete this book. Neil Walsh has been a phenomenal support throughout this process and has cooked the most delicious food. Without you, I would have been cast adrift. To our beautiful daughter for making me want to write something you will be proud of. Thanks also to my brother, for keeping me in laughter.

To my wonderful DPhil family, Dr Luke Rostill, Sarah Smith, Dr Katia Mandaltsi and Dr Diana Greenwald – you made the time researching this book much more fun. Thanks to my host of other friends who have been incredible cheerleaders, including Dr Kathryn Barush, Dr Helen Brookman, Dr Roxana Willis, Dr Insa Lee Koch, David Yates, Dr Shona Minson, Dr Harry Annison, and many other members of the Centre for Criminology, University of Oxford.

I am grateful too to Professor Jane Garnett and Dr Caroline Mawson for always having your doors open. Finally, my thanks go to Jeffrey Hackney and Laura Hoyano, my undergraduate tutors, who offered me a place to study law at Wadham over 20 years ago. That decision changed my life, and your counsel has remained invaluable ever since.

CONTENTS

PART I
HOW SHOULD AUTISTIC ADULT DEFENDANTS BE GOVERNED?

PART II
STRATEGIES OF GOVERNANCE: AUTISTIC ADULT DEFENDANTS AND AUTISM-SPECIFIC POLICY

TABLE OF ABBREVIATIONS

APA	American Psychiatric Association
APPGA	All-Party Parliamentary Group on Autism
AS	Asperger's Syndrome
ASC	Autism Spectrum Condition
ASD	Autism Spectrum Disorder
BCC	Birmingham City Council
CJS	Criminal Justice System
CPS	Crown Prosecution Service
CUREC	University of Oxford Central University Research Ethics Committee
DDA	Disability Discrimination Act
DED	Disability Equality Duty
DfE	Department for Education
DOH	Department of Health
DOHSC	Department of Health and Social Care
DSM	Diagnostic and Statistical Manual of Mental Disorders
ECHR	European Convention on Human Rights
E&HRC	Equality and Human Rights Commission
hfASD	High functioning Autism Spectrum Disorder
HMCTS	Her Majesty's Courts and Tribunals Service
ICD	International Classification of Diseases
LASS	Local Authority Social Services
LD	Learning difficulties
L&D Services	Liaison and Diversion Services in England and Wales

MOJ	Ministry of Justice
NAO	National Audit Office
NAS	National Autistic Society
NDTi	National Development Team for Inclusion
OMCCS	The Offender Management Community Cohort Study
PCC	Police and Crime Commissioner
PRT	Prison Reform Trust
SOPO	Sexual Offences Prevention Order
SSH IDREC	Social Sciences & Humanities Inter-divisional Research Ethics Committee
UNCRPD	United Nations Convention on the Rights of Persons with Disabilities
UPIAS	Union of the Physically Impaired Against Segregation
WHO	World Health Organization
YJCEA	Youth Justice and Criminal Evidence Act

TABLE OF CASES

TABLE OF STATUTES

1

Introduction: Autism, Criminality and the Criminal Justice System

Introduction

While feminist and race-critical criminologists have produced numerous examples of the law reflecting the 'subjectivity of the dominant white, affluent, adult, male' (Hudson, 2006: 30), analysis from the perspective of disability theory extends these critiques of 'legal man' to incorporate '"able-ism" as a key characteristic of rampant masculinist subjectivity' (Campbell, 2005: 112). Baldry et al highlighted the lacuna in critical criminology which, while taking account of race, gender and class, currently relegates disability 'to the status of an additional dimension of social disadvantage' (2008: 32). Their work aimed to move thinking beyond traditionally siloed disciplinary approaches, and consequently combined insights emerging from critical criminology with innovations from the discipline of critical disability studies (2008: 31) – most notably the 'social model of disability' (see above; chapter three). This model, upon which much of this discipline is premised, makes a distinction between impairment, a condition of the mind or body, and disablement, a form of disadvantage or restriction of activity, caused by the failure to take account of impairment. Such failure leads to barriers to participation in mainstream social activities, which are imposed on top of impairment (UPIAS 1976, in Oliver, 1990: 22). Criminological theory and criminal justice practice have often sought to categorise offenders with mental health problems through the reductive binary of 'mad' or 'bad', perpetuating a crude and 'false dichotomy' (Seddon, 2007). Building on the work of Baldry et al (2008; 2012), this book argues that there is descriptive and normative value in proactively categorising these groups as 'disabled' under the 'social model' of 'disability' (see chapter three). The development of this theoretical model provides a critical framework for the qualitative research in chapters four to eight and is vital in realising the normative objective of establishing how autistic defendants *should* be governed (see chapter ten).

This intellectual venture is timely given the entrenchment of this model in the Equality Act 2010 and the inception of the Autism Act 2009, Statutory Guidance and related policy which has brought the treatment of autistic adults to the fore in public policy-making over the last 15 years. The 2009 Autism Act and its accompanying Autism Strategy (2010; 2014) and Statutory Guidance (DOH, 2010; 2015) recognised the lacuna in provision of public services for autistic adults, and related social exclusion; it signalled a focus by legislators on enabling autistic individuals to live more fulfilling and rewarding lives in our society. The 2006 United Nations Convention on the Rights of Persons with Disabilities (UNCRPD) was ratified by the UK Government on 8 June 2009. Therefore, it is particularly germane to utilise the 'intellectual resources' available in critical disability studies to develop modes of theorising about the governance of autistic adult defendants in the English criminal justice system (CJS).

Section 1 below describes how this book integrates the 'governmentality' analytical approach (Foucault, 1984; Seddon, 2007; Lippert and Stenson, 2010) and together with the 'social model of disability', from disability studies, to formulate a more sophisticated theoretical model for understanding the governance of autistic adult defendants. The social model has also assisted in relating the various strands of 'psy' literature on autism and crime/autism and criminal justice to the studies within criminology. Section 2 defines terminology that will be used. Section 3 presents an interdisciplinary literature review, highlighting gaps in knowledge about how autistic individuals are governed in the English CJS, and Section 4 outlines the book's objectives and structure.

1. The Governmentality Analytical Approach and Research Questions

Drawing on Foucault, Seddon's work focuses on the 'dividing practices' that channel individuals into prisons, rather than on the field of 'mentally disordered offenders' as a whole. He sees the 'dividing practices' as a contextual tool to bring together three interconnected areas: the modes of objectifying, categorising and distinguishing human subjects; the social and human sciences which provide the language and discursive resources for these modes of 'knowing' human beings and making them subjects; and the modes of controlling, containing and regulating the subjects thus classified (2007: 14). While ultimately dismissing the dichotomy of 'mad' and 'bad' as 'a misleading simplification which leads to analytical imprecision', Seddon nevertheless acknowledges the value of 'dividing practices' which go beyond this dualism to 'encompass interconnected questions about responsibility, social order, cultural sensibilities, treatability, resources and risk management' (2007: 158–9). Although autistic offenders are not considered directly by Seddon, this work is useful in articulating the changing relationship between the penal and welfare domains for offenders with mental health problems. Since this has not been explored for autistic defendants, this conceptual tool can be used in analysis of the governance of this group. Seddon's critique of the mad-bad dichotomy can be used to question some of the assumptions and discussion within the 'psy' disciplines about the intrinsic link between the symptomatology of autism and violence/symptomatology of autism and crime. However, it fails to contextualise the dividing practices of the CJS within broader academic studies which have recorded the historically-differentiated construction of disability as a social category (Stone, 1985; Hughes, 2002).

Currently, there is limited work which considers autistic defendants from a disability perspective (see Rogers, 2019; Smith, 2023; Vinter and Dillon, 2023) and even more limited research examining their 'governance', compared to those with learning disabilities (see Baldry et al, 2009; Spivakovsky, 2014a, 2014b; Spivakovsky and Steele, 2021) and mental health problems (see Seddon, 2007; Dowse et al, 2009; Ben-Moshe, 2011; Steele, 2017). In posing the question 'how are autistic defendants governed through criminal justice policy and criminal court practice?' this book takes a governmentality approach as its mode of analysis. Utilising the notion of 'dividing practices', it deploys what Donzelot calls the three concepts of governmentality's research programme – strategies, technologies, and programmes of government (Donzelot, 1979) – while responding to Lippert and Stenson's call to incorporate 'the real' into the governmentality approach (2010; see chapter two). Thus, the governmentality approach enables analysis of the governance of this group on a number of levels, attending 'to the nexus between everyday practices and techniques, and more abstract technologies and broader political rationalities' while avoiding 'the political insulation characteristic of many micro-focused frameworks' (O'Malley et al, 1997: 503). Analysing this 'nexus' reflects the approach of the section 149 Public Sector Equality Duty in its application to policy and actions of decision-makers. Analogies can also be drawn between the concept of 'cumulative impact', which has been developed by the Equality and Human Rights Commission (E&HRC, 2012a: 15), and the three concepts of governmentality's research programme.

The shifting landscape of the clinical governance of autistic adults (see NICE, 2012; NICE, 2021) and research which indicates a failure to identify and address autistic peoples' disability within the CJS (Slavny-Cross et al, 2022) makes the governmentality approach highly relevant. The *Diagnostic and Statistical Manual of Mental Disorders, Fifth Edition*[1] (DSM-V) (APA, 2013) collapses the Asperger Syndrome (AS) category into 'a single category called Autism Spectrum Disorder' (NICE, 2012: 11) in parallel with the use of the inclusive 'umbrella' term 'autism' (see DOH, 2010). This continues in more recent policy documents (DOHSC and DfE, 2021), in order to ensure people with AS do not miss out on health and social care. Furthermore, AS was only recognised as a diagnostic category in 1996; before this time, professionals struggled to diagnose this group of individuals, many of whom received no diagnosis or were misdiagnosed (Haskins and Silva, 2006). The issue of dividing practices is particularly pertinent as autism is often referred to

[1] Two international classification systems set out the diagnostic criteria for autism used by clinicians: the American Psychiatric Association's Diagnostic and Statistical Manual version-V (DSM-V) and the World Health Organization's (WHO) International Classification of Diseases version-10 (ICD-10) (1992). Both systems define and diagnose autism in a similar way, based on the observation of behavioural traits.

as a spectrum condition, because of the 'range of ways it can impact on people and the different levels of support they may need across their lives' (DOHSC and DfE, 2021: 8). Autism's spectrum nature compounds the issues arising out of the controlling, containing and regulation of this group dependent on how individuals are categorised. Chapters four to eight describe how misunderstandings and misconceptions around the nature of this spectrum impact directly on the choice of disposal for autistic adult defendants; for example, the perception by criminal justice decision-makers that it is a spectrum of severity.

Strategies of government, later referred to as rationalities (Gordon, 1991: 3), comprise epistemological 'assumptions and a particular idiom that enables a problem to be translated into language that then makes it amenable to intervention' (Rose, 1999; Gilling, 2010: 1143). The '"market-consumer" or neoliberal discourse' heavily underpinned the austerity measures introduced by the previous Coalition and Conservative governments of the last 13 years, 'rather than the progressive agenda of the Disability Movement', is currently the 'main ideological driver of personalisation' (Ferguson, 2012: 56). This book, therefore, investigates which rationalities are applied in criminal justice policy and how these are translated into technologies of governance of autistic defendants. As Lippert argues 'the governmentality analytic promises to unearth aspects of human rights regimes and their interface with state crime and control that may themselves lead to progressive intervention' (2016). The Liaison and Diversion agenda – developed in parallel to the Equality Act 2010 and the Autism Act 2009 (see chapter five) – made offenders with mental health problems and learning disabilities (as a subset of the broader category of 'vulnerable defendants') a locale for the attention of policy-makers. Thus, what emerged from the current research was the dominant rationality of 'vulnerability'. Chapter four contends that the social model of disability provides a better analytical framework than the concept of 'vulnerability' in enabling the exploration of the 'social, political, cultural, and economic factors that define disability and shape personal and collective responses to difference' (Baldry et al, 2008: 32).

'Technologies' of government are 'intellectual and material means and routines that make different forms of rule possible', such as risk management techniques (Lippert and Stenson, 2010: 477; Dean, 1999; Lippert, 2010). 'Programmes' are 'prescriptions, plans or schema for acting on some aspect of social conduct'. These 'constitute a space within which the objectives of government are elaborated, and where plans to implement them are dreamed up' (Miller and Rose, 1990: 14). Rose et al explicate that 'analysis of governmentalities':

> seeks to identify these different styles of thought, their different formation, the principles and knowledges that they borrow from and generate, the practices that they consist of, how they are carried out, their contestations and alliances with other arts of governing (2006: 84).

Chapter five analyses the autism-specific 'programmes of governance' arising out of the Autism Act 2009 and how these apply to autistic defendants. From a governmentality perspective, Rose posits that 'it becomes apparent that each formulation of an art of governing embodies, explicitly or implicitly an answer to the following questions': 'Who or what is to be governed?'; 'How should they be governed?' and 'To what ends should they be governed?' (ibid: 85). These questions have been used to frame the book's primary research question: *how are autistic adult defendants governed through English criminal justice policy and criminal court practice?*

'Who or what is to be governed?' In posing the first subsidiary question, the present research sought to understand how the categories of defendants with mental health problems and learning disabilities were applied to autistic defendants. It explored whether they were considered in terms of their legal status as citizens with disabilities under the Equality Act 2010, or whether they were more commonly conceptualised as dangerous, 'risky', mentally disordered or vulnerable. In posing this question, the intention was to discern to what extent there was coherence between the legal framework provided by the Equality Act 2010 in its ambit covering criminal justice organisations (E&HRC, 2015: 13), and policies directed at defendants with mental health problems and learning disabilities. Where decision-makers have taken into account the defendant's autism, the language and diagnostic categorisation used have been analysed. For example, do decision-makers differentiate the category of autism and the categories of 'Aspergers' and what implications does this have for the outcomes for the defendant?

'How should they be governed?' The utility of the governmentality approach is that it provides 'the conceptual and analytical equipment for the critical engagement between theory and political practice' (O'Malley et al, 1997: 503) in order to render knowable the 'dividing practices' which are applied to offenders with autism and create space to make thinkable a normative position about how they *should* be governed. It is because the 'analytical tools developed in studies of governmentality are flexible and open-ended' that '[t]hey are compatible with many other methods' and 'are not hard wired to any political perspective' (O'Malley et al, 1997: 503). This makes them well-suited for integration with the disability perspective set out in chapter three and the normative venture that this book undertakes.

'To what ends should they be governed?' This line of enquiry leads us to understand more clearly how autistic defendants are 'juridical subjects whose conduct is to be limited by law, individuals to be disciplined, or, indeed, people to be freed' (Rose et al, 2006: 84). It also leads us to a further set of questions: at what point in the court process did the defendant's autism become relevant and to what extent? Is autism a relevant issue in mitigating or aggravating factors and decision-making around case disposal? How is autism considered in relation to fulfilling sentencing aims? To what extent does it impact on decisions about the appropriate disposal of autistic defendants by the courts? This perspective 'recognises that a whole variety of authorities govern in different sites, in relation to different objectives' 'instead of seeing a single body – such as the state – as responsible for managing the conduct of citizens' (Rose et al, 2006: 84).

As a result, a second question emerges: 'who governs what?' The case study at the opening of this book recorded the interface between the criminal justice, health and social care systems. The interaction between health and criminal justice is an issue which has been explored in great detail with regards to adults who have mental health problems (see Seddon, 2007) and learning disabilities (Talbot, 2008; Spivakovsky, 2014a; Spivakovsky and Steele, 2022). However, the interaction with, and influence of, the adult social care system has not been considered in the same level of detail and has only rarely been discussed (see Prison Reform Trust, 2012) in relation to autistic offenders. This book does not include a systemic analysis of the interface between criminal justice and social care. However, it does investigate the interaction between criminal justice and adult social care policy as a potential 'interconnecting variable' which may be one of a number of factors leading to the potential 'elevated prevalence' (Browning and Caulfield, 2011) of adults with autism in the English CJS. Further, the movement between these systems compels criminologists to examine changing epistemologies and better conceptualise individuals whose conduct is governed through the re-purposing of the adult social care system (see chapters eight and nine). This leads to questions about the role of expert witness statements in court cases and how decisions are made by the court in evaluating which service or institution is the most appropriate for their diversion or disposal.

'According to what logics?' At present, 'public services' within the CJS have no statutory obligations under the Autism Act 2009 and accompanying Statutory Guidance but are told to follow the guidance in order to 'help improve the delivery of the services they provide' (DOH, 2010c: 8; 2015a). Therefore, to what extent does criminal justice policy and criminal court practice acknowledge the Autism Act 2009 and its accompanying policy in their decision-making? Are there, in fact, any logics applied *per se* to autistic adult defendants?

'With what techniques?' There has been a modest but important growth of scholarship that has begun to 'show how civil and administrative processes are increasingly being repurposed so as to accommodate the goals of criminal law' (Spivakovsky, 2014a: 560). Drawing on Foucault's governmentality approach in relation to disabled people in the Australian jurisdiction, Spivakovsky calls for criminologists to 'explore the myriad ways by which operations of punishment and punitiveness are being recruited, reconfigured and repurposed across justice arenas in the name of governing the population' (2014a: 4). This research is delimited to looking at the governance through the criminal courts of autistic adult defendants up to and including disposal options but not beyond. Nevertheless, in understanding the kinds of techniques of governance that are used for adults with autism, it documents whether, for example, risk management techniques are recruited and whether criminal court disposals reconfigure or repurpose health and social care processes to accommodate the goals of criminal law (see chapters eight and nine).

2. Defining Key Terms

A. Autism

Terminology used to define autism varies across jurisdictions, between professions and professionals and among individuals who are themselves on the autism spectrum. Autism is a life-long 'spectrum condition' (Wing, 1995) because, although autistic people share the same difficulties, the condition affects people with autism in different ways (NAO, 2009: 4). In the United Kingdom, Autism Spectrum Condition (ASC) is often preferred to Autism Spectrum Disorder (ASD) by some authors and those individuals with a diagnosis themselves, because this group is neurologically different but 'not necessarily "disordered"' (NICE, 2012a: 18). Subgroup diagnostic categories such as autism, AS, pervasive developmental disorders and atypical autism are also used by professionals within research and practice (ibid). American psychiatrist Leo Kanner introduced the modern construct of autism (Kanner, 1943). A year later, the Viennese paediatrician Hans Asperger gave an account of a similar phenomenon, autistic psychopathy (1944), which formed the basis of the modern diagnostic construct of Asperger's disorder (or Syndrome) (Cashin and Newman, 2009). The development of the AS sub-category partly reflects divergence in parallel accounts of similar phenomena and partly historical clinical differentiation: while both conditions share what has been known as the 'triad of impairments' involving difficulties with social interaction, communication and a restricted and stereotyped pattern of behaviour (Wing, 1995; APA, 1994; 2000), in AS there is no developmental language delay and IQ is always >70 (NICE, 2012a). Whether or not 'autistic and Asperger's disorders are separate entities is a contentious issue' (see Cashin, 2006; Eisenmajer et al, 1996; Gillberg, 1998); nonetheless, the distinction played a marked role in allocation of resources and access to services in the English policy context (see DOH, 2010a; chapters four and five) in the period leading up to the first autism strategy and statutory guidance and beyond.

The DSM-V collapses the sub-categories of AS and autism into one single category called Autism Spectrum Disorder (ASD), now characterised by impairments in two domains: '(A) social-communication and (B) strongly repetitive behaviour/difficulties adjusting to rapid and unexpected change/unusually narrow interests' (NICE, 2012a: 18; APA, 2013). Specific difficulties in these domains are discussed below where they are relevant to the prevalence of offenders with autism, patterns of offending and association with violence and criminality. Sensory processing differences are also common, hypo-sensitivities across *all* sensory domains to a high degree which amount to exaggerated responses to one or more types of sensory stimuli (Schoen et al, 2008; see chapter seven below). Indeed, the All-Parliamentary Party Group on Autism (APPGA) inquiry highlighted evidence that autistic people often find prison environments overwhelming because they can be noisy, brightly lit and cause sensory distress (2019). In parallel, to the changes in clinical language, the inclusive 'umbrella' term 'autism' is used in recent legal and policy documents to cover all individuals on the autism spectrum, including individuals with AS (Autism Act 2009; DOH, 2010a, b, c; NICE, 2021; DOHSC and DfE, 2021). The term 'autism' is used in this sense here to create a nexus between the present research and these policy developments. However, when discussing original research studies, the specific terminology used by the authors will be cited. This will ensure the authors' work is accurately represented and reflects their potentially significant use of certain categorisations.

Although there are similarities in the key issues affecting offenders with mental health problems and learning disabilities, autism is given special attention in this book for a number of reasons. Firstly, it has particular features which challenge mainstream accounts of criminality and corresponding standard criminal justice responses. Secondly, as co-occurring mental health problems and learning disabilities are not always present, autistic adults often faced barriers in accessing services and support as they did not fit into health and social care provision support preceding the Autism Act 2009 and through the poor and uneven implementation of its provisions across English Local Authorities (see chapter five). This means the inter-connecting variables (Browning and Caulfield, 2011; see below) which lead them onto criminal justice pathways are likely to differ from those with mental health problems and learning disabilities. Thirdly, many adults with 'unrecognised autism' may only receive a diagnosis after coming into contact with the CJS as offenders or victims (Hare et al, 1999). Hence, they will have previously missed out on access to services that a diagnosis facilitates, making a governmentality analysis particularly apposite.

B. Person-First and Identity-First Language

Over the last five decades there has been an evolving debate around the use of person-first ('person(s) with disabilities') and identity-first ('disabled people') language in disability studies scholarship, in national and international law and policies on disabled people, by Disabled People's Organisations and, most importantly, by disabled people themselves. Originally, 'persons with disabilities' was proposed in the 1970s to signify that disability 'is one component of a person's identity, rather than the only defining feature', and as an 'alternative option to the standard identifiers "disabled" or "handicapped"' (Vivanti, 2019: 691). It is the phraseology used by the United Nations Convention on the Rights of Persons with disabilities (2006; 'UNCRPD') and was chosen at the time, to be in 'accordance with the approach adopted in the Standard Rules', because it had been suggested that the term 'disabled persons' might be 'misinterpreted to imply that the ability of the individual to function as a person has been disabled' (UN General Assembly, 1993; UN Committee on Economic, Social and Cultural Rights (CESCR), 1994: para 4; Schulze, 2010: 35). In placing the person before the disability, person-first language for 'people with autism', for example, 'conveys an emphasis on the person's unique combination of strengths, needs, and experiences (both related and unrelated to their disability)', and acknowledges that these 'might be different from those of others who happen to have the same diagnosis' (Vivanti, 2019: 691).

Furthermore, the term 'persons with disabilities' was perceived as expressive of the 'social dimension of disabilities' (as a collective group with shared experiences), as highlighted in the CESCR General Comment that:

> [t]hrough neglect, ignorance, prejudice and false assumptions, as well as through exclusion, distinction or separation, persons with disabilities have very often been prevented from exercising their economic, social or cultural rights on an equal basis with persons without disabilities. (1994: para 15)

Conversely, those who prefer an identity-first approach and use 'disabled people' do so because it connotes the fact that people with impairments are disabled by barriers constructed by society – reflecting the social cause, nature of exclusion and discrimination of those barriers – as opposed to being disabled by the impairment itself (Inclusion London, 2015). Thus, the person-first term 'people with disabilities' does not accurately reflect this disablement by society in the social model, 'confusing impairment and disability by implying disability is something caused by the individual' (DRUK, 2022). Putting 'disabled' before 'people', therefore, signifies 'identification with a collective cultural identity' (DRUK, 2022; Spectrum CIL, 2018: 5). Consequently, it is also preferred by many because it reclaims the term to allow people to positively identify as disabled, allowing for important recognition of the identity politics which form part of disability studies scholarship and the disabled people's movement.

Thus, for autistic people, that terminology, advances 'the idea that the diagnosis itself should be reason for pride and respect' (Vivanti, 2019: 691). Over the last 20 years, person-first language has been challenged by disabled people and Disabled People's Organisations (DPOs) generally (Inclusion London, 2015; DRUK, 2022; Spectrum CIL, 2018: 5), by autistic self-advocates specifically (see Sinclair, 1999) and scholars alike (Kenny et al, 2016; Gernsbacher, 2017). There has also been a change of usage in policy and practice relating to autism over the last decade from 'person with autism' in the earlier strategy and statutory guidance (DOH, 2010a; DOH, 2015) to 'autistic people' in the most recent iteration of the strategy (DOHSC and DfE, 2021).

There 'remains an open and passionate debate about appropriate language and terminology' (Smith, 2023). It should be noted that some have argued that the two terms are not mutually exclusive, can sometimes be used interchangeably (Goodley, In Press) and scholars writing about autism should use the term most relevant to the context in which they use it (Dunn et al, 2015; Vivanti, 2019). For this reason, where a direct quotation is used, the present book cites verbatim the term used in the source materials. In the remaining description and critical analysis herein, the book uses the identity-first language when referring to 'disabled people', 'autistic people' (as opposed to 'person with autism') and, where that person is a defendant (see below), 'autistic defendant(s)'.

Language has the power to drive change, and how society constructs disability (see Harpur, 2012). The terms 'disabled people' and 'autistic people' have been chosen because, in the context of the dominance of the conceptualisation of 'vulnerability' in criminal justice policymaking and practice, they help to purposively forge a conceptual shift to a social model approach to disability. These terms align with the growing consensus in the UK disability rights movement about the use of this language to counter the embedded ableism in society. Ableist language – such as evidence presenting autistic people as 'emotionless' (Mundy, 2009) – is language which 'assumes disabled people are inferior to nondisabled people' and perpetuates deficit discourses on autistic research participants, (Bottema-Beutel et al, 2021: 18). So, it is important not to perpetuate stigma, stereotype and attitudes which create further barriers to autistic people in society. For this reason, 'Autistic people' is also the house style and replaces 'people with autism' in the most recent 2021–26 Autism Strategy (DOHSC and DfE, 2021; see chapter five) and the NICE style guides for all guidelines because stakeholders commented that the latter term was 'ableist' (2021). In contrast, many people with learning disabilities use this person-first language, as the NICE style guide recognises, and that is utilised in this book. Indeed, they often 'prefer to be known as People First (a common term of many self-advocacy organisations run by and for people so-labelled who work for the rights and recognition of themselves and their comrades)' (Goodley, In Press). People 'with mental health problems' is used – as opposed to person with mental ill health or illness or the mentally ill – in line with the approach used by mental health charity, Mind, as many people who experience mental health problems have told Mind 'this feels helpful and appropriate for them' (2023).

Finally, identity-first language is also consistent with the notion of 'neurodiversity' (Singer, 1999), which considers autism as one (neurological) form within a diversity of human minds (Nicolaidis, 2012; Robertson, 2010; Kenny, 2016). Consequently, autistic people may choose terms such as 'neurodiverse', 'neurodivergent' or 'neuroatypical'; as Goodley notes, '[s]elf-definition can of course contrast with administrative definition]' (In Press). A balance has been sought here, therefore, between using terminology which reflects a general consensus amongst disabled people in different contexts and with differing impairments, which is now reflected in administrative usage, and critical analysis of administrative definitions. For further, detailed discussion on this topic, Botha et al (2023) and Bottema-Beutal et al's (2021) pieces provide further nuance to these discussions; particularly in centring autistic people's voices, increasing participation of those who do not communicate verbally and avoiding ableist language in research.

C. Autistic Adult Defendants

Autistic adult defendants are defined as individuals aged 18 or over who have received a diagnostic assessment (see NICE, 2012a; 2021) of autism, which has been disclosed to a criminal justice decision-maker and made known to the criminal court prior to or during the criminal court proceedings, and who have been charged with a criminal offence. There are, of course, difficulties in restricting the definition in this way. On one view, it means the book is establishing its own 'dividing practices' by giving pre-dominance to medical definitions of the condition. Professional controversies abound (see Baron-Cohen, 2008) in relation to parameters of accurate identification, assessment and diagnosis of autism. Criticism can also be levied at the primacy which is given to decision-making by professionals who, in some cases, may have given a diagnosis when the defendant was a child or whose prior diagnosis is later called into question. After all, there is 'wide variation in rates of identification and referral for diagnostic assessment, waiting times for diagnosis, models of multi-professional working, assessment criteria and diagnostic practice for adults with features of autism' (NICE, 2012a: 367). Also, these disparate 'factors contribute to delays in reaching a diagnosis and subsequent access to appropriate services' (ibid) and in turn may become one of the 'interconnecting variables' (Browning and Caulfield, 2011) that lead autistic individuals to come into contact with the CJS. What is, therefore, lost in using the above definition is the opportunity to capture data about the difficulties faced by individuals who may well have autism but have not been able to obtain a diagnostic assessment prior to or during the court proceedings, and by individuals who may have only certain features of the autism spectrum. Again, this decision was made to strengthen the nexus between the research herein on governance by CJS decision-makers and 'administrative definitions' used in law and policy on autism. Further research is needed on self-definition and this is outside the remit of the present book.

The requirement that the defendant's autism be disclosed to at least one professional in the court proceedings, and made known to the court decision-makers, means that certain interesting data will not be discussed in this book. Multiple factors inhibit the disclosure of a disability in the employment environment for people with mental health problems (Wheat et al, 2010) and by autistic adults (Mazurek, 2014). There is limited research on disclosure of disability by defendants in the CJS (Bromley Briefings, 2014) and autism in particular (see Crane et al, 2016). The very nature of autism means that autistic adults may find it difficult to articulate their diagnosis. Although the use of autism alert cards may facilitate this process in the CJS (Archer and Hurley 2013; NPAA), there are difficulties around acquiring these cards, achieving consistency in how professionals respond to them and there may be factors which inhibit autistic people showing them to aid disclosure (see Reveley and Dickie, 2023). Parents and supporters can also play an important role in assisting the individual to get an autism diagnosis, as well as determining the nature, timing and extent of the disclosure of autism to criminal justice decision-makers. However, some individuals only receive a diagnosis later in life, as late as retirement, after the death of their parents (James et al, 2006; Bates and Tully, 2022). The issue of disclosure for disabled defendants, especially 'invisible' disabilities, also requires further research. Under section 15 of the Equality

Act 2010, 'Discrimination arising from disability', it is possible to justify unfavourable treatment occurring from or in consequence of the person's disability if the public authority does not know or could not reasonably be expected to know that a person has a disability (see HM Government, 2010: para 69). Therefore, these restrictions are necessary to delimit clear parameters of this book.

D. Criminology, the CJS and Criminal Courts in England

How criminology is defined and what it should encompass as a discipline is a highly-disputed question. Criminology is principally thought of 'as the study of the causes, patterns, and nature of crime itself' (Zedner, 2004: 32). The challenge of resolving these issues moved scholarly attention to the state's response to crime; the discipline, therefore, has long included the study of crime control, its institutions and its effectiveness (ibid: 32–33). The present book starts from the premise that the nature of crime and its control are interrelated. Space precludes extensive discussion of the proper parameters of the discipline, and these debates are best found elsewhere (see Bosworth and Hoyle, 2011). Instead, it is contended that because criminologists have always grounded their analysis in 'a nuanced sense of the world as it is, and as it is becoming' (Garland and Sparks, 2000: 2), the development of a more clearly-conceived disability perspective is vital. Disabled people, within criminal justice frameworks and scholarship, are in a position of ambivalence, which leaves disabled people in the 'simultaneous and contradictory position of centrality and marginality' (Steele and Thomas, 2014). Disabled people's voices are often silenced or marginalised, while disabled people are over-represented in the CJS (Thorneycroft and Asquith, 2021). Thus, foregrounding disability in the discipline of criminology as a whole, and not just the sub-discipline of critical criminology, is important because the absence of such a perspective leads to 'theoretical blindspots', and – to the extent that criminology can affect criminal justice policy (ibid; Loader 1998; 2006) – to discriminatory practice. In 'disabling' criminal justice (see chapter three), this book adds to the important work on 'cripping' criminology (Thorneycroft and Asquith, 2021), 'disabling' incarceration (Ben-Moshe, 2013) and forensic mental health detention (Steele, 2017).

Criticism has, rightly, been levelled at the description of a uniform CJS (Zedner, 2010) and, in fact, this is not a system in the true sense but more of a loose association of bodies (Ashworth, 2011b) and organisations. References made here to the CJS are to the bodies and organisations involved in responding to the alleged crime committed by an autistic defendant at 'any stage of the criminal justice process: before arrest, after proceedings have been initiated, in place of prosecution, or when a case is being considered by the courts' (cf NACRO, 2006; Bradley, 2009). However, this is not to assume that siloed policy-making and practice does not still occur. This study is restricted to the governance of autistic defendants in the English CJS rather than England *and* Wales because although the Autism Act 2009 applies to Wales, the original and revised Autism Statutory Guidance (DOH, 2010c; 2015a) does not. The term 'English Criminal Courts' is used here to denote the process from the defendant's first plea and case management hearing at the Magistrates' Court through to any possible referral of the case to the Supreme Court as the final court of appeal for criminal cases in England.

3. The Relationship between Autism and Criminality and the CJS

A. The 'Psy' Disciplines

i. Prevalence

A number of extensive literature reviews have analysed studies conducted in the 'psy' disciplines on the prevalence of autistic offenders in the CJS (Cashin and Newman, 2009; Chester et al, 2022; King and Murphy, 2014), Collins et al, 2023) and whether elevated prevalence evinces an association between autism and violence/criminality (see eg Browning and Caulfield, 2011). No established protocol exists for the process of screening offenders for autism across the many services linked to the CJS (Underwood et al, 2013). Consequently, there is no definitive prevalence figure and individuals may be more likely to miss out on appropriate support and diversion. Prevalence of autism is increasing (Attwood, 2022), with current estimates of 1.1 per cent for the overall prevalence of autism in the general population in England (Brugha et al, 2011; 2016). However, O'Nions et al's research found that a further 0.77–2.12 per cent of the English population may be autistic but undiagnosed as of 2018 (2023). Further, autism is likely underdiagnosed in women using standardised tools, so autism prevalence estimates are likely to underestimate true prevalence (Brugha et al, 2016).

It is difficult to determine accurate figures for prevalence in the CJS (Attwood, 2022) but estimates range from 3 per cent with some over-representation (Collins et al, 2023, see below), to autistic people making up 6 per cent of those with intellectual disabilities hospitalised by courts in England (Glover and Brown, 2015) and a prevalence of 9 per cent for neurodevelopmental disorders amongst prison inmates (Young et al, 2018). In the period in which the Autism Act was going through Parliament, and early in the last decade, as it was being implemented, discussion around prevalence in the CJS circled around Asperger Syndrome or higher functioning autism (hfASD), rather than the broader category of autism. In parallel, there were concerns about access to a diagnosis of AS, its exclusion from earlier diagnostic manuals and changing clinical approaches to including it within the wider autism diagnosis. Indeed, difficulty for people with AS to access services was one of the drivers of the Autism Act 2009 (see NAS, 2008; chapter five). The DSM did not include AS until the publication of (DSM-IV) in 1994 and so 'many forensic clinicians were not formally trained in diagnosing this condition in adults'

(Haskins et al, 2006: 374). Perhaps the focus on the prevalence of AS in this context was a response to the availability of this diagnosis whereas, previously, as Haskins et al note, there had been a lack of diagnostic paradigm to subsume the 'clinical features with which [forensic clinicians had been] presented' (ibid), coupled with an assumption that those with low functioning autism would be identified at a much younger age, with their 'challenging behaviour'[2] being managed in communal care establishments (such as residential and nursing homes). Further, because individuals with the AS diagnosis were 'associated with more intellectually able and higher functioning individuals than many ASDs, this presents greater issues for their identification and treatment … if they come into contact with the [CJS]' (Browning and Caulfield, 2011: 166).

Studies examining the prevalence of AS among offenders suggested that there was a higher rate of individuals with higher functioning autism than is found in the general population (Browning and Caulfield, 2011). However, these studies had mainly 'been restricted to forensic hospital settings' and 'failed to establish the prevalence rates in the general prison population' and thus it has 'been hypothesised that a significant proportion of individuals with an ASD in custody are undetected or unidentified or are simply misdiagnosed, often with mental health diagnoses' (Cashin and Newman, 2009: 71–72; Allen *et al*, 2008; Schwartz-Watts, 2005). Scragg and Shah (1994) undertook the first prevalence study within a secure setting. They examined the case notes of the entire male population (n = 392), and interviewed staff and consenting patients in their study at Broadmoor Hospital (1994). Using the diagnostic criterion of Gillberg and Gillberg (1989; 1991) they found that 1.5 per cent (n = 6) of the sample had definite Asperger's disorder and 0.8 per cent (n = 3) had probable Asperger's disorder, giving a prevalence rate of 2.3 per cent. Cashin and Newman point out that 'the prevalence rate of Asperger's disorder may potentially have been significantly higher if the hospital had accepted patients with a diagnosis of a learning disability' (2009). Five years later, of the 1,305 patients screened by Hare et al in the three English special (forensic) hospitals, 2.4 per cent (n = 31) had a definite Autism Condition, 21 of whom were classified as AS; and a further 2.4 per cent 'uncertain' cases were identified for whom insufficient information was available to make a clear diagnosis of an autistic condition (1999). No comparative study was done in the general prison population; therefore, there may have been a higher concentration of this group in the forensic settings (rather than in the wider prison estate).

As a result, these studies were subject to criticism that they lack validity because their samples were 'highly selected' (Allen et al, 2008: 749) and simply reflected 'sentencing policies and practice, which use mental health, rather than criminal justice, facilities for the detention of violent offenders with ASDs' (Woodbury-Smith et al, 2006: 110; Browning and Caulfield, 2011). Interpreting

[2] The preferred language around this term is now 'People with behaviour that challenges services' (NICE, 2021). This book uses this terminology unless referencing a direct quotation to reflect shifts in dividing practices.

these studies in secure settings as demonstrating an elevated prevalence of AS amongst the offending population as compared to the general population is highly problematic. Despite highlighting this point (ibid) neither set of authors teased out what the 'policy and practice' of this era were, nor did they properly differentiate between prevalence studies carried out in England and other jurisdictions (Siponmaa et al, 2001 (Stockholm); Mouridsen et al, 2007 (Denmark)) on the basis of potential variations in such policies and practices in these countries.

To address their concerns that the earlier findings in secure settings could distort the picture of the criminality of people with AS by representing only the prevalence of very serious offending, Woodbury-Smith et al found that offending occurring within people with higher functioning ASD was significantly lower ($p<0.05$) than that of the neuro-typical population group (2006). Allen et al, whose study was carried out in Wales, found little evidence to support the notion that offending was a significant problem in people with Aspergers (2008). The inconsistency in both methodological and diagnostic approaches taken in these prevalence studies has produced dichotomous results (Browning and Caulfield, 2011) and failed to accurately assess the numbers of offenders with AS, let alone the numbers who would come under the wider category of autism that might exist in the English CJS.

Systematic reviews have identified similar problems and a definitive prevalence rate for the number of autistic people, as a wider category, in the English CJS remains elusive. King and Murphy (2014) subsequently reviewed research on the prevalence of autistic people coming into contact at various stages with the CJS, their findings suggesting autistic people were less likely to offend than other people of the same age and gender. Interestingly a recent systematic review found that offending by autistic people, was at a rate equivalent to, or lower than the general population/comparison sample, in the 15 studies assessing CJS involvement in autistic cohorts (Chester et al, 2022). However, the studies suggest that the prevalence of autistic people are over-represented within CJS settings, with Chester et al attributing possible explanations within three categories: pre-sentencing CJS factors, such as autistic people being more likely to be caught for their criminal behaviour, to enter a guilty plea, or to have difficulty advocating for their rights in court; 'autistic offender factors', whether autistic people who do engage in criminal behaviour do so in behaviour of a higher severity; and post-sentencing CJS factors – such as harsher sentences for autistic people, a lack of autism sensitive forensic rehabilitative programmes and risk assessments contributing to extended forensic placements (2022).

Collins et al's Systematic Review of Autistic People and the Criminal Justice System (2023), largely focused on UK-based research, also concludes findings suggest that autistic people may be somewhat over-represented in the CJS. In the 16 studies with biased samples, where participants were already hospitalised in psychiatric inpatient services and thus already identified as a risk, 13 per cent of offenders were reported to be autistic. Whereas, in the 7 studies to include prevalence data of autism derived from mostly unbiased samples, 3 per cent of offenders were reported to be autistic (Collins et al, 2023). The authors note the variability of diagnostic tools and that the 'biased samples and methodological limitations of the research conducted impact the reliability of these findings' (2023: 3170). Particularly because the samples recruited cannot be said to be 'truly unbiased' as prisons may provide lower prevalence of autism due to people being diverted away from custody, at an earlier stage, as well as difficulties associated with the accuracy of diagnosis (Collins et al, 2023: 3170) and uniformity of diagnostic procedures to make comparisons (Chaplin and McCarthy, 2022). As others have stated, more research is needed which utilises improvements in assessment methodology in forensic and custodial settings, which involve women, those from different ethnic backgrounds and studies that use comparison groups (Chaplin and McCarthy, 2022).

ii. The Association between Autism, Criminality and Patterns of Offending

Hans Asperger identified a variety of forms of antisocial behaviour in his seminal study (1994). Wing noted that four of the 34 cases of AS to which she referred had committed 'bizarre antisocial acts' (1981). Successive studies within the 'psy'-disciplines (Mawson et al, 1985; Baron-Cohen, 1988; Barry-Walsh and Mullen, 2004; Chen et al, 2003; Chesterman and Rutter, 1993; Cooper et al, 1993; Everall and LeCouteur, 1990; Fujikawa et al, 2002; Kohn et al, 1998; Haskins and Silva, 2006; Murrie et al, 2002; Schartz-Watts, 2005) used clinical studies to hypothesise the association between AS and offending (Allen et al, 2008), shifting the focus away from likely prevalence numbers within secure settings at any one time. Using case studies of one or more individuals, a number of these use retrospective analysis (Silva et al, 2004) to determine whether AS was present in people convicted of serious crime. Their contribution to the 'understanding of issues relating to the prevalence and pattern of law-breaking and offending' is 'limited' because none of these studies provided a 'detailed developmental history' making it uncertain whether 'the individuals meet the criteria for a diagnosis of an ASD, rather than some other disorder' (Woodbury-Smith et al, 2006: 109).

In the earlier studies which hypothesised this association, the focus was upon AS and violence, not criminality. First, Mawson et al speculatively hypothesised that the 'association between [AS] and violent behaviour is more common than has been recognised' (1985: 569). Ghaziuddin et al (1991) then examined this hypothesis by reviewing 21 papers, published between 1944 and 1991, relating to people with AS in order to determine the rate of violence among these individuals. Only 3 (2.3%) of 132 patients described had a clear history of violent behaviour. Using less conservative inclusion criteria for the publications reviewed, they found violence in 11 of 197 cases (5.6%). Comparing this figure to the rate of violent crime in the US population at this time (7%), they concluded that there was no significant association between violence and AS (ibid). Indeed, research has shown that 'patients with an ASD detained in high-security psychiatric care have been found to have lower index offence violence ratings compared to patients with schizophrenia or a personality disorder' (Murphy, 2002). At present, therefore, there is no evidence 'to support the "robust association" between ASD and violent behaviour', evidentially 'any association between autism and violence is small and poorly understood' (Murphy, 2010: 463). Further, Chaplin and McCarthy are also careful to point out that the risk for violent behaviour is 'no greater in autistic adults and is significantly reduced when commonly comorbid conditions that are associated with violent behaviour are controlled for' (2022: 47).

Other studies broaden out the original 'hypothesised speculation' to look at the association between AS and other types of offending (Barry-Walsh and Mullen, 2004; Haskins and Silva, 2006; Allen et al, 2006). The findings cited above by Woodbury-Smith et al are compatible with the argument made by Howlin (2004) that autistic people may adhere to lawful behaviour more consistently than their counterparts in the general population, but there is some early evidence of a difference in the patterns of offending. Earlier 'psy' literature, based on the small number of court cases and clinical case studies, recorded 'anecdotally' some 'preliminary data to support a portrait of Asperger's offending which is characterised by one of three criminal activities that tend to be engaged in: physical violence, sexual assault, and arson' (Freckleton and List, 2009). For example, despite showing higher levels of compliance with the law generally, the committal of violent acts achieves a slightly higher rating than those reported by their neuro-typical counterparts in a community-based study (Woodbury-Smith et al, 2006).

Over the last 15 years, the literature has investigated the association between patterns of offending and the broader category of autism. Collins et al's recent systematic review found the types of offences committed by autistic individuals varied and included arson, property crime, sexual offending, drug offences, traffic incident/driving offences, stalking, fraud, theft, and robbery (2023: 3171). Cybercrimes (see below) were also be added to these patterns by the literature (Chaplin et al, 2013), although the incidence of the latter may be magnified rather than real due to high-profile cases such as that of Gary McKinnon (see Mackenzie and Watts, 2010) and Brandon Fleury (see Chaplin and McCarthy, 2022: 48–49). There has also been limited research which explores risk factors for autistic and non-autistic people for different types of offending (Collins et al, 2023). Comparing 40 autistic male offenders and 40 non-autistic offenders to a community sample of 40 autistic and 39 non-autistic people without a history of offending behaviour, Payne et al found autistic offenders scored higher for risk factors related to mental health, 'conduct problems' and family/childhood adversity (2020). In fact, an increasing number of studies have found that autistic people are no more likely to engage in offending than individuals without an autism diagnosis (Cashin and Newman, 2009; King and Murphy, 2014) and that autistic people are disproportionately at higher risk of experiencing abuse and victimisation (Brown-Lavoie et al, 2014; Sevlever, Roth, and Gillis, 2013; Allely, 2022).

iii. The 'Symptomatology' of Autism and Criminality

Many of the aforementioned studies (for example, Baron-Cohen, 1988; Murrie et al, 2002; Barry-Walsh and Mullen, 2004) made subsidiary points about the 'individual components' (Haskins and Silva, 2006) of AS/high functioning ASD (hfASD) or 'symptomatology' of autism (Freckleton and List, 2009) which may be associated with criminality or type of offending for an autistic person. Making a segue from the inconclusive association literature, Haskins and Silva are clear that in describing the features of hfASD 'that would most likely be involved when criminal actions lack occur' this 'is not to say that having a developmental disorder enhances the likelihood of acting criminally *per se*' (2006: 377–8). Difficulties in 'social-communication' may reduce the ability of an individual to be aware of, and reflect upon, the affective, cognitive and perceptual life of others as well as the self (Clarke et al, 1989; Abu-Akel, 2003) and potentially misunderstand non-verbal cues (Patton, 2019). This led some to argue, therefore, that autistic defendants may be 'genuinely unaware of the harm they caused their victims' (Murrie et al, 2002: 66) or unable to prevent themselves from causing that harm. Authors also documented offences closely associated with particular difficulties in 'strongly repetitive behaviour' and 'unusually narrow interests' (NICE, 2012: 18; APA, 2013) for autistic offenders who commit sexual crimes (Haskins and Silva, 2006; Allely, 2016) but the evidence is variable (see Chaplin and McCarthy, 2022), stalking (Mercer and Allely, 2020), arson (Barry-Walsh and Mullen, 2004) and cybercrime (Payne et al, 2019; Higham et al, 2021). Finally, literature records 'difficulties adjusting to rapid and unexpected change' (ibid) or unexpected events and rigid rule adherence to official and unofficial social rules (Allely, 2022), which have triggered heightened anxiety leading, in some cases, to criminal damage and assault (Allen et al, 2008).

Chaplin and McCarthy undertake a thorough examination of the literature on the association of autism symptoms and characteristics of offending (2022). They conclude that autistic people do not commit more offences because of the association between symptoms of autism but evidence from both case studies and the media indicates 'that those with autism may be more likely to commit certain offences such as computer-related crimes that are associated with core' diagnostic domains for autism (Chaplin and McCarthy, 2022: 50). The authors are also careful to point out that some of these 'symptoms may be protective and reduce the likelihood of offending' and thus it is also important to acknowledge the 'heterogeneous variability' across autistic people (Allely, 2022). Whether certain features of autism may have contributed to an autistic person's engagement in offending behaviour are not a '"get out of jail free card"' but crucial in ensuring the 'individual receives a fair hearing and that appropriate diversionary measures' are put in place (Allely, 2022: 19).

iv. Difficulties Negotiating the Criminal Justice System

By virtue of AS being a pervasive developmental disorder, it has the 'potential to impact upon almost every aspect of criminal responsibility' (Freckleton and List,

2009: 30) and research has shown that 'people with this diagnosis who do fall foul of the law clearly struggle to negotiate the CJS' (Allen et al, 2008: 757). As a consequence, a number of pieces in the 'psy' literature published over the last 20 years (Allen et al, 2008; Murrie et al, 2002; Katz and Zemishlany, 2006; North et al, 2008) have considered how the 'symptomatology' of AS and autism has led to autistic people facing barriers in negotiating different aspects of the CJS (see Chaplin et al, 2017; Cooper and Allely, 2017; Burch and Rose, 2020; see also Allely, 2022).

There is growing literature on the way characteristics of autism such as: (i) social interaction and communication, and (ii) restricted and repetitive behaviours, can affect communication in investigative interviews (North et al, 2008; Gudjonsson, 2018) and court proceedings, leading to misconceptions by criminal justice decision-makers on the autistic defendant's culpability, guilt and remorse (Archer and Hurley, 2013; Mattison and Allely, 2022; Allely and Murphy, 2023). Mattison and Alley provide a comprehensive overview of these issues in relation to Theory of Mind (ToM) and alexithymia, sensory processing, verbal and non-verbal communication, compliance and suggestibility, and memory and recall (2023).

The relevance of Theory of Mind (Baron-Cohen et al, 1985), where an autistic person may find it difficult to imagine the thoughts and feelings of others, was explored early on in 'psy' the literature. From their review of six court cases of adult offenders with AS, Murrie et al discuss the implications that features of AS have for decision-making in the CJS, as well as for disposition and treatment (2002). Namely, the relevance of 'Impairments in Social Interaction', including what was termed 'Deficient Empathy' and the resultant potential for 'Immediate Confession' by the defendant or for police, prosecutors, or jurors to perceive this as a 'mitigating factor that elicits sympathy' from police, prosecutors, or jurors who 'feel compassion for a person with an impoverished emotional life' and 'deficient in one of the normal inhibitors against crime'. Conversely, it may be viewed as an aggravating factor, 'alienating the decision-maker and eliciting fear of future crimes' to 'the extent … that deficient empathy is seen as cold, heartless, and remorseless' (ibid: 66). Research on whether judges' perception of this characteristic in examining aggravating and mitigating factors in sentencing is limited and was undertaken in the US, see Berryessa (2016). Chapter seven explores this issue further through the court case observations.

Scholarship on autistic people's experience of empathy has become more nuanced in this context in recent years. More is now understood about 'alexithymia', a term used to describe difficulties autistic people experience in distinguishing feelings from the bodily sensations of emotional arousal identifying and describing their own emotions (see Hill et al, 2004; Berthoz and Hill, 2005; Mattison and Allely, 2022). Allely and Cooper underline that, rather than a lack of remorse, inappropriate or unexpected expression might not be indicative or reflective of what an autistic person is thinking or feeling (2017). Reveley and Dickie's work is useful on 'street' policing and the perceptions and preconceptions of police officers when interacting with autistic suspects in the community, as well as the strategies and guidance which have been introduced to train professionals to improve police interactions with autistic people (2023). In particular, on the concept of 'context blindness' (Vermeulen, 2012) – the difficulty some autistic individuals may have transferring knowledge in one context to another – may affect how an autistic person responds to the police in the community, whether they produce an autism alert card or 'self-declaration' of autism in custody (Hepworth, 2017, Crane et al, 2016). Milton's 'double empathy hypothesis' contends that it is the differences between autistic and neurotypical peoples' perceptual frameworks that mean both groups can at times struggle to accurately perceive and appreciate the perspectives of the other group (2012; 2018). Reveley and Dickie draw on this to posit 'that greater emphasis should be placed on increasing officers' awareness of perceptual differences to facilitate greater empathy and understanding of autistic and neurotypical perceptual frameworks' (2023). Arguably, this is relevant across the CJS and needs further research regarding implementing this approach in practice.

North et al concluded that suspects with hfASD may be 'more prone to respond compliantly to requests and demands' because they are 'more eager to please or to avoid conflict and confrontation than controls' during interrogative interviewing (2008: 331). Of the 26 individuals with hfASD and the 27 gender- and IQ-matched controls, the group with hfASD were rated as significantly more compliant than the controls in terms of 'the extent to which they yielded to misleading questions or changed their answers following negative feedback' (North et al, 2008: 329). They also had higher scores on measures of depression, anxiety, fear of negative social evaluation and paranoia. In some circumstances, the tendency to respond in this way in a police interview may disadvantage a suspect. Psychological tests of suggestibility and compliance could, therefore, be related to police transcripts and the manner in which questions were phrased and how the interviewee responded to challenges (ibid). This could supplement an assessment of intellectual ability, providing important information about the strengths and vulnerabilities of an alleged offender (Gudjonsson and Henry, 2003) and help evaluate the legitimacy of self-incriminating evidence obtained during interrogation (ibid; North et al, 2008).

Further research has highlighted how verbal and non-verbal communication patterns of autistic people, such as difficulties understanding non-literal language, metaphors and irony (Allely & Cooper, 2017) may affect the perception of CJS decision-makers, so need to be considered by those interviewing and cross-examining autistic defendants. Similarly, growing research has highlighted the divergence in autistic people's memory and recall, which may be relevant to responses to questions and giving evidence (see Allely and Murphy, 2023). While many autistic people have enhanced semantic memory (general knowledge) and non-social details (including objects and surroundings), they may have difficulties with episodic memory recall for specific events, and may have difficulty consciously recollecting past events (Crane and Goddard, 2008; Bigham et al, 2010), with episodic recall taking longer (Goddard et al, 2007; Crane et al, 2012). Consequently, it is essential that the CJS have an awareness of autistic people's memory and recall differences

(Mattison and Allely, 2022) and a need for further prompting in retrieving specific episodes (Crane and Maras, 2018).

Hyper and hypo-sensitivity can result in challenging or self-injurious behaviour as well as adverse effects on communication (Pellicano, 2013). Sensory issues may be relevant at every stage of the CJS, including in the unfamiliar environment of police stations and courts (Mattinson and Allely, 2022), and formal police interviews could cause sensory overload and distress, leading to a negative experience for the autistic person or 'a poor level of engagement' (Allely and Murphy, 2023). Chapter six below discusses the barriers in court room design which emerged as potentially problematic for autistic defendants and their engagement in the court process. Murphy set out areas which should be considered when an autistic person is being interviewed, covering: personal safety, and ensuring the interviewer addresses any potential triggers for the interviewee; addressing sensory issues within the interview space, such as light and temperature; difficulties with reciprocal social communication which mean 'rules' of the exchange should be set out, along with the potential option of using devices to facilitate communication, such as a laptop; the cognitive style of the neurodivergent individual should be supported with clear, concise questions, which avoid non-literal interpretation and inference; and the interviewer should identify the potential for co-morbidity (2018). This has been augmented by Mattison and Alley as well as key recommendations for professionals when questioning an autistic individual in forensic contexts (2022; see also Allely and Murphy, 2023).

Barry-Walsh et al consider Fitness to Plead and Legal Insanity in England, Australia and the US. They argue that offenders with AS have 'deficits that raise the likelihood that their disorder will render them unfit or be of exculpatory value' given that, in all five cases reviewed, 'the offending behaviour was not recognised by the offender as being wrong' and the general reduced ability of patients with AS to 'reflect on how their actions may impinge on others' (2004: 96; 105–6). Even though they concede the variability of AS and the 'uniqueness of each individual's capacities' means that some individuals 'will have sufficient understanding to be morally responsible for their offending behaviours', the offending and disposal of people with AS should be placed in the context of the core features of AS by the courts to 'form a basis for sophisticated assessment of the issues of disability and legal insanity' (ibid). Freckleton and List go into considerable detail about how 'the nature of Asperger's disorder goes to the heart of determining responsibility for the commission of criminal offences in terms of the intentional element of offending' and 'also impacts at a fundamental level on the evaluation at the sentencing phase of the criminal process' (2009: 35). Literature also highlights the necessity of guidance for judges, juries, and magistrates to counter 'the risks of drawing over-ready (and inaccurate) inferences from the unusual manner' and the 'eccentric, tangential and formal' language of individuals with AS (2009: 31; Berryessa, 2014). There is limited research on judges (Berryessa, 2014b; Berryessa, 2016) and jurors' perceptions of autistic defendants (Allely and Cooper, 2017; Maras, et al, 2019) and the impact of this on sentencing. Nevertheless, it has been posited that some of the characteristics of autism discussed above may be 'perceived negatively' and may affect outcomes for autistic defendants (Freckelton, 2013a; Kristiansson and Sorman, 2008; Allely, 2022) making the role of the expert witness an important one in educating the court (Berryessa, 2017). Guidance to counter such perceptions has now been produced for judges (Berryessa, 2021). Findings on jurors' perceptions of autism indicate knowledge of a defendant's autism diagnosis can result in more empathetic feelings towards them (Maras et al, 2019); leading Allely to have 'strongly recommended' that the court should be presented with diagnostic and psychiatric information about autism (2022).

Two recent pieces examine why it is important for the courts to recognise a defendant's autism in order to receive a fair trial (Allely, 2022), to identify an autistic individual as early as possible in the criminal justice process, to address court actors (mis)conceptions and provide adequate support for these defendants to have access to justice by adapting the process to enable them to participate effectively (Allely et al, 2023: 47). Such reliable screening and identification of autism are still yet to be developed and implemented in many cases (ibid). Alley et al argue for access to special measures for autistic defendants (see chapter four) and reasonable adjustments which allow the defendant to sit outside of the dock, with a family member, or to have the assistance of an intermediary. Data is unavailable on systematic usage of such adaptations at present and their effectiveness in practice for autistic defendants (Allely et al, 2023). In Slavny-Cross et al's research, defence lawyers across 12 nations completed an online survey regarding one case in which they had defended an autistic client between January 2015 and January 2020 (2022). Eighty-five per cent of the 93 lawyers who had one such case, were in the UK. Respondents reported less than half of the autistic defendants had an appropriate adult at the police stage and three-quarters of the autistic defendants they represented received reasonable adjustments. Court case observations in chapters six to eight reinforce the picture that the usage of reasonable adjustments for autistic defendants are largely overlooked by the courts.

Beyond the courts, research indicates autistic people find incarceration 'far more burdensome' and may be more likely to be exploited in prison as well as being financially, physically and sexually abused (Allely, 2022). Hence, the identification of autistic prisoners is necessary to ensure their health and emotional well-being is maintained (see chapter eight below), and to enable their ability to reduce their risk of re-offending (Bates and Tully, 2022). Standard screening processes are not in place in English and Welsh prisons and there is currently no specific autism tool validated for prisons (Archer and Hurley, 2013; Ashworth, 2016; Vinter and Dillon, 2023). Research has documented challenging experiences for autistic prisoners in relation to communication and social interactions; routines, rules and predictability; and sensory environment (Allely, 2015; Allely and Wood, 2022; McAdam, 2012; Newman et al, 2015; Vinter et al, 2020; see also Vinter and Dillon 2023). Negative experiences of being treated differently to other prisoners can lead to them becoming lonely and isolated (Allely, 2015; Newman et al, 2019; Talbot, 2009) and there is increasing recognition that autistic adults are potentially 'more vulnerable' to bullying (Newman, et al, 2019). Positive experiences have also been reported, with some autistic individuals becoming more socially active in prison (Vinter, 2020; Vinter et al, 2020). However, there remains a relative absence of studies on female autistic prisoners' experiences (Vinter and Dillon, 2023). While there is limited research surrounding prison-based rehabilitation of autistic prisoners (Vinter and Dillon, 2023), Vinter's empirical research highlighted the implications of 'the challenging and supportive aspects of the prison experience', which have important implications for the extent of autistic prisoners' engagement with rehabilitative interventions (2020). Melvin and Murphy critique offending behaviour programmes for autistic people (2022) and, internationally there are no accredited offending behaviour programmes designed specifically for autistic people available within prisons (Bates and Tully, 2022).

Although the medical model (see below) dominates the literature in the 'psy' disciplines on autism, criminality and criminal justice, Vinter and Dillon provide an overview of the experiences of custody and implications for custodial rehabilitation for autistic prisoners through a social model lens (2023). The NAS Autism accreditation of prisons is one example given as demonstrating a shift away from a medical model approach where it is implemented (Vinter and Dillon, 2023), designed as a quality assurance programme to ensure autistic defendants receive adequate support across these settings (Lewis et al. 2015; NAS, 2021). Reasonable adjustments which have been documented in meeting this autism accreditation are provision of low-stimulus rooms and permission to wear noise defenders, to enable de-escalation and support autistic defendants with noise sensitivities, and the roll-out of training (Hughes, 2019; Lewis et al, 2016). Mainstreaming prison-wide adjustments could benefit many prisoners but the literature is careful to note that the heterogeneity of autistic individuals means reasonable adjustments tailored to individuals will also be important (Vinter and Dillon, 2023). Ultimately, some authors posit that custodial sentences 'may not be appropriate' for many autistic people, as characteristics of autism mean incarceration is 'significantly more intolerable' for autistic prisoners than the non-autistic population, leading them to advocate for a community-based sentence with treatment as a more appropriate option (Bates and Tully, 2022). Evidence on what this might look like in practice is scant, and how to avoid the 'net-widening' and the responsibilisation of family members and supporters (see Spivakovsky, 2014a) in the context of current social care support should lead us to approach such sentences with a critical eye (see chapters eight and nine below).

Thus, while there has been a growth in the 'psy' literature over the last decade to better understand the barriers autistic defendants face, which acknowledges the wider policy context, and a smattering of pieces which draw on the social model of disability, this material makes limited critical analysis of the strategies and technologies of governance of decision-makers in the CJS nor of the wider programme of government in law and policy; it is to this the present research makes a significant contribution.

B. Criminology and Criminal Justice: Interconnecting Variables and Difficulties Negotiating the CJS

Like offenders with learning difficulties, research on autistic offenders is limited within 'mainstream' criminological analyses (see eg Macdonald, 2006; Mayes, 2003). Browning and Caulfield made a useful contribution to the field by making the connection between potential offending behaviour of autistic defendants being attributable to 'other risk factors commonly associated with offending within the general population such as social circumstances or co-morbid mental health issues' (2011: 170). Further, that any potentially 'elevated prevalence' within offender populations, rather than an 'innate predilection towards offending behaviour', may be 'better explained in terms of certain interconnecting variables', including an 'inadequate level of recognition and understanding within the police service, the Crown Prosecution Service (CPS), the judiciary and the various criminal justice agencies, along with current justice policy' (Browning and Caulfield, 2011: 175). It is this latter 'interconnecting variable' that the current book contributes to, focusing as it does on the governance of autistic adult defendants through criminal justice policy and criminal court practice.

Centring on court practice, the present book builds on the canon of court-based studies in criminology. The seminal study by Bottoms et al, *Defendants in the Criminal Process*, placed the defendant centre stage in research on the criminal courts (1976). They were the first to look systematically at the choices that defendants made in their participation in the English criminal court process and the quality of justice as it was assessed and experienced by the defendants themselves (1976). Through interviews with the defendants and court case observation, the authors investigated defendants' substantial decisions about plea, mode of trial, representation (legal or otherwise), choice of bail or custody and appeal. Their matrix for 'scheduled routes' (Bottoms et al, 1976: 7) through the court process was useful in guiding the court observation carried out in Phase 2 of the present research (see chapter two). Over the course of the last 30 years, criminologists have carefully researched the differential treatment and experiences of women defendants in the criminal court process (see Worrall, 1981). They have also produced accounts of the role of race and ethnicity in sentencing practices in the Crown Court (see McConville and Baldwin, 1982; Crow and Coive, 1984; Hudson, 1989; Hood, 1992) and Magistrates' Courts (Mair, 1986). A comprehensive review of this literature can be found elsewhere (see Shute et al, 2005).

After the 1976 study by Bottoms et al, much of the subsequent research which takes the defendant as the focal point has concentrated on his or her differential treatment in the conviction and sentencing stages of court procedure by reason of gender (Wilczynski, 1997), race (Kalunta-Crumpton, 1998) and ethnicity (Shute et al, 2005). Later research helped to address the absence of consideration of the treatment and experience of female suspects (see Edwards, 1984) by investigating, for example, the impact of sentencing practices on women and their families (Daly, 1989) and whether the sex of the defendant is related to the severity of the sentence in cases dealt with in Magistrates' Courts (Farrington and Morris, 1983). At the end of the last decade, two books have added significantly to this canon. Owusu-Bempah's monograph explores the changing role of the defendant as a participant in the criminal process and develops a normative theory which proposes that the criminal process should operate as a mechanism for calling the state to account for its accusations and request for official condemnation and punishment of the accused (2017). Jacobson et al's ethnographic research within the Crown Courts of England and Wales provides a valuable insight into the different players in the courtroom and explores the extent to which the court process is viewed as legitimate by these actors (2016). Although acknowledging some of the issues faced by participants with learning disabilities and mental health problems (see Jacobson et al, 2016: 35–37, 42–43) neither of these texts draw on a broader disability perspective in discussing the particular challenges to our understanding of participation and legitimacy brought by considering disabled defendants.

4. Objectives and Structure

A number of different objectives are explored across this book's ten chapters, bringing together disparate bodies of literature and adding value to material discussed in the previous sections. One of the 'strengths of an interdisciplinary discourse is the cross-fertilisation of ideas between specialisms that facilitates comparative study and knowledge transfer' (Quirk et al, 2010: 1). This is an important venture given that the very nature of disability (and autism) is 'complex and calls into question a web of discourses and institutional practices' (Goodley, 2011: xii). The social model's distinction between impairment and disablement enables us to comprehend, on the one hand, the aforementioned 'psy' literature which explores the link between the 'symptomatology' of autism and criminality (the 'impairment branch' of the distinction), in combination with the 'interconnecting variables' which may lead autistic offenders into the CJS; and, on the other hand, the inequitable experiences of autistic defendants and the barriers they face in the criminal justice process (the disablement branch of the distinction). Drawing on critical disability studies, chapter three will develop a theoretical framework to understand and critique the instruments and decision-making processes involved in the governance of autistic adult defendants.

Chapter two describes the 'cross-method' triangulation used in this research – carrying out different types of qualitative methodology to study the same phenomenon (Hoyle, 2000; Webb et al, 1966). A vibrant array of research on the criminal courts in England has given important insights into the operation of justice in the courts for certain groups of defendants (see Baldwin and McConville, 1977; Ashworth et al, 1984; Shute et al, 2005). This chapter utilises this scholarship to carry out the governmentality research programme discussed above and informs the three phases of this book's fieldwork: textual analysis of policy documents and official documentation of court cases; court observation, including interviews where possible with adult autistic offenders; and semi-structured interviews with practitioners and elite decision-makers.

By examining the wider policy context and integrating qualitative research with criminal justice decision-makers, chapters four and five conduct an analysis of how governance from above 'interacts with "governance from below"' (Stenson, 2008: 5). In the circumstances of the shift towards localism initiated by the Coalition government's 2011 Localism Act, and continued by the present Conservative government, navigation between these levels of governance recognises that 'there is discretion and choice' within 'local political cultures … in which political leadership and decision-making are crucial in shaping policy-making and practice' (Stenson, 2008: 5). These chapters triangulate a textual analysis of policy documentation with interviews conducted with elite decision-makers to better understand instruments of governance as applied to autistic adult defendants. In chapter four, the discussion moves from national rationales and strategies of governance of offenders with mental health problems and learning disabilities to decision-makers' perceptions of the application of the Equality Act 2010 in criminal justice policy and court practice. The dominance of the concept of 'vulnerability' emerged as a significant theme, particularly in the roll-out of liaison and diversion services.

Chapter five brings into focus the developments in autism-specific law and policy: the Autism Act 2009, the Statutory Guidance, *Implementing Fulfilling and Rewarding Lives* (DOH, 2010), and the subsequent 'refreshed' autism strategies (DOH, 2014; DOHSC & DfE, 2021). It is argued in this chapter that the first Autism Strategy and Statutory Guidance missed the opportunity for coherent policy and practice, as its statutory requirements do not apply to certain providers of public services, such as the courts, and the police and probation services are only expected to follow its requirements by reason of best practice (DOH, 2010c: 8).

The language and argumentation used by legal counsel, the judge or magistrate, the defendant and witnesses reveal much about the 'wider structures' of 'states, economies and legal orders, and the like' (Burawoy et al, 1991: 282). Chapters six, seven, eight and nine detail the rich qualitative findings from observation of the criminal court cases of eight autistic adult defendants. The nature and extent to which the defendant's autism is considered by the judiciary at the different stages of the decision-making process is examined, including its relevance to fitness to plead; as a mitigating or aggravating factor; the nature and length of sentence and the adequacy of disposal options available to the court for this group. The court observation of lower courts and qualitative interviews explored in chapters six to eight reveal that there is still truth in Galligan's remark that 'the reality of the CJS is numerous associated processes in which decision-makers generally act independently and in ignorance of the actions of one another' (2010; 1987). These disparate actions and siloed working practices are made evident when many of these actors come together in the courtroom and are highlighted by the scrutiny of the court. Chapter nine examines the collateral impact and 'symbiotic harm' (Condry and Minson, 2021) for autistic defendants' families, an important theme in understanding the governance of the defendants in the case study cohort.

Chapter ten makes the normative case that autistic defendants should be governed through a conceptualisation of disability. This concluding chapter connects the levels of governance and reflects on the interaction between national policy on offenders with mental health problems, learning disability and autism and court decision-making. Building on the intellectual resources garnered from the development of a disability perspective in chapter three, it posits that it is necessary to move away from the reductive mad-bad binary and the dominant conceptualisation of 'vulnerability' to the recognition of this group as disabled citizens. This, it is argued, would enable a more coherent and dignified approach to criminal justice decision-making involving this group.

Conclusion

Examining the collection of work within the 'psy' disciplines, this chapter argues there is a paucity of discussion on the governance of this group and limited work which draws on a wider disability studies perspective to utilise the social model. Further, 'mainstream' criminological analysis is scant on its inclusion of such perspectives generally and on autistic defendants in particular. The inception of the Autism Act 2009, subsequent policy (DOH, 2010a; 2010d; 2014; 2015a; DOHSC and DfE, 2021a) and clinical guidelines (see NICE, 2012; NICE 2021) over the last 15 years makes a study on the governance of this group especially relevant. Recent clinical guidelines have augmented this research venture. This makes it all the more pertinent for criminology to address the changing epistemologies and ensure that it responds to Spivakovsky's call to 'explore the myriad ways by which operations of punishment and punitiveness are being recruited, reconfigured and repurposed across justice arenas in the name of governing the population' (2014a: 563) for disabled defendants. An integral part of responding to this call is to develop a more clearly-conceived disability perspective within criminology.

2

Qualitative Methods and Inclusive Research Participation

Introduction

There is limited qualitative work (North et al, 2008; Talbot, 2010) on what criminal justice decision-makers know about autism and what informs their decision-making about the governance of autistic adult offenders. Further, existing research does not consider autistic offenders from a disability perspective. The governmentality approach enables an analysis which captures the interplay of policy and practice; attending 'to the nexus between everyday practices and techniques, and more abstract technologies and broader political rationalities' (O'Malley et al, 1997: 503). It deploys what Donzelot calls the three concepts of governmentality's research programme – strategies, technologies and programmes of government (1979). It also answers Lippert and Stenson's call to incorporate 'the real' into the governmentality approach (2010) by using contextually suitable methodologies to conduct 'case studies' to 'dissect … moral language and practices from above and below' and allow the public to reflect on such practices (ibid: 488). This approach is central to the qualitative methodology used in this book; which involves 'cross-method' triangulation (Hoyle, 2000; see Webb et al, 1966) using different types of methods, broken into three phases.

Section 1 of this chapter discusses Phase 1 of the research, the textual analysis of policy documents and reported Court of Appeal and Supreme Court criminal cases. Section 2 describes Phase 2, which involved court observation; including interviews with autistic adult defendants, family members and their legal representatives. Section 3 outlines Phase 3: semi-structured interviews with practitioners and elite decision-makers. The limited but important criminological literature on the criminal courts in England informed the methodology for these phases because of the paucity of research on autistic defendants in the courts. Retrieval of criminological studies on the courts was conducted by a purposive and thematic literature review. *The Trial on Trial* (Duff et al, 2007) and *Standing Accused* (McConville et al, 1994) were used to find other seminal texts in this field, identify relevant themes and to retrieve studies with analogous methodologies to this book's research. These themes provided keywords for electronic searches of relevant high-impact criminology journals, SSRN and Google Scholar. As a core set of texts emerged, their bibliographies were reviewed purposively for additional texts.

A review of this material was then conducted on the themes: pre-trial 'shaping'; court decision-makers; differentiating defendants; and vulnerable witnesses and vulnerable defendants. This material was used to develop the theoretical approach and research design. Section 4 describes the ethical considerations which arose in the research, including confidentiality and informed consent, and Section 5 gives a brief overview of research limitations.

1. Phase 1 – Textual Analysis

Advancing governmentality research is important in criminology because 'crime, security and justice' are central to politics at every level and 'criminology can provide intellectual techniques and a knowledge base for public agencies attempting to govern populations' (Lippert and Stenson, 2010: 488). In turn, incorporating 'the real' into governmentality research within criminology means 'embracing social constructionalism's lessons'. In methodological terms this means 'analysing multiple forms of data with a range of methodologies', a greater analysis of oral discourses and examining 'the interaction between governance from above and sites and practices of governance "from below"'(ibid). Phase 1, therefore, involved textual analysis of 'governance from above': examining national policy documents and reported criminal law cases tried at Crown Court level and beyond; informing methods of data collection on 'governance "from below"' in Phases 2 and 3 of the research.

Hansard transcripts of debates in the House of Commons and the House of Lords were analysed, for all stages of the passage of the Autism Act 2009 and references to related policy and guidance (see DOH, 2010a, b and c; NICE, 2012a and b). Finally, the oral and written questions of the Members of both Houses, who belonged to the Autism Bill Committee 2008/9 and Autism Quality Standards Bill 2010 and the Members of the All Parliamentary Group for Autism, were searched by the subject matters: 'autism', 'autistic', 'Asperger', 'learning disability', 'mentally disordered offenders', 'mental health problems', 'defendants' and 'crime'.

Data collection of *legal cases*, as differentiated from the *case studies* discussed in Phase 2 below, refer to those found in the All England Law Reports. Searches for Court of Appeal case law involving autistic adult defendants were conducted in Westlaw and LexisNexis in the 'free text' search box using the search terms 'autis!' or 'Asperger!'. The same process was conducted in LexisNexis and SSRN to retrieve additional journal articles citing cases involving autism. The free text search results were then individually filtered by the researcher to find cases involving an autistic *defendant*; cases involving a victim or other witness were excluded. These exclusions left a cohort of 72 reported Court of Appeal cases where the adult defendant had autism. Although space precludes these cases being discussed in this present book, analysis of these cases in Phase 1 were extremely important in informing methods of data collection and thematic analysis in Phase 2 (see below).

Phase 1 undertook the textual analysis of policy documentation and use of Dedoose software to code and analyse the sample of reported criminal cases retrieved through these searches. This provided the opportunity to explore whether there were any evolving programmes, strategies and technologies of governance for autistic adult defendants. The coding used a mixture of theoretical and grounded approaches. The research questions discussed in chapter one were distilled into codes, such as *description of autism*, *dangerousness*, *vulnerability*, *mitigation* and *disposal at sentencing*, and then 'open coding' was used to discern emerging themes like *adequacy of expert evidence* and *appropriateness of prison* by 'pulling together real examples from the text' (Ryan and Bernard, 2003: 280). This coding technique also enabled the author to develop a court observation matrix to use in Phase 2 of the research and to formulate questions to be asked in the semi-structured interviews in Phase 3.

Various limitations meant that reported cases found on legal databases were only those at the Court of Appeal and Supreme Court levels and this led to the decision to focus this research analysis on court observation in the lower courts. It was not possible to conduct a free text search of Crown and Magistrates' Court cases on the larger databases like Westlaw or LexisNexis with key terms to find out the number of Magistrate Court cases where the defendant had autism. It was, therefore, impracticable to obtain an exhaustive data set of the number of cases involving autistic adult defendants over a fixed time period. In order to obtain files for cases in both the Crown and Magistrates' Court, it is necessary to know the defendant's name in order to request their case files. So, while some may view the sample size retrieved in Phase 2 as small, these limitations made the court case observation in Phase 2 essential to the analysis of oral discourse in the sites of governance in the lower court; providing a valuable contribution to research in this field.

2. Phase 2 – Case Studies

Phase 2 involved observation of eight adult autistic defendants through their criminal court process over a period of up to three years in some cases. The court observations were supplemented, where possible and appropriate, with interviews with the defendant, their parent or carer, solicitor and/or barrister. In some circumstances, other professionals involved in the case were interviewed, such as the defendant's Offender Manager or social worker. 'Case study' is used here to mean '*an intensive study of a single unit for the purpose of understanding a larger class of (similar) units*' (Gerring, 2004; author's emphasis). A unit connotes a 'spatially bounded phenomenon' – here, an autistic defendant – 'observed at a single point in time or over some delimited period of time' (ibid: 342).

Case studies are included in the research for several reasons. Firstly, because of the paucity of criminological literature on this topic, understanding the governance of autistic defendants in the English CJS had to be largely 'exploratory' to constitute a 'generative moment' in the empirical research in this area (ibid: 349).

Case studies enjoy 'a natural advantage' (ibid) here, evincing a 'descriptive end product' which is useful in providing 'information about the unit of analysis at the centre of the research' (Jupp, 2000: 19). As exemplars of the governance of autistic defendants in the CJS, they build a picture of the extent of coherence of the governance across the system's disparate processes and institutional areas. Furthermore, case studies are used to provide insight into a topic which includes a 'multiplicity of shifting issues', choices and a 'plurality of truth claims' (Lippert and Stenson, 2010: 488). The multiplicity of shifting issues means analysis of these case studies cannot be exhaustive but they are illustrative of the 'messy' reality of governance and are intended to stimulate points of discussion for the reader and inspire future research.

A. Retrieving the Case Studies Sample

An individual Court Circuit was chosen as the primary area for case study retrieval, due to its geographical diversity and the author's network of contacts there. At the time of retrieving the case studies, there was no standard screening or survey tool used across England to gather data on autistic individuals entering the criminal court system; consequently, this study could not use systematic sampling methods to retrieve representative case studies of autistic adult defendants in the English Criminal Courts. Hence, recruitment of defendants for court case observation was done directly through self-selection or through third party professionals or 'gate-keeping' organisations: (a) the 12 Autism Alliance charities; (b) criminal justice agencies and criminal justice practitioners; (c) solicitors' firms and barristers' chambers; (d) local authorities. Two of the eight individuals were identified by their solicitor, one by a police officer, one by their social worker, three by an autism charity and one by the researcher while observing another case at court.

In all cases the consent of the defendant or, where this was not possible, their family's consent, to observe the case was sought. Where recruitment to participate was done through third parties, initial written and telephone requests were made to these agencies and once they had identified a potential participant, they were asked to share both types of Participant Information Sheets and Consent forms with them. This secured preliminary permission to take part in the research from the participants; continued consent was checked once the author had made direct contact with the defendant or their family member.

Charities may only hear about an individual coming into contact with the CJS in 'special' or 'difficult' cases; nevertheless, they often play a vital 'frontline' role in identifying problems in service provision before service providers themselves and were an important resource to retrieve case studies. The newly established local authority leads on autism and autism partnership board members were also helpful in identifying case studies as they were, at this time, engaged in developing local autism commissioning plans and collecting information about the 'number of adults known to have autism in the area' (DOH, December 2010: 24–5).

All barristers' chambers and solicitors firms in the chosen[1] sub-area of the selected Court Circuit were contacted by letter of introduction, to the senior Clerk or Criminal Defence Partner, and a follow-up telephone call. Two additional potential case studies were identified via this route but because of the sensitive nature of the defendants' offences, their families told the defendants that they did not want them to give permission to take part in the research for a fear of repercussions for them. When retrieving cases using this method, like sampling from charitable organisations, there is a possibility that the advocate is already dealing with the client's autism and related needs more sensitively or the 'special' nature of that client's case may be unrepresentative of cases involving autistic defendants more generally. However, this limitation was outweighed by the necessity to gather at least exploratory data on the governance of adult defendants in the lower courts and the difficulty of systematically identifying this group through criminal justice agencies and impossibility of searching electronic databases.

The decision to recruit participants through third parties, rather than direct advertising through, for example, social media, was made to ensure the defendant's autism was already diagnosed prior to their Plea and Case Management Hearing and disclosed to at least one professional in the court proceedings and made *known* to the court decision-makers. This is because it was important to understand how this group was governed when decision-makers were *aware* that the defendant had autism and to minimise the risk that the researcher's presence through court observation might influence the outcome of the case. The temporal limitations of the research meant that it would not have been feasible to include individuals who self-identify as having autism but had not received a diagnosis before the disposal of their case or persuaded the court of the need for expert evidence to this effect. Unsurprisingly, however, the nature of their 'autism' was differentially diagnosed and some had co-occurring conditions.

A number of other access routes were attempted to retrieve further case studies, including via the police, Magistrates' and Crown Courts and the CPS, and the then Probation Service. These routes ultimately led to dead ends, and difficulties in the systematic identification of autistic adult defendants through these agencies led to the small sample size. These dead ends reflect the fragmentation of the CJS and the limitations at each stage of the process in effectively identifying and tracking disabled defendants generally, and autistic defendants in particular. In itself, an important finding.

B. Court Case Observation

Court case observation included shadowing the autistic defendant and their solicitor/barrister during adjournments in proceedings, observing their case

[1] Detail of this locality removed to protect anonymity of participants.

from the public gallery of the court and conducting informal semi-structured interviews with these parties. Although criminal courts are open to the public, access is a matter of degree. Special rules prevent discussing the case with jurors (in the Crown Court) and observing the process of sentencing decisions made by the magistrates and judiciary (Baldwin, 2007: 375). Access to informal discussions and exchanges that occur between various parties during adjournments were also restricted; given the difficulty in identifying cases, it was not feasible to obtain permission and, ultimately, access to these discussions. Nevertheless, court observation proffers numerous benefits. It is a site which makes the intersection of multiple issues and criminal justice pathways (of both the defendant(s) and victim(s)) visible and observable. It may even be the first time since the original criminal event that all parties involved are in close proximity to each other. Subtle and sometimes unrestrained exchanges between parties may reveal much about the parties themselves and the decision-makers involved in their case. Hence, it was a valuable environment to gather data on the 'interconnecting variables' (Browning and Caulfield, 2011) which lead autistic adults into the CJS.

The disparate criminological literature on the English criminal courts was useful as a guide to the court observation and in coding fieldwork notes. There has been a paucity of fieldwork in the courtroom in recent decades; making early works particularly informative on data collection on the court process. Bottoms et al's seminal study (1976: 7) was helpful on the framework for 'scheduled routes' through the court process. They investigated defendants' substantial decisions about plea, mode of trial, representation (legal or otherwise), choice of bail or custody and appeal (ibid). Understanding scheduled routes is especially important for autistic adult defendants as they move erratically through the court system and, sometimes between the court, mental health and adult social care (see chapters six to eight). Lord Bradley's 'simplified diagram of the offender pathway' for offenders with mental health problems and learning disabilities was also useful in mapping this process (2009: 24).

Research on the exercise of the police and prosecution's discretion (Ericson, 1982; McBarnet, 1981; McConville and Baldwin, 1981; McConville, Sanders and Leng, 1991) has demonstrated 'that the prosecution case is not the result of discovery of some objective reality, an entity which exists outside and apart from the process itself; rather, prosecution is a process in which cases are *constructed*' (McConville et al, 1994: 10). *Standing Accused*, however, was the 'first major study of the organisation and methods of criminal defence lawyers in England and Wales' and found that: 'the nature of criminal defence practice … is overwhelmingly reactive in character and incorporates methods which parallel and even mock those of the police and the prosecution' (ibid: 70). This research could not look extensively at the construction of the defence case but these studies alerted the author to the need to analyse the logics by which solicitors and barristers argue the relevance of the defendant's autism at different stages of the case.

Shapland's research, with 30 barristers, into the process of constructing mitigation (1981) 'suggested a considerable variation in the factors selected and put forward by [barristers] in mitigation and a considerable variation in [their] knowledge of and views about different kinds of sentence' (Ashworth et al, 1984: 45). Speeches in mitigation were also found by Ashworth et al to be 'influential on the determination of the sentence', leading those authors to warn that 'any analysis of sentencing decisions which neglects to study [such] speeches … is likely to be defective' (ibid). Consequently, a decision was made to focus on the role of aggravating and mitigating factors in the case study observations (see chapter seven). Ashworth et al employed a number of strategies to discern why judges sentence in the way that they do: they undertook interviews with 25 judges; asked the judges to provide their sentencing decisions on a sample of 'sentencing vignettes'; completed periods of observation of court cases and 'attachment' to individual judges; and conducted document analysis of the sentencing records of these judges to understand how they approached sentencing and past practices. This combined approach helped to overcome the individual shortcomings of each isolated method, provided a thorough examination of the processes that they explored (Ashworth et al, 1984), and influenced the triangulated methodology used in this book.

Jacobson and Talbot produced a comprehensive review of the treatment of vulnerable defendants within the criminal courts of England and Wales and the use of Special Measures for vulnerable defendants 'in recognition that court proceedings can be particularly difficult for these individuals' (2009: 5). As such, the use of Special Measures for autistic adults is not the central question of this research. Rather, data on Special Measures was collected as an indicator of the way autistic defendants are governed and whether this group is consistently identified as being vulnerable or disabled (see chapters four and six).

C. Background Features of the Eight Case Studies

The data collected while observing the court cases of the eight individuals became a rich but intricate array of source materials: field notes when the court was in session and in meetings outside the courtroom, interview transcripts, notes of telephone calls and expert reports. The use of longitudinal case studies 'provides the ability to capture and explain change, conceiving of legitimacy views as part of a developing process rather than a stable state of thinking or acting' (Pennington, 2015: 904).

Chapter six triangulates these data to set out a composite summary case study for each of the eight individuals followed through the criminal court process. However, readers will find it helpful to have some introduction to them at this stage. Of the eight individuals observed through the court system, seven are male and one is female. Seven of the cohort were aged between 18 and 25 and one was aged between 35 to 41 at the time of the final follow-up. The crimes for which the group were charged were as follows: two cases involved possession of a knife ('Claire' and 'Noah'), one possession of class B drugs ('Ollie'), one the downloading of illicit images of children ('Miles'), one sexual assault ('William'), one racially aggravated assault and theft ('Patrick') and one of domestic violence ('Robert'). These are the crimes which were on the indictments for the cohort when fieldwork observation began. As described above, apart from Henry, seven individuals in the cohort had an antecedent history and Miles reoffended during the period of time in which his case was followed.

One of this book's subsidiary research questions was to explore 'who or what is to be governed?' This was posed to find out how the categories of defendants with mental health problems and learning disabilities were applied to autistic defendants (see chapter one). For example, do decision-makers differentiate the category of autism and the categories of 'Aspergers' or 'high-functioning autism'? Where the latter categories dominate, what implications do they have for the outcomes for the defendant? That there is 'wide variation in rates of identification and referral for diagnostic assessment, waiting times for diagnosis, models of multi-professional working, assessment criteria and diagnostic practice for adults with features of autism' (NICE, 2012: 4) was discussed in chapter one.

The nature of an individual's diagnosis and the stage at which it was discovered by, or disclosed to, decision-makers in the criminal justice process had implications for decision-making about and disposal of their case. Miles' diagnosis was one of high functioning AS; Robert had a diagnosis of AS along with Semantic Pragmatic Disorder and Obsessive Compulsive Disorder. Henry and Patrick also had a diagnosis of ADHD. Ollie had AS. William and Noah were both recorded as having a co-occurring learning disability and low IQ (<70 and <100, respectively). Indeed, chapter one noted that the disparate 'factors [in identification] contribute to delays in reaching a diagnosis [of autism] and subsequent access to appropriate services' (ibid) and in turn may become one of the 'interconnecting variables' (Browning and Caulfield, 2011) that lead autistic individuals to come into contact with the CJS. The change in the diagnosis given to Claire, from AS to autism, as her IQ was later assessed as being lower than previously thought, had a direct impact on her access to local authority support and how her case was processed through the CJS (see below in chapter six).

3. Phase 3 – Semi-structured Interviews

Phase 3 involved conducting semi-structured interviews with elite decision-makers and practitioners. The research questions discussed in chapter one and the grounded themes which emerged from research in Phases 1 and 2 were used to develop the interview schedule for semi-structured interviews. Semi-structured interviews enabled the author to make thematic comparisons while allowing 'more opportunity for probing and giv[ing] the respondent considerable freedom to expand on a given question' (Huitt and Peabody, 1969: 28–29). It also reduced the risk of 'potential power imbalance between researchers and their elite interviewees' (SSH IDREC, 2008: 4) and the interviewee dictating interview content. The objective of this part of the qualitative research was to provide substantive evidence of what rationale, if any, drives the governance of autistic adult defendants at the national policy and legislative level. Elite decision-makers are those who were chosen because of the senior 'public role they hold' and 'are likely to have had more influence on political outcomes' than the general public, including 'Government Ministers … associated with a particular piece of legislation' (Richards, 1996: 199). Other criminal justice decision-makers and practitioners were 'chosen not because of their particular role but because of their general position', such as senior prosecutors (SSH IDREC, 2008: 4).

The 15 interviewees included Senior Civil Servants at the DOH, senior psychiatrists who had acted in an advisory capacity for autism-specific policies, Members of the House of Lords and Members of Parliament, the CPS, Court of Appeal judges and magistrates and senior police officers. These individuals were identified through purposive selection, based on research conducted in Phase 1 and followed by snowball sampling across the hierarchy of the CJS to give: 'an insight into the mind-set of the actor/s' who shaped policies in this area and the 'interviewee's subjective analysis of a particular episode or situation' (Richards, 1996: 199–200).

Interviewees were not, therefore, selected to represent generalisations of all decision-makers in their particular profession but because their specific 'features or characteristics … enable[d] detailed exploration and understanding of the central themes' in this book (Ritchie et al, 2003: 78). They were recruited through a personalised letter of invitation, with follow-up emails and telephone calls to secure the interview. All interviews, except those conducted by telephone, were carried out in person. Face-to-face interviews were chosen over written correspondence to assuage the risk of 'potential power imbalance', enabling researchers 'to manage senior people … so that they do not terminate interviews early' (SSH IDREC, 2008: 4).

4. Ethical Considerations

Assuring anonymity and confidentiality was essential in Phases 2 and 3 of the research. Anonymity was guaranteed to participants in both phases as the respective Information for Participants, and the University of Oxford guidelines on special considerations for data on film/video/CD/audiotape were followed (2012: 1). The reporting of all data and results conformed to the principles of anonymity and confidentiality.

Chapter three makes the case for a more coherent disability perspective in criminology. Given so much criminal justice research focuses on society's most disenfranchised groups, dialogue in our profession about the ethics related to marginalised individuals (Dupont, 2008: 201) should not be limited to the substantive research but necessarily involves inclusive research methods too. This means more research by disabled researchers and about disabled research participants who are victims, witnesses or defendants. Participatory research embodies 'the idea that research can, and should, be empowering and directly useful to research participants' but has been 'limited to the margins of a few social science disciplines' (ibid). Service user engagement is a central consideration of recent autism-specific policy developments (DOH, 2010d; NICE, 2012a: 15).

Hence, obtaining informed consent of autistic adult defendants and their families, which incorporated principles of participatory action research and service user engagement, was paramount in getting permission to follow an individual's case through the courts. However, autistic adults can have 'impaired executive function' (Goldberg et al, 2005; Hughes, Russell and Robbins 1994; Landa and Goldberg 2005) which affects working memory – the 'ability to maintain or hold information "on line"' (Attwood, 2007) – and repetitive patterns of behaviour and interests (see APA, 2013). The approach of the Mental Capacity Act 2005 is to assume individuals have capacity unless there is sufficient evidence to the contrary. Further, compared with 'neuro-typical' individuals, autistic adults can have difficulty in making decisions where those decisions have to be made quickly, outside their routine and/or involve talking to others (Luke et al, 2012). Such difficulties can be exacerbated by increased levels of anxiety and depression (ibid: 7). The following strategies, recommended to better support autistic adults in decision-making, were implemented in the process of obtaining ongoing consent:

> addressing general stress and anxiety present at the time of the decision;
>
> providing additional time to make decisions;
>
> minimising irrelevant stimuli;
>
> presenting closed questions;
>
> providing encouragement and reassurance;
>
> and acknowledging the person's strengths in decision-making (ibid: 8).

Further, consent to participate was broken into two stages. Once potential autistic participants had been identified by a particular agency, direct written or telephone contact was made to the individual to request their participation. Participants then had a minimum of a week, between the invitation to participate and the court appearance that the researcher requested to observe, to consider their consent to participate. Where the court listing was brought forward, they were given a minimum of 24 hours.

The Mental Capacity Fact Sheet for Social Scientists emphasises that it is 'important to avoid the possibility that compliance is wrongly taken to imply consent' and that '[d]emonstrable steps should be taken to ensure that the respondent is able fully to comprehend or retain information about a research study' (DOH, 2009: 4). Therefore, it was assumed that a potential case study subject had capacity to decide to participate in the research but positive action was taken to increase capacity. Others have recommended presenting information as separate elements instead of an uninterrupted form (Nind, 2008) and adapting social and environmental factors (Harris, 2003). Consequently, the format and communication of information materials were adapted by providing a *Participant Information Sheet*, written in both standard and 'Easy Read' forms. Easy Read documentation included *Change Pictures* (2012), with an explanatory image placed next to each block of text. Text met the *Flesch Readability Test* criteria for readability and Mencap's accessible language principles (Mencap, 2009; DOH, 2010g). Hard copies were given to potential participants prior to the signing of the consent forms, and were also explained orally by the researcher.

Each individual was given time to process each question on the consent form, because autistic people can make literal interpretations (Happe, 1993). 'Checking questions' were asked about what the participants understood the research to involve, why they were asked to participate and what the interviews with them would be used for. Participants were then asked if they consented to take part and signed a consent form.

The same process was taken in obtaining consent to conduct interviews with case study subjects, following their court observation. Participants were made aware that breaks could be taken during the interview and, to establish ongoing consent, the interview was periodically paused to check that they were happy to proceed. This protocol reflects provisions in the Mental Capacity Act 2005 Code of Conduct that decision-making should be delayed until a time when the individual is less anxious. In cases where an individual was deemed not to have competence to give informed consent to take part in *interviews*, permission to make that decision was not sought from other parties because empowerment through participation is central to the paradigm of this research. In line with the DOH Guidance on 'research which does not wish to involve people without capacity', reasonable steps were taken to prevent the inadvertent inclusion of such people in interviews (2009: 5). However, where in all situations the individual was deemed not to have competence to give informed consent for the researcher to take part in the *court observation*, such consent *was* garnered from parents/guardians of the autistic person. This differentiation was made because of the public nature of the court proceedings and the public benefit of the research; had this not been the case, the research was at risk of excluding cases where fitness to plead was an issue.

Measures were also taken to minimise risks of negative consequences of participation for autistic participants, their parents and carers, of recalling the events which led to the autistic defendants coming into contact with the CJS. The participants were signposted to relevant support agencies and were also permitted to have a supporter present during the interviews to reduce their risk of distress and anxiety. The Participant Information Sheet explained the researcher's professional experience working with autistic people to reassure them of credibility and to facilitate access but made it clear the researcher was unable to provide legal advice, to ensure the outcome of their case was not affected by their participation in the research. Further, whilst preliminary questions were asked to establish the facts of the case and court proceedings arrangements, the defendant, their parent or legal representative were only interviewed after sentencing.

Autistic adults can express behaviour which is described as 'challenging' when it affects the person's or other people's quality of life and or jeopardises their safety and includes 'stereotypic behaviour (such as rocking or hand flapping), anger, aggression, self-injury, and disruptive or destructive behaviour' (NICE, 2012b: 46). It can result from the interaction between individual, social and physical environmental factors, including triggers from: relationships with family; sensory factors; coexisting mental disorders; communication problems; and changes to routine (ibid: 8). The stressful nature of court proceedings and the type of crime the defendant had committed, made triggering behaviour that challenges services a risk to the participant and the researcher's physical safety in this fieldwork. Consequently, the researcher was careful to discuss potential triggers with the defendant's solicitor, barrister or other agency that had identified the participant, along with the defendant's parents or supporters. To avoid these triggers, participants were given sufficient personal space and adaptations were made to the sensory environment of the interview setting.

5. Research Limitations

The practical limitations of pursuing a cross-method research strategy for the present research, originally for a doctoral thesis, meant that each phase of the research had to be circumscribed. The research would have benefitted from more interviews with members of the judiciary and senior civil servants. However, the problems inherent in retrieving the sample of case studies, as described above, meant that this was not feasible. Then again, whilst the sample of case studies is small, the retrieval of each case was hard sought and revealed much about endemic problems in the identification of autistic defendants along the criminal justice pathway. Although repeated attempts were made to interview all the autistic defendants, their parent(s) and a legal representative for each of the case studies, it was not always possible or appropriate to do so. Nevertheless, that some of these studies comprised between one (Henry, Patrick, Ollie and Claire) and three (William, Noah, Robert and Miles) years of observation provided a longitudinal perspective with a rich array of source materials.

Although courts are open to the public, access is a matter of degree, thus limiting the observation method. Access to the informal discussions and exchanges that occur between various parties during adjournments may also be restricted and we, as researchers, cannot be omnipresent. We have to make choices about '"whose side we are on" at all stages of the ethnographic process' (Becker, 1967; Corcoran, 2005) and recognise the impact that such choices may have on our findings as well as our research participants. Nevertheless, as the site in which the power of the state is levied against its citizens, rendering justice more visible and accountable in our democracy, court observation has much to offer our discipline. The perceptible decrease in ethnographic research in this area is to the detriment of criminology.

On balance, the limitations outlined in this section are outweighed by the value of using a mixed-method approach, which has sought to incorporate 'the real' into criminological research by conducting specific case studies 'using contextually suitable methodologies to dissect effectively moral language and practices from above and below' (Lippert and Stenson, 2010: 488).

Conclusion

The limitations inherent in systematic sampling of case studies, as outlined in Section 2 above, mean that the observed case studies may not be representative of the governance of all cases involving autistic adult defendants. However, because of the paucity of criminological literature on this topic (see chapter one), understanding how autistic defendants are governed through criminal justice policy and criminal court practice has had to be largely 'exploratory'; aiming to constitute a 'generative moment' in the empirical research in this area. Allowing a 'flexible, exploratory approach' (Palys and Atchison, 2008: 145), Phase 1 provided the opportunity to generate themes to be explored in Phase 2 and formulate questions to be asked in the semi-structured interviews in Phase 3.

It is difficult to describe the disparate research on the criminal courts in England as a cohesive body of material, with each study building on the last to reflect a linear progression of knowledge about these important public institutions. This is partly because the English criminal courts are complex social institutions administering justice through a variety of actors, for a variety of offences and to a diverse range of victims, witnesses and defendants. It is also because much of the research starts from different theoretical perspectives. Nonetheless, a vibrant array of research has given important insights into the operation of justice in the courts. Over the last 15 years, there has been a reduction in the use of court case observations, surveys and interviews in criminological studies of the courts. Aside from two notable exceptions (Jacobson et al, 2016; Owusu-Bempah, 2017), instead, there appears to be a trend towards greater use of qualitative and quantitative analysis of pre-sentence reports (see earlier examples Gelsthorpe and Raynor, 1995; Cavadino, 1997), case files and court reports in investigating the mechanics of the courts and the roles of participants in the court process. It is unclear whether this trend reflects more restricted research access by governmental bodies, the appetite for analysis of much larger data sets, or the more limited availability of financial and other resources for multi-method longitudinal research. More methodological research is needed but it is likely that the pandemic has exacerbated barriers to research within the physical courtroom space and, perhaps counter-intuitively, with new digital barriers blocking access to the virtual criminal court process for researchers and members of the public alike[2] (see chapter seven).

Whatever the reason for this apparent decline, there is a risk that the sort of rich data, gathered in studies such as the 'pilot study' by Ashworth et al, Baldwin and McConville's *Negotiated Justice* and McConville et al's *Standing Accused*, are not captured. Consequently, as criminologists and citizens, we miss out on such studies' insight into law in action and the empirical evidence that justice is being done in our criminal courts. Thus, validating the use of court observation in this book.

Participants' aspirations for change and their desire to tell their story to 'put things right' are well-documented motivations for participation in qualitative research on criminal justice institutions (Bosworth et al, 2005). Engaging autistic defendants and their families through court observation and interviews was designed to be directly 'empowering' to them as research participants (Dupont, 2008: 200). Maximising the public benefit of this research has been a guiding principle of this book's methodology and substantive content. The research's involvement of elite interviewees and practitioners may have encouraged these groups to consider issues raised by the interview schedule; potentially improving the exercise of the professionals' role. By combining textual analysis, a rich set of eight case studies and 15 elite interviews in one research design, it is possible to illustrate a contemporary picture of the governance of autistic adult defendants. This data has informed the development of a normative framework to determine how they should be governed and why Disabling Criminology is so important.

[2] Professionals seeking permission to attend a video-enabled hearing remotely must email the court's nominated email address for Cloud Video Platforms (CVP) with their reason for the request, this must be no later than 24 hours before the hearing or, for magistrates' remand hearings, on the morning of the hearing (HM Government, 2018; 2021).

PART I

How Should Autistic Adult Defendants be Governed?

3

Disabling Criminal Justice: Developing a Theoretical Toolkit

Introduction

Foucault, the progenitor of the governmentality approach, 'distinguished two lines of critical philosophy descended from Kant: 1) an inquiry into the conditions of possibility of true knowledge and; 2) a practical, historical critique of our present selves that makes thinkable and assists the creation of other possible ways of living' (1984; O'Malley et al, 1997: 506–7). It is to 'this second sense of critique that Foucault attaches his own work' (ibid). Sections 1 and 2 of the present chapter draw upon the intellectual resources available in critical criminology (Baldry et al, 2008; Dowse et al, 2009; Hudson, 1998b; 2002) Disability Studies (see Goodley, 2011), most notably the 'social model of disability', and to formulate the latter kind of critique and the development of a more sophisticated theoretical model of the governance of autistic defendants in the English criminal courts. In so doing, it builds on the emerging scholarship, discussed in Section 3, which have begun to develop disability as a conceptual lens, 'disabling' criminology, to facilitate a more critical engagement with the concerns of disabled people in the criminal justice system (see Ben-Moshe, 2013; Steele and Thomas, 2014; Steele, 2017; Thorneycroft and Asquith, 2021).

As described in chapter one, the social model, upon which much of critical disability studies is premised, makes a distinction between impairment, a condition of the mind or body, and disablement, a form of disadvantage or restriction of activity caused by the failure to take account of impairment. The present chapter argues that there is descriptive and normative value in proactively categorising these groups as disabled under the social model of disability in order to move criminology away from the 'mad-bad' dichotomy and to critique the growing dominance of the concept of vulnerability in scholarship about offenders with mental health problems, learning disabilities and autism, and used as a dividing practice in criminal justice policy and decision-making. Thus, foregrounding disability in the discipline of criminology as a whole, and not just the sub-discipline of critical criminology, is important because the absence of such a perspective leads to 'theoretical blindspots' and – to the extent that criminology can affect criminal justice policy (ibid; Loader, 1998; 2006) – to discriminatory practice.

It is salient to remember that conduct prohibited by the Equality Act 2010, and its duty to provide reasonable adjustments, applies to criminal justice organisations (E&HRC, 2015: 13). Further, elements of the social model of disability are already 'grounded' in the Equality Act 2010 in the section 6 definition of disability and in the iterative process required by the section 149 Public Sector Equality Duty. Writing in relation to the then Disability Discrimination Act 2005 (DDA), Talbot and the Prison Reform Trust (PRT) found that, in general, there was a failure by both criminal justice staff and those responsible for criminal justice services 'in their duty to promote equality of opportunity and to eliminate discrimination and, as such, [they were] not complying with the requirements of the DDA 2005 and the DED [Disability Equality Duty] in particular' (Talbot/PRT, 2008: 62). The present research found that the Equality Act 2010, under which the DDA 2005 has been subsumed, is still largely overlooked in criminal justice policy and decision-making (see chapter four below). Furthermore, there has been a failure by criminologists and criminal justice scholars to problematise the role and application of the Equality Act 2010 to criminal justice organisations. Consequently, it becomes even more relevant for criminology to evaluate the social model and the application of the Equality Act 2010 to criminal justice organisations. These 'grounded' elements will be discussed in Section 4 below, alongside a brief overview of the Act and related guidance. The development of this theoretical model will also help to provide a critical framework for the qualitative research which will be discussed in chapters six to eight and will be generative of a normative position about how autistic defendants *should* be governed in chapter ten of the book.

1. Conceptual Roots: Doing Justice to Difference

In the past, the criminological 'mainstream' has failed to adequately differentiate between criminals. Despite so-called critical perspectives, inconveniencing 'a criminology imbued with male, adult, mentally healthy, formerly non-victimised values' (Peay, 2007: 501), few scholars take intersectional approaches. Moreover, even within intersectional approaches, disability is too often considered as an afterthought or not considered at all (Sokoloff and Dupont, 2005; De Coster and Heimer, 2006). Yet, as Steele and Thomas point out, it is central to criminal law in a number of ways, including: being explicitly apparent in criminal law doctrines across numerous stages of criminal legal process; being a separate system of regulation and punishment – the forensic mental health system – for disabled people found unfit to plead or not guilty by reason of mental illness; having implications for definitions and our understanding of capacity and rationality; an overrepresentation of disabled people in an empirical sense in the criminal justice system as offenders and victimisation; and being the subject matter for the attention of law reform, such as mental health defences (2014: 358–9).

The way forward, Baldry et al argue, both for criminological theory and criminal justice practice, requires mental health problems and learning disabilities to be moved 'from a categorical or diagnostic attribute to a central location in the conceptualisation of the individual who presents to the CJS' (2008: 42). Peay contends that because the category of the 'mentally-disordered offender' is not fixed – and presupposes a 'category of mentally-ordered offenders' – it should not be considered separately by analogy with race, gender, youth and victims. She warned that this would perpetuate 'the fantasy that we are all whole' and that such disorder is prior to other aspects of identity. Nonetheless, she acknowledges that lessons can be learned from consideration of this and other 'marginal groups' for subject matters regarded as central to criminology (Peay, 2007: 502). It is argued here that a more integrated disability perspective would shed important light on the *dynamic* aspect of disability (see below) and how its trajectories – the intermittency of mental disorder for example – lead to entry to the CJS. Given the sheer numbers of offenders with mental health problems and learning disabilities in the CJS, these are certainly not 'marginal groups'. While their identity is multi-faceted, the specificity of needs created by their impairments and the disablement they experience through barriers to navigating the CJS (see chapter one above) should be focused upon more sharply, as criminology needs to expand its conceptual toolkit to understand disabled people's experiences more effectively.

An analogous argument can be levied in relation to autistic offenders. Autism is life-long (NICE, 2012a) but features of diagnostic domains are not fixed for an autistic person: key life events can impact on an individual's experience of autism, leading to increased anxiety and reduced ability to cope (ibid). Thus, the work below on the *dynamic* aspect of disability is helpful in understanding the governance of this group on the pathways into and out of the CJS. While the identity of autistic people is also multi-faceted, the specificity of needs created by their impairment and the particular barriers which exacerbates their disablement in the CJS should be brought to the fore. Critical disability studies are premised upon the fact 'that the disadvantage typically experienced by those who are disabled reflects primarily the way society defines and responds to certain types of "difference"' (Baldry et al, 2008: 31). This relates well to pre-existing conceptual elements in criminology in Barbara Hudson's work on 'doing justice to difference', and helps to integrate the thesis of Baldry et al with broader criminological debates. In a number of articles, Hudson (1998b; 2001; 2003; 2007; 2008) looks at the nature of justice in modern democratic societies, societies which are 'divided by gender, race, ethnicity, socio-economic status, lifestyle, religion and so on' (2008: 276). Because 'citizens of modernity' do not live in homogeneous societies, they must respond to difference and diversity. She differentiates these terms (2007: 158–9) by arguing that 'difference' has negative connotations, implying 'not only dichotomy, but also hierarchy'. On the other hand, 'diversity' has neutral or positive connotations, suggesting 'a range of options from which to choose, a spectrum of lifestyles and attributes to enjoy and appreciate' (ibid). Hudson therefore argues that it is imperative for criminology 'to expose and critique the politics and policies of criminalisation and crime control which are grounded on an ideology of difference, rather than on an acknowledgement of diversity' (ibid). She does not, however, problematise disability as a social construct and only fleetingly refers to offenders with mental health problems (1998b; 2001), but her work provides useful theoretical tools for reappraising the criminal conduct of autistic offenders, along with offenders with mental health problems and learning disabilities, while taking their particular needs into account.

Chapter one states that this book, in part, will answer Spivakovsky's call for criminologists to 'explore the myriad ways by which operations of punishment and punitiveness are being recruited, reconfigured and repurposed across justice arenas in the name of governing the population' (2014: 563). This is especially relevant in analysing the use of disposal options in chapters seven and eight. Criminologists have, over the last three decades, attributed the 'responsibilisation strategy' (O'Malley 1992; Garland, 2001: 124) as central to such re-purposing of punishment and punitiveness. Responsibilisation was central to the broader New Labour agenda which applied authoritarian versions of contractual and communitarian[1] principles by delegating an increasing number of policy functions to families and communities – akin to processes of 'governing through the family' described by Donzelot (1979; Squires and Stephen, 2005: 4–5; see also chapters eight and nine). Individuals and communities are supported in achieving their aspirations (Squires and Stephen, ibid) only if opportunities are seized and in return for their own contributions (Social Exclusion Unit, 2001: 3). Reflecting the new 'politics of conduct' (Flint, 2003) which conceived of individuals as active, autonomous and rational agents (Foucault, 1991), 'responsibilisation' strategies, therefore, achieve governmental aims through self-regulation (Flint, 2006). Consequently, as Nixon et al point out, failure 'to conform to normative standards of behaviour' – shaped by the government and the media – make the citizen subject to an increasing range of interventions, disciplining and punitive sanctions (2007: 38).

For autistic defendants, responsibilisation strategies represent what Glaser and Deane refer to as the 'normalisation paradox' (1999). 'Normalisation' involves making 'available to [the disabled] patterns of life and conditions of everyday living which are as close as possible to or indeed the same as the regular circumstances and ways of life of society' (Nirje, 1985: 67). With the promise of citizenship comes the same acceptance of responsibility as non-disabled citizens held accountable for their actions through criminal justice sanctions. Consequently, 'a myth of equality' (Glaser and Deane, 1999: 351) develops in sharp contrast to the discrimination and disadvantage actually experienced by autistic defendants. 'Responsibilisation' therefore denotes what Hudson critiques as the 'philosophical expulsion of difference' by Western theories of justice, 'reflected in

[1] For a detailed philosophical perspective on the problematic application of the social contract to disabled people, see Nussbaum, 2006.

law's model of the abstract subject of law, with all legal subjects constructed equal in their possession of agency and free will' (2001: 162). Clearly, it is crucial not to argue that autistic defendants should be deemed entirely incapable of taking responsibility for their actions. But there needs to be a more nuanced understanding of responsibility, and recognition that, in reality, many will have limited freedom of choice because of what Hudson called 'personal-socio circumstances' (1998a: 207).

Being aware of the way evolving responsibilisation strategies act to blur the boundaries between social care and social control and are used for autistic defendants is, therefore, important in answering Spivakovsky's call to recognise the re-purposing of punishment and punitiveness (2014a). The case studies of 'Claire' and 'William', discussed in detail in chapter eight, reveal how social care placements and community orders perform such responsibilisation. The case studies of 'Noah', 'William' and 'Miles' also evince processes akin to 'governing through the family' (Donzelot, 1979). Nixon et al argue that such strategies often fail to recognise that attempts by parents to 'access special educational support or behavioural interventions' for children whose 'behaviour may be disturbing and distressing' are often thwarted by the difficulty of navigating complex complaints procedures (2007: 45). Rejecting the conceptualisation of such governance as a form of secondary victimisation, chapter nine conceives of these strategies as causing 'symbiotic harm' (Condry and Minson 2021) to the family members compelled into this familial 'net-widening' which extends mechanisms of control beyond the autistic defendant. Such strategies represent what Hudson terms 'an ideology of difference' rather than an acknowledgement of diversity, repressing difference 'in those [subsequently] defined as abnormal [or] incapable or dependant' (Hudson, 2007; 2001). After rendering such ideologies visible, it is necessary to examine intellectual resources which might enable us to create 'other possible ways of living'. Previous court studies, which differentiated the treatment and experiences of certain groups of defendants (see chapter one above), have often failed to connect 'governance from below' – technologies applied to certain groups of defendants in the court process – to macro-level policies. The present research aims to overcome this schism.

2. Critical Disability Studies and the Social Model of Disability

In the culture of modernity, medical models of disability – influenced by Enlightenment rationality – conceived of disability as a derogation from the norm (Handley, 2003); something that needed to be cleansed and controlled (Hughes, 2002). According a privileged position to medical knowledge in defining disability assumes medicine's 'value-free objectivity' (Handley, 2003: 110). Critics argue (Oliver, 1996; Barnes, 1991; Oliver, 1990), however, that policy prescriptions based upon the medical model 'focus upon rehabilitation and cure to "fit" the disabled individual "into" society as much as possible' (Handley, ibid). The 'counter-culture' from which the 'disability movement and the social model of disability and (by extension) disability studies' originate (Hughes, 2002: 578) came from rejection of this 'medicalisation' of disability which had put the 'fate of disabled people solely in the hands of professional experts' (Barnes et al, 1999: 67; O'Grady et al, 2004). The 'social model' of disability 'is the formalised articulation of a set of "principles"' advanced in the 1970s by a group of disabled activists – the Union of the Physically Impaired Against Segregation (UPIAS) – to counter 'individual' or 'medical' conceptions of disability (Tremain, 2005: 9). Medical models tend to see any social disadvantage experienced by the individual as a result of a direct 'common-sense' causal link to their functional limitation (Handley, 2003: 110). Proponents of the social model, however, make a crucial distinction between impairment and disability: impairment is 'a condition of the individual body or mind (such as experiencing schizophrenia, intellectual disability or brain injury)'; disability is the 'experience flowing from the presence of impairment, including the range of barriers to full participation that exist in a society which privileges "normalcy" and marginalises difference' (Oliver and Barnes, 1998; Baldry et al, 2008: 32). This impairment-disability dyad is sometimes advanced by analogy with the distinction between sex and gender (Shakespeare, 2006a). Such an analytical framework enables an exploration of the 'social, political, cultural, and economic factors that define disability and shape personal and collective responses to difference' (Baldry et al, 2008: 32), and hence attempts to redress the power balance, empowering disabled people as citizens with rights (O'Grady et al, 2004: 260).

With respect to offenders with mental health problems and learning disabilities, Baldry et al submit that the value of the social model is that it permits a conceptualisation of 'the intersections of the social, systemic and individual dimensions which operate to structure' their experience of criminal justice (Baldry et al, 2008: 31). Therefore, the potential for integrating critical criminology and critical disability studies lies in the concept of social exclusion. Perceiving 'crime and social responses to it as deeply political, cultural and critically challengeable matters', critical criminology locates 'the reasons for crime within wider structural and institutional contexts' (ibid); including socio-economic, class-based, cultural, racial and gender contexts (Anthony and Cunneen, 2008: 1). Drawing on British Social Exclusion policy, Baldry et al (ibid: 32) point to 'what can happen when people experience a combination of linked problems such as unemployment, poor skills, low incomes, unstable housing, high crime environments, poor health and family breakdown' (Social Exclusion Unit 2001). This exclusion, 'when combined with other disadvantages, funnel[s] people into the CJS' (Baldry et al, 2008: 32–3). Consequently, Baldry et al argue (32–3) that this requires 'an iterative process of identifying, understanding and removing obstacles to resources, combined with a deeper analysis of the dynamics of both impairment and disability'.

Some have contended within critical disability studies that the categorical distinction between impairment and disability is problematic because even though proponents assert that impairment neither equals nor causes disability (Oliver, 1996), the 'implicit premise of the model' that one cannot suffer disablement without the existence of an impairment, makes the distinction a 'chimera' (Tremain 2001; 2002). However, by highlighting the distinction between impairment and disablement, the social model allows for a more nuanced understanding of the fact that, as Baldry et al note, 'the combination of stressful life events is also likely to be linked to the episodic occurrences of impairment … in both a causative and consequential sense' (2008: 39). As argued in chapter one, the social model of disability and its distinction between impairment and disablement is helpful in comprehending the literature which explores the link between the 'symptomatology' of autism and criminality (the 'impairment branch' of the distinction) in combination with literature on the 'interconnecting variables' which lead autistic defendants into the CJS and their inequitable experiences because of the barriers to justice in the CJS (the disablement branch of the distinction). The social model, therefore, has unitary force; enabling the 'deeper analysis of the dynamics of both impairment and disability' and the impact that they have on the governance of autistic defendants in the CJS.

The present book does not follow those proponents (see eg Oliver, 1990; Barnes, 1998) who, in 'splitting impairment and disability', attempted to sever the link between the two (Goodley, 2011: 27). Instead, it argues that it is helpful to distinguish between the two branches of the social model but not to exclude consideration of impairment. Proponents such as Barnes severed this link to turn 'attention away from the personal tragedy model of impairment to the public problems of disablism' (ibid) but such a move creates an intellectual impasse arising from the 'reality' of impairment; the relationship between impairment and culture, and the effects of impairment (Goodley 2011: 28–9). Firstly, following responses by disabled feminists (see French, 1993; Crow, 1996; Morris, 1991) to the 'strong social model' of disability, who asserted that impairment effects such as pain and tiredness were intrinsically disabling, Shakespeare argues that the social model 'can only explain so much before we need to return to the experiential realities of "impairment" as object(s) independent of knowledge' (Shakespeare, 2006b: 54). These 'experiential realities' are differential between impairments as some 'are static, others episodic, some degenerative and others terminal' (Shakespeare and Watson, 2001). Recognition of the differential experiential realities of autistic adults not only helps us to better understand their criminality and governance, it also enables a subtler normative account of how they should be governed. In turn, offering policy recommendations grounded in an acknowledgement of 'diversity' rather than 'difference' (Hudson, 1998) and validating the approach here of engaging autistic adults at every stage of fieldwork research (see chapter two above).

Furthermore, acknowledging the 'reality of impairment' enables an analysis of the dynamic aspects of disability (Burchardt, 2000), which are in turn connected to the increased likelihood of justiciable problems (O'Grady et al, 2004), both of which are relevant to criminological theory and provide tools to improve criminal justice practice. Burchardt noted that disability, in general, is still understood only in its *static* sense. Yet, as stated above, disability is not fixed in nature. Research needs to distinguish between 'disability trajectories', avoiding the conflation of 'different experiences of being disabled and improving "the design" and evaluation of effective policies' (2000: 645–6). Where medical research does acknowledge these fluctuations, 'the dynamics of disability from a social policy perspective [i.e. the impairment-disability distinction] remain underexplored' (ibid: 649). Burchardt emphasised the need to view disability dynamically in order to permit analysis of the 'different processes by which disabled people become socially excluded'. Such a perspective enables the identification of 'key points in the trajectories individuals follow', supporting more precisely-targeted interventions, for example, during 'the transition to adulthood for those who become disabled in childhood' (2000: 665). In research, a longitudinal view of disability needs to be taken, as those with 'intermittent or fluctuating conditions – especially mental health problems – are significantly under-counted in cross-sectional measures' (ibid). Burchardt applied this analysis to the employment environment, but such a disability dynamic could analogously be applied to criminological discourses, which would reveal important insights into the nature and impact of these trajectories of disablement upon an individual's entry to the CJS and the fluctuating experience of impairment on, for example, desistance, in a similar manner to the age-crime curve. This is not to say that there is an inevitable link between either a person's disablement and crime nor impairment and crime but, rather, the necessity of applying an 'iterative process of identifying, understanding and removing obstacles to resources, combined with a deeper analysis of the dynamics of both impairment and disability' (Baldry et al, 2009).

However, if different groups following different trajectories within the disabled population are not differentiated, just as within the employment context, 'the disadvantage disabled people encounter will be underestimated' (Burchardt, ibid). This means that '… people who are disabled for a relatively short period face less severe pressures on their income and in general experience less severe dislocation from the mainstream' (ibid). Consideration of such trajectories for autistic defendants has existed at the peripheries of analysis in criminology (see Browning and Caulfield, 2011) and in the 'psy' disciplines. This underlines the rationale of this book to specifically examine the governance of autistic defendants from a disability perspective, rather than through the lens of broader categories such as mentally disordered offenders. This validates the approach taken in this research of applying this iterative process in investigating the governance of this group, through the court observation of the cohort of eight case studies of autistic adult defendants (see chapters six to eight).

Secondly, the exclusion of a discussion of impairment from an analysis of disability leaves a 'theoretical vacuum' 'which is filled by those who adopt an individualistic and decontextualised perspective' (Goodley, 2011: 28–9). This risks ascription to strict medical models which do not acknowledge that, far from being purely natural, impairments are 'an embodied experience shaped by culture' (Hughes and Paterson, 1997; 2000; Hughes, 1999; 2000; 2002a, b; 2004; Paterson and Hughes, 1999; Jung, 2002; see Goodley, 2011: 28–9). The importance of this point is reflected in the shift towards a preference for identity-first language (see chapter one). In self-identifying in this way, autistic people are making a purposive shift away from 'deficit' models of autism towards an 'aspiration' model which highlights the talents of 'non-neurotypical' thinking.

Thirdly, Thomas has called for a more dialectical analysis of impairment and disablism because 'in any real social setting, impairment and disablism are thoroughly intermeshed with the social conditions that bring them into being' (2007; see Goodley, 2011: 29–30). This analysis is reflected in the emphasis on the link between 'stressful life events' and 'episodic occurrences of impairment' as described by Baldry et al (2008). Such analysis is implicit in the National Autism Strategy's discussion about the kinds of crises which can lead autistic defendants into the CJS (DOH, 2010a: 37; see chapter five) but has not been properly translated into criminal justice policy.

O'Grady et al argue that different elements of exclusion interact to increase barriers for disabled people and perpetuate exclusion, leading to a spiralling of 'justiciable problems' (2004: 261) – such as debt, difficulties with housing and welfare benefits – which can potentially be addressed by the legal system (Genn, 1999). They can have an 'additive effect' compounded by barriers to seeking help from professional organisations (O'Grady et al, 2004: 265). Were criminologists to be alert to such differentiating issues, they could address the relationship between the fluctuating impact of autism on the adult individual, stressful life events and patterns of criminality. Applying a dialectical analysis of impairment and disablement/disablism to the governance of autistic defendants in order to tease out the 'additive effects' of the interaction between policy and decisions by elite decision-makers in the CJS is highly pertinent. It resonates with the Equality and Human Rights Commission's development of the concept of 'cumulative impact' (see Section 4 below).

As mentioned in chapter one, the medical model of disability is the dominant model in autism studies (Graby, 2016) in general and in the 'psy' literature on autism, crime and criminal justice (Vinter and Dillon, 2023). Utilising the social model also resonates with Woods' exposition which explores how the social model of disability can be re-invigorated for autism (Woods, 2017). The dominance in autism discourse by autism being conceptualised as a disorder and a deficit (Graby, 2016), has led to the 'systematic discrimination and oppression of autistic individuals by Predominant Neurotype society', creating a 'profound type of barrier' which has to be tackled by using the social model of disability (Woods, 2017: 1092, 1094). Thus, Woods argues, shifting autism research away from 'causes and biological effects' onto exposing barriers within services and systematic oppression in social issues will 'also assist autistic individuals by exploring the impact of living in Predominant Neurotype society' (Woods, 2017: 1091).

In turn, 'stopping the negative discourse of autism ... along with proper application of The Autism Act 2009 and The Equality Act 2010, the social model can be used to achieve autism emancipation by creating positive societal attitudes towards autism' (2017: 1094). In doing so, this model transfers 'the imbalanced burden of adapting away from autistic individuals onto Predominant Neurotype institutions' (ibid).

3. 'Disabling' Criminal Justice

Drawing on the analytical tools in critical disability studies in the way described in the previous sections and utilising these resources to centre disability in subjects to which criminology attends has been described as 'disabling' (Steele, 2017) this discipline. In doing so, the present book builds on an emerging scholarship which has worked to 'disable' criminology (Dowse et al, 2009), our understanding of criminal justice and the criminal law (see Steele and Thomas, 2014; Minkowitz, 2014; Harpur and Douglas, 2014; Weller, 2014; Gormley and Watson, 2021), incarceration (Ben-Moshe, 2013; Dodd et al, 2022), forensic detention (Steele, 2017) and court diversion in Australia (Steele, 2020). Bringing together analytical tools in critical disability studies, drawing on the social model in particular, and our criminological enquiry, ensures the focus of our research is on the barriers faced by disabled people which serve to overlook, compound and further punish their disability (Ben-Moshe, 2013; Gormley and Watson, 2021; Dodd et al, 2022) bringing attention to the ableist features of criminal justice and carceral environments.

In 'Cripping Criminology', aligning their work with the shift to queer and queering criminology, Thorneycroft and Asquith apply an analytical lens to 'subvert and disrupt criminology from the inside in order to expose its ableism and disablism' to 'open up spaces of possibility in which (crip) lives can be lived' (2021: 190). 'Cripping' comprises disrupting and subverting abled assumptions, practices, and effects (Sandahl, 2003). Thorneycroft and Asquith claim that the CJS and criminology are 'institutionally and theoretically ableist', with criminologists, even critical criminologists, continuing to theorise about crime 'as if the actions of offenders and victims can be explained through the lens of abledness' (2021: 195). Consequently, they tease out the previously under-explored concepts of ableism and disablism in criminology (2021). As they explain, ableism is premised upon the notion that the abled body is 'natural and normal', the 'corporeal standard' and 'species-typical and therefore essential and fully human' (Campbell, 2001: 44; Thorneycroft and Asquith, 2021). Thus, ableism 'works to (re)produce the abled body as the norm, and in so doing produces disablism; the belief that disabled people constitute inferior ways of being' but these terms 'should not be used interchangeably or conflated' (Thorneycroft and Ashworth, 2021: 190; 191), for they 'render quite radically different understandings of the status of disability to the norm' (Campbell, 2009a: 5). Whereas disablism produces ideals around disability, ableism produces ideals surrounding abledness (Campbell, 2009c). To this end, Thorneycroft and Asquith 'explore the ways in which disabled bodies and lives are constituted, regulated, governed, and violated by criminal justice frameworks' (2021: 190).

They explicate that the tasks of a 'crip' criminology might operate to: include crip people in criminological research and scholarship; produce new knowledge about their experiences; and shed new light on the ableism inherent in criminological theories (2021: 195–8). Three case studies, situated in the Australian justice system, are used to highlight ableist criminology and criminal justice frameworks: jury service; the multiple voices of victimization; criminal responsibility, insanity and unfitness to plead. Their exposition also sets out the subjects of a crip criminology, which includes:

1. disabled people who (are more likely to) commit crimes or are victimized;
2. people disabled as a consequence of criminal behaviour or victimization;
3. people iatrogenically harmed by the criminal justice system (such as the onset or exacerbation of mental health disablement arising from imprisonment and victims' participation in criminal (in)justice processes);
4. ableist criminal justice systems;
5. ableist criminological theory. (Thorneycroft and Asquith, 2021: 1990)

As with the earlier work of Baldry et al (2008) and Dowse et al (2009), discussed in the last section, Thorneycroft and Asquith's recent piece has been an extremely important contribution to the field. It has been helpful in the present book perceiving exacerbation of disablement by the CJS, as well as giving the analytical tools to further critique ablism within the CJS and criminological theory.

The UNCRPD has made an important shift in international law which expedites the need for us to 'disable' criminal justice. The scholarship of 'lived experience' and the expertise of disabled people is increasingly being recognised as an important counter balance to the dominance of 'objective' professional knowledge upon disabled people's lives, and was integral in the reformulation of human rights law (Weller, 2014) through the development of the UNCRPD. As a signatory of the UNCRPD, the UK is compelled to take steps to ensure that disabled people have equal access to justice under Article 13. The equality principle threaded through and throughout the UNCRPD is embedded in Article 1 in the objective that disabled people should have 'full and effective participation in society on an equal basis with others' (2006). Consequently, the 'radical feature' of its social participation is its point of reference setting the participation enjoyed by disabled people against the 'measure of comparison as the rights and entitlements enjoyed by non-disabled people' (Weller, 2014: 502). Yet, disabled people 'accused of a crime are disadvantaged by a system that neither acknowledges nor understands their needs' (Gormley and Watson, 2021: 494), as the Equality and Human Rights Commission (EHRC) states in its Inclusive Justice report, urgent reforms are needed to ensure equal and effective participation for disabled defendants (2020).

Chapter one argued that a 'disabling' criminology perspective aligns well with governmentality perspectives, which themselves 'provide a fruitful way to analyse the complex interactions between disability and the law' recognising as the literature does, 'the law is implicated in the truths, knowledges, rationales and practices through which disability is rendered known and knowable' (Weller, 2014). Weller utilises a governmentality framework to consider the complex and contradictory relationships between capacity, disability and law, in the Australian legal system, to analyse the concept of legal capacity in Article 12 of the UNCRPD and the challenge it presents to the understanding of mental capacity in Western legal systems. In so doing, Weller elucidates the perpetuating impact of 'paternalistic paradigms' in disability, health and welfare laws, on the one hand, and the 'disappointing impact of anti-discrimination laws on the other' (2014: 499). Following their qualitative research in Scotland, Gormley and Watson, draw together criminology and disability studies to argue the failure of criminal justice systems and practices to 'acknowledge' disability as an equality issue, in itself creating disabling barriers in the CJS which further marginalise disabled people (2021). In the context of the English CJS, with autistic defendants as the case study, the present book investigates what strategies, rationalities and technologies of governance had a role in perpetuating these paternalistic paradigms, generating disabling barriers and creating the conditions for the 'disappointing' impact of the Equality Act 2010. It is argued that the dominant conceptualisation of 'vulnerability' is a strategy of governance which has been 'the dominant frame' to construct disabled people in the CJS (Roulstone and Sadique, 2013) in preventing CJS systems and practices acknowledging disability as an equality issue (see chapters four and ten).

The principle of progressive realisation within the Convention means States Parties are not required to ensure that the obligations contained within it are met all at once, and this can be context specific (see O'Sullivan and McNamara, 2021). Crowther and Sayce, in light of the Inquiry by the Committee on the Rights of Persons with Disabilities on the UK, note that '[l]ooking back over the period since 2009, it sometimes appears that ratification of the CRPD (2006) represented the high watermark for UK disability rights' (2020: 298). The UK government has not been through a full harmonisation with the provisions within the UNCRPD nor have they made the UNCRPD directly applicable in law. The focus here on the Equality Act 2010, therefore, is to understand the barriers in governance which have de-limited its implementation in the CJS. It is also to clear the ground to better understand what will need to be tackled in the future in order for criminologists to problematise how we bring into being the *effective* implementation of the UNCRPD.

4. The Equality Act 2010, the Public Sector Equality Duty and the Courts

The Equality Act 2010 replaces previous equalities legislation, streamlining all legal requirements on equality that the public, private and voluntary sectors need to follow, and sets out protection against discrimination on the basis of eight protected characteristics for people who use these services: age; disability; gender reassignment; pregnancy and maternity; race; religion or belief; sex; sexual orientation. Section 6(1) incorporates the definition of disability (see above) previously found in the DDA 2005 and premised upon the social model of disability (Hunter et al, 2007) with its emphasis 'on the effect that an impairment has on a person's ability to carry out normal day-to-day activities' (Talbot and Riley, 2007: 155). As previously noted, autism, including AS, would come under this definition. Under the Act, 'service providers', defined as a person (including an organisation) 'concerned with the provision of a service to the public or a section of the public (for payment or not)' (Equality Act 2010, section 29(1)), and employers, must treat their service users (and employees) fairly.

In relation to disabled service users/employees, the Equality Act 2010 prohibits service providers/employers from the following main forms of conduct: direct discrimination by treating a person with a protected characteristic less favourably than it treats or would treat others (ibid, section 13); indirect discrimination in applying to a person with a protected characteristic a provision, criterion or practice which is discriminatory in relation to a relevant protected characteristic (ibid, section 19); discrimination arising where a person is treated less favourably because of a combination of two characteristics (ibid, section 14); discrimination arising from disability where a disabled person is treated 'unfavourably because of something connected with their disability when this cannot be justified' and through 'failure to make reasonable adjustments for disabled people' (see ibid, sections 15 and 21; EHRC, 2010: 4). The restriction in section 14 is an important one because it prevents a claim of direct and indirect discrimination being combined in one ground and restricts applicants to two grounds where only a combination of two relevant protected characteristics can be included in these grounds. It was a compromise made by the Labour Government 'in the face of opposition from the business lobby … who opposed any provision on multiple discrimination' as being unnecessarily 'burdensome' (Hepple, 2010: 16). It may also be true that analysis of multiple-discrimination would have been cumbersome for the judiciary who have indicated a preference for claims which involve only one protected characteristic because analysing the cumulative impact of discriminatory practices across the intersection of an individual's protected characteristics is difficult to quantify. To an extent, therefore, the current position of the law limits the development of jurisprudence on intersectionality. Although legislative strictures should not circumscribe academic analysis, this does, however, justify the need to focus on disability as a protected characteristic and as a focused perspective in criminology and criminal justice studies. Indeed, the incorporation of the social model of disability into the Act provides a site for analysis of the structural features that affect the entry and treatment of certain groups of defendants. The social model, therefore, provides a useful mechanism for intersectional approaches in future academic research.

Other prohibited conduct includes: harassment, which involves 'unwanted conduct which has the purpose or effect of violating someone's dignity or which is hostile, degrading, humiliating or offensive to someone with a protected characteristic or in a way that is sexual in nature' (Equality Act 2010, section 26); victimisation, which involves '[t]reating someone unfavourably because they have taken (or might be taking) action under the Equality Act or supporting somebody who is doing so' (Equality Act 2010, section 27); and discrimination arising out of someone 'wrongly [perceiving] them to have one of the protected characteristics' or discrimination because 'they are associated with someone who has a protected characteristic', for example, someone who is caring for a disabled person (ibid). Such conduct is also prohibited where a person is exercising 'a public function that is not the provision of a service to the public or a section of the public' (section 29(6)).

Equality and Human Rights Commission (E&HRC) Guidance makes it clear that this prohibited conduct applies to criminal justice organisations – a 'person or organisation who is involved in the criminal … justice system, whether what they are doing counts as a service or as a public function' – 'service providers' for the purposes of the Equality Act, include: the police; prisons and similar institutions, such as young offender institutions; probation services and criminal justice social work services; national security; criminal courts, civil courts and tribunals (2011: 4–7). The Equality Act also imposes an anticipatory duty for service providers, encompassing the aforementioned criminal justice organisations, to make reasonable adjustments for disabled service users. This duty comprises three requirements 'to take such steps as it is reasonable to have to take to avoid the disadvantage': firstly, 'a provision, criterion or practice of the service provider's' (section 20(3)); secondly, a 'physical feature' (Section 20(4)) puts a disabled person at a substantial disadvantage in relation to a relevant matter in comparison with persons who are not disabled; or, thirdly, 'where a disabled person would, but for the provision of an auxiliary aid, be put at a substantial disadvantage in relation to a relevant matter in comparison with persons who are not disabled, to take such steps as it is reasonable to have to take to provide the auxiliary aid' (section 20(5)). Where the first or third requirement relates to the provision of information, ensuring that information is provided in an accessible format is included in the steps which it is reasonable for a service provider to take to avoid disadvantage (section 20(6)).

The anticipatory nature of the duty to make reasonable adjustments means that service providers should not 'wait until a disabled person wants to use a service that they provide before they give consideration to their duty to make reasonable adjustments' (E&HRC, 2010: 103). Consequently, service providers should 'anticipate the requirements of disabled people and the adjustments that may have to be made for them'; this 'applies regardless of whether the service provider knows that a particular person is disabled' (ibid: 103–4). The compulsion for service providers – criminal justice organisations for our purposes – to anticipate the requirements of disabled people, strengthens the argument levied in this chapter. Not only is there descriptive and normative value in categorising autistic defendants as citizens with the protected characteristic of disability, there is a legal imperative to do so. The social model of disability is incorporated in the Equality Act 2010. This Act places a legal duty on public service providers to remove barriers which place disabled defendants (autism for the purpose of this book) at a substantial disadvantage in the courts compared with people who are not disabled. *Think Autism*, the 'refreshed' Autism Strategy for England (see chapter five), dedicated one of its *Priority Actions for Change* to ensuring reasonable adjustments are made to enable autistic adults to benefit fully from mainstream public services (DOH, 2014: 17). The *2021–26 Autism Strategy* also sets out national training and awareness raising on reasonable adjustments in standard police practice and for Her Majesty's Courts and Tribunals Service (HMCTS) in its section on improving understanding of autism across the criminal and youth justice systems (DOHSC and DfE, 2021a).

The problem is that it seems, in practice (see chapter six), especially in the lower courts, that defence solicitors and barristers are unaware of these resources or do not use them effectively with their autistic clients. Chapter six describes in detail the poor visibility and audibility from the dock in a Victorian Magistrates' Court where an autistic defendant was tried. It is argued there that the impact of these environmental factors on the exercise of the principle of orality should not be underestimated. As the case studies in chapters six to nine reveal, the problem is that autism is often identified only later in the court proceedings. Even when it is known about before the plea and case management hearing, there are no standard procedures for counsel to make arrangements for such a court visit prior to the defendant's first appearance. Where the defendant's autism is known to the counsel, difficulties around court listing and bail arrangements may also mean reasonable adjustments are overlooked (see chapter seven) and the anticipatory aspect of the duty to make reasonable adjustments is not fulfilled in practice. Thus, asking decision-makers in Phase 1 of the research, about what reasonable adjustments they have made or would be willing to make in their respective roles, and asking autistic defendants about reasonable adjustments they have actually received or requested to receive in Phase 2, formed an important line of investigation in understanding the governance of autistic defendants in the courts (see chapter four and six, respectively).

Section 149 of the Equality Act 2010 replaces the Disability Equality Duty with the Public Sector Equality Duty (PSED). Nevertheless, the 'iterative process' was still incorporated in the PSED which consists of 'the "general equality duty", which is the overarching requirement or substance of the duty, and the "specific duties" which are intended to help performance of the general equality duty' (E&HRC, 2012: 6). Applying to those 'public authorities' listed in Schedule 19 of the Equality Act and 'other organisations that … are carrying out public functions on behalf of … [these] public authorit[ies]' (ibid: 7), the purview of bodies subject to the PSED is narrower than the provisions for prohibited conduct and the duty to make reasonable adjustments. So, although Ministers of the Crown and government departments, the NHS, local government and the Police are encompassed by Schedule 19, exceptions in respect of the PSED, Schedule 18 include, for example, under section 3(1) judicial functions and functions 'exercised on behalf of, or on the instructions of, a person exercising a judicial function'. The general PSED requires those authorities, in the exercise of their functions, to have due regard to the need to:

> (a) eliminate discrimination, harassment, victimisation and any other conduct that is prohibited by or under this Act;
> (b) advance equality of opportunity between persons who share a relevant protected characteristic and persons who do not share it;
> (c) foster good relations between persons who share a relevant protected characteristic and persons who do not share it. (Equality Act 2010, s 149(1))

Public authorities must have due regard to all three of these PSED aims to comply with their general equality duty (E&HRC, 2012). In respect of the second aim of advancing equality of opportunity, section 149(3) explains that due regard to this involves the need to:

> (a) remove or minimise disadvantages suffered by persons who share a relevant protected characteristic that are connected to that characteristic;
> (b) take steps to meet the needs of persons who share a relevant protected characteristic that are different from the needs of persons who do not share it;
> (c) encourage persons who share a relevant protected characteristic to participate in public life or in any other activity in which participation by such persons is disproportionately low.

Section 149(6) states that 'compliance with the duties in this section may involve treating some persons more favourably than others'. Thus the 'iterative process' to which Baldry et al (2009) refer, formerly present in the DDA 2005 and incorporated in the social model of disability's aim to 'understand and dismantle the barriers which exclude and limit the life chances of disabled people' (Disability Rights Commission, 2006: 9) is still entrenched in this Act. Also pertinent to the development of the argument in this chapter is the requirement for public authorities to have due regard to the aims of the general equality duty 'when making decisions and when setting policies' (E&HRC, January 2012b: 5–6). Understanding the effect of their policies and practices on people with protected characteristics 'is an important part of complying with the general equality duty' because it can help those public authorities 'to consider whether the policy will be effective for all sorts of different people' (ibid). 'Policy' is used as shorthand for the full range of a public authority's 'policies, practices, activities and individual decisions', falling into three main categories: 'Organisational policies and functions' (for example, 'stop and search procedures'); 'Key decisions' (for example, 'a government department developing new legislation'); 'Policies that set criteria or guidelines for others to use' (for example, a local authority setting criteria about school admissions) (ibid: 7).

Even more pertinent for the governmentality approach used in the present book is that having due regard across all functions of a public authority 'may also involve assessing the impact on equality of decisions that are made together …' which would mean 'ensuring that [public authorities] have sufficient information to understand the cumulative (or combined) impact of these decisions' (ibid: 8). It seems that this 'cumulative impact' assessment needs to be undertaken across policies that a particular public authority has developed but they will also 'need to understand the impact on equality when implementing a policy that has been developed elsewhere' by, for example, other government departments (ibid). So, while 'responsibility for the policy itself will rest with the department that developed it', in making choices about how to implement it, the public authority must consider 'whether any mitigating measures or alternative ways of delivering [their] policies are required in order to minimise any negative impact on people with different protected characteristics' (ibid).

The ability of the governmentality approach to attend 'to the nexus between everyday practices and techniques, and more abstract technologies and broader political rationalities' (O'Malley et al, 1997: 503) connects well with the approach of the section 149 Public Sector Equality Duty and its application to policy and decision-makers. It also validates the explicit inclusion of questions to decision-makers about their normative considerations in the qualitative research carried out for this book. Further, analogies can be drawn between the concept of 'cumulative impact' which has been developed by the Equality and Human Rights Commission (EHRC, 2011) and the impairment-disability dyad discussed by Baldry et al (2008). In turn, this validates this book's objective of developing a disability perspective within criminology to better understand and critique the governance of autistic defendants in the English CJS.

Conclusion

This chapter has argued that central to the utility of developing a disability perspective in criminology is the need to provide a theoretical framework to analyse the governance of autistic defendants. There is descriptive value in proactively categorising these groups as 'disabled' under the 'social model' of 'disability'; enabling an enquiry into conditions of possibility – the first of the two lines of critical philosophy descended from Kant as discerned by Foucault. Rioux and Riddle note that 'broader social values and assumptions about disability are embedded in legal understandings, frameworks and jurisprudence' (2011: 2). Such an intellectual venture is timely, given the entrenchment of this model in the Equality Act 2010 and the inception of the Autism Act 2009, Statutory Guidance and related policy.

Disability has been 'presumed to be a static state' and there has been 'too little attention paid to conceptualising the impact of the legal construction [or lack thereof] of disability' (Rioux et al, 2011: 2). Critical disability studies render visible the fact that disabled people have been viewed as 'objects of pity, as recipients of charity and welfare' because of 'the nature of legal and social constructions of the status of disability' rather than as individuals 'entitled to rights' (ibid). The theoretical framework set out in this chapter of 'disabling' criminal justice is, therefore, also generative of the normative position discussed in chapter ten about how autistic defendants *should* be governed. An important response to the exclusion of disabled people from activities of daily living, social and cultural pursuits and the denial of their rights 'is to have recourse to law and for legal interpretation to be considered in light of disability' (ibid: 3). Rioux et al argue that the human rights principles of dignity, equality, inclusion and participation provide tools to critically assess the exercise of the law itself and 'offer insight into justice' for disabled people (ibid). Therefore, drawing on this work, chapter ten utilises the kinds of 'intellectual resources' available in critical disability studies and in the emerging literature on 'disabling' criminology to develop modes of theorising and forms of empirical enquiry to assist criminology in coming 'to terms with the social and legal worlds that it aspires to comprehend and in which it intends to intervene' (Garland and Sparks, 2000: 2–3).

PART II

Strategies of Governance: Autistic Adult Defendants and Autism-specific Policy

4

Disability vs Vulnerability in Liaison and Diversion

Introduction

Early literature on the courts demonstrated the potential barrier of pre-trial 'shaping' of cases to interpreting data gathered during court proceedings (Baldwin, 2007: 383) and the value of understanding the procedures and decision-making in the earlier stages of the criminal process. This is evident in research on the pressures placed upon defendants to plead guilty (Baldwin and McConville, 1977), the impact of legal advice and assistance for defendants in police custody (Sanders, 1989; McConville and Hodgson, 1993) and the correlation between motivation for arrest and conviction (Phillips et al, 1998). The Liaison and Diversion agenda (L&D agenda) was borne out of the recommendations of the Bradley Report 2009, developed in parallel to the Equality Act 2010 and the Autism Act 2009 (see chapter five). It is this agenda which made offenders with mental health problems and learning disabilities, including autism, a locale for the attention of policy-makers. Therefore, this chapter explores the influences of the broader policy context towards offenders with mental health problems and learning disabilities on pre-trial shaping and reflects on the relevance of these instruments on the governance of autistic adult defendants. It does so by triangulating a textual analysis of policy documentation with interviews conducted with elite decision-makers.[1] Thus, facilitating an understanding of the connection between 'wider structures', in particular 'legal orders' relating to disabled defendants, and decision-making about autistic defendants in the court process, as explored in chapters six to eight.

A series of policy documents, Reports and Commissions proceeded the Bradley Report, working to implement its recommendations (see CPS, 2010; MOJ, 2011; Judicial College, 2013; Adebowale, 2013; HM Inspectorate of Probation and HM Inspectorate of Prisons, 2015; DOH, 2015b). A full rollout of Liaison and Diversionary Services (L&D services) was finally achieved in England by 2020. Section 1(A) gives an overview of the L&D agenda, which had been 'accepted' by the Coalition government 'to be carried forward into the cross-departmental Health and Criminal Justice Programme' (NHS England, 2013: 2). One of the

[1] Excerpts of interview responses are quoted in italics, followed by the professional status of the interviewee in brackets.

precepts of the governmentality approach is that how groups are categorised determines how their conduct is governed. As we saw in chapter three, autistic people come within the definition of disability used by the Equality Act 2010; conduct prohibited by this Act and the duty to provide reasonable adjustments applies to 'criminal justice organisation[s]' (E&HRC, March, 2011: 4–7). Section 1(B) of this chapter charts the shift from the original Bradley Review category of offenders with Mental Health and Learning Disabilities, including autistic defendants, to a broadening out of this group to the category of *vulnerable defendants* in the Service Specifications for L&D Services. This category is a rationality of government comprising epistemological 'assumptions and a particular idiom that enables a problem to be translated into language that then makes it amenable to intervention' (Rose, 1999; c.f. Gilling, 2010: 1143). Additionally, the section critiques the influence of 'Localism' on the implementation of the L&D agenda. This strategy of government moved decision-making about local services away from '*central-command*' (Senior Civil Servant 1) to local councils and community organisations (Holdaway, 2013: 220).

Whilst the categorisation of *vulnerable defendants* may assist in improving attitudes towards and awareness of their needs, it is problematic from the perspective of the social model of disability. Many defendants, including autistic defendants, incorporated into the categorisation of vulnerability have the protected characteristic of disability. The divergent categories of disability and vulnerability do not sufficiently relate to each other and attract different sets of policies, procedural protections and substantive outcomes. Section 2(A) argues that this divergence derives from the origin of the concept of the 'vulnerable adult' and its close association to the 're-balancing' of the CJS towards the victim (see Home Office, 2005). Whereas, 'disability' has its origin in the disabled people's movement, which lead to the Disability Discrimination Acts of 1995 and 2005, ultimately subsumed into the Equality Act 2010. As such, while there is a body of literature on strategies of governance centred on 'risk' and 'dangerousness' in relation to offenders with mental health problems and learning disabilities (see Seddon, 2008), these were not central to the development of the L&D Service Specifications (NHS England, 2014b & 2019b). Thus, section 2(B) analyses the dominance of the rationality of 'vulnerability' in the development of policy in this area and in elite interview responses. An under-researched topic in relation to defendants, the section also interrogates whether the concept is appropriate in its application to disabled defendants.

Section 3 presents interview data on how elite decision-makers perceived the role of the Equality Act 2010 in its application to criminal justice organisation (E&HRC, 2011: 4–7) and whether they perceived autistic defendants as having the protected characteristic of disability under the Act. Interviews revealed that the concept of vulnerable defendants created an oblique amnesia that defendant sub-groups within this categorisation, including autistic defendants, have this protected characteristic of disability. They were not considered as disabled citizens under the Equality Act 2010. Chapter four argues, therefore, that the concept of *vulnerability* perpetuates this 'oblique amnesia' because of its origins in the protection of victims and witnesses and the 'rebalancing' of the CJS towards the victim. In turn, this has sustained the asymmetrical access to Special Measures and Intermediaries between disabled victims and witnesses and defendants. Thus, resulting in an abrogation of responsibility towards these defendants in their access to legal protection under the Equality Act 2010 in the criminal courts and incoherence between this legal framework and policies directed at defendants with mental health problems and learning disabilities, which also apply to autistic defendants.

1. The Liaison and Diversion Agenda: The Locale for Policymaking Around Offenders with Mental Health Problems and Learning Disabilities

A. The Development of the Liaison and Diversion Agenda

In 2007, Jack Straw, as Secretary of State for Justice, commissioned Lord Bradley to undertake an independent review of 'the extent to which offenders with mental health problems or learning disabilities could, in appropriate cases, be diverted from prison to other services' (Bradley, 2009: 7). Lord Bradley was tasked with exploring barriers to diversion and making recommendations to government, particularly on the organisation of effective court L&D arrangements and the services needed to support them (ibid). He broadened the remit of 'diversion' in its 'traditional sense – i.e. schemes set up in courts' – to a diversionary agenda which considered 'the whole offender pathway' (2009: 7), moving policy and practice beyond their typically isolated development. Building on NACRO's definition of 'diversion' as a decision-making process and the National Policing Improvement Agency's (2008) definition which covers 'diversion' *from* the CJS as a whole, he defined diversion as:

> A process whereby people are assessed and their needs identified as early as possible in the offender pathway (including prevention and early intervention), thus informing subsequent decisions about where an individual is best placed to receive treatment, taking into account public safety, safety of the individual and punishment of an offence (Bradley, 2009: 15–16).

In mapping 'offender pathways' (2009: 24), Lord Bradley made 82 recommendations about the diversion of offenders with mental health problems and learning disabilities within the CJS of England and Wales. He uncovered incongruence between organisations, caused in part by the variety of definitions applied to these groups and lack of common understanding about assessment tools and identification (Bradley/Westminster Policy Forum, 2009). Consequently, the processes of identification, assessment and diversion were 'happening too far along the criminal justice pathway' (2009: 24); leading to a lack of proper information-sharing between organisations. This resulted in poor 'continuity of care', with no-one taking responsibility for the individuals, leaving them to bounce from one organisation to another (ibid: 7).

A 'flurry of activity' (Peay, 2013) greeted his report as criminal justice organisations discharged their obligations under its recommendations. The MOJ established the National Health and Criminal Justice Programme Board and a Delivery Plan was produced (see DOH, 2009). As jurisdiction shifted from the MOJ to the DOH, this Delivery Plan set out the 'programme of work' to implement the Report's recommendations. The 'single biggest change' they proposed was to establish L&D Services to work with the police and the courts to ensure that mental health problems and learning disabilities were 'identified as early as possible on the offender pathway' (ibid: 40).

Since 2009, sustained work has been done to keep this policy agenda on the political and organisational map. After the general election in 2010, the intention to implement the Bradley Report recommendations had been reaffirmed by the Coalition Government (NHS England, 2014; MOJ, 2011), and three bodies were set up to try to monitor the progress of L&D with a view to a national roll-out of the pilot schemes in 2015/16. The Bradley Group, comprised of organisations from the voluntary sector, has helped the government to shape the framework in which L&D Services will be established. In addition to this body, the Care Not Custody Group – looking at the alternatives to custody within L&D Services – and The Bradley Commission were established, both chaired by Lord Bradley. The latter took certain aspects of the original Report, which required further attention, and gathered evidence to establish what the core elements of the L&D agenda should be (Centre for Mental Health, 2014: 5), such as women, employment and the high prevalence of black and ethnic minority communities with mental health and learning disabilities in the CJS (Research Interview, Member of the House of Lords).

The historical development of L&D activity and the tensions and potential contradictions across the three phases of L&D rollout can be read elsewhere (Roch and Hean, 2021), as can an evaluation of the extent to which Lord Bradley's recommendations have been acted upon (Centre for Mental Health, 2014). Our task is to examine under 'what logics' autistic adult defendants are governed, throughout the 'offender pathway', including L&D services. The implementation of the Autism Statutory Guidance (DOH, 2010) sat within the jurisdiction of the DOH during the development of the wider L&D agenda. Yet, as discussed in chapter five below, its statutory authority over the CJS was limited in legal terms. Consequently, the elite interviews sought to elicit how this agenda and wider policy initiatives (Bradley, 2009; DOH, 2009; Adebowale, 2013; DOH, 2014) for defendants with mental health problems and learning disabilities applied to autistic defendants. It also sought to understand how these policies operated at the interfaces between the CJS, health and social care systems. Understanding the interrelationship between these systems is important in appraising the logics which inform decision-making surrounding autistic defendants in the criminal court process. For instance, a Senior Civil Servant and a Member of the House of Lords recognised the imperative that the 'link' between these systems should not be broken. Indeed, a Member of House of Lords perceived policies for offenders with mental health problems and learning disabilities must involve the CJS as part of a '*wrap-around*' response in order to sustain public support for the evolving L&D Services.

B. L&D Service Roll-out and 'Logics' Applied to Autistic Defendants

The first Liaison and Diversion Service Standard Service Specification ('The Service Specification', 2013/14 NHS) established the core requirements for the L&D Services that were initially piloted in 10 areas, covering 13 police forces. The Core Team workforce required that the L&D Services include an Adult Liaison and Diversion Practitioner, Learning Disability Practitioner and Speech and Language Therapist. Additionally, 'some' L&D Services would 'offer specifically a referral pathway for people with autism' (Senior Civil Servant 1), dependent upon the competencies of the particular local Extended Workforce Team. These teams were intended to provide extended capabilities which would involve the '"knitting together" of L&D with existing services' through coordinated 'local commissioning' (NHS, 2014: 19). Such services included: Psychiatry, Psychology, Social Work, Learning Disability and Autistic Spectrum, Police, Probation and HMCTS.

The then Home Secretary, Rt Hon Theresa May MP, said they were to 'be rolled-out across England by 2017', with '£25 million of government funding commissioned from NHS England' (11/07/2014). Ultimately, 100 per cent coverage of L&D Services across England was achieved by March 2020 and the Service Specification was updated in September 2019. The latter Specification builds on the first, 2014, iteration which shaped the operating model for L&D services: identification, screening, assessment, referral to other services and outreach. The L&D Service does not involve a whole population screening of defendants whose case reaches a plea and case management hearing in court. Instead L&D teams proactively check clients identified by them, or referred by other criminal justice agencies, who are in scope for the L&D service, against relevant databases (NHS England, 2015: 5; 2019: 10). Where an individual is in scope, they are offered a second stage screening appointment with a L&D practitioner to determine levels of 'risk' and 'urgency' for that individual to have of further involvement of or assessments by other organisations (NHS England 2014: 7; 2019: 11). For such individuals, a report is then provided to the court on the person's 'vulnerability', their ability to plead and/or participate in court proceedings, an assessment of potential needs, and any reasonable adjustments which will enable them to 'understand and engage in youth and criminal justice proceedings' (NHS England, 2014: 7, 8). As an interviewee explained, the L&D practitioner may subsequently make a 'referral to suitable [healthcare] services' for 'a limited period of case management and follow up by the core [L&D] service' (Senior Civil Servant 1). Multi-disciplinary teams, including peer support and recovery workers, provide outreach with people in community settings, alongside any ongoing criminal proceedings, to address issues such as housing and financial advice (NHS England 2019; see Disley et al, 2021: 2).

Explicating the logics towards autistic defendants, within the Service Specifications for L&D Services since their rollout, is crucial and illuminates these rationalities of governance applied to autistic defendants in L&D Services. What emerged from analysis of these policies and research interviews was the dominance of the concept of vulnerability and, in general, a greater emphasis on the liaison, rather than diversion, strand of the L&D agenda. The latter was likely impacted by localism, a strategy of government that influenced the implementation of this agenda and inter-agency working. Further, Localism had an associated influence on the changing epistemologies applied to autistic defendants.

The shift from the original Bradley Review category of offenders with Mental Health and Learning Disabilities, to a broadening out of this group to the category of *vulnerable defendants* under which autistic defendants are subsumed, is evident in both Service Specifications. The 2014 Service Specification's 'threshold' category of 'vulnerability' covered those with mental health, learning disability, substance misuse and other vulnerabilities, listing those 'service users most likely to be referred to and benefit from the service' (NHS England, 2014b: 4; 10). Screening and addressing the needs of defendants with an 'autistic spectrum' condition was specifically mentioned in the requirement for the Core Liaison and Diversion Team (NHS England, 2014b: 6; 7). Identification involves criminal justice agencies, working with the Police and Courts, recognising 'possible signs of vulnerability in people when they first meet them' and then alerting their local L&D service (NHS England, 2019b). Thus 'vulnerabilities' were the starting point in determining access to these services and not the pertinent protected characteristic, such as disability. The Liaison and Diversion Operating Model 2013/14 ('The Operating Model'), along with the updated Service Specification, provided for the delivery of an 'all age' L&D Service across all points of intervention in the youth and criminal justice pathways which must '**be relevant to those with protected characteristics as set out in the Equality Act 2010**' (NHS England, 2014a: 5; emphasis added; NHS England, 2019a). This language of 'relevance' to those with protected characteristics under the Equality Act 2010 is weak and does not denote the language of rights. A new section on 'Equity of Access', strengthens the recent Service Specification by requiring service providers must 'document consideration of how it meets the needs of people with different protected characteristics under the Equality Act and the Public Sector Equality Duty' (NHS England, 2019a: 5; 26). However, whilst this is reinforced by the Equalities Statements on protected characteristics, in the supplementary practical guides for L&D Practitioners, the totality of Equality Act provisions relating to disability are not covered and vulnerability remains the dominant rationality (see NHS England, 2019b & c).

Coupled with this shift, research interviews and policy analysis also revealed that the focus of the L&D Service has better operationalised the *liaison* arm of the L&D agenda. As a result, this reflects more closely the deontological objective of Lord Bradley's definition of diversion as a 'process whereby people are assessed and their needs identified as early as possible in the offender pathway' (2009: 16). The teleological objective of gathering this information to inform 'subsequent decisions about **where** an individual is best placed to receive treatment' (ibid; emphasis added) has been sidelined. In other words, diversion *out of* the CJS at various points along the pathway was not the objective of the L&D services. One Senior Civil Servant in the DOH perceived that the police '*thought*' that L&D Services were going to come into police stations and 'mop all these people up'; whereas 'it's much more' that these services are 'the point at which a health professional can … make sure that your vulnerabilities are being met' (Senior Civil Servant 1). The implication is that these 'vulnerabilities' are to be met *within* the CJS. This focus on *liaison* reflects the imperative to maintain the 'link' between health, social care and the criminal justice system. Again, this was mirrored in the original Service Specification which stated that '[d]iversion should be interpreted in its *wider sense*, referring to **both** diversion "out of" and "**within**" the youth and criminal justice systems' (NHS, 2014b: 4, emphasis added).

The first Service Specification's emphasis on the function of *liaison* was also manifest in responsibilities for the services' L&D practitioners including: informing decision-making; advice on making reasonable adjustments; and mobilising multi-agency care (ibid: 18). The 'information flow', facilitated by the liaison function of L&D practitioners, proffered an opportunity to do justice to individuals in scope of this service and promote closer working between CJS organisations. However, the original Service Specification and Operating Model omitted to mention important elements to embed this effectively. L&D Practitioners' role in obtaining Special Measures or appointing intermediaries in supporting vulnerable defendants to 'participate in court' were excluded. These *are* both now included in the updated Service Specification's expanded responsibility for L&D practitioners to provide advice to decision-makers within criminal justice agencies, such as recommendations for referral for an assessment of fitness to plead (NHS England, 2019: 14). Unfortunately, informed consent was not a prerequisite of this information sharing in the original Service Specification either and, where the offer of a screening assessment was declined, a 'risk alert form' could be completed and noted on file, indicating refusal to be screened (NHS England, 2014). Although now rectified (see NHS England, 2019: 31), the recent Service Specification does not ensure data sharing by defence lawyers with L&D Practitioners is in the best interests of their client. Such steps are vital to preventing disclosure of information which may be prejudicial to the defendant's case and so that L&D services incorporate the social, rather than the medical, model of disability, treating individuals in scope of the service as subjects with rights (see section 3(C) below).

The focus on diversion *within* the CJS was, according to a Senior Civil Servant in the DOH, driven by the MOJ's 'silo mentality' as 'some of the Ministers in Justice haven't liked' the 'diversion bit' of L&D Services because it suggests that 'the individual is being diverted away from the punishment they deserve for the offence they have committed' (Senior Civil Servant 2). Consequently, this Civil Servant perceived that 'sometimes … different paradigms' are being used (Senior Civil Servant 2). This is despite the central aim of the L&D service to enable an individual's effective participation in the CJS process (NHS England, 2014b: 5). This MOJ 'paradigm' is evident in the 2014 Service Specification's statement that access to L&D Services by, individuals meeting the threshold of vulnerability, '**does not imply** that they will **avoid appropriate sanctions**' imposed by the CJS (ibid; emphasis added). Instead, that the CJS process will be better informed and that there will be improved access to appropriate health and social care interventions (ibid). The 2019 Service Specification replicates this language, adding 'social care, education and training' in expanding the list of interventions aimed at diverting individuals, where appropriate, out of the youth and criminal justice systems (NHS England, 2019a: 8).

In doing so, however, neither Service Specifications make reference to the Care Act 2014 in improving access to social care interventions for such defendants. This is disappointing given the relevance of the Care Act in this context, which defines the requirements for local authorities to meet the care needs of children and adults (section 8) and provides the reformed eligibility criteria for social care (sections 9–13). Importantly, for our purposes, the Care Act also updates the aftercare requirements (section 75) following the discharge of a patient who may have been detained under a Hospital Order under the Mental Health Act 1983 and provision for an adult being released from prison (section 76; see chapters eight and nine). Moreover, the six practical guides for L&D Practitioners do not refence either the Care Act 2014 nor the Autism Act 2009. While the practical guide on *People with a learning disability, autism or both* does provide actions to support these groups, most are types of reasonable adjustments (NHS England, 2019c, 13–14; 16–17), it does not strengthen the detail on the role and responsibilities of L&D practitioners to divert individuals *into* social care.

This matters both to the access autistic defendants have to social care at the interface of the health, social care and criminal justice systems and to them as disabled people with rights. Chapter eight considers how cases could have benefitted from a more coherent and integrated approach. One example is that of 'William', an autistic adult who was given a Community Order which stipulated that he could only use public transport if he was accompanied by an adult aged over 18 who knew about his previous convictions. William had no adult social care support from his local authority. He was ashamed of his convictions and did not want other people to know about them. This meant that his mother, who was in her seventies, had to travel everywhere with him. The lack of social care support and the restrictive nature of the Community Order in William's case led to an imbalance between protection of the public and restriction of his and his mother's freedom. His case is illustrative of the problem of incoherent access to social care and governing defendants through the service language of vulnerability, rather than of the rights which flow from the status of being disabled citizens.

More coherent practice at the interface between health, social care and the criminal justice systems also matters in relation to ethical considerations which arise for disabled defendants at this intersection and the changing epistemologies which are applied to them. These changing epistemologies will be entrenched by the expectation that L&D Services are to treat and manage individuals 'within a whole care pathway approach with services working collaboratively' (NHS England, 2019: 5). This is an approach underpinned by the *Mental Health Crisis Care Concordat* (the 'Concordat'; DOH, 2014), designed to achieve a parity of esteem between mental health and physical health (DOH, November 2013: 15). The 'Concordat' was a blueprint for the ways in which statutory and voluntary services work together with NHS Offender Health and bolster the operation of L&D pathways. As one interviewee recalled, its *raison d'être* was for commissioners to better identify and support 'a particular group or section of society [that] is reaching crisis point at a disproportionate rate' or only 'accessing mental health services through involvement with the CJS' (Senior Civil Servant 1). This evinces a recognition of the 'interconnected variables' noted by Browning and Caulfield (2011), which lead autistic adult defendants into the CJS (see chapter one).

Analysis of elite interviews indicate that the origins of the Concordat was to address such 'variables' and reveal the influence thinking around the Concordat had on expanding L&D Services in tackling 'vulnerabilities'. According to a Senior Civil Servant in the DOH, the Concordat 'started from concerns of the police' about 'picking up a lot of people who haven't committed a crime' or, where they have, their needs 'are really mental health' coupled with offenders with 'substance misuse problems' (Senior Civil Servant 1). Local services explained to the DOH that things go 'wrong' for these individuals 'when you don't have very responsive mental health services'; and the 'the wider vulnerabilities' affecting such individuals who needed to 'get the right service as quickly as possible' (ibid). For instance, it was not just 'about the police' but about making 'a big difference' to 'the person who rings the crisis team saying "I need some help" and by the time they are rung back they've been sectioned' (Senior Civil Servant 1). Chapter six discusses the problems that arise when multi-agency engagement either does not happen or happens too late along the criminal justice pathway. These case studies came to court prior to the roll-out of NHS England's new operating models for L&D Services and the Concordat's implementation. However, there is cause for pessimism about the extent of real change for cases involving autistic defendants, especially when these case studies are seen in conjunction with the numbers of autistic people in inpatient care (see chapter five).

C. Localism's Influence on L&D Services

Both policy document analysis and interviews with relevant actors revealed Localism was a significant strategy of government that shaped the implementation of these L&D services in practice across the country. The Localism Act 2011 and related policy (see DOH, 2010d & e) heralded significant alterations in the relationship between the disabled citizen and the state (see Lewis, 2011) and led to a greater diversity of organisations involved in the governance of offenders with mental health problems and learning disabilities. Thus, the former Coalition Government of 2010–15 and subsequent Conservative government's style of localism – bound up with the Big Society agenda (Cameron, 2010; 2011) – had a pervasive impact on the way that government departments have made policy over the last decade. The Big Society was seen as a vague slogan by some (see Mulgan et al, 2010), criticised by others as an insidious smokescreen for austerity measures (see Evans, 2011) and as a mask to hide the State's withdrawal from central areas of public policy (see Reiner, 2013). Its 'hands off' approach (Nicholson, 2011), which assumes 'that citizens are "competent" and "capable" and should be able to do the things the state "used to do"' (Lent, 2011), lead Goodley to ask what becomes of the 'citizen who is judged to fail to match up to the dominant ideal-type?' (2011). Runswick-Cole and Goodley suggest that this is an example of 'ableism in motion' where the 'shrinking state and disappearing rights' lead to the 'further oppression of disabled people' (2011).

In practical, policy-making terms, a Senior Civil Servant described localism's 'different approach', following the change of government in 2010, in 'the operational side of health' which 'is run at arm's length from the Department' and the Coalition 'government's view towards cross-governmental working' (Senior Civil Servant 2). The interviewee recalled how this shaped the Department of Health's implementation of the L&D agenda and Autism Strategy (DOH, 2010b; 2014) because 'some of the architecture which existed previously about cross government issues doesn't exist anymore' and the 'nominal lead that certain departments had on some cohorts … is … not really happening …' (ibid). This interviewee also ascribed this shift to 'the reduction in central government department's size' (Senior Civil Servant 2) and the abolition, by the Coalition government, of Labour's Public Service Agreements (PSAs). Although 'of variable effectiveness …', the interviewee saw PSAs as 'a mechanism to get people together on a shared set of outcomes' (Senior Civil Servant 2). Another interviewee cited this as significant for Liaison and Diversion by 'pushing everything down to the localism approach' which made what they were trying to achieve and 'how you achieve it quite different' (Senior Civil Servant 1). The Coalition government approach was described by another civil servant in the DOH as 'less direct … [with] less scope to be central and use central command' (Senior Civil Servant 2). Indeed, according to a Senior Civil Servant in the DOH, the L&D Service Specification was introduced to better evaluate data on L&D Services, which had been set up 'at the time when localism was pre-eminent' and schemes were established without any standardisation, and the DOH found they 'couldn't compare apples and turnips!' (Senior Civil Servant 1). The justification for 'localism' was to allow 'local councils and community organisations to make decisions about local services and significantly influence their work' (Holdaway, 2013: 220). In practice, however, moving from 'central command' down to the 'localism approach' drove a differential implementation, across local authorities, of the roll-out of L&D Services (Senior Civil Servant 1; Senior Civil Servant 2; NHS England, 2014b; 2019a) and of subsequent iterations of Autism Strategies (DOH, 2010a & 2014a; DOHSC, 2021).

Where implemented, research shows L&D services lead to increased numbers of local team referrals; which may reduce court adjournments, the overall amount of time spent attending court and some evidence of an association with improved mental health among both adults and young people (McGlaughlin, 2021). A recent evaluation found that L&D Services successfully engaged people with a broad range of vulnerabilities, appearing to intervene at a point of crisis, when people are most in need of support, with the likelihood of service users receiving a custodial sentence is halving following their involvement (Disley et al, 2021). However, there was substantial variation between L&D services in the types of interventions offered, they do not appear to reduce offending and court processes are not significantly affected by these services (ibid). This impacted local authorities' effectiveness in achieving the outcome of ensuring autistic adults received support in the CJS (NAO, 2012: 28; see chapter five below) and reinforces the present research's interview data on the influence of localism.

Chaplin et al found an absence of robust epidemiological studies into L&D populations and making prevalence estimates for autism difficult to establish in this context (Chaplin et al, 2021a, 2021b). At present, there is considerable variation in the assessment of autism across L&D services; thwarted by a lack of diagnostic and screening services and dependent upon the availability of specific expertise and local policy arrangements (Allely et al, 2023). Case studies in chapters six to eight illustrate this, indicating that inconsistency in health and social care provision, driven by localism, has likely affected the aforementioned 'interconnecting variables' which lead autistic adult defendants into the CJS. This in turn influences court practice because the adequacy of local social care assessments and the availability of hospital placements affects the courts' use of disposal options – in particular those options available under the Mental Health Act 1983, Mental Health Treatment Requirements and Community Orders (see especially William and Claire's cases).

These findings are validated by research on variation in practice of the implementation of L&D models, which found they were 'largely left to local interpretation' (Chaplin et al, 2021: 118). This is largely because the range of different agendas of agencies involved partly underpin the inconsistent adaptation of practices and information transfer (Chadwick and Wesson, 2020). It has been posited that service variation could be in part due to the differing priorities of Police Crime Commissioners (PCCs) (Walsh, 2018) and local L&D services were adapting the policy 'to their local circumstances'; meaning implementation 'has not galvanised improved collaboration between L&D sites, and between L&D and neighbouring services in criminal justice and welfare systems' (Rocha and Hean, 2021: 158). Disley et al recommend that L&D services could be improved through 'increased capacity for onward referrals' (ibid: xi–xii). Thus, further detailed work needs to be done to model good practice around onward referral to adult social care in future versions of the Service Specification. As there is currently an absence of an agreed L&D model for autistic defendants, Allely et al also advocate further discussion on how L&D services are offered to autistic defendants and what 'essential components' are required to be integrated into existing systems and pathways (2023: 61). More research is also needed on the role of localism and variations in local implementation in L&D services, on whether defendants in the scope of these services were diverted *within* the CJS rather than *outside* of it.

2. Vulnerable or Disabled Defendants?

A. Understanding the Divergence

So, what are the origins of vulnerability in this context and why is this significant for the governance of disabled defendants and autistic defendants in particular? The concept of the 'vulnerable adult' derives from a Consultation Paper, *Who decides?*, issued by the Lord Chancellor's Department (1997). It refers to a person who is aged over 18 and:

> who is or may be in need of community care services by reason of mental or other disability, age or illness; who is or may be unable to take care of him or herself, or unable to protect him or herself against significant harm or exploitation (Home Office and DOH, 2000: 8–9).

It was entrenched in the provisions for and definitions of vulnerable and intimidated witnesses in Part II of the Youth Justice and Criminal Evidence Act 1999 and in the joint guidance issued by the Home Office and DOH (2000), *No Secrets*. Under this Act, the vulnerable and intimidated witnesses eligible for Special Measures include children under 17 (section 16(1)(a)); those witnesses whose quality of evidence is likely to be diminished by reason of mental disorder, significant impairment of intelligence and social functioning (section 16(2)(a)(i), (ii)) or a physical disability or a physical disorder (section 16(2)(b)). Witnesses likely to experience particular fear or distress in testifying are also eligible, by reason of the nature and circumstances of the offence, and the age of the witness (section 17(2)(a), (b)). Interestingly, the court may also consider a number of other matters in deciding whether the witness is likely to experience particular fear or distress, namely, their social and cultural background and ethnic origins, domestic and employment circumstances and religious beliefs or political opinions (section 17(2)(c)(i), (ii) and (iii)), along with any behaviour towards the witness by the accused, the accused's family members or associates of the accused, or any other person who is likely to be accused or a witness in the proceedings (section 17(2)(d)(i), (ii) and (iii)). Finally, victims and witnesses of sexual offences are eligible for Special Measures unless they wish not to have access to them (section 17(4)).

Introducing the first mandatory Special Measures for vulnerable and intimidated witnesses, the Youth Justice and Criminal Evidence Act (YJCEA) 1999, when 'taken as a package' of measures, signified 'the most radical rewriting of the orthodox rules for treatment of witnesses in the adversarial trial system in the common law world' (Hoyano, 2009: 345). Special Measures for these vulnerable and intimidated witnesses, introduced by the YJCEA 1999, consisted of screens in the courtroom between the witness and defendant (section 23); giving evidence over live TV link (section 24); giving evidence in private (section 25); the removal of wigs and gowns by counsel and the judiciary (section 26); video recorded evidence-in-chief (section 27); video recorded cross-examination (section 28); examination of a witness through an intermediary (section 29) and aids to communication (section 30). The *No Secrets* guidance was intended, in part, to bolster the provisions of the Act by developing and implementing multi-agency policies and procedures to protect vulnerable adults from abuse (Home Office and DOH, 2000).

No Secrets set out how commissioners and providers of care services should protect vulnerable adults through the development of local multi-agency codes of practice. Agencies responsible for the codes of practice, underpinned by this guidance, included the police and 'other relevant law enforcement agencies (including the CPS)' (ibid: 14). These agencies were expected to protect two corpora of vulnerable adults: those individuals receiving adult social care and support and vulnerable or intimidated victims and witnesses. Thus, the category of *vulnerability* acted as a driver for access to Special Measures Directions in the courts and multi-agency bodies working between criminal justice, health and social care organisations in respect to these corpora of individuals. Consequently, in criminal justice policy and practice, vulnerability became bound up with concepts of 'victimhood' and the 'rebalancing' of the CJS towards the victim (see Home Secretary et al, 2002). In light of this, it is easy to see the legal, conceptual and cultural difficulties in the development of the concept of the vulnerable *defendant*. Whilst impairment is a central feature to each of the three factors determining the eligibility of witnesses who may access Special Measures on the grounds of incapacity (see YJCEA 1999, section 16), this categorisation ties the concept of vulnerability closely to the group of victims eligible for these measures on the grounds of risk of harm and exploitation.

Further, section 16(1) of the YJCEA explicitly excluded defendants from the 'special measures' provisions; leading to an 'asymmetrical' application of measures to enable effective participation in court for vulnerable witnesses. This was out of step with the disability discrimination provisions of the DDA 2005. Hence, it is important to note here Jacobson and Talbot's review of the treatment of vulnerable defendants within the criminal courts of England and Wales recommended that the HMCTS should ensure its provision was fully compliant with the then DDA 2005, making the courts fully accessible to vulnerable defendants (2009). Indeed, as Jacobson et al explain, this asymmetrical approach to vulnerable defendants has been gradually eroded (2016: 40–2), thanks to pressure from academics and CJS professionals (see Hoyano, 2009; Bradley 2009; Talbot, 2012), by subsequent legislative amendments and a more recent Practice Direction. Thus by 2006, a 'vulnerable accused' was, where certain conditions are met, permitted to give evidence to the court (YJCEA 1999, s 33A[2]) and the right to support from an intermediary in court was extended to vulnerable victims in 2009 (YJCEA 1999, s 33AB[3]). The subsequent Report *Fair Access to Justice?* sets out the legal framework governing these defendants in the courts and how to better implement Special Measures for vulnerable defendants (Talbot/PRT, 2012). Practice Direction III.30 within the *Consolidated Criminal Practice Direction* (MOJ, 2013c), albeit non-statutory, sets out a range of measures to support vulnerable defendants in making the environment of court less intimidating and aiding their comprehension of the court process and capacity to communicate.

Studies on the effectiveness of the implementation of Special Measures can be read elsewhere (see McEwan, 2013; Plotnikoff and Wilson, 2009, 2014). The use of Special Measures for autistic adults was not, therefore, central to the present research; instead, it sought to understand the relationship between the categories of vulnerable and disabled defendants and how autistic defendants are being characterised. The legislative and common law asymmetry of protections for vulnerable defendants is discussed in more detail elsewhere (Hoyano, 2009; 2015). What the present research revealed was that, despite the changes to access to intermediaries and Special Measures for vulnerable defendants in law and policy, the perception that they applied asymmetrically was pervasive; exacerbated by professional misunderstandings and the operation of court practice (see chapter six). One of the sources of the misunderstanding in this area may originate from the drafting of the original *No Secrets* Guidance (Home Office and DOH, 2000), because, although its Appendix signposts readers to the DDA 1995, it does not expressly state the confluence of its protection and that legislative schema. Differentiating the origins and conceptualisation of *vulnerability* and *disability* as a protected characteristic helps to make sense of the divergent development of protections afforded to vulnerable witnesses. In particular, it helps us to make sense of the concept of the vulnerable defendant on the one hand (Home Office and DOH, 2000) and, on the other, those protections available to disabled persons when using the services of criminal justice organisations through the DDA's of 1995 and 2005 and the subsequent Equality Act 2010. The apparent consequence of this divergence is that CJS professionals have overlooked the Equality Act 2010 in securing access to special measures and intermediaries as reasonable adjustments for disabled defendants appearing before the court. Further, from the case studies

[2] Inserted by the Police and Justice Act 2006.
[3] Inserted by the Coroners and Justice Act 2009.

research, it appears that ground rules hearings to establish the use of an intermediary for vulnerable defendants (Criminal Procedure Rules 2013, rule 3.8(4)(d)) are underutilised, possibly as a result of pervasive perceptions of the asymmetrical application to vulnerable defendants.

B. Vulnerability: An Appropriate Concept for Disabled Defendants?

Over two decades on, this divergence between the categories of vulnerability and disability has also contributed to confusion about the application of the Equality Act 2010 to defendants with a protected characteristic of disability. What emerged from analysis of the policy surrounding the L&D agenda and data gathered in the research interviews, was vulnerability's conceptual appeal. Its expansiveness and flexibility for criminal justice and clinical governance strategies towards certain groups of defendants made it attractive as a pragmatic response to individuals with a range of needs. Vulnerability encapsulates the multiplicity of complex health conditions and 'problematic' socio-economic circumstances presented by individuals coming into contact with these services. Senior Civil Servants from the DOH commented that these common factors required an expansive concept which allows service-led intervention because the Department of Health leads on 'a range of vulnerabilities … learning disability, autism, dementia …' for adults in health and social care (Senior Civil Servant 2). Conversely, 'for younger people, a lot of other vulnerabilities are to do with family circumstances' (Senior Civil Servant 1). Consequently, interviewees said it 'wouldn't be feasible for all staff and all services to have in-depth training in all those areas; you've got to recognise who are the critical people and think about … [how] to raise awareness and understanding' (Senior Civil Servant 2). In the research interviews the Senior Civil Servants working on L&D Services and autism policy perceived that the police and other agencies were more comfortable in responding proactively to the concept of the vulnerable defendant. As opposed to defendants with a specific impairment, such as autism, or the notion of a defendant with a disability, recalling that:

> [Senior Police] are talking a lot more about [the Autism Strategy], in relation to the training at the police training college about … **knowing how to react to vulnerability rather than the Adebowale talk about training in Mental Health** (Senior Civil Servant 1; emphasis added).

This Senior Civil Servant observed that, for the police, the concept of vulnerability has more resonance as its opaque quality prevents the need for them to become 'quasi-mental health professionals'; allowing them to 'think' about the person's 'vulnerabilities' (ibid). One Senior NHS-Police Inspector, who worked across the policymaking in this area, supported this observation educing that the concept enabled the police to 'know how to respond to the situation in front of them'

(Senior NHS-Police Inspector), whatever the underlying cause of that behaviour or vulnerability might be. A Senior Civil Servant also gave the use of restraint as another prominent area where they perceived the concept of vulnerability enabled the police to see 'the person as a whole person' rather than 'regarding them as behaving oddly and need[ing] to be held down' (Senior Civil Servant 1). Describing the implications of the Independent Commission on Mental Health and Policing (the 'Adebowale Report' 2013), vulnerability was stated as assisting the police in understanding when restraint is necessary or exacerbated by 'police officers' in uniform 'who hold [a defendant] down' (Senior Civil Servant 1).

Yet the predominance of the concept of vulnerability sits awkwardly with the principles which underpin the social model of disability. In the context of disability hate crime, scholars have argued that it is inherently disablist to refer to disabled persons as vulnerable because it automatically conflates disability with vulnerability (Quarmby, 2011). One Member of Parliament expressed their concern about this conflation and 'misuse of the concept of "vulnerability"' by citing former DPP, Ken Macdonald, who 'fully rejected the idea that disabled people are per se vulnerable'. This Parliamentarian explained that where there may be situations where a disabled person may 'become vulnerable' because their disability means they 'can't get away from a scene as quickly' but that Lord Macdonald 'quite rightly warned against the glib assumption' that people were intrinsically vulnerable. This Member of Parliament explained if you do that, you start asking questions about why vulnerable people are '"going out at night"' or '"going clubbing?"' Comparing this to attitudes towards women taking responsibility for their risk of being raped, he believed that this 'is the wrong way to look at disability' because:

> disabled people don't get up in the morning and say they are vulnerable. They say – 'yes, I have got a disability but I'm a human being and I've got a right to access mainstream life like everyone else'. … 'why should I be sectioned off because I am "vulnerable" in a generic sense?' (Member of Parliament)

Connotations of weakness have led others to mount the critique that the designation of groups as vulnerable, in their provision of services and the deployment of their responsibilities, is an inherently paternalistic process undertaken by the powerful majority group (Roulstone *et al*, 2011). Nevertheless, vulnerability is a concept which is still perceived as helpful by academics and criminal justice decision-makers alike. A vulnerability-centred approach in the context of hate crime, for example, does not automatically establish an association with disability and features of defenceless passive victimisation (Chakraborti and Garland, 2012: 507). Instead, proponents of this approach direct attention towards those individuals who fall through the cracks in current policy frameworks and facilitates better recognition of the intersectionality of identities that can be targeted by perpetrators of hate crime. Finally, the lens of vulnerability is important in the global context of austerity measures which make cuts to welfare and public services (ibid: 507; 509). Analogous arguments were made by architects of the L&D Services who were anxious to 'address vulnerabilities' outside a person's mental health because that issue 'might not be the most risk to somebody who has come into contact with the police and the CJS' (Senior Civil Servant 1).

This quote acknowledges the structural factors and the wider interconnecting variables that may lead defendants with mental health problems and learning disabilities into the CJS. However, it is contended that the social model of disability provides a better analytical framework than the concept of vulnerability in enabling the exploration of the 'social, political, cultural, and economic factors that define disability and shape personal and collective responses to difference' (Baldry et al, 2008: 32). This model provides a counterweight to the aforementioned connotations of weakness imbued in both legislative and professional conceptualisations of vulnerability. As discussed in chapter three, the social model of disability attempts to redress the power imbalance, empowering disabled people as citizens with rights (O'Grady et al, 2004: 260). The impairment-disability dyad of the social model is helpful in achieving this by shifting the analysis away from individual weakness towards an 'iterative process of identifying, understanding and removing obstacles to resources' (Baldry et al, 2008: 32–33). As discussed in chapter six, one of the unforeseen consequences of the dominance of the rationality of vulnerability is that, in criminal justice practice, disabled defendants are dislocated from the legislative protections which are available to them as citizens with a protected characteristic of disability.

3. The Protected Characteristic of Disability: The Perceived Utility of the Equality Act 2010 for Disabled Defendants

This research aimed to determine whether autistic defendants were considered in terms of their legal status as disabled citizens under the Equality Act 2010 (chapter one). The intention was to discern to what extent there was coherence between the legal framework provided by the Equality Act 2010, whose ambit covers 'criminal justice organisation[s]' (E&HRC, 2011: 4–7; chapter three), and policies directed at defendants with mental health problems and learning disabilities. Further, it was hoped to establish what operative role the Act had on decision-making about policies and practices in relation to autistic adult defendants and to capture how interviewees considered and applied the provisions for citizens who have the protected characteristic of disability when they come into the CJS as defendants.

What the responses revealed was a lack of understanding, demonstrating the need for better implementation of this legislation by criminal justice organisations. Across the strata of interviewees most acknowledged the general relevance of the application of the legislation in the CJS but there was a lack of specific knowledge about the provisions of the Act for defendants, particularly in court. One civil servant acknowledged that 'the awful thing about the Equality Act, you only register non-compliance …' (Senior Civil Servant 2). Another Civil Servant noted that such compliance must be proven, which they attributed in part to 'these things' taking 'time to change and people do talk about it much more' (Senior Civil Servant 1). These interviewees, working across the L&D agenda and autism strategies, also ascribed 'a lack of awareness' about its application for 'non-physical disability[ies]' and 'suspect[ed]' that 'people are not clear whether' they are 'included or not' (Senior Civil Servant 2). In particular, 'where people have a mental health [problem]' they had 'been in discussions where people have been confused whether it is or isn't encompassed' in the Act and if it 'should be defined as a disability' for example, 'someone said' to them:

> 'well the universal symbol for disability is a picture of someone in a wheelchair'. People find it hard … to think in terms of disability more broadly … they might get as far as sensory impairment but getting any further is a stretch (ibid).

Whilst many saw the Bradley Report had been influential in directly and indirectly highlighting the relevance of the Equality Act 2010 to the court process, there remained a lack of awareness and confusion about the Act's role in this context. For example, two Senior Civil Servants responded that '… it's difficult to comment on that question' (Senior Civil Servant 1); and 'you're better asking the courts and what they think' because there is 'probably more information they can provide' (Senior Civil Servant 2). Interviewees often paused before responding to the question, saying things like this Senior NHS-Police Inspector:

> … whether we should have cognisance of the duty under the Equality Act in a criminal justice process, I've got to say yes because that's what it's about but having said ethically that's the right answer, I'm not sure what that means in practice.

In some cases, respondents gave no answer or, like this Chief Crown Prosecutor, said: 'No, sorry, I don't think I can answer that question'. One Member of Parliament, rather tellingly, retrieved their mobile device, scrolled down the legislation on its screen and said:

> well if you look at it, the protected characteristic of disability, you are protected at work, in education and as a consumer when using public services. I would have thought that the definition will cover attendance at or appearance in court …

On the one hand it may well be impracticable to expect all senior decision-makers to have exhaustive legal knowledge on the application of this Act to the CJS, on the other, the important work being done on improving the interfaces between health, social care and criminal justice makes this awareness all the more pertinent. This is particularly the case if we believe it is normatively important to sustain the social model in these contexts and move away from the predominance of the medical model of disability. Yet, as the following response from a Senior NHS-Police Inspector shows, there is still a discrepancy in institutional paradigms based on the predominance of the medical model:

> Mental health is in itself a disability and when you talk to NHS colleagues about diversity and equality, they will talk about … gender issues [but] [t]hey won't talk about mental health because they see that as a clinical condition. If you look at where ACPO cited their work around mental health and disability, it was in an equality and diversity work stream so they're coming at it from a different agenda.

Further, a Member of Parliament did not 'think' that the Equality Act 2010 was at the forefront of the minds of the decision-makers in court 'at all' when 'it comes to the defendant', though 'it might be in terms of the victim or the witness'; reinforcing the arguments levied above.

When prompted about whether the provisions of the Act should take more of a central role, this Parliamentarian thought 'it could do but I don't think any of us want to use these things as a sort of cloak to allow defendants with a disability to escape responsibility'. This is significant: implicit is the association that the application of the Act is about escaping responsibility, when actually it is a matter of accessing their procedural rights, such as the right to a fair trial and proportional punishment. Uncertainty about whether or not the provisions applied to disabled defendants was a recurrent theme in other interviews too. The assumption was that there was differential applicability and relevance of the Equality Act's reasonable adjustments and 'duty to pay due regard', for example, for disabled victims and witnesses as opposed to disabled defendants: that it applied to the former but not the latter. It seems that this is borne out of a canteen culture (cf Fielding, 1994) which was based on the original asymmetrical application of Special Measures for victims and witnesses and not defendants (above). Perhaps it is because these measures foreground procedural adjustments for vulnerable defendants, that the Equality Act 2010 and its requirements surrounding reasonable adjustments were overlooked. The duty to provide reasonable adjustments in the Equality Act 2010 is, in fact, asymmetric towards disabled people (as opposed to the non-disabled comparator group): 'the differential treatment of people with disabilities is necessary to achieve equality' (Fredman, 2011: 98; chapter three). It expressly recognises 'that, instead of requiring conformity to the able-bodied norm, modification of the environment or of existing policies or practices is essential if people with disabilities are to have genuine equality of opportunity' (ibid). Thus, the courts have a duty to 'make adjustments to enable the full participation of disabled people' (Judicial College, 2022: 79).

Another subtext which emerged was that practitioners adopted different approaches to accessing protection under the Equality Act 2010 for a disabled defendant, depending on the association between the defendant's autism and whether this impairment was a direct cause of the individual's criminality. In other words, for a Senior NHS-Police Inspector, it was 'a fundamental question' to ask:

> Do we treat people with autism differently depending on whether it was a driver of the offence? What you're effectively saying is we want to reduce re-offending; we want to provide a better service for people with mental ill-health because … by addressing those health inequalities we will also be reducing crime … [I]t is predicated with almost the

> unwritten assumption that it is mental health that is in part one of the drivers of the offending and what we're talking about here is something that, therefore, particularly around autism is something that may not be part of the offending cycle of the rationale of the offending.

This Senior NHS-Police Inspector went on to explicate three scenarios in the treatment of defendants, based on whether autism: (a) 'definitely is' such a 'driver' of the offending; (b) it definitely is not a driver of the offending; (c) and when 'you don't know whether it has a relationship to the offending or not'. In relation to the first formulation, where there is an association between the defendant's offending and their autism, the interviewee framed that as a 'Liaison and Diversion issue and that decision has to be made in the round'. The interviewee also noted that in relation to 'those clinicians where we're developing a skill set, do they know how to identify autism or know who to refer to? I'm not sure'. The paucity of treatment and probation programmes for autistic defendants is discussed elsewhere (Archer and Hurley, 2013) and as chapters seven and eight show, the dearth of specific clinical knowledge available at earlier stages of the CJS has a material impact on the disposal options available for this group.

In the second scenario – the 'person who has committed the offence but they happen to have autism' – this interviewee asked rhetorically: 'do I think they should be treated differently under those circumstances because of the Equality Duty?' They answered: 'I suppose the Liaison and Diversion process would respond [to them] but you're already picking up on my gap in terms of knowledge'. This Senior NHS-Police Inspector knew what L&D is in 'terms of the service it needs to provide' but 'could not describe' the 'decision-making process that a mental health clinician should make' in reaching 'a decision …' (Senior NHS-Police Inspector).

This material highlights an apparent legal and conceptual disconnect between the L&D agenda and Equality Act duties to challenge discrimination and promote equality for people with the protected characteristic of disability, including autistic defendants. The interviewee also thought it would be 'interesting', as L&D Services 'go through this process' of implementation 'how the courts will react' and 'comes back to the question of how flexible' the CJS is 'from a cultural perspective?' and 'we'll have to back it up with some other stuff and quite meaningful interventions or adjustments' (ibid). The researcher was asked directly by the interviewee what reasonable adjustments had been detected in court observation for autistic adult defendants. The defendant sitting outside the dock, next to their counsel and an appropriate adult was given as an example. '[T]hose are on an ad hoc basis made by a well-meaning judiciary' responded the interviewee; implying that a more coherent and systematic resource to describe types of adjustments was needed. The Equality and Human Rights Commission Guidance (2012) and *Equal Treatment Bench Book* (Judicial College, 2013), operative at the time of interview, fell short of providing sufficiently comprehensive guidance for disabled defendants (see chapter three). An updated version of the latter is now more comprehensive on these issues (Judicial College, 2022).

The likelihood of a cultural shift, however, was obstructed by the disruption caused by changes to Legal Aid, *Transforming Rehabilitation* (MOJ, 2013) and the Criminal Prosecution Service's balancing towards the victim based on the view that the rights to a fair trial are 'a zero-sum game' (Hoyano, 2015). Subsequent research showed these factors contributed to a disparity for 'mentally vulnerable defendants', who struggle to effectively participate in their trial, between the magistrates' courts where they are not receiving the same protection as those who stand trial in the Crown Court (Howard, 2021).

The second category, identified by the Senior NHS-Police Inspector was '[t]he person who has autism but we're pretty clear that it has nothing to do with the offending …'. They had 'never considered' what that means 'in terms of the Equality Duty' and were 'not disputing it' but asked '[w]hat does that mean … in practical terms?' That 'we should consider it, yes' but '[i]f you [consider] the CPS' and 'the police' who each have 'their decision-making process[es]', they thought that 'in terms of the way … they're handled by the police it comes back to disproportionate impact again and what that means …' (ibid). Finally, in the last scenario, where there is a defendant that 'we're not sure about, I'd give them the benefit of the doubt …' (ibid). For this interviewee, the differentiation between the three scenarios was not one based on any prejudice they held against the third group, where autism was not the driver of the offending. Instead, it evinced a concern with practical outcomes of applying the Equality Act 2010 because they had 'seen many policies go through that don't actually reach the ground'. Therefore, it was 'all well and good saying that we will treat people differently but if there is no practical way of treating people differently then I don't know … the answer' or whether it was 'helpful to carve them up into' those 'three cohorts'. The interviewee wanted 'to understand what … in terms of making that reasonable adjustment … practical things we can do and how flexible the CJS is' as a 'notoriously inflexible system' because 'the CJS has got the balances and the woman with the blindfold on …' (ibid).

The Equality Act's section 6 definition of the protected characteristic of 'disability', as supplemented by Schedule 1, does not incorporate the concept of a deserving and un-deserving disabled person, nor does the Equality Act 2010 import the concept which predicates the disabled person's access to its protections on whether the individual self-identifies as a disabled person. There are issues around the reasonable identification of the service user's disability by the public authority (see chapter three). However, the Equality and Human Rights Commission Guidance on the application of this legislation to 'criminal justice organisation[s]' does not envisage a schema of provision for disabled defendants that differentiates protection on the basis of the association between the service user's disability and their alleged or actual offending (2012). Indeed, courts and tribunals are expected to 'adapt normal trial procedure to facilitate the effective participation of witnesses, **defendants** and litigants', by taking 'every reasonable step to facilitate the participation of any person, including the defendant' in preparation for trial. (Judicial College, 2022: 79; emphasis added; Criminal Procedure Rules 2020). To that extent, it is not 'helpful to carve them up into three cohorts'.

Nevertheless, the Senior NHS-Police Inspector's narrative articulates a set of assumptions that were evident in the culture of the court process and were consistently observed in the fieldwork for this research (see chapter six). Along with the Member of Parliament above, there is evidence of a confusion between equality of process, and a more substantive form of equality where adjustments are made to accommodate difference, the essence of the Equality Act 2010, as Fredman points out (op. cit.). Both interviewees appear to see this as differential treatment, almost as affirmative action, rather than making adjustments to assure all are in the same position. As the Equal Treatment Bench Book notes, fair treatment 'does not mean treating everyone in the same way: it means treating people equally in comparable situations' (Judicial College, 2022: 7).

Unfortunately, however, the waters have been muddied by the interpretation of the Upper Tribunal Administrative Appeals Chamber of Regulation 4(1) of the Equality Act 2010 (Disability) Regulations 2010 ('Regulation 4(1)') in *X v The Governing Body of a School (SEN)* [2015] UKUT 0007 (AAC). Regulation 4(1) outlines other conditions which are *not* to be treated as impairments for the purposes of the meaning of disability under section 6(1) of the Equality Act, including 'a tendency to physical or sexual abuse of other persons' (section 4(1)(c)). *X v The Governing Body of a School* was an appeal by the parents of a child, 'S', against the decision of the First-tier Tribunal (Health, Education and Social Care Chamber (Special Educational Needs and Disability)). The First-tier Tribunal had dismissed the appellant's claim of disability discrimination against S, their daughter. The discrimination claim involved a school employee who gave S, an autistic child, six fixed-term exclusions of up to four days when S, a six-year-old child, was violent to teaching staff and other children over a three-month period. The issue on appeal was the interpretation of regulation 4(1) and whether it applies where the conditions specified therein arise as a consequence of an impairment that is *already* protected under the provisions of section 6 of the Equality Act 2010 ([2015] UKUT 0007 (AAC): para 6). The Upper-tier Tribunal dismissed the appeal because they were satisfied that S's behaviour demonstrated a tendency towards the physical abuse of other persons, which amounted to an excluded 'condition' under regulation 4(1). They dismissed the argument, made by the appellant's counsel, that regulation 4(1) 'only applies to "freestanding" conditions and not to consequential symptoms of an already protected impairment' (ibid: para 62).

In doing so, they found that the Article 1 definition of disability of the UNCRPD added little to the analysis (ibid: para 51). Instead, by reason of paragraph 7.3 of the Explanatory Memorandum to the 2010 Regulations, they read the prescribed conditions of regulations 4(1) as having been excluded by Parliament for 'public policy reasons', for example:

> to avoid providing protection for people where the effect of their condition may involve anti-social or criminal activity and thus have an impact on others, whether by potential or actual harm to their health and safety, or to their property (ibid: para 40).

Drawing on the Equality Act 2010 Guidance (see Office for Disability Issues, 2012: para A13), they held that it was not Parliament's intention 'to exclude only a free-standing impairment and not the manifestations of an already protected impairment' ([2015] UKUT 0007 (AAC): para 93). They found that 'regulation 4(1) does apply where the conditions specified therein arise in consequence of an impairment that is already protected under the provisions of section 6 of the 2010 Act' (ibid: para 101). Therefore, because the alleged discrimination – the school's fixed term expulsion – was a result of the excluded condition, 'tendency to cause abuse', under regulation 4(1), S was not entitled to the protection of the Act in relation to the discrimination she experienced even though this tendency was a consequence of an already protected impairment, S's autism (ibid: para 92). However, the court did find that the First-tier Tribunal had erred in law in 'failing to make sufficiently specific findings of fact about any tendency to physical abuse' (ibid: para 115).

Pursuant to determining whether a person has a 'tendency to physical … abuse', the Upper-tier Tribunal said that this is an issue of fact and the Tribunal must consider the circumstances of the individual case. They set out guidance in this regard, stating that, firstly, there 'must always be an element of violent conduct' but this conduct on its own was not sufficient to amount to a 'tendency to physical abuse'. Rather, 'the greater the level of violence, the more readily it will fall within the meaning of "physical abuse"' (ibid: 116). Secondly, because the regulation is concerned with the manifestation of behaviour, 'there is no requirement for any knowledge on the part of the perpetrator that what they are doing is wrong' (ibid: 117). Thirdly, it was noted that a finding of physical abuse in the absence of some sort of misuse of power or coercion 'would … likely … require careful justification' (ibid: 118). Fourthly, while children are included within the ambit of regulation 4(1)(c), 'the child's development is a factor which will be considered in deciding whether or not that particular child has a condition to bring it within the remit of the regulation' (ibid: 119). Finally, in their fifth point of guidance, and most worryingly, the Upper-tier Tribunal said that:

> It is not necessary for a tendency to physical abuse to be manifested frequently or regularly. It may be that the tendency is only displayed in response to certain trigger events, but that does not mean that it is not present at other times (ibid: 120).

They did, thankfully, limit the interpretation of the regulation so that 'it is only to the extent that such disorders manifest themselves in the tendency identified in the regulation that they are excluded' from the Equality Act 2010's protection (ibid: 94; 131). Therefore, the person would still be protected in relation to any discrimination which is *specifically related to the actual impairment* under section 6 that does not arise from the excluded effects of their condition under regulation 4(1).

Although the decision of the court was made in the context of the education system, there is a risk that analogous arguments could be run with respect to bodies within the CJS. If the court had not restricted its decision in this way, there would have been a risk that the application of the Equality Act 2010 to bodies within the CJS, with respect to autistic people who are shown to have any of the excluded conditions under regulation 4(1), may have left them outside the ambit of the Act's protection. This would be contrary to the Equality and Human Rights Commission's Guidance (see 2012c), the Equal Treatment Bench Book (Judicial College, 2022), the Advocate's Gateway Toolkit on autism (2015) and the (Criminal Procedure Rules 2020). Nevertheless, the interpretation of regulation 4(1)(c) by the court *in X v GB of a school* was problematic. It would be easy to see how – without properly understanding that the application of regulation 4(1) is an issue of fact relevant to the individual circumstances of a particular discrimination claim – misinterpretations of this case could have perpetuated the misconception that the Equality Act 2010 does differentiate protection on the basis of the association between the defendant's disability and their alleged or actual offending. Moreover, the Upper-tier Tribunal's fifth point of guidance on the meaning of 'tendency to physical abuse' (see above) is in conflict with the 2012 NICE Guidance on working to reduce triggers for 'challenging behaviour'[4] for autistic people. The Upper Tribunal's interpretation risked acting as a disincentive to public bodies to make environmental changes that would prevent this kind of tendency towards abuse being triggered. It also undermined the spirit of the Revised Autism Statutory Guidance and the most recent iteration of the 2021–26 Autism Strategy on 'challenging behaviour' (see chapter five).

Thankfully, the case of *C and C v The Governing Body of a School and Others* [2018] UKUT 269 (AAC) rendered the guidance in regulation 4(1)(c) obsolete. The Upper Tribunal Judge accepted the argument that, in the context of a child in educational provision, it was contrary to Article 2 of the First Protocol and Article 14 (prohibition of discrimination) of the European Convention on Human Rights. Judge Rowley was 'firmly of the view' the regulation came 'nowhere near striking a fair balance between the rights of children such as L [an autistic child]' and 'the interests of the community on the other' ([2018] UKUT 269 (AAC): para 89). Further, in his judgment, the Secretary of State had failed to justify maintaining a provision 'which excludes from the ambit of the protection of the Equality Act children whose behaviour in school is a manifestation of the very condition which calls for special educational provision to be made for them' (ibid: para 90).

This is exactly why criminology needs to attend to the wider debates in disability studies to better critique restrictions to the legal definition of disability and its understanding of the aetiology of behaviour which may be considered as criminal. In parallel, why we also need to attend to attitudes of criminal justice

[4] Note the NICE (2021) style guide change in language to 'People with behaviour that challenges services' (as above).

decision-makers which conflate the aetiology of such behaviour with the access to protection under the Equality Act 2010 for disabled defendants. As we saw in chapter one, there is insufficient evidence in the 'psy' literature to show that there is an association between autism and violence. These tendencies are not core attributes that would lead to a diagnosis of autism. Instead, the 'psy' literature is careful to explain that there are certain circumstances in which the symptomatology of autism may 'likely be involved when criminal actions occur' but this 'is not to say that having a developmental disorder enhances the likelihood of acting criminally *per se*' (Haskins and Silva, 2006: 377–78).

The opening of the current section in the present chapter set out the purpose of investigating the application of the Equality Act 2010 in the court process: to establish what operative role the Act had on decision-making about policies and practices in relation to autistic adult defendants. Many interviewees noted the role of reasonable adjustments and, as discussed above, highlighted the gap that they perceived between the requirements of the Equality Act 2010 in relation to disabled defendants and the practical application of its provisions in the criminal justice process and the courtroom in particular. Interviewees also identified a specific lacuna in relation to its application to autistic defendants, where 'reasonable adjustments could be used more frequently' and in terms of 'what would be more appropriate' for autistic people 'maybe that is already covered but the fact that we needed the Autism Act suggests that the previous legislation was not enough' (Senior Forensic Psychiatrist 1). Yet, as will be seen in chapter five, the restricted jurisdiction of the Autism Act 2009 failed to cross-reference provisions of the Equality Act 2010, which were being developed contemporaneously to the Autism Act, in extending its statutory application to criminal justice organisations.

4. Liaison and Diversion and Changing Epistemologies

The 2009 Bradley Report's recommendations and the subsequent L&D agenda have created the potential to significantly change the ways in which the English CJS responds to defendants with mental health problems and learning disabilities, including autistic defendants. They present clear challenges to the epistemological framework within which criminology has developed; making the need for a clearer disability perspective particularly germane. Baldry et al argue that, by integrating the traditionally distinct disciplines of critical criminology and critical disability studies, we can re-conceptualise the complex matrix of concerns which affect the marginalised group of offenders with mental health problems and learning disabilities (2008). In doing so we can represent 'an interconnected and fluid continuum encompassing social, systemic, community, institutional and criminological processes with individual experiences of impairment, disability and social discrimination, disadvantage and exclusion' ((Baldry et al, 2008: 31).

The mapping of offender pathways within, out of, and often back into the CJS is a useful starting point in recording this 'matrix of concerns'. Such projects inevitably introduce 'a range of dilemmas which cross boundaries from the theoretical, methodological, ethical and political, to the institutional and personal' (ibid). It is argued here that the 'dilemmas' to which Baldry et al refer are borne out in practice with respect to some key changes heralded by the embedding of L&D Services. Thus, there is value in importing the intellectual resources of critical disability studies into the criminological mainstream, and not merely into critical perspectives; raising important issues for research and policy implementation.

'Dividing practices' have historically influenced the longstanding political tensions between the DOH and the MOJ (Seddon, 2007: 61). The Bradley Report built on broad definitions of mental health problems and learning disabilities: broader than strict medical models but not directly referring to the social model of disability in the then DDAs of 1995/2005. In doing so, it demarcated a new 'dividing practice' for governing offenders in these categories. It is significant, therefore, that while the MOJ commissioned the Report, and the Government set up a Health and Criminal Justice Programme Board to oversee delivery of its recommendations (DOH, 2009: 14) – comprising cross-government departments and agencies – ultimate competency for implementing the Report rested with the DOH which had the main responsibility for funding (Bradshaw/Westminster Policy Forum, 2009)). Augmenting the transfer of prison health services in 2003 to PCTs (DOH, ibid), along with the increased responsibility given to the DOH and NHS England in implementing the Report's recommendations means that medical models of mental health problems, learning disabilities and autism have prevailed as they have been subsumed under the broader category of vulnerability. The relevance of such models is not entirely dismissed, but they should be supplemented by the kind of analysis found in critical disability studies which shows that they are not based on value-free ideology.

Moreover, this shift does not mean that criminological theorising about crime control, its institutions, and its effectiveness should end when the offender is diverted out of the CJS. On the contrary, the diversion into health and social care services adds to developments over the preceding four decades which have undercut the viability of the specific 'institutional epistemology' of criminology within which it has operated for most of its existence, ie the institutions of the criminal justice state (Garland and Sparks, 2000: 19). Responses which divert vulnerable defendants 'within' and 'out of' the CJS are still modes of regulating crime, and will have an impact on how crime is experienced by both offender and victim. As argued in chapter three, a clearer disability perspective could help criminologists to reconsider the nature of the criminality of autistic defendants and indeed of the crimes with which they are involved. The broadening of the L&D Services beyond offenders with mental health problems and learning disabilities to cover the 'threshold' category of vulnerability – which includes autistic defendants – embeds this dividing practice for these defendants.

Conclusion

In attempting to envisage a disability perspective for criminology, this book does not take an abolitionist approach to prisons; instead, it has taken one guided by a principle of penal moderation (Loader, 2009). The L&D agenda proffers a step towards this moral approach; especially as early evaluations indicate the likelihood of L&D service users receiving a custodial sentence is halved (Disley et al, 2021). However, support is qualified by awareness that L&D Services could imbue old problems present in the CJS. Studies within criminology on 'mentally-disordered' offenders have periodically documented the fact that 'problems of due process dog the diversion arena' (Peay, 2007: 507). Such concerns are not wholly assuaged by the L&D Service Specifications, neither of which mention due process (NHS England, 2014b & 2019a). In developing these services, boundaries need to be drawn to prevent oppressive control by alternative modes of regulation. In diverting individuals *within* and *out of* the CJS, there needs to be consideration of the increased risk of 'net-widening'. Hence, a disability perspective is necessary for the development of models of justice which inform the treatment of disabled defendants as they move between the complex pathways of health, social care and the CJS. Autistic defendants are affected by these dividing practices, coming under the remit of both the Equality Act 2010 provisions and as a specific sub-group included in the vulnerable cohort covered by the L&D agenda. One reason for this disjuncture is that the different categories applied to these defendants attract different sets of policies, procedural protections and substantive outcomes. Rather than disabled citizens, they are characterised as *vulnerable* in the policy framework which underpins the establishment of the L&D Services. Although not given primacy in this framework, technologies of identifying risk are also present in the L&D Service Specification (see NHS England, 2019: 20).

The conceptualisation of these groups as *vulnerable defendants* may assist in improving attitudes towards and awareness of the needs of these defendants. However, as argued in this chapter, use of this terminology may actually perpetuate the asymmetrical access to Special Measures and Intermediaries for *vulnerable defendants* in contrast to vulnerable victims and witnesses. It also seems to sustain an oblique amnesia that many individuals have protected characteristics under the Equality Act 2010 and thus facilitates an abrogation of responsibility towards these defendants in accessing this Act's legal protection (see chapter three). Beyond legal protection, this oblique amnesia, created by the predominance of the rationality of vulnerability, sustains the dominance of medical models of disability and the mad-bad binary. The predominance of the broad category of vulnerability also obfuscates the social model of disability which, as we saw in chapter three, is embedded in parts of the Equality Act 2010 and entrenched in the UNCRPD. This masks the paradigm shift made by this important international legislation in 'comprehensively and emphatically [viewing] persons with disabilities as subjects with rights, rather than objects of charity, medical treatment or protection' (Fredman, 2011: 98).

It is true that, as discussed in chapter three, the Equality Act 2010 does not entirely 'measure up' to the UK's international commitments to the UNCRPD (Butlin, 2011), particularly in transposing the social model into legislation. However, as the primary source of domestic equalities legislation on disability, it provides an important starting point for understanding when and whether defendants are conceptualised from the perspective of this particular legal status. It creates space for a criminological critique from a disability perspective, informed by critical disability studies and the social model of disability.

Chapter five considers how the statutory requirements of the Autism Act 2009 do apply to bodies within the CJS and furthermore, why this Act's statutory parameters do not effectively mirror the reach of the Equality Act 2010. Further, it traces the rationalities, programmes and technologies of governance for autistic defendants through the Act's consecutive Statutory Guidance (DOH, 2010c & 2015b) and Autism Strategies (DOH, 2010a & 2014b; DOHSC, 2021). Operating at the interface between health, social care and the CJS, their dominant paradigm does not treat autistic defendants primarily as 'subjects with rights' but recipients of 'equal access to care and support where needed' (DOHSC, 2021: 35).

5

Mapping the Legislative Landscape: The Autism Act 2009, Autism Strategies and Statutory Guidance

Introduction

The interconnectedness of the health, social care and criminal justice systems was noted in chapter four. The failure of local authorities to provide adults with timely diagnoses, assessment and support were the *raison d'être* for the Autism Act 2009 and its subsequent Autism Strategy (DOH, 2010a; 2014; DOHSC & DfE, 2021a) and Statutory Guidance (DOH 2010d; 2015a). This programme of government brought the issue of the provision of effective services for autistic adults to the fore in public policymaking (DOH, 2010a & c). Early intervention and support were seen as ways of preventing the kinds of crises which may lead this group to come 'into contact with the CJS' (DOH, 2010a: 37). However, the statutory status of the Act's accompanying Statutory Guidance (DOH, 2010d; 2015) were not extended to cover public bodies within the CJS. This means that recourse to this guidance, and the subsequent iteration of it (DOH, 2015), does not effectively alleviate the inconsistent and problematic processing of the cases of autistic adult defendants in the criminal courts. Chapters six to eight discuss the knowledge deficit of criminal justice decision-makers in adult social care provision and how this plays a role in increasing criminalisation of autistic adult defendants. The present chapter, therefore, aims to lay a foundation for that discussion, in explaining the disjuncture in the interfaces of these systems and the incoherent approach to the governance of this group. As such, it records a 'history of the present' (Seddon, 2007; Foucault, 1991) by integrating an analysis of qualitative data taken from legislation, Hansard and policy documents with a narrative informed by interviews with elite decision-makers. A number of central themes are examined.

The chapter critiques the Autism Act 2009, along with the three autism strategies and two iterations of autism statutory guidance, and the relevance of these policies for the treatment of autistic defendants in the CJS over the last 15 years. Section 1 interrogates why the statutory remit of the Autism Act 2009 and its accompanying Statutory Guidance (DOH, 2010d; 2015) *does not* mirror the Equality Act 2010 and apply to bodies in the CJS. It appears that this was a missed opportunity for legislative coherence. The Autism Act 2009 went through Parliament contemporaneously to the Equality Act 2010, and the original Autism Strategy, *Fulfilling and rewarding lives*, explicated that it was 'built on the Bradley Report' and 'other policies' (See DOH, 2010a: 19). Further, the original Statutory Guidance, *Implementing fulfilling and rewarding lives* (2010d), did not comprehensively relate to the Bradley Report (2009), or the subsequent DOH policy on liaison and diversion (DOH, 2009). This disconnection is surprising because while the Bradley Report had been under the jurisdiction of the MOJ, the DOH – which led on the autism strategies – became responsible for the operationalisation of the Report's recommendations. However, policy-makers *did* look at extending the scope of the first Autism Strategy and Statutory Guidance to CJS Bodies after Royal Assent of the Autism Act 2009. Section 1(B) and (C) analyse this context and the bases for widening the ambit of the Statutory Guidance to organisations in the CJS in future. These subsections also chart the changing political rationalities as implementation of the Autism Act shifted from administration by the Labour to the Coalition government.

Section 2 extrapolates the changing programmes and technologies of governance for autistic defendants over the period 2011–22. Section 2(A) interrogates what interviewees thought appropriate management of autistic adult defendants might look like in practice, in order to elicit what logics drove the governance of this group in the first part of this period. Section 2(B) analyses the 2014 'Refreshed' Autism Strategy for England, *Think Autism*, the *Revised Statutory Guidance* (DOH, 2015a: 4) and *The National Strategy for Autistic People, Children and Young People 2021 to 2026* ('2021–26 Autism Strategy'; DOHSC & DfE, 2021a). In doing so it identifies key themes across these policies and the underlying rationalities and technologies of governance for autistic defendants. In particular, it notes the shifting scenery from the Coalition to Conservative government, including reversal in the privatisation of the probation service.

The present chapter argues that the first Autism Strategy and Statutory Guidance were not sufficiently focused on policymaking and practice on autistic defendants because the statutory requirement of this guidance does not apply to public bodies within the CJS. The courts, police and probation services were only expected to follow its requirements by reason of best practice (DOH, 2010c: 8). Even for the institutions where the Statutory Guidance has statutory force, its provisions were weakened by the absence of the language of mandate. The subsequent autism strategies (DOH, 2014; DOHSC & DfE, 2021a) have assisted the consideration of issues affecting autistic defendants who come into contact with the CJS. However, the *Revised Statutory Guidance* (DOH, 2015) statutory ambit remains unchanged, leaving many significant issues unresolved.

1. Mind the Gaps: The Autism Act 2009 and Organisations within the CJS

A. The Autism Act 2009 and 2010 Autism Strategy and Statutory Guidance

Widely welcomed and frequently celebrated as the first piece of legislation to focus on a specific disability, the Autism Act 2009 was brought to Parliament as a Private Members Bill by Conservative MP, the late Right Honourable Cheryl Gillan (HC Deb 21 January 2009, c754WH) after she came top of the Backbench Business Committee Ballot. The Autism Act 2009 places two main requirements on the Secretary of State for Health. Firstly, to produce an 'autism strategy' which meets 'the needs of adults in England with autistic spectrum conditions by improving the provision of relevant services to such adults by local authorities, NHS bodies and NHS foundation trusts' (section 1(1) & (2)). Secondly, in order to secure the implementation of the autism strategy, the Secretary of State is required to issue guidance to local authorities on the exercise of their social services functions and to NHS bodies and foundation trusts in the 'exercise of their functions concerned with the provision of relevant services' (section 2; 2(a) & (b)).

The first national Autism Strategy (DOH, 2010a) set out the agenda for long-term change to achieve the goal of a society that accepts and understands autism. It also aimed to create opportunities to help individuals on the autism spectrum to live fulfilling and rewarding lives. The strategy identified five specific areas for action between 2010 and 2013:

1. increasing awareness and understanding of autism among frontline professionals;
2. developing a clear, consistent pathway for diagnosis in every area … followed by the offer of a personalised needs assessment;
3. improving access for adults with autism to the services and support they need to live independently within the community;
4. helping adults with autism into work, and;
5. enabling local partners to plan and develop appropriate services for adults with autism to meet identified needs and priorities.

It highlighted that autistic adults only 'come to the attention of services when they reach crisis point [including]: a severe mental health problem, physical illness, homelessness **or coming into contact with the CJS**' (ibid: 37; emphasis added). The Strategy further noted that when the needs of autistic adults are recognised earlier, and are responded to with autism-specific strategies and support, 'crisis can be prevented; this is beneficial not only to them and their families but also to wider society' (ibid). The requirements in the subsequent Statutory Guidance *only* apply to local authorities and NHS bodies (DOH, 2010d) and not the CJS. Therefore, other public service providers, such as the police and probation services 'are not legally required to have regard to it' (DOH, 2010c: 8). Instead, they are encouraged to follow the guidance to 'help improve the delivery of the services they provide' (ibid). This is despite the Autism Strategy's frequent references to the problems experienced by autistic adults entering the CJS (DOH, March 2010: 37; 43–4; 68) and the Delivery Plan's focus on rolling out autism awareness training, through the DOH's 'National Learning Disability Offender Steering Group … to all staff in the criminal justice sector' (DOH, 2010c: 13).

As the Autism Act 2009 only explicitly mentions local authorities, NHS bodies and NHS foundation trusts as subject to the guidance, for the purpose of implementing an autism strategy, to improve the provision of relevant services to autistic adults (sections 1 & 2), it would be difficult to extend the 'duty to act' (section 3) to other public bodies without revising the Act itself. Whilst the Autism Act 2009 is a hugely positive step forward, it could have mirrored the Equality Act 2010 to apply across public bodies more broadly or extended to cover the exercise of certain functions of criminal justice agencies. It is surprising that it did not because the Bradley Report (2009) elucidated problems which arise from siloed disciplinary working (see chapter four) for offenders with learning disabilities and mental health problems, including autistic defendants. Indeed, the Health and Criminal Justice Programme Board's 2009 Delivery Plan for the Bradley Report acknowledged the 'interdependencies' of the health, social care and criminal justice sectors and their policies; recognising this plan should not be isolated from other Government policies, specifically citing the autism strategy (DOH, 2009: 17; 18).

Further, had the scope of the 2010 Statutory Guidance's requirements been extended, more coherent practice across the boundaries of health, adult social care and criminal justice could have been facilitated. For example, the requirement that general autism awareness training should be available for everyone working in health and social care could have been extended to those working in the CJS. The training aimed to ensure staff in health and social care were able to identify 'potential signs of autism' and to make reasonable adjustments in their own behaviour, communication and services for people with an autism diagnosis or who display those characteristics (DOH, December 2010: 13). Implementing this for staff in the CJS could have helped to overcome some of the problems recorded in the literature discussed elsewhere in this book (see chapters one, six and seven).

The 2010 Statutory Guidance said that '[l]ocal authorities, NHS bodies and NHS Foundation Trusts should develop local commissioning plans for services for adults with autism' and collect information on the 'number of adults known to have autism in the area' (DOH, December 2010: 24–5). Research reviewed in chapter one shows that prevalence data in the CJS is inconclusive; therefore, extending data collection requirements to the police and other criminal justice bodies would have provided a clearer picture of where (and how many) autistic defendants are governed within the CJS.

The 2010 Statutory Guidance also required that '[e]ach area should put in place a clear pathway for diagnosis of autism, from initial referral through to assessment of needs' and the 2012 NICE Guideline set out a model care pathway in its clinical guideline for autistic adults 'concerned with the diagnosis and management of adults on the autism spectrum in the community and in prison' (DOH, March 2010: 14–15; NICE, March 2012: 13). Amongst their extensive recommendations, NICE stated that Autism Strategy Groups should have representation from the CJS, and be responsible for developing, managing and evaluating local care pathways that 'promote a range of evidence-based interventions' including 'people in the CJS' (ibid: 162; 168). These pathways should 'provide an integrated programme of care across all care settings' and 'establish clear links (including access and entry points) to other care pathways …' (ibid: 162). So, even though service providers in the CJS were only *encouraged* to follow the Statutory Guidance to achieve best practice and were not subject to its statutory requirements, the NICE Guideline increased the overlap between the programmes of governance for autistic adult offenders on clinical and criminal justice pathways. Taken in conjunction with the diversionary agenda for offenders with mental health problems and learning disabilities, these Guidelines augment challenges already made to the 'institutional epistemological' (see above) framework that has developed within criminology (see Garland and Sparks, 2000: 19; chapter four above). This legitimates the governmentality analysis undertaken here and the relevance of autistic defendants as a case study for the utility of disabling criminology as a critical perspective. It also begins to tell us why it matters that organisations in the CJS were excluded from the statutory ambit of the Autism Act 2009 and Statutory Guidance.

B. Why were Organisations within the CJS Excluded?

At the time the Autism Act 2009 progressed through Parliament there was a bustle of legislative and policy-making activity in relation to the Equality Act 2010 and the Liaison and Diversion agenda. So, why was the remit of the Autism Act 2009 not extended to cover organisations in the CJS? Analysis of the Parliamentary debates about the 2009 Autism Bill and elite interviews revealed that this was, in part, due to the focus of the National Audit Office (NAO) and NAS reports, along with the nature of the legislative instrument which led to its introduction to the house. It was also influenced by legislative pragmatism driven by the limited time available to achieve Royal Assent for the Private Member's Bill and the looming 2010 general election.

The origins of the substantive content of the Autism Bill in its 2009 form can be charted back as far as 2000, when Ivan and Charika Corea, the parents of an autistic child, began an autism awareness campaign and worked with the Labour government to initiate the first 'autism awareness year' in 2002 (HC Deb 9 Jan 2002, c226WH). By 2008, the Autism Awareness Campaign UK, in collaboration with the NAS and other leading autism charities, were successful in securing two Early Day Motions, 1359 and 705, calling on the government to launch a cohesive 10-year national strategy for autism and the setting up of an Autism Taskforce to address the serious education and health issues facing parents, carers and people with autism and AS (HC Deb 26 April 2007; 15 January 2008). Building on the work already done by the Autism Awareness Campaign UK, the NAS's report *I Exist* (2008) played an important role in shaping the substantive content of the proposed national autism strategy and in calling for related guidance. The NAS had, in 2005, published a *Guide for Criminal Justice Professionals* who may come into contact with people on the autism spectrum – as victims, witnesses, suspects or offenders – but this issue was not integrated into the *I Exist* report. It focused on four core areas where changes needed to be made in Health and Social Care in order to transform the lives of autistic people by: counting prevalence of autistic adults nationally and individual local authorities recording data; improving access to diagnosis and social care assessments; increasing funding of local support services and improving leadership in government by introducing statutory guidance to improve local authority commissioning (NAS, 2008).

In turn, the report also shaped the remit and content of parliamentary questions on autism that year (HC Deb 25 Feb 2008, c1189WH), along with the Adults with Autism Bill 2008 (HC Deb 20 May 2008, C163WH) and the later 2009 Autism Bill, which was ultimately enacted. Angela Browning MP's first reading of the 2008 Adults with Autism Bill, under the Private Members' Ten-Minute Rule, was an early attempt to convey to the House the need to change the law in this area. *I Exist* highlighted the discrepancy 'between the increasing recognition of the need to provide support to people with autism and the action taken to meet that need' (HC Deb 20 May 2008, c163WH). Once the 2009 Autism Bill began its journey through the Commons, the NAS worked with both the DOH and the Department for Children, Schools and Families 'to develop the new policies' that were central to the Parliamentary debate on the Bill (Phil Hope MP, HC Deb 27 Feb 2009, c539WH). The expert external reference group, which included a coalition of 15 charitable organisations, led by the NAS's Mark Lever, drew heavily on *I Exist's* four areas for change to develop the 'four pillars of reform' in the proposed strategy, (HC Deb 27 February 2009 c483; 543–4). The first pillar was 'better specialist and mainstream health services', and the second tackled 'social exclusion, including employment …'. The third was 'improved choice and control for adults with autism …', through the personalisation of services, and the fourth was 'improving the skills and knowledge of the staff who work with adults with autism' (ibid).

The NAO report, *Supporting people with autism through adulthood*, also heavily 'informed discussions' around the 2009 Bill (HC Deb 29 April 2009, c5WH), in particular, in providing an evidence base for the first and second pillars noted above. It focused on 'the extent of existing services and how they meet the needs of adults regarding health, social care, employment and carers' (HC Deb, 27 Feb 2009 c523WH) and assessed the efficiencies in public spending in these areas. It found that the costs of increased funding of specialist autism services in these areas could 'over time be outweighed by overall public expenditure savings' (NAO, 2009: 5). Although the NAO's survey showed that there were some court diversion services at that time, which aimed to minimise the inappropriate entry of vulnerable adults into the CJS, such services 'were reported in only 33 per cent of areas, and less than one in eight of these have specialised autism support' (ibid: 25). It further noted that the limited research available suggested that 'high-functioning autism and AS may be disproportionately represented among the prison population; and that a proportion of these detentions could potentially have been avoided through appropriate early intervention and case management' (ibid: 51). Unfortunately, however, the NAO's economic model did not 'take into account potential savings from avoiding inappropriate interactions with the CJS' (ibid).

Certainly, parliamentary debates on the Bill raised the issue of extending its substantive contents beyond these four pillars and expanding its statutory remit. In the second reading of the Bill, Dr Stephen Ladyman MP remarked that '[s]urprisingly, the four pillars do not include law and order and the CJS' (HC Deb 27 Feb 2009, c544WH). He went on to request that Phil Hope MP, the Minister of State at the DOH, ask the Home Secretary and the Lord Chancellor to 'issue the same sort of guidance as he is talking about for the health services and social care to' professionals responsible for 'autistic people when they enter the criminal justice system'. In response, Phil Hope MP agreed that he had 'raised an excellent point' and would draw the comments to the attention of '… members of the external reference group' who would take into account 'the plea that he has made about a possible further pillar of reform'. In particular because 'the national external adviser' was 'concerned about what happens to … people with autism who end up in our CJS as offenders' where '[t]heir needs are not understood and they are in completely the wrong place to deal with the issues' that they have 'in their lives'(ibid).

On the Autism Bill's third reading in the Commons, Ann Keen MP, the then Parliamentary Under-Secretary of State for Health, noted the Bradley review was 'worth mentioning' and that the government would 'be convening a special event … on the CJS and autism as part of the programme of stakeholder engagement to support the consultation on the strategy' (HC Deb 19 Jun 2009, c578WH). On its second reading in the Lords, Baroness Tonge highlighted that where some people's autism was not recognised in childhood, in adulthood they '… end up in the criminal justice system and … often go to prison' (10 July 2009: Column 894). Consequently, she asked what was being done 'to identify these people before they get into trouble?'

Nevertheless, the entry of autistic adults into the CJS did not became a fifth pillar of the strategy. Instead, the 2010 Autism Strategy depicted such entry as a failure in the operation of the health and social care systems when an individual had reached 'crisis point'. The influence of the substantive considerations of the *I Exist* report and evidence base available to the NAO, in developing their model for maximising the efficiency of public expenditure on specialist services for autistic adults, prevailed. These materials revealed that legislators were 'starting from an extremely low base' across the four pillars originally identified. Indeed, the NAO had reported that 74 per cent of local authorities did not have a 'commissioning strategy for adults with autism' and that was 'one of the biggest challenges to shifting the culture' (Browning, 19 June 2009: Column 550). This was also true of employment, where the DWP had 'a long way to go to get up to speed' (ibid). The 'low base' in service provision at that time appears to have led to legislative pragmatism and overtook the objective of legislative coherence in terms of the breadth of public bodies subject to the Act's statutory remit.

Such pragmatism is also likely driven by the type of legislative instrument that the Autism Bill was, and the timing of its passage through Parliament. Debates in Hansard reference the concerns of members of both Houses that, as a Private Members Bill, brought by a backbencher, it had more limited parliamentary time than a Bill brought by a cabinet member would have done (HC Deb 27 Feb 2009, c494WH; 29 April 2009, c6WH; 13 May 2009, c29WH). As a result, there was a risk that it would not reach Royal Assent in time for the last Parliamentary session before the 2010 General Election campaign began (ibid: 27 February 2009, cc495–6WH). Further, while the Labour government supported having an autism strategy and statutory guidance, already set in play by the Early Day Motions and earlier Adults with Autism Bill 2008, they thought the same outcomes could be achieved without recourse to legislation. Legislating for such a strategy and guidance created 'the risk of rigidity, inflexibility and inability to deliver change that might be unintended consequences of' this measure (Phil Hope MP, HC Deb 27 February 2009, c540WH). Indeed, at the second reading of the 2009 Autism Bill, the Labour Government had already made 'cast-iron reassurances about the Government's intentions' to produce an autism strategy and statutory guidance (ibid: c540WH). They believed that these outcomes could be achieved by properly including autistic people in other interdepartmental initiatives and the Guidance could, instead, be placed on statutory footing under section 7 of the Local Authority Social Services (LASS) Act 1970 (ibid: c544WH). The Government was defeated and the Bill went through to the third reading. So, by the first sitting of the Bill Committee, it was made clear that the Autism Bill garnered 'cross-party support' (Rt Hon. Cheryl Gillan MP, HC Deb 29 April 2009).

That the strategy and the statutory guidance were incorporated into this primary legislation may have been a feature leading to the ultimate ossification of the range of public bodies covered by these measures. In its final manifestation, the Autism Act 2009's prescription about the content of Statutory Guidance issued under section 2(5) excluded reference to the CJS. Under section 2(1)(a), the Act prescribed that when issuing guidance to secure the implementation of the autism strategy, it was issued to local authorities within their meaning under the LASS Act 1970 and 'to NHS bodies and NHS foundation trusts about the exercise of their functions concerned with the provision of relevant services' (section 2(1)(b)). This was done in order to ensure that local authorities and NHS Trusts would be subject to judicial review if these bodies did not follow the Autism Statutory Guidance. Why was this technicality important? Parliamentarians were keen that the guidance had 'bite'. As Phil Hope MP explained to the House, utilising the section 7 provisions within the LASS Act 1970 was helpful because it gives 'the Secretary of State powers to issue general guidance', 'commonly referred to as statutory'. Case law has established local authorities 'are then required to exercise their social service functions in accordance with that guidance … unless they can show compelling reasons not to do so'. The 'obligation to act in accordance' with guidance issued under section 7 is 'very strong', with this requirement 'is more than simply taking account' of such guidance because if a local authority 'ignored' it 'or arbitrarily chose to disregard it, would be acting unlawfully' and could find itself subject to judicial review or default action by the Secretary of State (HC Deb 27 February 2009, cc481 548WH).

The reliance on the LASS Act 1970, however, makes it difficult to extend the ambit of the statutory guidance to public bodies in the CJS. This may have caused inadvertent ossification, with the provision being interpreted as an exhaustive list of statutory bodies under a duty to act. Responses from elite interviewees (see below) indicate that this prevented further statutory extension in the *Revised Statutory Guidance* (DOH, 2015b). A more coherent approach in terms of application to public bodies could have been by doing what was done through section 3(5) of the Autism Act (Northern Ireland) 2011. This section is drafted so that the 'Department' 'may make regulations as regards the content of the autism strategy'. Under section 4(1), 'Northern Ireland department' is given in list form and includes 'the Department of Justice'.

Strangely, the Equality Act 2010, which started its journey as a Bill through the House of Commons on 4 April 2009 – just over two-and-a-half months after the Autism Bill 2009 – was not discussed specifically in either the Commons or Lords' debates on the Autism Bill; nor, indeed, were the provisions of the 2005 Disability Discrimination Act. There may be something in the fact that responsibility for the Autism Bill 2009 sat with the DOH, where conceiving individual impairments in terms of medical models of disability prevailed, rather than as disabilities as defined in equality legislation (see chapter four above). It is noteworthy that the Report stage and third reading of the Autism Bill in the Commons was on 19 June 2009. Considering that, by this time, the Equality Bill had progressed through 16 sittings at Committee stage, it is peculiar that the debate in the Commons on the Autism Bill pays such scant attention to it. Although autism is regularly referred to as a 'disability', its legal status under the then Disability Discrimination Act 2005 or the then forthcoming Equality Bill 2010 was not discussed directly. Perhaps this was because the timing was so precarious: there may have been a lack of clarity about the final enactment of the disability provisions that had been in the Disability Discrimination Act 2005 as they were to become subsumed into the Equality Act 2010. Therefore, it may have been easier to legislate on autism on its own terms. Whether it was right for the Bill to prioritise the needs which arise from one particular impairment, autism, was a concern raised in debate (Sharon Hodgson MP, 27 February 2009, c486WH).

Perhaps the lack of focus on the disability provisions in the DDA 2005 and in the Equality Bill indicates that there were fears that the momentum for improvements for autistic people would be slowed down by attaching provisions to this legislation. It may have also risked losing the focus on the specific impairment of autism to the prevailing multifarious needs of disabled people as a category of protected characteristic. There is some evidence to suggest that these concerns were justified. The Equality Act 2010 did not come into force until 1 October 2010, with some provisions and guidance delayed until April and September 2011. Further, research on the number of cases involving individuals with AS, between October 2010 and January 2014, found that the Equality Act 2010 had not 'made a great impact' on how courts deal with individuals with AS in case law (Foster, 2014). Indeed, there was only one such case involving AS in the 'legal domain' of the CJS (ibid: 62).

C. Extending the Scope of the Autism Strategy and Statutory Guidance to CJS Organisations after Royal Assent of the Autism Act 2009?

The research interviews included in this study took place before publication of *Think Autism* and the *Revised Statutory Guidance* but remain insightful on the policies' underpinning rationalities and programmes of governance between 2009–2021. Whilst the subsequent autism strategy (DOHSC & DfE, 2021a) includes more in-depth priority actions on criminal justice-related issues, the *Revised Statutory Guidance* remains unaltered. That the 'duty to act', under section 3 of the Autism Act 2009 only applies to local authorities and NHS bodies, pursuant to their section 7 duties under the LASS Act 1970, is directly referenced in it (see above; DOH, 2015a: 6). However, research interviews, undertaken with senior civil servants and clinicians, revealed that policy-makers did consider widening the parameters of the statutory requirements of the Autism Statutory Guidance to apply to the DOH in exercising its functions in relation to offender health and to public bodies or organisations in the CJS. According to one Senior Clinical Advisor, who worked closely with the DOH, they wanted the Statutory Guidance '*to mirror the [Autism] Strategy*' and understood '… that people with autism were not recognised in the CJS and it was not working but there were no resources or expertise … therefore, we focussed on the health and social care system' (Senior Clinical Advisor).

This interview explicated that there was a sense that drafters 'were under time pressure, had to do a lot of consultation' and they never 'caught up with Bradley' (Senior Clinical Advisor) in the process of developing the Statutory Guidance, despite this being considered in Parliamentary debate. A research interview with Lord Bradley revealed that, when asked what role he had in contributing to the 2010 Autism Strategy and Statutory guidance, he responded:

> None. I wasn't asked. … [M]y report was commissioned by the government as an independent review, with particular terms of reference, which was completed and reported to the government who … ran with … [its] recommendations. Those were not specific to any particular condition and … I was not charged with particular activity … [beyond] that.

It is pertinent to note that the Autism Strategy (DOH, 2010a) and the first year Delivery Plan (DOH, 2010b) were published under the Labour Government before the 2010 General Election, while the Autism Statutory Guidance (DOH, 2010c) was drafted after the election under the Coalition Government. Civil servants in the DOH working on the guidance, said they 'were under too many time pressures' which impacted on the ambit of the Statutory Guidance because they 'were unsure what would happen with the change of government' so 'wanted to capture what the next government would like to do' and had difficulties in 'cross department working' (Senior Civil Servant 1). Whilst they met 'other government departments' and 'tried to work with' the MOJ, 'it was hard to get meetings with them' (ibid).

As the administration of this policy shifted from Labour to the Coalition government, implementation also moved from a 'government that did things at a national level' – such as 'Valuing People, [Mental Health] service contracts, establishing NICE' – rather than regulation at 'a local level' with 'local priorities and understanding … and [l]ocal resource diversion' (Senior Clinical Advisor). Consequently, the 2010 Autism Strategy 'was written by the government' with 'national standards for policy' distilled 'through networks'; whereas 'the Statutory Guidance was written for local level driven upwards' (ibid). This shift to localism, further prevented expansion of the Guidance's statutory remit and had implications for efficient progress. Although the DOH held 'the ring as a department on issues like learning disability and autism' the way in which they did that was 'much softer' and 'much more about influencing and negotiating' as saying 'we're the lead department' did not 'hold much water …' (Senior Civil Servant 2).

The DOH were also aware that the NICE Guidelines were going to focus 'around challenging behaviour', which includes 'anger, aggression, self-injury, and disruptive or destructive', that is 'seen as challenging when it affects the person's or other peoples' quality of life and or jeopardises their safety' (2012b: 52). It is surprising that responses to 'challenging behaviour' was left to clinical guidance 'intended to improve the process and outcomes of healthcare' (NICE, 2012a: 9) but without statutory effect. Consequently, drafters of the 2010 Statutory Guidance 'focussed on training, diagnosis, general mental health service responsibilities … and reasonable adjustments' in GP services which still 'felt like … too much to do or to ask' but they 'wanted a win on some things' and '… needed to take one step at a time' (Senior Clinical Advisor).

However, all interviewees expressed their regret that the statutory parameters of the Guidance were constricted in this way. The Senior Clinical Advisor to the DOH thought autistic defendants who were in prison were disadvantaged in their access to diagnosis and assessment and thought 'people underestimate[d] how much' they were 'subject to abuse' and 'how much their offending behaviour is related to their core diagnoses'. This lack of awareness has an impact on resource allocation because criminal justice decision-makers 'will say "that costs money and this group is only small …" [but] there are more people than you would expect' (ibid). Prevalence estimates still vary widely of the prison population who have autism (see Chapter 1; Fazio et al, 2012; Underwood et al, 2016; Tyler et al, 2019). The Senior Clinical Advisor to the DOH felt that if the statutory requirements of the Guidance did cover organisations in the CJS then the 'prison staff would better understand the health needs of someone with autism'. Without the parameters of these requirements being extended, this interviewee was concerned that prison staff would not be compelled to make reasonable adjustments for them. These concerns have finally filtered through to the *2021–26 National Autism Strategy*, which evince a shift in both resource allocation and focus on prison healthcare (see Section 2(c) below). However, the 2015 Statutory Guidance remains without teeth to back this up.

Indeed, one of the general criticisms of both iterations of the Statutory Guidance has been the weak language of mandate adopted during the drafting process. This is likely to have been another factor in barring the extension of remit to criminal justice organisations. A Senior Clinical Advisors, who worked with the team drafting both the 2010 and 2015 Guidance, recalled that:

> We wanted to put in some obligation. But the whole statutory document was written to make sure that there was [sic] no mandated phrases. It then had an equality impact assessment and this all had to go to the Treasury.

Further, senior civil servants, overseeing the process of updating policy, said that the *Revised Statutory Guidance* would be 'more of a refresh and a revisit'. They did not have 'any plans to' extend it to apply to criminal justice organisations as they did not 'even know whether that [was] possible' but intended 'the scope of it won't be much broader than it already is' (Senior Civil Servant 2). This has been borne out in practice because the *Revised Statutory Guidance* does not extend the scope of its statutory requirements. It only 'recommend[s] that other providers of public services, such as … [the] police, probation and the CJS look to follow the guidance to help improve the delivery of the services they provide to adults with autism …' (DOH, 2015: 10). In echoing the 2010 version, that by following the guidance 'those bodies could help improve the delivery of the services they provide' (ibid), it appears that what was intended to … be a non-exhaustive list of bodies with a duty to act has in fact ossified into an exhaustive list.

Thus, although there is not a duty to act under the Guidance, nor has there been a reform of the Autism Act 2009 to enable this, there may 'well be … existing statutory obligations to [criminal justice organisations] to do this' and it 'would be a fertile line of inquiry [to] … invoke those provisions under … the 2010 Equality Act' (Member of Parliament) because autism is a disability as defined by section 6 of the Act. It is possible, therefore, to invoke the Public Sector Equality Duty (PSED) in section 149 of the Equality Act 2010 to require CJS organisations to follow the Statutory Guidance in order to comply with their general equality duty to have due regard to the need to:

(a) eliminate discrimination, harassment, victimisation and any other conduct that is prohibited by or under this Act;
(b) advance equality of opportunity between persons who share a relevant protected characteristic and persons who do not share it;
(c) foster good relations between persons who share a relevant protected characteristic and persons who do not share it (Equality Act 2010, s 149(1)).

To put it another way, the material in the *Revised Statutory Guidance* adds detail to what it means to achieve these three PSED aims for autistic individuals; individuals who have the protected characteristic of disability under the Equality Act 2010. Thus, the Guidance can be read to provide further detail to the provisions of the Equality Act 2010 on what it means to be protected against indirect discrimination under sections 13, 14, 19, and direct discrimination under section 15, and the nature of reasonable adjustments for autistic people under section 21 of the Act.

A senior Member of Parliament extolled the virtues of utilising this interpretation instead of 'passing new laws when there's no need to' and 'to use what we've got'. This may be especially helpful if it is not viable to redraft sections 2(1) and 3 of the Autism Act 2009 itself to mirror the spread of public bodies which are included under the Equality Act 2010. However, in light of the more detailed coverage of criminal justice related issues in Chapter 8 of the *2021–26 National Autism Strategy*, the Secretary of State for Health should be compelled to make such an extension in carrying out their statutory appraisal of the 'extent to which the guidance has been effective in securing the implementation of the autism strategy' (Autism Act 2009, section 2(3)). For this to be practicable there would have to be a clear determination from the MOJ for an extension in the scope of the guidance.

In addition to these points about legal interpretation, interviewees noted a number of other barriers that would limit the ambit of their drafting of the *Revised Statutory Guidance.* Not surprisingly, the availability of both financial and professional resources was cited. The availability of sufficient training, the time available for professionals to interact with individual defendants and sufficient specialist expertise were all such examples (Members of Parliament; Senior Clinical Psychiatrists; Senior NHS-Police Inspectors). One interviewee explicated that there was 'also a lack of capacity in the system to actually deal with people when they may be on sentence' and to 'ensure that' support services for 'mental health and learning disabilities', which 'obviously includes' autism, are 'available' on 'a daily basis' (Member of the House of Lords). Public opinion was identified as a potential problem if autism was being used as 'an excuse', 'get out of jail free card' or using 'disability as some sort of barrier to responsibility' (Member of House of Lords; Member of Parliament; Senior NHS-Police Inspector). However, as long as there was effective public education, interviewees thought 'the public themselves would say "we want a CJS that is efficient"' by better identification and diagnosis of autism, leading to more effective support and a reduction in re-offending and by the CJS 'acting in the public interest' (Member of House of Lords; Senior Clinical Psychiatrist 1; Member of Parliament). Therefore, one Member of Parliament thought the public would 'understand' that 'making sure the public interest test [in criminal cases also] takes into account disability' was 'the right thing to do'.

The Autism Act 2009 uses the 'umbrella' term for autism to include AS and high functioning autism. Chapters six to eight, on the governance of autistic adult defendants in Magistrates' and Crown Courts, describes the issues which arise from the misconceptions made by criminal justice professionals of the autism spectrum as a scale of severity. Therefore, interviewees were also prompted on whether the spectrum nature of the condition posed a potential barrier to extending this policy's coverage. Responses expressed the importance of raising public awareness about the condition in this regard. Interviewees also referenced 'a fundamental clash of perspectives' in the health and criminal justice systems and the way 'those systems … are designed' as a barrier to extending the Statutory Guidance to CJS organisations because:

> … the focus of the CJS is on the act that has been perpetrated … rather than the person, whereas the health and social care system is supposed to be about the person; although it's often about the condition rather than the person … (Senior Civil Servant 1).

A Senior Civil servant in the DOH described this dissonance between the clinical and criminal justice paradigms as leading to discord around categorisation of individuals as 'once you've got a mental health diagnosis, it could be anything from depression through to schizophrenia' the MOJ 'see them as all the same'. This interviewee said there was 'an issue' for defendants who have 'gone into a mental health hospital' about 'whether they have to go back into the prison system' and 'the ability' of the MOJ 'to actually see' this as an issue about 'continuity of care'. This Senior Civil Servant described the dichotomy in the MOJ's approach to defendants with mental health problems, where 'it's either':

> [1] they need to stay in the mental health hospital because we [the CJS] can't possibly care for them …; or [2] if they are ready to be discharged they can just go anywhere … it's that lack of understanding … and being unable to see that person with a range of needs … you've either got the mental health label or not. (Senior Civil Servant 1)

The perspective conveyed here, by the DOH professional, of the governmentality approach of those working within the MOJ, reflects the mad-bad binary view of offenders with mental health problems or learning disabilities. A dividing practice which subsumes autistic defendants, this was also reflected in the comments made by a Senior Police Officer working in Offender Health who said policymakers 'like to put things in different cohorts and organisational buckets' but autism is 'not an on/off issue – either you are or you're not [autistic] – it's a spectrum'. That interviewee described the 'ideal approach' would be if someone told them

'"I am autistic"... [I] would say: what does that mean in terms of how we need to interact to get the best out of you?'

A Senior Crown Prosecutor, in discussing the particular challenges posed to prosecutorial decision-making, also raised the spectrum nature of autism and compared it to a 'learning difficulty or mental condition' where:

> you may need to get into ... [whether it's] a lower-level issue, rather than if it is something very serious, [you might ask]: is that an issue which could impact on proving essential elements of the offence because of the mens rea ... ? ... [I]t is challenging because you've got Aspergers at one end of the spectrum. ... [I]t is very difficult for busy prosecutors, who are dealing with a whole host of cases, to fully understand ... the intricacies of this in cases.

Implicit here is the primacy given to the seriousness of the offence rather than the relevance of a condition such as autism, in determining whether the defendant has the *mens rea* for the offence, and the decision to prosecute. It also reflects misconceptions by criminal justice professionals of the autism spectrum as a scale of severity determined by IQ. The assumption is that the higher the person's IQ, the less 'severe' a person's autism. This view is at odds with the NICE Guideline, which highlights that the 'potential discrepancy between intellectual functioning as measured by IQ and adaptive functioning as reflected, for example, by difficulties in planning and performing activities of daily living including education or employment' (2012: 11). It is also at odds with what the Autism Act 2009 and associated policy sought to achieve. By including autism as an umbrella term, drafters of the Act recognised that for too long, people with AS, having an IQ >70, had fallen between the gaps of mental health and learning disability provision (DOH, 2010a: 10; 35). Yet a Senior Psychiatrist, who had acted in an advisory capacity for the Autism Strategy, stated that 'policymakers' in the CJS **could** 'work around the fact it is a spectrum condition'; the 'limiting factor is the evidence base', nevertheless his 'group all share core difficulties' and its spectrum nature 'is no excuse not to do it'.

A senior Member of Parliament with specialist knowledge in this area corroborated this view: whilst the autism spectrum is 'always a problem' because 'there's no typical case of someone with autism and ... you can't make sort of glib assumptions about "... he's autistic so he takes a literal view of every word that's said"... [t]hat being said, where there has been a diagnosis then there has ... to be a system whereby that ... [is] flagged to the authorities'. Rather, the issue was the system not being able to properly 'cater for the undiagnosed person, of which there are many ... by the time you get to sentence' the judge may realise '"there's something not right here; I want a medical report ..."' and then 'you ... see there's a diagnosis of ASD' and 'think "... if only that had been worked out years ago"' (Member of Parliament). As a member of the House of Lords explained, there is also a tension between the egalitarian allocation of resources to defendants who are deemed to be vulnerable within the CJS and the '... the quality and sensitivity of the assessment tools' available 'at different stages of identification' for specific conditions like autism. Such tools in the CJS were not that 'sophisticated', so 'you have to start' by 'getting an agreement for a common assessment tool' and 'a multi-agency' agreement on the 'validity and consequences' of diagnosis. Then 'people with expertise on specific needs' should 'refine and develop [these tools] for those particular purposes' (Member of the House of Lords). Continued progress in the operation of L&D Services (see chapter four) will also have an impact on the successful identification and assessment of autistic adult defendants. Nevertheless, there is still greater work to be done here in the later stages of the CJS pathway, as the *2021–26 Autism Strategy* acknowledges (see below).

Thus, beyond the limitations of legal interpretation, these research interviews shed light on a number of other barriers that constrained the application of the Autism Act and related policy to the CJS. The mad-bad binary (Seddon, 2008) categorisation of autistic defendants, the nature of autism as a spectrum condition, the contrasting organisational culture between the DOH and MOJ and low baseline of expertise in the CJS to identify autistic defendants were all such factors. Any future reform in this area will need to consider how to overcome these obstacles to ensure more coherent statutory application to institutions in the CJS.

2. 2010–2022: What are the Rationalities, Programmes and Technologies of Governance for Autistic Defendants?

This section analyses the implementation of the first Autism Strategy and its subsequent iterations (see DOH, 2014; DOHSC & DfE, 2021). A number of interesting themes emerge around the changing 'political rationalities', 'programmes' and 'technologies' of governance for autistic defendants. There is a noticeable shift from no-longer 'managing inappropriately' the risks of autistic defendants to *Think Autism's* awareness raising and signposting to services, backed by limited additional resource. In turn followed by a focus on 'improving support' in the CJS, the community and inpatient settings in the *2021–26 National Autism Strategy*. On the latter, there is an important move towards de-institutionalisation of autistic people in inpatient care by bringing forward changes to the Mental Health Act 1983. Proposed changes would mean that this group should only be admitted to 'inpatient mental health settings if absolutely necessary' (DOHSC & DfE, 2021a: 30). The shift to 'improving support' for autistic defendants focuses on meeting the healthcare needs of autistic defendants in the healthcare system, access to reasonable adjustments in the CJS and 'improving the understanding' of CJS professionals. So, whilst there are the green shoots of a more disability rights-based approach indicated in the language of the 2021 Strategy, this is not comprehensively embedded across the CJS pathway by its chapter 8 or in the accompanying action plan (see DOHSC & DfE, 2021b). In particular, these documents fail to incorporate recommendations embedding such an approach in procedural decision-making in the courts in a way that is needed (see chapters six to eight below).

A. No Longer 'Managed Inappropriately'?

The DOH published a *Local Self-Assessment Framework* for local authorities, NHS organisations and their partners to implement the Statutory Guidance in their localities (2011). Its Quality Outcome 5 was that 'adults with autism are no longer managed inappropriately in the CJS' (DOH, 2011: 7) and asked these organisations two specific questions to assess progress in their local area: 'are you engaging the CJS as a key partner in your planning for adults with autism'? 'Have you considered joint planning for community-based interventions?' (ibid) The NAO's *Progress in implementing the 2010 Adult Autism Strategy* reported that only 135 of 152 local authorities responded to the self-assessment exercise (2012). Under the RAG (Red/Amber/Green) rating system, only 4 per cent of local authorities rated themselves as Green in achieving the Quality Outcome 5 and 36 per cent rated themselves Amber for putting a plan in place to achieve this outcome (ibid: 28). A large proportion, 29 per cent, said they had no such plan to achieve this outcome and 31 per cent of local authorities did not answer (ibid). Thus, even on the measures for success the DOH set, there was inadequate levels of local planning to support autistic adults coming into contact with the CJS. The lack of resource for local authorities to work with autistic defendants and absence of a statutory duty placed on their criminal justice partners, is likely to have stymied partnership working in this area.

Thus, it was crucial for research interviews to catechise the meaning of 'adults with autism are **no longer managed inappropriately** in the CJS' and what *appropriate management* might look like, in perceiving the rationalities, programmes and technologies of governance for autistic defendants. The phrase was explained by a Senior Clinical Advisor as 'short-hand for adults with autism being recognised' in the CJS and 'treated appropriately' so that: 'reasonable adjustments are made for them … [and] [t]hey should potentially be diverted out into community mental health services'. Consequently, Senior Civil Servants said it was deliberately left 'for people in the operational organisations … to define' (Senior Civil Servant 2) and agreed that this was 'a cross government strategy rather than the pathways of care' (Senior Civil Servant 1). The Senior Clinical Advisor to the DOH, described inappropriate management as only identifying autistic defendants 'in their 50's, who have been revolving around prison because no-one picks them up' and all of whom have 'been bullied'. However, deliberately leaving the phrase undefined in Quality Outcome 5 and *Think Autism* (DOH, 2011: 7; emphasis added; DOH, 2014a) reflected the shift towards localism, concerns about the spectrum nature of autism and the implementation of the Autism Strategy following the change of government in 2010.

A number of elements emerged in interviewees' responses to how autistic defendants *should* be managed appropriately. All interviewees acknowledged the need to improve identification through better screening tools, training and to ensure 'assessment at any level [is] comprehensively employed and consistently and systematically used' (Member of the House of Lords). Senior clinicians – who had worked in an advisory capacity in this policy area – believed that existing screening tools did not work well in the CJS context. For example, as a Senior Clinical Advisor stated, '[e]ven ADOS (Autism Diagnostic Observation Schedule) needs to be adapted', despite being the main diagnostic assessment tool recommended by NICE (2012). The tool was perceived as being problematic for use on adults because it was designed to assess children and aspects of this schedule rely on interviews with the parents of the autistic person to chart their childhood development. A Senior Psychiatrist pointed out, '[a] lot of people [with autism] are disinherited from an early age' and, as a result, 'an adapted screening and diagnostic tool is needed' for autistic adults.

As with treatment of offenders with mental health and learning difficulties in Lord Bradley's 2009 Report, there was a view that managing autistic offenders appropriately involved a cross-system model with apposite disposal pathways connecting individuals to access in health and social care systems. If an autistic defendant finds 'themselves in the CJS …' whether the 'disposal option is a community sentence', 'custodial sentence' or in the 'the healthcare system' depends 'on the nature of the offence … then that condition has to be properly … recognised, supported and treated' in the particular setting (Member of the House of Lords). This Member of the House of Lords emphasised that such support and treatment should be 'axiomatic' for autistic defendants in the 'the [general] healthcare system' but more has to be done in 'prison healthcare'. Further, this interviewee pointed out that community sentences were 'only effective if all the complex needs of the individual are recognised and are supported' and autistic adults 'are connected to services not only whilst they are on the community sentence but at the end of [it], because there is no point in cutting support for someone with health needs' (Member of the House of Lords).

Early identification was seen as essential, both at the gateway to the CJS and at the interfaces with community-based services so that 'if the condition is recognised … at police custody' and the nature of the offence does not necessarily require a court appearance' then it is 'necessary to either connect or reconnect with services in the community' (ibid). A Member of Parliament commended identification as necessary in the courts and 'is something which can be done quite efficiently' in the Plea and Case Management Hearing by asking an 'extra question' in the questionnaire: 'does the defendant suffer from any disability, including hidden impairment?' This would be helpful for the judiciary, this interviewee noted, because:

> If the box is filled with autism/ASD the judge can ask counsel: … Is there any potential relevance to court sittings or the issues in the case that this condition gives rise to …?

> [T]he judge, with training, can [then] ask counsel: how the disability relates to the management of the case or the issues in the case?
>
> [Y]ou could do that fairly easily with a revised practice direction. To a certain extent it's done – if judges see someone with a hearing impairment or blindness they say well 'how are we going to manage the case?' … [I]t does happen but the hidden (though I don't like 'hidden' as it implies some sort of intent), the invisible impairments, I really don't think we've cracked that.

Indeed, the 2013 Equal Treatment Bench Book, which applied at the time the case studies below took place, stated that judges should not only be able to 'recognise the existence of a mental disability if not informed of it' but they should also be able to 'identify its implications in the court or tribunal setting and understand what should be done to compensate for areas of disadvantage without prejudicing other parties' (Judicial College, 2013: 97). This earlier version of the Bench Book also stated that where a disability is 'indicated on court or tribunal pro-formas both the administration and the judiciary should act on this information' by 'requesting further documentation or arranging a directions hearing to consider requirements arising out of special needs' (Judicial College, 2013: 100). This documentation may then reveal that there is 'a duty to make reasonable adjustments under the Equality Act 2010' (ibid). Furthermore, during this period, a specific guide for solicitors, barristers, and judges on cross-examining autistic defendants was available on The Advocate's Gateway (2015). This guide also emphasised that courts were 'expected to make reasonable adjustments to remove barriers for people with disabilities' (*op. cit.*: 1). Yet, as chapters six to eight evince, there is often a paucity of good practice, despite being recommended in these materials, in individual cases in the lower courts. This material is expanded in the *2022 Equal Treatment Bench Book*, in the examples of adapting procedures (disability) and in the specific section on 'Autism Spectrum condition in the Disability Glossary: Impairments and reasonable adjustments' (Judicial College, 2022: 87–88; 396–400). Further research is needed on the impact this has had to autistic people accessing reasonable adjustments in the courts.

In terms of training, interviewees gave examples of training for 'all the staff that are working with' people 'with personality disorders …', called '"psychologically enabled environments"', about how to 'handle and support' them (Senior Psychiatrist). This interviewee suggested analogous professional practices which could be advanced for autistic people (ibid). Beyond improving professional awareness of autism across the offender pathway, the 'essence of the [Autism] Strategy needs to be applied'. Thus, this Senior Psychiatrist said that 'managing defendants with autism appropriately' should be underpinned by the principle of 'public services treating people fairly' (ibid). However, as a Senior Civil Servant from the DOH pointed out, it 'would be impossible for a strategic document [like the Revised Statutory Guidance] to define' in 'detail' the term 'managed inappropriately' because there 'are so many scenarios that you can imagine' and types of 'offences that people have committed' (Senior Civil Servant 2). Instead, that Senior

Civil Servant believed such a strategic document should be underpinned by the principle that people are 'better cared for in a healthcare environment than in prison' and 'they should be looked after in those settings in a way' which enables them 'as far as possible to be rehabilitated and recover, rather than stay there' indefinitely 'without the support to address' the 'behaviours … of concern' (Senior Civil Servant 2). Another Senior Civil Servant observed 'quite a lot of the prisons' at this time were 'concerned about the social care bit' of the Care Act 2014 because 'it open[ed] up the fact that … some older prisoners' have a 'disability' which requires making 'the prisons a different environment'; and 'wonder[ed] if there is something coming down the track [for autism]' (Senior Civil Servant 1; see chapters eight and nine). This is now a key work strand of the *2021–26 Autism Strategy* but took nearly a decade to get there.

A shift to localism and the managerialism of 'inappropriate' behaviour towards autistic defendants were the dominant rationalities in this period. What is interesting in interrogating the normative intention behind the concept of 'managed appropriately', was the limited reference to CJS agencies' Public Sector Equality Duty. In particular in paying due regard to this duty, the need to 'take steps to meet the needs of persons who share a relevant protected characteristic that are different from the needs of persons who do not share it' (section 149(3)). This further indicates the necessity to strengthen the interface between the Equality Act 2010 and policies in this policy area.

B. Think Autism, the Revised Statutory Guidance and the 2021–26 Autism Strategy

The present section identifies key themes raised across the last two iterations of Autism Strategies and in the *Revised Statutory Guidance* (DOH, 2015), teasing out the underlying rationalities and technologies of governance for autistic defendants. Whereas *Think Autism* built on rather than replaced (DOH, 2014: 5) the first *Autism Strategy* (DOH, 2010a), *The national strategy for autistic children, young people and adults: 2021 to 2026* (the '*2021–26 Autism Strategy*', DOHSC & DfE, 2021) augments *and* replaces the 2014 policy. This new strategy broadens its scope to children and young people for the first time, ensuring autistic people have access to diagnosis and receive the right support as early as possible and across their lifetime.

The *Revised Statutory Guidance*, supports the implementation of *Think Autism* and the subsequent *2021–26 Autism Strategy*, in setting out the role of local authorities and NHS bodies with respect to how they should work with the CJS (DOH, 2015: 55). However, as argued earlier in the present chapter, the asymmetrical application of its statutory remit, leaves an imbalance in implementation because bodies within the CJS are not compelled to reciprocity in working jointly with local authorities and NHS bodies. Two specific sections relate to autistic adults coming into contact with the CJS: section 7 on supporting people with complex needs and section 9 'Working with the CJS'. The language of mandate in the *Revised Statutory Guidance* was strengthened (see NAS, 2014) in its application to local authorities and health bodies, who 'must . . follow the relevant sections' of the guidance 'or provide a good reason why they are not doing so'. If they do not do so, they may be liable to judicial review or action by the Secretary of State' (DOH, 2015: 6). Mandatory language was also strengthened in section 9 on working with the CJS but still uses 'should' rather than the imperative 'must'. The weak language of 'should seek to' and 'consider' was likely a factor in perpetuating the low rate of planning to support autistic adults in the CJS reported by Local Authority Self Assessments discussed above (2012; see also DOH, 2016). This should be strengthened in future versions of the statutory guidance.

Think Autism's key strategy areas focused on enabling inclusion of autistic people in the community through better joined up advice and information, along with local innovation in 'new models of care' to support those who did not meet statutory eligibility (DOH, 2014: 9). These strategic areas were augmented by 15 'Priority Challenges for Action'; three of which were relevant to the governance of autistic people within the CJS. Priority Challenge 5 focused on community safety and autistic people being 'free from the risk of discrimination, hate crime and abuse' (DOH, 2014: 20). It set out enhanced services for 'vulnerable victims' under the new Code of Practice for Victims of Crime, including those with a mental disorder or 'a significant impairment of intelligence or social functioning' (CPS, 2013), highlighting the police duty to provide early assessments of these victims. Priority Challenge 12 reiterated many of the actions set out in *Transforming Care*, and the *Winterbourne View Review* (DOSC, 2012), emphasising reducing 'reliance on in-patient care for this group' (DOH, 2014: 36–37). Priority Challenge 13 covered the role of criminal justice system institutions to 'think about autism and to know how to work well with other services' (DOH, 2014: 38). Neither the key strategy areas nor Priority Challenges developed the concept of 'managing' autistic adult defendants 'appropriately'.

Across the strategy, there was evidence of a move away from centralised service delivery, towards localism and the 'asset-based commissioning' so redolent in policymaking associated with the Big Society agenda. Personalisation, a strand of this agenda, was enhanced by *Think Autism* – building care and support around an individual's strengths and needs, rather than trying to fit them into predetermined service designs (Marshall-Tate, 2019; SCIE, 2012). Personalisation has been criticised as disproportionately emphasising improvements in individual autonomy through personalised support whilst 'lacking reference to structural oppression or the need for collective forms of action that bring about structural change' (Dodd, 2011: 260). Further, on the one-hand, the strategic emphasis on 'signposting' autistic people to services was designed to overcome siloed practice. On the other, this coincided with a failure to allocate resources for advice services, rather than doing justice to difference and meeting autistic people's social care needs.

The focus and actions of the *2021–22 Autism Strategy* was informed by the findings of an APPGA inquiry into the Autism Act (2019), as well as a review of *Think Autism*, which was launched alongside a public call for evidence in 2019 (DHSC & DfE, 2021a). These reports, along with findings from autism charities' *Left Stranded*, showed 'that the pandemic exacerbated many of the inequalities autistic people already faced', including social exclusion and isolation (ibid: 7; National Autistic Society, 2020; Pais and Knapp, 2021). Six themes formed the basis of *2021–26 Autism Strategy*, derived from the challenges identified through this process. Improving the understanding and acceptance of autism within society was central, as well as access to education and transitions into adulthood for autistic children and young people, support into employment and tackling health and care inequalities for autistic people all being priorities. Two additional themes had particular relevance to autistic defendants: building the right support in the community and supporting people in inpatient care; and improving support within the criminal and youth justice system (DHSC & DfE, 2021a: 10). The latter is covered by chapter 8 of the *2021–26 Autism Strategy*. The vision to improve support in this context aims to ensure that all staff understand autism and how to support autistic people. Demonstrable progress is expected in autistic people having equal access to care and support across the CJS pathway. Finally, the vision to achieve this involves providing autistic people who have been convicted of a crime with additional support to 'engage fully in their sentence and rehabilitation' (DHSC & DfE, 2021a: 35). Actions in the *Implementation Plan* for 2021–2022 (DHSC & DfE, 2021b) will support achieving this vision. The final chapter of the *2021–22 Autism Strategy* includes factors which will enable strategic delivery: improving autism research, data collection and monitor implementation, as well as strengthening governance, leadership and accountability (DHSC & DfE, 2021a: 38).

Whilst the two strategies both broadly cover key institutions in the criminal justice system, *Think Autism* has more of an emphasis on the police and earlier stages of the CJS process, while the *2021–26 Autism Strategy* has more substantial material on the probation services and prisons, as well as resourcing support for autistic people in inpatient care. The identification of autistic adults by these services and role of L&D in referring autistic defendants to other services was a theme considered to varying extents by these policies. The *Revised Statutory Guidance* explicates the role of health bodies in earlier identification of autistic adults in the criminal justice process (2015: 55, para 9.7-8), and where 'appropriate', for the 'CJS to refer people with autism' for 'health and care support to divert them from offending … and prevent re-offending' (ibid). One Member of Parliament interviewed stressed the need for 'a flagging system', on the 'national computer', to be built into proceedings at the 'earliest stage', so that 'there is an awareness of their condition' from 'the outset of the investigation' by the police. This interviewee explained this would enable CJS professionals to look up that individual, where 'the person is known to the police', and see 'there is autism' and 'who they can refer [them] to' (Member of Parliament). While the interviewee stressed 'that autism is not always relevant to the allegation[s]', early identification 'could affect' the 'progress of the case' as 'a factor in the decision to charge …' (ibid) and the appropriate management of autistic defendants in the CJS. It is also necessary in ensuring the reasonable adjustments are provided for. Under the Equality Act 2010 no duty arises to provide 'reasonable adjustments' if the public authority 'does not know or could not reasonably be expected to know that a person has a disability' (EHRC, 2010: 9).

The Member of Parliament who raised the issue was right to be pessimistic about how long it would take to put a digital flagging system in place. *Think Autism* was vague on actual detail, proposing only that the Metropolitan Police use such a system. The *2021–22 Autism Strategy*'s plans developing a new 'data categorisation list on disability, which will include autism' for NHSE/I patient records, to improve identification and screening of autistic adults in prison through a HMPPS digital prison management system (ibid: 37). Digital identification alone is insufficient, however. As chapter four noted, L&D Services were supposed to be 'available in every police custody suite and criminal court in England by 2017/18' (DOH, 2014: 39) and their Standard Service Specification required a validated screening tool for autism (NHS England, 2014). To support this, *Think Autism* Priority Challenge 13 recommended that autism awareness training for staff and the police, the CPS, probation and courts should 'ensure that they have access to expertise to support adults with autism' suspected of committing a crime. Whilst the 2014 strategy recognises that such expertise 'can change the way that the police or courts view a situation' (DOH, 2014: 38), the *2021–26 Autism Strategy* bolsters the diversionary approach to 'find alternatives to prosecution and custody' (DHSC & DfE, 2021a: 37). It commits to funding research to 'provide insight about how police use Out of Court Disposal of autistic people' and to drive better access to health and social care services for this group (ibid).

Over the last decade training for CJS professionals has been about increasing professionals' 'awareness' of autism and autistic people's specific needs, to aid identification of autistic defendants in the CJS. The most recent strategy sets out 'the development of a toolkit to educate frontline staff about neurodiversity' (DHSC & DfE, 2021a: 38). For police officers, this will now reflect guidelines on the reasonable adjustments they require (ibid: 37). The *2021–26 Autism Strategy* also makes increasing awareness of professionals in the prison and probation service a particular focus, including a dedicated autism session which will be included for new prison officers and youth custodial specialists in England and Wales. Further, a new Neurodiversity Support Manager role will be introduced in education services in up to five prisons (ibid). Although better identification and flagging systems, along with liaison and diversion proffer many benefits, training must go further in making explicit that care should be taken to ensure digital systems do not lead to 'pre-crime technologies' (Zedner, 2007) for autistic defendants and result in net-widening.

On the latter point, none of the iterations of autism strategies over the last decade have dealt satisfactorily with the aetiology of crime and legal classification of behaviour which is associated with the symptomatology of autism. An issue identified through a review of the 'psy' literature in chapter one of this book. Such behaviour – in contexts like residential homes and supported living environments – may be deemed to be 'challenging' (Hayes, 2006) requiring professionals to adapt the support, services and care planning (see DOH, 2014: 36) while, in other contexts, it may be prosecuted and the individual treated as a criminal offender. Nevertheless, although the *Revised Statutory Guidance* (2015) builds on the *Winterbourne View Review* neither this, *Think Autism* nor the *2021–26 Autism Strategy* unpack this issue or the point on the relationship between the symptomatology and criminal offence. For example, *Think Autism* set out a work plan on 'preventing disability-related harassment on public transport' through working with the Department of Transport on a national scheme to prevent cyber bullying by teaching pupils about e-safety (DOH, 2014: 21). However, there were no proposals to work with autistic defendants around understanding the boundaries of internet use or to look at how to deal with this type of offending in either *Think Autism* nor the *2021–26 Autism Strategy*. This is unfortunate, as shown by the case study on cybercrime in chapters six and seven below; complex issues arise out of the interaction between the symptomatology of autism and the nature of the offending and cyber-crime.

Beyond training, identification and referral, there is limited detail on the strategic role of the police, or indeed the Police and Crime Commissioners (PCCs), or CPS in relation to autistic defendants. Apart from PCCs engaging with local Autism Partnership Boards (APBs) in commissioning emotional and practical support services for victims of crime, to (DOH, 2014: 20), neither *Think Autism*, nor the *2021–26 Autism Strategy* elaborates on their role. This is disappointing; chapter eight below outlines an innovative example of how a PCC intervened in the processing of a case of an autistic *defendant* and is a missed opportunity. *Think Autism* signposted the court process and availability of Special Measures for Victims and Witnesses and an 'aide-memoire'[1] for prosecutors on implications for the 'prosecution process and sources of support for people with autism' (DOH, 2014: 20). However, there is no additional material in the *2021–26 Autism Strategy* to reinforce what should be considered by the CPS in relation to the needs of autistic defendants. Indeed, improved understanding of the implications of the defendant's autism on the prosecution process will only happen if, first, they include disabled defendants in future Business Plans. Second, the CPS would need to pivot from the asymmetrical protection of vulnerable victims without equivalent support for vulnerable defendants in criminal cases (see chapter six). Signs of this are now evident in the CPS 2021–22 Business Plan proposals for an 'At Risk

[1] See the Legal Guidance, 'Mental Health Conditions – Neurodevelopmental disorders', part of the *Psychological Evidence Toolkit – A guide for Crown Prosecutors*.

Defendants Strategy' on 'defendants who have additional needs or vulnerabilities, or who may be at risk of disproportionality, are treated fairly' (2021).

Across the autism strategies and statutory guidance of the last decade, there has been little to change guidance on temporising, dispositive and processual decision-making in the courts (see chapter six below). *Think Autism's* section on the courts did note that '[c]ases involving offenders with autism often involve an application for Special Measures' (DOH, 2014: 38). In practice, the present research found a disjuncture between policy and practice: Special Measures were not provided for any of the autistic defendants observed in the case studies discussed in chapters six to eight below. Some of the barristers and solicitors interviewed for the purposes of this research required an explanation of what was meant by 'Special Measures'. When participants did know about these measures, it was evident that they had not considered the use of these resources or did not know how to access them for their clients (see chapter six). The *2021–26 Autism Strategy makes* no mention of Special Measures specifically. However, it is strengthened by its emphasis on convicted autistic people receiving additional support to fully engage in their sentence and rehabilitation; deriving in part from Equality and Human Rights Commission research (EHRC, 2020). It found that because disabled people's needs, including those of autistic people, were not identified early enough, reasonable adjustments are not made and so they often struggle to participate in processes like sentencing. These findings are further corroborated by the case study research in this book (see chapters six to eight below). Work to tackle this by staff in the courts and tribunals service, through making reasonable adjustments and more 'autism-friendly' courtroom environments, is set out more comprehensively in the *Implementation Plan*, than in the *2021–26 Autism Strategy* itself. These changes will be carried out through the planned 'Hidden Disabilities Scheme', introduction of mandatory learning in this service and by to employing a 'national neurodiversity advisor for the Community Sentence Treatment (CSTR) programme' (DHSC & DfE, 2021b: 22; 2021a: 37).

However, guidance on dispositive decision-making by the courts at sentence, in relation to hospital orders, is weak across the three autism strategies and two statutory guidance of the last 13 years. This is despite the *Revised Statutory Guidance's* emphasis on the 'reduction in reliance on inpatient care for people with autism' (2015: 4). *Think Autism* does restate the DOHSC's planned programme to 'reduce the use of restrictive practice and promote safe, positive and therapeutic environments' (2014a: 36). Nevertheless, *Think Autism* makes no mention of the use of hospital orders for autistic people generally (see NAO, 2015) or those made by the criminal courts for autistic defendants in particular. This missed opportunity impacted on the institutionalisation of this group over the last decade, with the number of people identified as being autistic in inpatient mental health services increasing during this period (DOHSC, 2021: 7). Although between 2015 to June 2021, 'a net decrease in inpatient numbers of 28%' was made towards the target of a 50 per cent reduction people with a learning disability or autism in these settings (NHS Digital, 2021; DOHSC, 2021: 30). Compared to other groups, however, the number of autistic people in inpatient mental health settings remained stubbornly at 1,200 at the end of June 2021 (NHS Digital, 2021).

Interviewees, in particular a Senior Civil Servant, Member of Parliament and Senior Clinical Advisor, expressed disquiet about the use of sections 37, 41 or 47 of the Mental Health Act 1983 for autistic people, and Civil Servants were interested in 'any case studies, where [autistic defendants were] disposed under the Mental Health Act and where they have languished …' (Senior Civil Servant 1). William's case in chapter six below is one such example. The Member of Parliament from the All-Party Parliamentary Group on Autism 'hoped that the vast majority of autistic people would never be made subject to Section 37, or, God forbid, [section] 41 because this would be a wholly inappropriate use of resources'. Since there must be evidence from two qualified psychiatrists, under section 12 of the Act, that the person either has a personality disorder or a mental health disorder that is capable of treatment, he argued that the Mental Health Act 'should be largely irrelevant when it comes to defendants with autism'. That is, in this Parliamentarian's view, '… unless the person with autism has a co-morbid, diagnosable mental health condition that is capable of treatment'. This Member of Parliament did not believe that consultant psychiatrists, considering the pressures on resources, '… are in the culture of misdiagnosis or diagnosis for the sake of it …' (Member of Parliament). A Senior Clinical Advisor emphasised that discharge is the 'biggest barrier as there are no autism-specific community services to discharge people with autism to' and the 'the opportunities' for 'local specialist autism services … are likely to be limited by the lack of expertise'. This barrier remained intractable for autistic adults during this period.

Indeed, the research discussed in chapters six to eight shows that such orders *are* being given to autistic defendants, who do not have a dual diagnosis. This, it must be emphasised, is not attributed to psychiatrists being in a 'culture of misdiagnosis'. Rather, it is argued therein, that psychiatrists recommend and courts utilise such orders where prison is seen to be inappropriate or ineffective. The case study research found they are also used where community sentencing provisions either will not facilitate access to specialist support or are insufficient in expressing the court's cognisance of the risk management required for a particular offender. It has taken over a decade, since the first Autism Strategy, for legislative reform, through the Mental Health Act White Paper, to propose changing 'the detention criteria so autistic people can only be admitted if there is a probable mental health need' (DOHSC & DfE, 2021: 31; DOHSC, 2021). It is welcome that the *2021–26 Autism Strategy* intends to 'modernise the Mental Health Act' so that 'autistic people are only admitted to inpatient mental health settings if absolutely necessary', along with the additional funding allocated to accelerate discharge (see DOHSC & DfE, 2021: 30–31). Nevertheless, it is disappointing that the *2021–26 Autism Strategy* remains scant on detail in relation to criminal court ordered hospital orders (see below). Especially, as chapter eight illustrates, the lack of available specialist services in the community means some autistic defendants spend protracted periods in special hospitals under court ordered hospital orders (see William's case).

Only time will tell whether the publication of the draft statutory guidance for Mental Health Units (Use of Force) Act 2018 and any enactment of the Mental Health Act White Paper's proposals will materially improve the care given in secure mental health inpatient settings to autistic adults with offending behaviour. The planned guidance on the use of injunctions, for families of people in inpatient care to more easily access information about the patient's care, will also help. However, the *2021–26 Autism Strategy* would have been strengthened in this area if it had made recommendations about any further roll-out of the NHSE/I Forensic Outreach and Liaison Service (FOLS), which provides specialist, forensic mental health care for autistic people who have been admitted to secure inpatient care.

The Revised Statutory guidance emphasises access to a 'timely' autism diagnosis and healthcare support in commissioning health services for persons in prison or detention (ibid: 57), with *Think Autism* outlining the role of mandatory assessment of function skills of all prisoners, from 2014, in identifying autistic prisoners (ibid: 13.5). The *2021–26 Autism Strategy* gives greater focus on achieving progress on autistic people getting equal access to care and support in the prison and probation services, by improving their access to reasonable adjustments and by making the environments of prison and probation services more autism friendly. These institutions will be encouraged to undertake NAS Autism Accreditation, with improved safety training for prison staff and will be underpinned by forthcoming guidance on meeting the needs of autistic people in prison healthcare (DHSC & DfE, 2021b: 25). There is, however, no cogent message about the use of imprisonment for this group more broadly nor are there any supplementary guidelines on the substantive reasonable adjustments which could be made in this context.

The MOJ's *Transforming Rehabilitation* strategy reformed England's Probation Service so that it was split-up by apportioning certain levels of risk between public services on the one hand and private services on the other (MOJ, 2013). Key functions remained within the ambit of the public sector, 'including the direct management of offenders who pose the highest risk of serious harm', while low risk cases were contracted out to 21 private Community Rehabilitation Companies (see also the Offender Rehabilitation Act 2014). This left the Probation Service's senior forensic psychologists working only on the high-risk caseload. These reforms were overturned in 2021 and have been described as 'fundamentally flawed' by an HM Inspectorate of Probation chief (Grierson, 2021). Dividing the service on the basis of risk presented serious consequences for autistic adult defendants in this period. According to a Senior Probation Service Psychologist, interviewed for this book, the service fragmentation presented an additional barrier to effective identification and improved support of autistic adult defendants. This interviewee explained that those deemed to be 'lower risk' missed out on the expertise of the National Probation Service's senior forensic psychologists, who only worked on the high-risk caseload. This approach also created additional obstacles to these 'lower risk' individuals being referred for adult social care assessments and was out of step with section 9 of the *Revised Statutory Guidance*. Under the Care Act 2014, 'local authorities must assess the care and support needs of adults (including those with autism)' in prisons or other forms of detention in their local area, and meet the needs for 'those who are eligible' (DOH, 2015: 56). Chapters six to eight below discuss the difficulties that the cohort of defendants had in accessing social care. Whilst a diffuse probation service was likely to be one barrier to such access at the dispositive stage of decision-making, more research is needed on the barriers to social care support for autistic defendants in the earlier stages of the CJS more generally. In one of the case studies below ('Claire'), a PCC ended up intervening and funding a social care package for the autistic defendant, so frustrated were they by the inability of the relevant local authority to pick up the tab.

After a decade of austerity and the COVID-19 pandemic, public spending on services and interventions for autistic adult defendants is another important theme to note. Knapp et al's economic modelling estimated the comprehensive costs of autism spectrum disorders (ASDs) in the UK was £28bn; including those who entered the CJS because they had not had the right support in the community (2009). Some movement away from austerity policies of the Coalition and earlier Conservative governments is a notable shift between *Think Autism* and the *2021–26 Autism Strategy*. Although neither committed dedicated spending on work in the CJS, where *Think Autism* included a total of £5.7 million of spending (DOH, 2014: 9; 33), the order of funding mentioned in the *2021–26 Autism Strategy* is greater. The newest strategy included £31 million for autistic people and people with a learning disability,[2] especially on inpatient care and facilitating discharge from these services (DHSC & DfE, 2021a). However, much of it had already been allocated before the strategy was produced and, clearly, additional funding to support social care in the community is needed to facilitate autistic adults staying out of inpatient care in the long-term. Further research to model the sufficiency of spending in this area, and elsewhere in the strategy, and what 'ought' to be spent to enable access to reasonable adjustments in the CJS and the social care support autistic defendants need would also be helpful.

This is important in ensuring the social model of disability is applied in practice for autistic defendants in the CJS. Woods emphasises the social model should be 'more widely implemented for all neurodivergent labels' (2017). The energy expended by autistic people in assimilating with the Predominant Neurotype demands and expectations, often causes undue psychological harm to themselves (Beardon, 2008; 2017). Whilst the strengthening of the *2021–26 Autism Strategy* on its emphasis on the use of reasonable adjustments in the CJS, there may be more work to support self-advocacy and to dismantle the 'profound' barrier (Woods, 2017) of the perception of autistic individuals as diminished versions of the perfect

[2] This includes spending to enable inpatient settings to become more autism-friendly, on crisis prevention, avoidable admissions, increased community support through a 7-day specialist multidisciplinary and crisis support for this group in every area of the country' (DHSC & DfE, 2021: 31).

Predominant Neurotype person (Campbell, 2008). To do so, future public policy-making in this area will have to more effectively wrestle with the complexity of 'behaviour that challenges services' which is associated with the symptomatology of autism. This will require more sophisticated social care support both in the community and across the CJS pathway.

Conclusion

The present chapter has sought to explicate the limits of the Autism Act 2009 and related policy and explain why the lack of statutory application to the CJS sustains the sort of siloed working that the L&D agenda has sought to avoid. We have seen an improved substantive focus on autistic adults coming into contact with the CJS in the more recent iterations of Autism Strategies (DOH, 2014; DOHSC & DfE, 2021) and Statutory Guidance (DOH 2015) However, there remains a lack of coherence in properly connecting the interfaces of the CJS, through statutory requirements, with social care and health services. The shift from 'managing appropriately' autistic defendants to better healthcare and support of their needs in the CJS is welcome. A lack of ambition in proactively integrating a disability rights-based approach in procedural decision-making endures. Chapters six to eight below illustrate an urgent review is needed of policy on temporising, dispositive and processual decisions in the courts to integrate such an approach. This would facilitate strengthening governance, leadership and accountability with respect to the CJS. In turn, this would be embedded by strengthening the statutory application of the guidance to institutions in the CJS when the Autism Statutory Guidance is updated again (see DOHSC & DfE, 2021: 9).

Chapter one described the analysis of the incidence of adult defendants as acting like a barium test on the CJS; revealing problems in the way it operates for disabled defendants in general. Expanding the statutory parameters of the operation of the Autism Act 2009 and subsequent policy, via mechanisms within the Equality Act 2010, may provide a helpful example of a schema for entrenching the L&D agenda in an existing legislative framework for disabled defendants. Such an approach could enable a shift away from the rationality of the vulnerable defendant discussed in chapter four. Following on from the arguments developed in chapters four and five, there is descriptive value in proactively categorising these groups as 'disabled' under the 'social model' of 'disability' in order to move discussion away from the rationality of 'vulnerability'. Circumscribing the focus of statutory guidance to local authorities and health bodies – and not extending it to criminal justice – actually risks further sustaining the mad-bad binary for this group in criminal justice practice while also ensuring the predominance of the medical model of disability.

Given that the Autism Act 2009 was the first impairment-specific piece of legislation in England, it could have derived more from the foundation provided by the

Equality Act 2010. That it did not do so is certainly in a large part due to when it was on the legislative agenda and nervousness that it would not complete its journey through Parliament before the 2010 General Election. In these circumstances, there is a lot to be learnt by legislators, legal academics and campaigners, who propose new impairment-specific legislation in future. Opportunities and pitfalls of the need to ensure confluence between existing Equality Law should be considered when tabling impairment-specific bills in future. To that extent, such ventures should be proactive in also ensuring such proposals are harmonised with the UNCRPD and integrate the social model of disability in their drafting. The Autism Act 2009's pragmatic approach to improving access to services for autistic people was laudable but it may have set a trend towards impairment-specific legislation which further embed medical models of disability. The recent Down Syndrome Act 2022 has already received such substantive criticism (Rose, 2022). Arguably, more purposive harmonisation and legislating for the direct implementation of the UNCRPD may have achieved more comprehensive social inclusion for autistic and Down Syndrome people alike. On the other hand, the very ratification of the CRPD may have been the 'high watermark for disability rights' (Crowther and Sayce, 2020); with the political reality making strengthening the legal foundation of the UNCRPD unlikely, even if doing so remains a normative necessity.

In the wake of the publication of the Bradley Report, Baroness Stern commented that the 'high number of people with mental health problems and learning disabilities in prison is a clear sign that something is going wrong'. She strongly criticised the use of our 'punishment system to deal with failures in the health and welfare system[s]' (Westminster Policy Forum, 2009). As Hayes points out in discussing offenders with learning disabilities, the fact that these individuals are 'missing out on support and services which might reduce or prevent offending behaviour does not only have consequences for the individual' (2007a: 152). The impact extends to families, service providers, and society more generally because the 'community as a whole suffers, socially, ethically and economically' (ibid). It is such failures in these systems for autistic people which led to the enactment of the Autism Act 2009. However, as described in chapters six to nine, autistic adult defendants are still 'missing out' on such support and this is having a grave impact on them and their families.

PART III

Technologies of Governance: Criminal Court Practice

PART III

Technologies of Governance: Criminal Court Practice

6

Pre-trial Shaping: The Police, the Crown Prosecution Service and Decision to Prosecute

Introduction

> I make no apologies when I say that the CJS is seriously letting people like myself, who are on the Autistic Spectrum, down badly (William, Letter Correspondence).

Chapters four and five explored the rationalities of governance of autistic defendants through autism-specific policy-making and policies on vulnerable defendants, including in L&D Services. Chapters six to eight examine the reality of governance of autistic defendants through eight case studies,[1] set out in Section 1 of the present chapter, as they were processed through the Crown and Magistrates' Courts. The inadequacy of recognition and understanding of autism by criminal justice decision-makers are borne out in these case studies, in the 'prescriptions, plans or schema for acting' used by the police, the CPS and the judiciary to control these defendants. These vignettes are illustrative of the complex reality of autistic defendants' interaction with the CJS and court system. Drawing together rich data into written case summaries[2] demonstrates the variation in level and quality of legal advice, family support and interactions in court.

A distinction can be drawn between three types of decision at the pre-trial stage (Ashworth and Redmayne, 2014: 416). Firstly, 'processual decisions' are 'concerned with the progress of the case from arrest through to court' or up to the point that the case moves through the criminal process. This is the subject of the analysis of the case studies in the current chapter. Discussion on 'pre-trial shaping' in Section 2 examines what logics are applied to autistic defendants and what dividing practices are utilised to manage their conduct (*cf* Rose et al, 2006) in decision-making by: (i) the police, and (ii) the CPS in their decision to prosecute. Secondly, 'dispositive decisions' involve diverting 'a case from the process

[1] All individuals have been given a pseudonym to protect their anonymity.

[2] Consistency has been sought in producing these case studies as units of analysis. However, length and detail vary somewhat due to adhering closely to qualitative research data and because of the intricacy of particular cases.

of prosecution and trial'; they may also dispose of the case 'through some kind of undertaking or penalty' (ibid). None of the cases observed in the present cohort were diverted from the process of prosecution in this sense. Thirdly, the 'temporising decision' of remand 'determines whether or not the defendant should be at liberty between first court appearance and trial' (Ashworth and Redmayne, 2014: 416). Chapter seven considers remand, followed by discussion of the influence of occupational culture on plea.

As Ashworth and Redmayne note, these three types of decisions should not be regarded as 'discrete rational determinations': each decision-maker is subject to rules and guidelines and, importantly, 'may be influenced as much by the power relations between the parties as by the law'. Indeed, they may also be 'influenced by an occupational culture and the expectations of others both within and outside the system' (Ashworth and Redmayne, 2014: 416). Several themes emerge, in the current chapter, which demonstrate the impact of these power relations and occupational culture on the decision-making applied to autistic defendants. Despite the policies in place at the time, Section 2(A) reveals poor identification of autism by the police remained, along with discriminatory treatment on arrest, detention in custody, in interview and in obtaining legal advice. Section 2(B) finds poor consideration, by the CPS, on the effect of a prosecution on the defendants' mental health in deploying the public interest test, and an 'oblique amnesia' about the defendants' rights as disabled people. It is argued across the present chapter and the next that there is a lack of preparedness to examine the relevance of the defendant's autism by the prosecution at these earlier stages of processual decisions. Instead, the 'guilty plea culture' has shifted emphasis to examine the relevance of autism in dispositive decisions: essentially, in mitigation at sentencing, discussed in detail in chapter eight.

1. The Eight Case Studies

Case 1, 'Henry'

'Henry' and a friend were walking home together one evening. While they were looking down at Henry's mobile, two youths ran towards them and punched him in the face. Henry fell over onto a wall. Then, one of the youths jumped 'a metre in the air' and landed on Henry's head, kicking it numerous times. The same youth took Henry's wallet and Autism Alert card from his pocket. A woman witnessed this scene from her lounge and banged on the window to disperse the youths.

Henry remained on the ground unconscious, the witness thought he was dead. The police and ambulance services were called. When the police arrived, they asked Henry whether he wanted to press charges he replied '"I just want to go home"' (Henry's father, 'Bill', Research Interview). They asked him what had happened and he said '"I fell on the wall" which is literally what had happened' (ibid)*. The witness,* *who observed the incident, from her home asked the police at the scene whether they were going to press charges. The Police Officer told her 'no, [Henry] doesn't want to' (ibid). The witness protested and said she saw it all, and would be witness to it. She told the police officers that they could still have caught the 'two lads that have beaten him up, one went to [the] top of the road and the other [was] hiding in the graveyard' (Douglas, Autism Expert, Research Interview). However, this was not pursued by the police.*

When the paramedics arrived on the scene and spoke to Henry, rather than asking him what he wanted to do, they told him to get in their ambulance so that they could see to his injuries. No one addressed his repeated requests to go home. On arrival at hospital, Henry kept telling staff that he had autism but this 'factor was not fully acknowledged' (Bill, Interview). At no point was he assisted by staff to call home.

While sitting in Accident and Emergency (A&E), Henry continued to ask medical staff about going home, including two police officers in attendance for a separate incident. After they kept refusing to take him home and told him to stop asking them, 'he got very agitated and started swearing' (Mr McKinnery, Solicitor, Interview). One officer told him that he could not swear in A&E and asked him to leave. Henry stood up and the officer pushed him from behind towards the door which made him get more agitated; the policeman then took him by the arm towards the exit. Henry then had a 'meltdown' (Bill, Interview) and there was a scuffle. Henry was accused of pulling the officer's ear. The officers then bound Henry's ankles and hands and he, allegedly, bit one of the officers. They then 'threw him head first' (Bill, Interview) into the police van and threatened to taser him. Henry was arrested and charged with assault on two police officers. He was held at the police station for 16-and-a-half hours.

At the Plea and Case Management Hearing, Henry pleaded not guilty to the two alleged assault charges. The case went to trial in the Magistrates' Court in front of a District Judge. In the intervening period, Henry's defence solicitor had instructed a psychiatrist to produce an expert witness report, which set out the detail of Henry's autism. The CPS had approved the psychiatric report commissioned by the defence; this is significant as it is open to the CPS to order their own report. The consultant psychiatrist said that Henry was not fit to stand trial. At court, the District Judge opened proceedings by asking whether the prosecution was going to 'proceed with a view to conviction or on a fact-finding basis under Section 37(3)' (District Judge, Court Observation). The District Judge told the 'claimants' (the two police officers) that he 'didn't want them to confuse fact finding where they seek to put matters forward to make a Hospital Order, with a public interest test to bring a conviction' (District Judge, Court Observation). Further, the District Judge said that the prosecution:

> *[c]ould not, under a reading of S37(3) [of the Mental Health Act 1983] proceed with both trying to get a conviction and, if there was an acquittal, seek a Hospital Order. It was in the public interest that it was one or the other' (Court Observation).*

The Judge then requested that the CPS 'show the claimants [the police officers] the psychiatrist's report'. The CPS Solicitor said that he had shown one claimant the report but they wanted to proceed regardless. The other claimant had not seen it and the CPS Solicitor said that he would have to show it to his superior. The District Judge asked whether it was 'in the public interest to proceed with the prosecution of assault in the knowledge of [the defendant's] autism.' Further, the District Judge said that if it was the guidance of the CPS solicitor's superior 'to proceed then there would be an abuse of process application' and reiterated that if they 'proceeded with fact finding then the Magistrates' Court would not make a finding to lead to a Hospital Order' (Court Observation). The District Judge told the CPS that 'no doctor would say that [Henry] needs a Hospital Order and [they, the CPS] already decided they did not want to get a second expert opinion' (ibid*). The case was adjourned for an hour or so while the solicitor saw the claimants' Superintendent. When he returned, he had been instructed to offer a bind over; this was rejected by the defence. After a further short adjournment, the CPS solicitor informed the court that they 'had no evidence to proceed with the case'. The District Judge agreed that this was 'the right decision' (Court Observation). The case was dismissed.*

Case 2, 'Ollie'

Ollie went to a diagnostic assessment for autism with a psychologist at a Mental Health Service. During the process of Ollie's assessment, his psychologist repeatedly asked the same question framed in a certain way. Gradually, Ollie proceeded to get more and more agitated. Eventually, he had 'an outburst of frustration and smashed the laptop in half' (Autism Social Worker, interview). This led to Ollie being charged and convicted of common assault and criminal damage. For these offences, he was given a community order and fine. The latter was paid out of the disability benefits he received: Disability Living Allowance and Employment Support Allowance.

Six months later, 'Barney', Ollie's friend who owed him money, asked Ollie to pick up some 'wraps' of cannabis. Barney had told Ollie that if he collected them successfully, Barney would give these cannabis wraps to his other friend, 'Gerard', who in turn owed Barney money. Barney had promised Ollie that this friend, Gerard, in return, would give Ollie petrol to fill up his motorbike. Ollie's motorbike was important to him, so he agreed to do what Barney asked.

Ollie went to this house to collect the cannabis wraps. However, unbeknown to him, this house was being watched by the police drug squad. Ollie was observed by the police officer, who was watching the house, shouting over the fence of that house. Ollie appeared agitated and the police officer asked 'what's in the bag?' Ollie answered 'a book and a drink'. Ollie's bag was searched and inside there was a book which had contained within it a compartment with two wraps of herbal cannabis. He was then asked whether the bag was his. 'Yes, it is mine' he replied. In Court, his solicitor clarified that 'it was not his cannabis but it was his bag'; in other words, his literal response, explained the solicitor, was in relation to the bag itself rather than the drugs.

When the police interviewed the defendant, there was an appropriate adult present but not a solicitor. Ollie explained in court that the officer had offered a solicitor but 'didn't say I **had to** *[have one]' and because the officer 'was so nice', Ollie 'asked him what he thought'. He said "well it's only possession isn't it?" And I had an appropriate adult so' Ollie did not 'think he needed [one]'. Ollie was charged with possession of two wraps of cannabis and one resin, and pleaded guilty. The Magistrate Court gave him a £75 fine and made him pay £40 for costs along with a £20 victim surcharge. They allowed the conditional discharge to continue. The fine was added to his existing fine for the previous assault and criminal damage; these funds were to be subtracted from his benefits.*

Case 3, 'Noah'

Noah lived with his parents. Between the ages of eight to eleven he went to a special school, near his home, for people with moderate learning disabilities. At this school, he was taught by a teacher, 'Mrs Wood', 'who had seemed to bully' Noah (Noah's Father, 'Leo,' Interview). After she married a male teacher at the school, 'Mr Wood', she would bring her husband into her classroom and she would verbally humiliate Noah in front of him (Leo, Interview). These incidents emerged only years later. Noah would 'see [the teachers] when out in town and wanted to know why they did not acknowledge him when he walked past them down the street' (Leo, Interview). Noah wrote to them years later saying that 'that he wanted to be able to say "hello" when he saw them … [but] got no response' (Leo, Interview). Noah 'harboured all of this until, on the day of the incident', when, while his parents were out of the house, Noah watched a moderately violent film (Leo, Interview). He had been 'very stable for days' so his parents 'did not think twice about leaving him and therefore [this day] was not unusual' (Leo, Interview). After watching the video 'he got angry and wound up with adrenalin … and grabbed … a butter knife and went to his teacher's house' (Leo, Interview). When his parents arrived home to find Noah was not there, they 'knew where he [must have] gone' and his father drove to the teachers' home.

When Noah arrived at the teacher's house he had kicked at the door. This was a glass door, the teachers 'would have been able to see who it was' and that Noah was carrying a [butter] knife' (Leo, Interview). Noah saw that the couple 'were not opening the door', and walked over to their cars and 'scratched the door of one of them' (Leo, Interview). At this point, Noah's father, Leo, arrived as Noah was scratching the car. Leo started calling Noah to get into his car. Then the male teacher came out of the house, shouting at Noah. Mr Woods 'lost it' and pushed Noah to the 'floor and punched him up' (Leo, Interview). Mrs Woods, the other teacher, then 'called the police' (Leo, Interview). Leo managed to get Noah to sit in the car and they waited at the scene until the police arrived. As the police were 'responding to an incident' where someone was described as 'wielding a knife … three police cars turned up'

(Leo, Interview). Noah and his father went home with one of the officers and told them that Noah had a learning disability and autism.

At the incident, 'the police said "oh this will never ever go to court: he has got autism"' and they kept on reassuring Noah's parents that this would not happen (Leo, Interview). However, Leo 'was very worried' because he knew that Noah 'had been carrying a knife' and as parents they needed to 'demonstrate that [they] had taken it very seriously' (Leo, Interview). Therefore, his father 'took him to A&E to see if he needed to be admitted to hospital'. Leo thought 'a stay in hospital might demonstrate a) that we had taken it seriously and also because b) psychiatric services might need to do something to put resources into [Noah's case] at this stage' (Leo, Interview). Noah was admitted as a voluntary patient but requested to go home. Therefore, it was decided to section him under section 2 of the Mental Health Act for 28 days. After a week, the doctors and nursing staff wanted to discharge him but the 'police said "No, we don't want him discharged until we have taken his statement"' (Leo, Interview). The police took the statement while he was still on the section 2 Order.

Noah appeared before the Magistrates' Court in 2011 for criminal damage, assault and possession of an offensive weapon, represented by the duty solicitor, Mr Jenkins, who had accompanied him at the police interview. Prior to this Plea and Case Management Hearing, his parents had obtained an expert witness statement from a consultant psychiatrist. 'Mr Grundy', the solicitor who was later instructed to replace the duty solicitor, explained that the 'report made it abundantly clear' that Noah 'was not capable of understanding the proceedings or responding to questions' from lawyers. Further, nor would Noah be able to 'follow the proceedings at all' and 'wasn't capable of giving instructions or making decisions' (Mr Grundy, Solicitor, Interview). However, despite this report, Noah's father recalled that, at the first appearance at the Magistrates' Court, 'nothing happened'. The duty solicitor did not utilise the report to apply for Noah to be deemed not fit to plead' (Mr Grundy, Solicitor, Interview). Instead, as Mr Grundy clarified, the duty solicitor, Mr Jenkins, told Noah's father Leo that he rang the local prosecutor and said:

> *we have got this young man, he is autistic, he has appeared before the court for criminal damage, assault and possession of an offensive weapon, if I then persuade him to admit the offensive weapon and the criminal damages, will you drop the assault [charge]?*

As a consequence of this exchange, Mr Jenkins, the duty solicitor, told Noah and his parents the '"good news"' that this assault charge was dropped. In turn, Mr Jenkins advised if Noah 'pleads guilty to the remainder of the offences because [he] was guilty of those offences, [then] I can get the case dealt with for you today' (Mr Grundy, Solicitor, Interview). As Mr Grundy explicated, Noah and his father agreed because 'most importantly' they thought it would 'get the stress away' from Noah and 'get the case dealt with' that day. Instead, however, 'shock horror, best laid plans and all' this went 'to tatters' because of the guilty pleas for the remaining offensive weapon and criminal damages charges, and failure by the duty solicitor to apply for unfitness to plead. Consequently, Noah was committed for sentence to the Crown Court (Mr Grundy, Solicitor, Interview).

So concerned were Noah's parents with the prospect that Noah might go to prison, they sought a second opinion from Mr Grundy, who took over his case. Mr Grundy then took proceedings to make an application to vacate the plea. He said this was 'done reasonably quickly and the courts were moderately good in getting it listed … for September 2011' (Interview). However, the first appearance at the Crown Court did not take place until the summer of 2012 and the case was not finally listed for trial until July 2013, over two years after the original incident. At these proceedings, the Judge made an order that Noah was unfit to plead. There followed proceedings for a jury to determine whether Noah 'did the act or made the omission charged against him as the offence' (section 4A(2) of the Criminal Procedure (Insanity) Act 1964). The jury were 'agreed that the defendant did the acts alleged' (Court Observation). This left the judge to decide whether to give 'a Hospital Order, a Supervision Order [or] an absolute discharge' (Judge, Court Observation). The defence barrister, Mr Reilly, who explained to the judge that Noah had now been given 'an increase from 35 hours' social service support to 67 hours, from social services, to keep him in as much as possible' (Court Observation). Following this assurance, the judge gave Noah a two-year Supervision Order.

Case 4, 'William'

'William' had previously been convicted of two separate offences of sexual assault. The first offence occurred on a bus where he struck up a conversation with a woman he did not know, and subsequently slid his hand up her leg on top of her clothing without her consent. The second offence occurred at a railway station, where he began a conversation with a woman as he was exiting the station, on an escalator and then touched the woman on her bottom. For the latter offence, William was given a Supervision Order and a Sexual Offences Prevention Order (SOPO) in 2011. The SOPO prohibited William from:

> *[T]ravelling on any form of public transport including train, bus, tram and metro or being present at any location where public transport is accessed or exited, including railway and coach stations, bus, tram, metro or underground stops, unless accompanied by an appropriate adult who was over 18 years old and who had knowledge of his previous convictions (District Judge, Court Observation).*

The third offence occurred in August 2013. William was waiting outside the job centre where he met a young woman, 'Jean', who had gone outside for a cigarette, and was standing outside the entrance doors. They had a short conversation and William stood right next to her. He stared at her breasts and did not look at her face. She was 'wearing a strappy top' and William asked if her breasts were 'natural' (Court Observation). He attempted to start talking about breast implants and asked her where her bras were from. Jean began talking about her boyfriend as William kept asking her 'increasingly personal questions' ('Mr Minelli', Defence Barrister, Interview). William stroked her arm down to her hand and she pulled her hand away; and he continued to stare at her breasts. He spoke about her freckles and asked her age; he said he thought she was 'only 17 or 18'. Jean began to move away, trying to distract him, and walked back into the job centre but felt William's 'hand on her bra strap and then felt his finger around to the side of the breast, he did not squeeze but left his hand lingering there' (Mr Minelli, Defence Barrister, Interview). He continued to stare at her and she became frightened. She told an official in the job centre what had happened and the police were called. William was charged with sexual assault in August 2013.

William lived with his mother, Alice, who was in her seventies. At the bail hearing in September 2013, Alice refused to have him back living with her because it had become 'too much' and she wanted him to 'get proper help' (Alice, Interview). His application for bail was unsuccessful and he was remanded in prison. He pleaded guilty at his Plea and Case Management hearing, in October 2013. His sentencing in the Crown Court was listed for February 2014. His legal team sought a section 37 Order for him but his solicitor had only arranged one medical report by the time of those proceedings. The case was adjourned until the end of April 2014. At sentencing, the judge made a section 37 Hospital Order, under the Mental Health Act 1983, and William was placed immediately in a forensic hospital. This was even though William had already been on remand for eight months up to that point. A SOPO was also put in place for seven years. However, the judge changed the terms of this order to prevent the 'draconian' (Judge, Court Observation) impact of the original terms of the SOPO on William's mother, Alice. As of April 2016, two years after the court ordered it, William remained on the section 37 Order. In the summer of 2016, Alice, William's mother had been told that discharge under section 117 of the Mental Health Act 1983 'may be considered when he has completed another course with his psychologist' (Alice, Interview).

Case 5, 'Robert'

'Robert' lived on his own in a housing association flat, two miles away from his mother, 'Nicola'. He had been housed there since the age of 16 because his prior aggressive and violent behaviour had been viewed, by social services, as a risk to his younger sister, 'Christina'. Robert had one previous conviction for violence against his mother. He also had one previous conviction for growing cannabis in this flat, along with his three other co-accusees, for which he had been given a four-month suspended sentence.

On the afternoon of the third offence, he had been at the pub with his school friend, 'Tyler', and Tyler's girlfriend, 'Lauren'. At 11.25pm, he went around to his mother's house, knocking on her window saying 'Alright mum, they're taking the piss [out of me] and Tyler's girlfriend came over and said she doesn't "like me"' (Nicola, Interview). Robert told Nicola that Tyler said '"you don't understand that people have homes to go to"' at the end of the evening, which upset Robert (Nicola, Interview). So, Nicola let Robert in because he was threatening to break the window, which 'he had done before' (Nicola, Interview). They sat talking in Nicola's living room, and she told him that she had to be honest with him that 'you demand a lot and you cling on [to people]' (Nicola, Interview). Then Robert 'got a bit aggressive' and started saying '"oh Mum, you don't understand"', and she suggested that he 'go up to bed and calm down' (ibid)*. Robert went on to say '"I've got nobody, I've got no friends, you kicked me out when I was 16"'. Nicola 'left it then as [she] did not want an argument'. However, Robert threw a telephone at Nicola, followed by a stool, then he walked over to her and 'kept punching' her and she got up. Then he threw the lamp at her (Nicola, Interview). She managed to call the police but it got 'worse' and Robert 'called her everything under the sun'. Nicola reported that 'he got at me so much with fear' that she wet herself all down her trousers (Interview). Nicola's right breast was 'black and blue and he kept punching [her] at the back of the head' (Interview).*

When Nicola got through to the police on the telephone they 'could hear him being abusive' and arrested Robert when they arrived (Nicola, Interview). Nicola was so frightened that her blood pressure was extremely high and had to be taken to hospital in an ambulance. Nicola made a statement about the incident to the police. However, she later retracted it, two weeks after his arrest, 'because of [Robert's] autism' and as his main carer, she did 'not want him to get locked up' (Nicola, Interview). Robert pleaded not guilty at the Plea and Case Management Hearing but, on the day of the trial, a guilty plea was entered. Rather than activating a breach on the suspended sentence for the second offence, the Magistrates' Court extended Robert's suspended sentence to 18 months and gave him a community order.

Case 6, 'Patrick'

Patrick had been arrested a total of 16 times and, in 2011, was convicted of affray. In April 2013, charges were brought against Patrick for criminal damage to three vehicles and possession of cannabis. He denied these charges. In May 2013, before his 18th birthday, Patrick was also charged with common assault and racially aggravated assault in May 2013. He pleaded guilty to that charge of common assault and not guilty to racially aggravated assault. In June 2013, after he had turned 18 years old, Patrick was also charged with theft of copper piping and cylinders, for which he pleaded guilty. The timing of these offences meant that he had proceedings listed for his property offences in the Magistrates Court in early August 2013 and a trial in the Youth Court for the assault charges in the Youth Court, later that same month.

At the Plea and Case Management proceedings in the Youth Court 2013 for the assault charges, District Judge 'Howdle' thought that it would have been 'wrong' for the court to deal with the matter of the property offences on that same day as it was 'important that the court [had] all the information' (Court Observation). Therefore, she decided to adjourn Youth Court proceedings until his Magistrates Court trial was 'over' (Court Observation). This District Judge also requested that the sentencing for the property offences was listed for the afternoon after Patrick's trial in the Youth Court (Court Observation).

Patrick was found guilty by a District Judge in the Magistrates' Court for all charges relating to property offences and was to be sentenced for them in early August 2013. District Judge 'Holdroyd' 'had concerns with sentencing' Patrick on that day before his trial for the assault charges in the Youth Court had taken place (Court Observation). So those sentencing proceedings, were adjourned until after the trial for the racially aggravated assault, reflecting the request of District Judge Howdle in the Youth Court.

When the trial in the Youth Court was reconvened in mid-August 2013, the facts of the racially aggravated assault were set out as follows. Patrick, then aged 17, attempted to gain entry to a nightclub at a Pride event in his local city centre. A female bouncer denied the defendant entry to the nightclub, raising 'concern[s] about his ID and age' (Prosecution Witness, Court Observation). Patrick was, according to the victim, the male head bouncer, 'subsequently rude and abusive' (CPS Solicitor, Court Observation). The head bouncer intervened, asking Patrick's 'friends to take him away' and 'pointed towards the police officers' at the exit (Victim, Court Observation). However, Patrick struggled as his friends tried to take him out of the venue. The head bouncer put his arms up 'in a welcoming gesture' and 'asked again if they could take him home' and put his arm 'out again … and [Patrick] pushed the bouncer' (ibid)*. The Bouncer then 'felt something on [his] face'; it was spit, and then asked Patrick '"what did you do?"'* (ibid)*. The bouncer alleged that Patrick 'then said: "fuck off nigger" and ran off from the police'* (ibid)*. Patrick admitted in court to 'jumping up and spitting' at the head bouncer 'because he had been pushing' him and Patrick 'had had a little to drink' (Court Observation). Patrick ran off, he said in court, because he 'saw a copper looking straight into [his] face' (Court Observation). Patrick denied saying 'anything after spitting' at the bouncer and 'never said the "N" word … at all' because '[i]t's racist innit? I've got black friends and my sister has got mixed race kids and I've got mixed race friends'* (ibid)*.*

Patrick was found guilty of the racially aggravated assault. After some deliberation and confusion as to why the proceedings were being tried in the Youth Court, District Judge Howdle decided to sentence Patrick for all the charges alleged against him. All matters were dealt with together and the sentencing proceedings that were to take place later that afternoon in the Magistrates Court, were cancelled. For the racially aggravated assault, he was given a 12-week community order with supervision and a 11pm to 6am curfew requirement for this period under section 177(1)(e) of the Criminal Justice Act (CJA) 2003. He was also ordered to pay £150 and a £250 contribution towards prosecution costs. For the remaining offences, she gave him a 12-month community order and ordered him to pay £60.

Case 7, 'Miles'

In 2009, Miles' father discovered pornographic images of children on Miles' computer and encouraged him to report these to the police. At court, Miles pleaded guilty to downloading and being in possession of indecent images of children. He was sentenced to a three-year Community Order with supervision and intervention requirements. Miles was also subject to a Sexual Offences Prevention Order and put on the Sex Offenders' Register for five years.

Miles reoffended between November 2011 and May 2012 by accessing hundreds of indecent images and films of children. He received specific counselling and help to address his sexual offending from an Autism Spectrum Specialist, before going to court for these offences. His solicitor 'Mr Griffiths' advised him not to enter a plea at the Magistrates' court. Miles' solicitor explained this was to allow the defence 'more opportunity to investigate his condition and circumstances surrounding his offending before the matter was finally sentenced in the Crown Court' (Interview). The case was adjourned three times in the Crown Court 'for various reports to be finalised, in conjunction with the probation service, so it was a lengthy process' (ibid*). The case went before the Crown Court for sentencing in April 2013. Miles was given an extension to his Sexual Offences Prevention Order, as well as a Community Order. This had a requirement for him to undergo psychiatric support from a specialist, 'Dr Toale', in the town where he was studying at university.*

Miles then returned to university and a local Offender Manager was assigned to check his internet usage. However, Miles' university accommodation was not his primary domiciliary residence. Consequently, he had to get a referral to Dr Toale, the psychiatrist, from Primary Care in his university town. Which meant arranging an appointment there with a local GP. However, with him living at university, away from parents, Miles 'failed to organise the appointments and wasn't given the support to do so' and did not get the referral to Dr Toale ('Amanda', Miles' Mother, Interview).

During this intervening period, his Offender Manager discovered that Miles had begun to download images again. Miles' 'mental ill-health deteriorated' (ibid*) and he was sectioned under section 3 of the Mental Health Act 1983. In June 2013, against Miles and his parents' wishes, he was moved from the hospital placement in his university town to a mental hospital placement, in a different local authority, where his family lived and classed as his main residence. This occurred as Miles' local authority would not pay for his out of area placement at his university town. Five months later, he was moved to a specialist Asperger hospital placement. In January 2014, the Mental Health Review Tribunal decided to take Miles off the section 3 Order but 'the [Local] Mental Commissioner said there was no place for him' and wanted to 'turf him back into the community' (Amanda, Interview).*

Six months later, Miles was discharged from hospital on a section 117 procedure. At this stage, he was 'guaranteed support' by the Local Community Psychiatric Nurse and Mental Health Trust (ibid*). However, Miles was 'never given psychiatric help and the Mental Health Trust said that it was not their job now' (Amanda, Interview). Although he had been given 'the right kind of probation support', Miles' parents made a complaint to the Trust that he had not had 'adequate psychiatric support' after being discharged and 'made it clear' that if there was no support 'he would reoffend'* (ibid*).*

*In September 2014, Miles did reoffend. A type of 'triage software' – a system used for rapid collection, analysis and reporting of computer files and artifacts – was attached to his computer by his Probation Officer. It discovered that two types of software had been downloaded by Miles: a memory eraser and CCleaner software to erase internet history. Forensic analysis using Iris software – an intelligence request and information system – 'revealed' that Miles had used 'open-source peer-to-peer sharing apps to retrieve data artefacts' (Prosecution Solicitor, Court Observation). Miles had 'viewed six videos with sexually suggestive titles regarding sexual exploitation of children and toddlers' (*ibid*). Miles pleaded guilty to the charges in the indictment and to breaching his SOPO by erasing his web history and downloads. He was sentenced in the Crown Court to a 12-month sentence which, 'with understandable hesitation' by the District Judge (Court Observation), was suspended for two years with 200 hours of unpaid work as an additional requirement. The judge did, however, modify Miles' SOPO, making it indefinite. He also added a further prohibition not to use any device capable of accessing the internet, including, but not limited to a personal computer, laptop, unless internet capability is disabled and unless you make the device available to the police when requested. Under this Order, Miles was prohibited until further notice from:*

1) *using any device capable of accessing the internet unless internet capability has been disabled;*
2) *deleting any internet history;*
3) *possessing any device capable of accessing the internet unless [he] disable[d] that [function on the] device;*
4) *prohibited from any contact with children under the age of 18, whether inadvertent or unavoidable, without the consent of the child's parent or guardian who [themselves] know about [his] offending history (Court Observation).*

Case 8, 'Claire'

*'Claire' became known to the police in 2008 when she started to 'attend' local police stations. 'DC Kim', was a Detective Constable from the Integrated Offender Management Service, who was working with Claire as an Offender Manager. DC Kim described how Claire would turn up and 'just wait around the public areas of the [police] station' until an officer began an interaction with her (Interview). Gradually, this behaviour 'escalated with her entering the "private" areas of the station,' such as the staff car park, and 'causing criminal damage to officers' vehicles' (DC Kim, Interview). Sometimes, when Claire 'attended' the police station, she would produce a Stanley knife, which she would hold in her hand and refuse to let go of (*ibid*). Claire had been given 'short prison sentences' for possession of a bladed article and public disorder offences for these incidents. She had also been detained under the Mental Health Act but Mental Health Services said Claire did 'not suffer from any "treatable mental illness" and was "not in crisis" so they [did]*

not section her' (DC Kim, Interview). However, 'nothing' had 'worked' and she kept 'coming back' and the 'local CPS' said they were 'not interested in prosecuting her' (DC Kim, Interview).

Claire described hearing 'voices in her head telling her to go the police station' and could not 'hear anything else over those voices' and, therefore, was 'compelled to be at the police station' (CPS Solicitor, Court Observation). Following these occurrences, she would not remember being at the police station and said she was not able to 'let [the knife] go' as if 'she had no control' (ibid*). The police were told by an expert psychologist that this was dissociative behaviour: 'trauma symptoms', related to being touched inappropriately, caused by earlier incidents of sexual abuse (DC Kim, Interview). Consequently, when she was anxious, she felt 'safe at the police station'* (ibid*).*

This went on for a further two years before Claire was diagnosed with Asperger's Syndrome in 2010. However, she was later assessed by a consultant psychologist who 'changed her diagnosis to autism' because they assessed her to have an IQ of <70; lower than that of an Asperger's diagnosis because of the low IQ' and at a level which would be considered a learning disability (DC Kim, Interview). Nevertheless, the 'learning disability services just didn't want to know'; she 'failed' various social service 'tests and assessments' of her needs (DC Kim, Interview). Therefore, the 'local social worker found her not to meet their eligibility criteria' for care and support (ibid*). These changes of diagnosis and the failure of local authorities to provide support continued to impact upon Claire.*

By 2013, Claire had been 'arrested 68 times' (CPS Solicitor, Court Observation) prior to being charged with two counts of possession of a bladed article: the incidents which led to the court proceedings observed for the present research. Claire pleaded guilty to both counts of possession at the Magistrates' Court Plea and Case Management hearing. When Claire's case came to court for these offences, the police had recorded that Claire had taken up over '1,000 hours of police time' and sought advice from a consultant forensic psychologist, 'Dr Wilkie'. Dr Wilkie recommended Cognitive Behaviour Therapy along with a supported living package from her local authority. Despite this, the Integrated Offender Management Service 'found it impossible for the local authority and mental health services to give [Claire] support' (DC Kim, Interview). Accordingly, as a result of her high rating on their Independent Offender Management scores, and the 'intense level of resources' needed to support her, DC Kim worked with the CPS to pursue 'prosecution rather than diversion' (Interview). They did so because they were concerned that if the court did 'not require her to attend the psychological sessions' then she would 'not attend' them (ibid*).*

During the period before sentencing, Claire's Offender Manager, DC Kim, contacted their local Police and Crime Commissioner asking for their support and to 'speed up and push counterparts at other agencies' (ibid*) in order to secure funding from social services to work with them. DC Kim had told the Commissioner that it costs £2,500 'every time [Claire] is arrested' (Interview). Thus, at sentencing proceedings, the CPS, as instructed by the police, and Claire's defence solicitor,*

Mr Maxted, obtained a four-week adjournment in order for DC Kim to seek funding for cognitive behaviour therapy and 'residential care through the Police and Crime Commissioner' (Court Observation).

When Claire was sentenced a month later, at the request of both legal teams, the presiding judge sentenced her to a twelve-month Community Order along with a twelve-month Supervision Order. They also put in place a six-month Mental Health Treatment Requirement to engage with the named psychologist to undergo Cognitive Behaviour Therapy, and a six-month residency requirement for her to be domiciled at the supported living placement that would be paid for out of the Police and Crime Commissioner's budget.

2. Pre-trial Shaping: To What Ends are Autistic Defendants Governed?

A. Police

The police, in most cases, as with other disabled defendants, are the first point of contact within the CJS for autistic defendants; with the legal responsibility of identifying mental health needs in custody resting with the custody officer. Thus, police intervention and liaison to engage services provides an early opportunity to avoid future problems (Bradley 2009). However, as discussed in chapters one and two, barriers still arise in preventing early identification of autism for those charged with a criminal offence. Nevertheless, Chapters four and five elucidated policies which are supposed to help overcome such barriers through the Service Specification requirements for L&D Services and under the Autism Act 2009 and accompanying Strategies and Statutory Guidance. Yet, in the case studies explored here, the police and health services' decision-making did not apply the logics of these defendants being vulnerable or disabled adults nor as an autistic adult. Consequently, relevant policies were overlooked; impacting on how their case was progressed by the CPS and the courts.

All the defendants' autism in this cohort had been diagnosed prior to arrest and disclosed to police on arrest, this is unusual. Mr McKinnery, Henry's solicitor, said it was 'rare' for the person's autism 'to be diagnosed or diagnosed correctly' nor identified expediently or appropriately because clients who are 'not behaving "normally"… often [get] diagnosed with ADHD, or learning difficulties …' (Interview). This solicitor explained it was only when you 'are using your experience … as a defence advocate … you appreciate it is more than ADHD' and such identification of autism impacted upon how he built his defence case:

> … it is important that you don't write them off; it is very easy to accept a 'diagnosis' e.g. I am ADHD or [whatever] … particularly the time constraints we have at the moment [and] financial constraints (ibid).

Other defence solicitors raised the need to systematise identification for cases involving 'a vulnerable defendant' where 'there is a specific unequivocal diagnosis' because 'a mark' on the case file 'help everybody' because everyone in court 'knows how to react and approach [such] individuals' (Mr Griffiths, Solicitor, Interview). This solicitor drew an analogy to the early identification of 'domestic violence case[s]' but acknowledged that using an unequivocal diagnosis of autism as the threshold for such a marker, 'in itself might cause a problem because in many cases you can be … [defending] people who haven't had a diagnosis' yet (ibid). Another solicitor raised concerns about police attitudes towards defendants who self-disclosed that they had autism using autism alert cards as a barrier to identification. Whilst such cards have 'been useful, if you can get the officer to look at it' and 'the officers are aware of them' 'it's a question of how the officer reacts' as alert cards are not 'the panacea' (Mr McKinnery, Solicitor, Interview). This solicitor thought an officer may not 'take any notice' when 'the client says, "I have a card that I can show you"' where that officer perceives the person '"not behaving how … [they] would expect [them] to behave"' and takes 'hold' of the autistic person who does not '"like being touched"' and feels "threatened"', escalating the situation (ibid).

Henry's pathway into the CJS began with him being the *victim* of an assault, not the offender. This illustrates the problems which arise from the failure of the police and other agencies to properly respond to autistic individuals and identify a defendant's autism prior to arrest and charge. Henry's literal response to language influenced how his case was processed because when the police asked him what had happened, he replied '"I fell on the wall"', and on asking if he wanted to press charges, Henry responded '"no, I just want to go home"' (Bill, Interview). Although the 'woman who had witnessed the incident from her downstairs window had informed the police' that she '"saw it all, [and would] be witness to it"', the police told her that they were not going to press charges because '"[Henry] doesn't want to"' (ibid). Conversely, when the paramedics spoke to Henry, 'rather than asking him what he wanted to do, [they] told him to get in the ambulance because of his injuries' (ibid). Henry got into the ambulance and was then taken to A&E because he 'was taking instructions rather than being asked' (ibid).

When Henry and his friend were in A&E, both patients and medical staff, who witnessed the incident between the police complainants[3] and Henry 'were given the impression that [he] was behaving in a very violent way towards the police officers' (Mr McKinnery, Solicitor, Research Interview). His solicitor explicated:

> [Henry's] shirt had been covered in blood, so [he] had taken the shirt off … Of course, just the appearance would suggest aggression, a young man stripped to the waist being noisy in a hospital was bound to attract attention … it started off by [Henry] going up to the police officer … saying: 'take me home'. Just a demand, which again would seem aggressive in ordinary circumstances but [his] Dad [Bill] explained to me: 'no, that's

[3] Different officers to those who responded to the assault on Henry.

> what we have told him. If he gets lost, ask a policeman, look for a policeman, tell him you're lost and then ask him, can he take you home'. So everything that [Henry] did could have been explained by Dad … (Mr McKinnery, Solicitor, Interview).

The perception of Henry's behaviour masked what happened: he and his friend 'had been assaulted which is why they had gone to the hospital in the first place' and his autism alert card was stolen along with his wallet in the attack. His solicitor, Mr McKinnery, therefore, believed that Henry was charged 'on the basis that there was an awful lot of evidence against him; they were satisfied that they could prove the case' (Interview). Thus, the failure of the police and the medical staff to properly identify Henry's autism and call Henry's relatives to support him, led to the escalation of the incident at A&E. When the police arrested Henry they bound his ankles and hands and he, allegedly, bit one of the officers (Court Observation). His father then described how they 'threw him head first into the police van and threatened to taser him' (Bill, Interview). After which, Henry was held at the police station for 16-and-a-half hours without inducting 'him properly as a vulnerable adult' (Bill, Interview). The positive association with autism and over-responsivity to touch experienced by autistic people means this was particularly problematic for Henry (see chapter seven below). Had the case gone to trial, Henry's defence team would have drawn on the psychiatric report and called Henry's father to explain 'the sorts of things that cause stress and anger, asking why he might have reacted when he was taken hold of by a stranger' (Bill, Interview).

It never should have reached this point, however. When this incident occurred, the Autism Statutory Guidance (2010c) was already in force and its provisions applied to NHS bodies and NHS Foundation Trusts for all staff working in health and social care. Autism awareness training should have already been carried to enable staff to identify potential signs of autism and understand how to make reasonable adjustments in behaviour, communication services and services for those displaying signs of autism (DOH, 2010c: 13). Therefore, the onus would not have been upon Henry to disclose his autism; the absence of his alert card was no excuse for non-identification. There is no duty to disclose placed upon an individual who has a disability such as autism.

Henry's case also reflects the findings of the Adebowale Report that the 'police on the street lacked understanding of mental health issues, including vulnerability and adults at risk' and failure to 'grasp' the significance of information from family, bystanders and their own observations deciding on 'an appropriate response' (2013: 18). The *Mental Health Crisis Care Concordat* recognised that 'problems' often result at the points where services meet, when people transfer from one service to another, about the 'support that different professionals give one another' (2014: 6). The police response was the antithesis of the *Concordat's* approach that professionals should treat people needed help 'with respect, compassion and dignity' (2014: 18). Henry was not at the A&E because of a mental health crisis; he was there because of injuries suffered by the earlier assault. Nevertheless, the response of the police failed to properly identify that he was a vulnerable adult. There was also a failure to follow guidance on restraint (See NPIA, 2009) and Section 8 of Code C of the PACE Code of Practice on conditions of detention for 'mentally disordered' or 'mentally vulnerable' defendants (Home Office, 2014).

Analogies can be drawn between Henry's treatment by the police and *ZH v Commissioner of Police for the Metropolis* (2013) EWCA Civ 69. In that case, during a school trip, a 19-year-old autistic man with epilepsy became fixated with the glistening surface of the water and jumped back in the water fully clothed after the police officer touched him on the shoulder. The police officers forcibly took him out of the pool, physically restrained him and used handcuffs and leg restraints before removing him from the building via an emergency exit. He was then placed alone in a cage in the rear of a police van, still in handcuffs, leg restraints, and soaking wet. The court found that the police had breached the duty to make reasonable adjustments under the Disability Discrimination Act 1995[4] to normal practice, policy or procedure and that the way ZH was restrained and placed in the police van amounted to inhuman or degrading treatment, in breach of Article 3 of the ECHR. Despite the arguments levied by the police in that case, about the necessity to prevent ZH from drowning, the court held that even if the purpose and intention of such actions were considered, there was a breach of Article 5 ((2013) EWCA Civ).

Similarly, no reasonable adjustments were made by the officers towards Henry and their actions in restraining him amounted to inhuman or degrading treatment. Their failure to recognise his 'mental vulnerability' (*sic* Home Office, 2014) and the preceding assault on him, meant that their interventions created a shift from Henry being a victim to the offender. Studies have shown that the experience of victimisation may precipitate offending (Reid and Sullivan, 2012; Ford et al, 2010; Manasse and Ganem, 2009). There is, however, a lack of robust research on the police's interpretation of an autistic person's behaviour and their impact on the escalation of that behaviour – whether at the scene of the crime or over a longer period of engagement with the individual, nor whether such interpretation influences police categorisation of that individual as a victim or offender. Unlike Henry, Claire's shifting status from victim to offender, in her treatment by the police, took place over a longer period. As Claire's Offender Manager, a Detective Constable from the Integrated Offender Management Service (IOMS), explained Claire had 'trauma issues'. DC Kim's 'personal opinion' was that Claire 'started coming' to the police because when she first went to the police 'about serious sexual offences', committed on her, it was the police who 'tried to trip her up' (Interview). The '[p]olice messed up' and Claire's relationship with the police 'became unhealthy' because her case was 'not dealt with properly' when she asked 'for help' and this 'led to her hating us' (ibid).

[4] This was applied as the facts took place in 2008, before the DDAs of 1995 and 2005 were superseded by the Equality Act 2010.

DC Kim thought that if Claire 'was not suffering from autism' she did not 'think' they would see her at the station. Attitudes of police officers towards Claire and understanding of autism was an issue as 'other officers who just don't know how to treat her' and did not 'believe she's suffering from anything'; while some were 'understanding' there were 'officers who don't believe her and muck her [about]' (Interview). The Offender Manager attributed that to 'a complete lack of knowledge' but thought this 'might have changed now because' she brought Claire to the 'custody block here' (DC Kim, Interview).

DC Kim would 'be in the same boat' if she did not have someone in her family with autism herself. The issue of dividing practices in the processing of Claire's case was manifest in the disagreement within the police teams in determining whether '[s]he should go to the vulnerable adult team' and 'not' be labelled as an 'offender but [a] victim' or dealt with by the IOMS team as an offender. Ultimately, the IOMS team 'kept her because the boss' asked DC Kim to 'sort' Claire's case 'once and for all'; they were 'not equipped' to 'be able to deal with her properly' and would still 'be here in five years' time' (Interview).

When asked whether the police had considered diversion, DC Kim responded that the IOMS team 'would employ simple tactics' because they are 'not trained' and were '[n]othing more than a bunch of cops having a go at it' (Interview). Indeed, rather than using L&D Services 'the only diversionary practice was the buses'; if they 'were lucky' her 'favourite driver would be on the bus' (ibid). DC Kim emphasised that they were 'not experts in autism; we're cops, we're supposed to be out catching thieves' but they had 'to do something' for Claire, especially when the health and social care systems were not supporting her. This is further discussed in chapter eight but a better understanding of her autism and proper social care support, when she first reported her sexual abuse, could have prevented Claire's shift from victim to offender. The police's difficulty in unravelling Claire's victim-offender status at this pre-trial stage, because of her complex needs, clearly directly influenced the schema for acting upon her conduct, from arrival at the police station to the processual and dispositive decisions about her. This, in turn, impacted on the treatment of Claire as a juridical subject whose conduct was to be limited by law and an individual to be disciplined through the disposal of her case, including through increasingly invasive governance of her actions (see chapter eight).

Like Henry, Ollie's literal interpretation of language impacted on the processing of his case; compounded by police failure to ensure Ollie exercised his right to free independent legal advice during police interview, as required by the Police and Criminal Evidence Act 1984 (PACE) (see Home Office, 2014: 12). These issues are revealed in an exchange between Ollie and his defence solicitor after his Magistrates' court proceedings:

Solicitor: Now there are two lessons to be learned today aren't there?

Ollie: Yes.

Solicitor: First never carry anything [illegal] because even if it's not yours, you will still be in possession [of it]. [She demonstrates] If I give you my pen, it's still my pen but it is in **your** possession. The other lesson is: always ask for a solicitor!

Ollie: But the [Police Officer] said I could [have a solicitor] but didn't say I **had to** and, because he was so nice, I asked him what he thought. He said 'well it's only possession isn't it?' And I had an appropriate adult so I didn't think I needed [one].

Solicitor: The police do a different job [to me] and this is why we had three versions of events – I had to be quite careful because otherwise it can look like you were lying. Remember, you should always ask for [a duty solicitor]. We have to turn up within 45 minutes of being called if you are going to have … [a police] interview. Our job is to be there for you; that's different to the police's job (Court Observation; emphasis added)

The right to legal advice applies to all detainees. Indeed, the PACE Code of Practice[5] explicates that 'no police officer' should 'do or say anything with the intention of dissuading any person' from 'obtaining legal advice' (Home Office, 2014: 22; 2019: 27). Further, and pertinently for Ollie's case, PACE makes clear that for 'mentally disordered or otherwise mentally vulnerable' persons, '**an appropriate** adult should consider whether legal advice from a solicitor is required' (Home Office, 2019: 28). Crucially, where such a person, like Ollie, indicates they do not want legal advice, the 'appropriate adult has the right to ask for a solicitor to attend' where this is in the person's 'best interests' (*op cit.*: 21).

In Noah's case, at the scene of the incident, 'the police said "oh this will never ever go to court; he has got autism"' and kept 'reassuring' his father that 'it would not go to court' (Leo, Interview). However, Noah's father, Leo, 'was very worried' and thought 'that psychiatric services might need to do something'. So Leo took Noah to A&E 'to see if he needed to be admitted to hospital' because he 'knew that Noah had been carrying a knife and [he] needed to demonstrate that [they] had taken it very seriously' and Noah was admitted as a voluntary patient (Interview). In the subsequent days, Noah requested to go home but he was sectioned, under section 2 of the Mental Health Act 1983 (MHA 1983); an order for the admission to hospital for assessment for up to 28 days. After being there for a week, the doctors and nursing staff wanted to discharge him 'but the police said: "no, we don't want him discharged until we have taken his statement"' (ibid).

It was understandable, though not required, that Leo felt a hospital placement was necessary for Noah. However. at the scene of the incident, a police constable could have decided to remove Noah to a place of safety if he had been deemed to be 'suffering' from a 'mental disorder' and in immediate need of care or control' (MHA 1983, s 136). If they had thought it 'necessary to do so in the interests of that person', or 'for the protection' of others, they could have done so for a 72-hour period, for him to be 'examined by a registered medical practitioner' and interviewed by an 'approved mental health professional' to make any 'necessary arrangements for his treatment or care' (ibid). This did not happen. Medical professionals later decided to detain Noah under a section 2 hospital order because he was no longer willing to remain as a voluntary patient, and the police expressly told medical staff that they did not want him to be discharged until they had

[5] Language in Code C, in place at the time of the case studies, and the 2019 revised version are consistent on these points.

taken his statement. For the police to block discharge and encourage detention is problematic, especially as they had previously given assurances that the case would not go to court. Making this assessment order is a clinical decision to be made by two registered medical practitioners. Thus, the police have no power in making recommendations for detention or discharge from this order to facilitate their investigations. Nor is requesting the detention of someone for such purposes part of the criteria of the two grounds for the order to be issued. Namely, that the individual is 'suffering from mental disorder of a nature or degree which warrants the detention' in a hospital for assessment and 'ought' to be detained in the interests of their 'own health or safety' or for 'the protection' of others (MHA, 1983, s 2(a) & (b)). Worryingly, it is unclear that Noah met these criteria for detention for assessment or treatment. Further, his compulsory hospitalisation, under these circumstances, appears to have circumvented the proper process that the police should have followed in deciding to arrest him, and determining whether or not to deny bail under their 1976 Bail Act powers (see also Section 2(C) below).

PACE does not give specific guidance about police interviews undertaken while a suspect is on a section 2 Hospital Order. However, it does give guidance on interviewing detainees where an appropriate health professional is called in accordance with section 136 of the Mental Health Act 1983 to examine or treat a detainee. In these circumstances, the custody officer shall ask the professional's opinion about risks or problems which need to be considered in decision-making on the detainee's continued detention, when to carry out an interview and 'the need for safeguards' (Home Office, 2014: 31; para 9.13). A section 2 order has a higher threshold for and period of detention than the section 136 order. By analogy, as a minimum, the police should have considered this guidance in requesting Noah's continued detention and in deciding the timing of the interview. The police involvement in this decision-making is an example of bad practice carried out for the sole purpose of securing Noah's prosecution, in turn, frustrating the expectations engendered for Noah's parents at the scene of the incident. Utilising a section 2 Order in this way subverts its objectives and re-purposes it to achieve goals of the criminal law.

The issue of the police failing to conceptualise these defendants as 'disabled' and properly apply PACE was also evident in William's case. When William 'showed the Custody Officer [his] autism alert card' at the police station, he was asked 'what it was [and] took one look at [it]' and 'gave it back' but 'didn't look all that interested' (Letter Correspondence[6]). The police officer's actions are contrary to PACE because where an officer 'has any suspicion, or is told in good faith', as they were by William, that a person 'may be mentally disordered or otherwise mentally vulnerable' the person shall be treated as such 'in the absence of clear evidence to dispel that suspicion' (Home Office, 2014: 5). In addition, PACE states any person in custody should be 'released as soon as the need for detention no

[6] William wrote letters to me recording his experiences documenting his arrest through to his time on a section 37 order.

longer applies' but William was detained for 16 hours and the custody officer did not expeditiously inform the appropriate adult nor ask them to come to see him (ibid). Instead, when William was first detained, a male police officer searched him 'from the neck down to [his] waist by rubbing down both shoulders and both [his] arms [and legs]' (Letter Correspondence). William described this as 'very uncomfortable' especially 'the way that [his] groin' and body 'was searched', which 'wasn't a gentle rub down … [but] can only be described as ruthless and painful' (ibid). Given the over-responsivity to touch positively associated with autism, such actions seem to breach PACE's guidance and the requirements to make reasonable adjustments under the Equality Act 2010. The conditions of William's stay in the police station cell were also startling as he 'was only allowed out' of his cell 'once'; he 'wasn't allowed to wash' his hands after going to the toilet which he thought was 'completely unhygienic' (Letter Correspondence). William asked '[o]n many occasions' if he 'could have a wash and a shave but this is something else' he was 'denied' and 'was told that the shower at the police station was broken', all the while he 'was locked up' William 'was extremely hot and there was no ventilation' (ibid). Such treatment falls short of PACE, which explicitly states that the conditions of detention must be 'adequately heated, cleaned and ventilated …' and '[a]ccess to toilet and washing facilities must be provided' (Home Office, 2014: 29).

PACE is explicit that when officers are carrying out their functions under the Equality Act, they must pay due regard to their section 149 Public Sector Equality Duty (ibid: 5). Yet, in the cases of Henry, Claire, Ollie, William and Noah, there is evidence of a proliferation of bad practice by the police in relation to their treatment of autistic defendants. This evinces systemic breaches of both their duties under section 149 of the Equality Act 2010, and PACE for failure to ensure 'powers and procedures' in the Code of Practice are used 'fairly, responsibly, with respect for the people to whom they apply and without unlawful discrimination' (ibid). Worryingly, police conduct shows flagrant disregard of the guidance provided therein towards persons who are 'mentally vulnerable', including autistic defendants, and amounting to discriminatory governance.

B. The CPS and the Decision to Prosecute

Chapter two explored the problems of systematic identification, flagging and differentiating disability on the electronic Case Management System (CMS). Following the Bradley Report, the CPS's own research on the prosecution of offenders with mental health problems or learning disabilities recommended the CPS to work with the police to improve monitoring data on the disability of offenders (Magill and Rivers, 2012). Perhaps surprisingly, this CPS research found 'little need' for further training of prosecutors to assist them in cases involving mentally disordered offenders because they found the decisions taken were in accordance with the evidential and public interest stages (ibid).

We must remember, that the 'availability of sufficient evidence should not automatically result in prosecution' (Sprack, 2012: 80). The Code for Crown Prosecutors sets out public interest factors tending for and against prosecution (CPS, 2013: 4.12; 2018: 4.14). Prosecutors should have regard, when considering culpability, 'whether the suspect is or was at the time of the offence, affected by any significant mental or physical ill health or disability, as in some circumstances this may mean that it is less likely that a prosecution is required' (CPS, 2018: 4.14(b)[7]). Prosecutors will also need to 'consider how serious the offence was, whether the suspect is likely to re-offend and the need to safeguard the public or those providing care to such persons (CPS, 2018: 4.14). Further, CPS Guidance, applicable during at the time the case studies were in court, emphasised 'there should be no presumption either in favour of or against the prosecution of a mentally disordered offender' (CPS, 2012). More recent Guidance reiterates the point that 'the fact that someone has a mental health disorder or condition may be relevant to the offence, but it may not' and prosecutors 'should approach each case on its own facts and merits'; assessing the nature, extent and effect of the condition on an individual and the circumstances of the particular offences (CPS, 2019).

However, there was no mention whatsoever of defendants, suspects, or offenders in the annual CPS Business Plans of the period 2012–20, let alone disabled or autistic defendants or those with mental health problems or learning disabilities. Conversely, making their 'Service to victims and witnesses central to everything [they] do' was CPS' strategic objective in this period (see 2015: 4). Further, the category of vulnerability is only used by reference to their achievement goals to increase the uptake of 'Special Measures in all appropriate hearings involving vulnerable witnesses' (ibid: 7). Central to achieving this goal was ensuring that the way the CPS explain their 'decisions and interact with victims and witnesses takes account of their needs, is more open and direct, and shows empathy' (ibid). Here, the CPS strategic approach represented a 'rebalancing' towards the victim. Since 2020–21 the Business Plans began to include outcomes to ensure 'defendants are treated fairly by the CJS', supported by a policy statement on 'rights of defendants with additional needs' (CPS, 2020: 7; 24). In more recent years, plans have evolved to include an *At-Risk Defendants Strategy*, covering improved procedural guidance on 'personal characteristics' (CPS, 2021). Others have noted how the presumption of the 'zero-sum' relationship between victims' and offenders' rights has a populist edge (Doak, 2008; Tonry, 2010) but it 'does not necessarily follow that the interests of victims and offenders will always conflict' (Doak, 2008: 247). Enhancement of the rights for both parties can be provided 'without loss to either side', especially because 'the categories of 'victim' and 'defendant' are not mutually exclusive but overlap in various respects' (Jacobson et al, 2016: 10).

[7] The 2013 Code was in place when case studies were in court and uses the same language on this point.

Nevertheless, the case studies are illustrative of how the rationality of re-balancing in favour of the vulnerable victim and witness during the last decade contributed to creating an 'oblique amnesia' (see chapter four) about the factors relevant to the interest to prosecute where the defendant had autism.

Henry's experience is a case in point. On the day his case was listed for trial, the CPS Solicitor had already seen the psychiatric report that his defence team had ordered and had approved it, deciding not to get a second expert report. However, the CPS 'were having none of it' (Mr McKinnery, Solicitor, Interview) and they certainly did not appear to consider the above factors tending against prosecution. Thus, the District Judge opened proceedings by asking whether 'the claimants were going to proceed with a view to conviction **or** on a fact-finding basis under Section 37(3)' of the Mental Health Act 1983. Addressing the CPS solicitor, the District Judge said they 'could not, under a reading of S37(3)', proceed with both: 'to try to get a conviction and if there was an acquittal seek a Hospital Order'. It was 'in the public interest that it was one or the other' (ibid). He explained that he did not 'want [them] to confuse fact finding, where they seek to put matters forward to make a Hospital Order' under section 37(3), 'with the public interest test to bring a conviction' Court Observation). The District Judge was emphatic in asking the CPS whether it was 'in the public interest to proceed with the prosecution of assault' on the two police officers 'in the knowledge of [Henry's] autism?' (Court Observation).

Subsequently, the judge instructed the CPS Solicitor to show the claimants, the two police officers, the psychiatrist's report. Whereby, the CPS Solicitor responded: 'I have shown one claimant the report but he wanted to proceed. The other claimant has not seen it and I will have to show it to his [the police officers'] superior' (Court Observation). The District Judge referenced *R (on the application of Singh) v Stratford Magistrates' Court*, which explains that section 37(3), taken with section 11 of the Powers of Criminal Courts (Sentencing) Act 2000, **only** applies to a defendant who is mentally ill when he appears before the court ([2007] EWHC 1582 (Admin), para 23). In view of these provisions, the District Judge was unequivocal that if they proceeded with fact finding there was 'no way that the court would make a Hospital Order' because he agreed with 'with the consultant psychiatrist' that Henry 'does not need to be in hospital' (Court Observation). He informed the CPS Solicitor that if it was 'the guidance' to choose to continue with the 'prosecution' it would 'be an abuse of process to carry on with the trial' because the 'consultant psychiatrist has said that he is not fit to stand trial' (Court Observation).

The court adjourned whilst the CPS solicitor spoke to the police officers' superior. When he returned, he informed the District Judge that the CPS had been instructed to offer a bind over. Henry's solicitor refused to accept this and the case was adjourned again. When Court reconvened, the prosecution said that they 'had no evidence to proceed with the case' (ibid). The District Judge said that this 'was the right decision' (Court Observation). Whilst there 'was no criticism in bringing a case of public disorder', the CPS 'should have taken the decision not to proceed' in light of the psychiatric report 'it was not in the public interest' and 'the Police should take on board' the court's decision (Court Observation). CPS handling of Henry's case, implies that there may be a culture of attaining successful prosecutions over achieving equitable outcomes in cases like Henry's, which meet factors tending against prosecution in the Code of Practice, and where the impact on the offender is such that it is 'far greater than is warranted by the offence' (Ashworth and Redmayne, 2014: 206).

In Claire's case, her Offender Manager, had been told by the psychologist that they had been instructed to assess Claire because she 'needed treatment' (DC Kim, Interview). DC Kim recalled while the 'Crown is not interested in prosecuting' her, they sought prosecution 'rather than diversion' to 'make the most of this situation to get help for her from services' having 'taken it upon ourselves to sort it out' (ibid). The IOM Team, therefore, had worked with the CPS because they were 'concerned that if the court [did] not **require** her to attend the psychological sessions' she would not 'attend' them (ibid). Claire's Offender Manager stressed that she did not want her to go to prison because of her 'vulnerability' but that they 'have to use "bad" [i.e. sentencing] to do some "good", [i.e.] to secure psychological support"' (DC Kim).

This is concerning when coupled with an apparent determination to continue prosecutions against autistic defendants, where it may not be in the public interest, or where prosecutions are pursued as the only means to obtain support from public services. Thus, despite the CPS Guidance for mentally disordered offenders, the focus on 're-balancing' towards victims in the CPS Business plans over the course of a decade indicates a culture which obfuscated the rights of disabled defendants. Hence, the CPS must divide the public interest test into two and consider particular 'harms of prosecution' to mental health and other consequential losses separately (see Rogers, 2006: 775). More also needs to be done to educate Crown Prosecutors, the police and defence solicitors on community care law and adult social care support to disavow them of the assumption that these services can only be achieved through criminal court-ordered requirements.

Conclusion

Court observation was piqued with poignancy where it became apparent that autistic adult defendants, and their families, did not have access to adequate legal or professional advice about the available options and protections at each stage of the criminal justice process. Failure by the police to ensure Ollie had an on-duty solicitor for his interview and in the arrest and prosecution of Henry, were two such examples. Moreover, as with Claire's case, many decision-makers lacked awareness of available alternatives too. Despite the entrenchment of the social model of disability in the Equality Act 2010 and the UNCRPD, the case studies demonstrate the predominance of the medical model of disability in the pre-trial stages of the court process. Thus, the defendants in this cohort were governed according to logics of this model; situating 'problematic aspects of disability firmly within the individual' and perpetuating 'the illusion that the state or society has no role in this' (Clough, 2014: 2). Even more worryingly, are examples of the police's policies, on vulnerable defendants, and CPS' guidance on the public interest test being overlooked. Defendants in these case studies, therefore, were even unable to receive the procedural protections from being categorised as vulnerable. Further compounding the 'oblique amnesia' (see chapter four) of the police and CPS in adequately identifying and responding to the defendant's disability, autism, under the requirements of the Equality Act 2010.

Chapter three cited the value of the work of the late criminologist Professor Barbara Hudson, who looked at the nature of justice in modern democratic societies, societies which are 'divided by gender, race, ethnicity, socio-economic status, lifestyle, religion and so on' (2008: 276). Because 'citizens of modernity' do not live in homogeneous societies, she argued, our CJS must respond to *difference* and *diversity*. Hudson differentiated these terms. 'Difference' has negative connotations, implying 'not only dichotomy, but also hierarchy' (2007: 158–9). While 'diversity' has neutral or positive connotations, suggesting 'a range of options from which to choose, a spectrum of lifestyles and attributes to enjoy and appreciate' (ibid). She argued, therefore, that it is imperative for criminology 'to expose and critique the politics and policies of criminalisation and crime control which are grounded on an ideology of difference, rather than on an acknowledgement of diversity' (ibid). As a modern democracy, we must work to achieve justice in ways which reflect the heterogeneity of our humanity and move disability away from a 'diagnostic attribute' to a 'central location in the conceptualisation of the individual who presents to the CJS' (see above, Baldry et al, 2008: 42). The following chapter moves from this pre-trial shaping to examine governance through the court process.

7

To What Ends are they Governed? Negotiating the Courtroom, Remand and Plea

Introduction

> I don't see being in court as any different as being in this room [interview room in Courthouse]. Well, except when I walk into the courtroom it all comes together in one place and at one time ('Miles', autistic adult defendant).

This quote reflects the imperative that motivated the court case observations of the Magistrates' and Crown Courts: the language and argumentation used by legal counsel, the judge or magistrate, the defendant(s) and witnesses reveal much about the 'wider structures' of 'states, economies and legal orders, and the like' (Burawoy et al, 1991: 282). Miles' perception that 'it all comes together' in the courtroom, conveys their role as sites which make the intersection of multiple issues and criminal justice pathways (of both the defendant(s) and victim(s)) visible and observable. Courtrooms are spaces where justice is administered and where the symbolic nature of their 'transparency and ease of access resonates deeply with many groups who have been marginalised in society, including people with disabilities' (Flynn, 2015: 83). The way the justice system responds to disabled people, therefore, is represented in both a substantive and symbolic way by the existence of barriers in the physical space of the courtroom. These physical barriers amount to technologies of governance; representing material means that impact upon modes of controlling, containing, and regulating autistic defendants as juridical subjects. Section 1(A) of the present chapter situates the case studies in the courtroom and discusses barriers for defendants, in both physical and virtual courtrooms. Section 1(B) explores issues in negotiating information and communication in their access to, and participation in, their criminal court process. Section 2 examines the 'temporising decision' of remand and to what ends autistic defendants are governed through expert witness evidence. Section 3 considers the dominant skew towards guilty pleas.

In this chapter, court observations record the defendants' governance along the CJS pathway as erratic and nonlinear. Long interruptions in getting cases listed in court, adjournments, remand in custody, and deferred decision-making awaiting expert witness statements all led to delays in processing the defendants' cases. Accordingly, it is argued that defendants and their families were left in a liminal state of incomplete or delayed decisions about their future. In turn causing anxiety and frustration which exacerbated the collateral impact and 'symbiotic harm' of the criminal justice process on the defendants and their families which is discussed in chapter nine.

1. The Context: The Courts and Access to Justice

A. Difficulties Negotiating the Courtroom

i. Courtroom Design and its Physical Barriers

Pat Carlen observed Metropolitan magistrates' courts for two years. She argued that the social relations between Magistrates, the police and court personnel, along with the physical layout of the courtroom, behaviour of the bench and arduous waiting times, combine to produce 'staged' Magistrates' justice. Accordingly, this 'atrophies the defendants' participation in proceedings', rendering as 'absurd' the 'judicial rhetoric of an adversary justice' (1976a; b). Carlen's visceral account predated most studies on measures for vulnerable witnesses and defendants by 20 years (see chapters one and four). Yet it continues to resonate; a particular allocation of people in space is fundamental to any exercise of power (Foucault, 1984), thus compelling us to attend to the impact on autistic defendants of the material reality of the courtroom, the technologies of governance within this space and the social interaction between its actors. This begs the question of the extent justice can be done in these circumstances. Feminist scholars explicate the symbolism of the physical space of the courtroom and how 'architectural design' can 'influence' the 'interpretation, application and upholding of the law in court' (Flynn, 2015: 88). Architecture such as the high gothic Victorian Law Courts in Birmingham is deliberately imposing, imbued with symbols of the state that encourage participants 'to reflect on the gravity of law and legal proceedings' (Mulcahy, 2007: 387). Not to say 'that surveillance and discipline in the courtroom are inappropriate *per se*' but we must acknowledge it is not the depoliticised space it is sometimes assumed to be (*op cit.*). Instead, we must appreciate 'how spatial dynamics can influence what evidence is forthcoming, the basis on which judgments are made and the confidence that the public have in the process of adjudication' (ibid: 384). Indeed, Mulcahy argues that 'the shape of a courtroom, the configuration of walls and barriers', the height of partitions, positioning of tables, and 'even the choice of materials' are 'crucial' to a more 'nuanced understanding of judgecraft' (2007: 385).

Flynn augments this work by considering how courtroom design impacts upon disabled people's access to and participation in justice by sending implicit and, sometimes, explicit signals of whether disabled people are fully welcomed or excluded (2015: 88). The types of barriers which disproportionately affect disabled people's access to justice and participation in court are, broadly, 'the physical accessibility to court buildings and infrastructure, access to court procedures and evidentiary barriers' (ibid: 83). Court observation of the eight case studies for the present research took place in both modern and 'historic' courts of the HMCTS estate. Physical accessibility is particularly apposite for autistic defendants, in relation to their possible 'over-responsivity' to the courtroom; potentially impacting upon their participation in proceedings. 'Over-responsivity' refers to hyper and hypo-sensitivities across *all* sensory domains to a high degree which amount to exaggerated responses to one or more types of sensory stimuli (Schoen et al, 2008). As such 'daily life experiences' like clothing labels (tactile domain) or clocks ticking (the auditory domain) are 'uncomfortable or distressing' for autistic individuals (Tavassoli et al, 2014: 429). The discomfort and distress of over-responsivity can compromise an autistic person's quality of life and is linked to high rates of depression and anxiety (Kinnealey et al, 2011; Kinnealey and Fuiek, 1999).

There is limited research on the impact of over-responsivity to the courtroom space on autistic defendants' or witnesses' participation in their case, one study found a lack of support and adaptation in court for sensory issues (Maras et al, 2017). Difficulties navigating this space emerged as a sub-theme in fieldwork observations. In one of the historic courts, where two of the cases were sentenced (those of Robert and Patrick), a wooden trellis encased the dock. This obscured visibility for the defendant of the Magistrates' Bench, the positions of the defence and prosecution solicitors in the court and those in the public gallery. The trellis also obscured visibility for the family members in the public gallery. Shadows were cast across the austere Victorian courtrooms; further reducing visibility for those with visual hypo-sensitivity. In the modern Crown and Magistrates' Courts – which were used in the cases of Claire, Ollie, Henry, Miles, Noah and William – the multiple bright lights would likely bleach out the faces and detail for those with visual hyper-sensitivity. The public gallery, in the Crown Courts where Miles' and Noah's cases were heard, was high above the court with a glass window separating the gallery and the main courtroom. This meant that the defendants' family and supporters were not visible to the defendants.

In the high-ceilinged Victorian courtroom, the acoustics were poor and there was no microphone or electronic sound system. As the Magistrates' and solicitors' pronouncements did not project well into the space, parents commented that it was difficult to follow what was going on. Observation field notes record Robert becoming restless in the dock and his mother, Nicola, commenting that her son 'was not listening' (see below) to the proceedings. In the busy modern courtroom, clocks tick, fluorescent lights burr, barristers shuffle their briefs, the keyboard of the Crown Court note-taker clacks, members of the public whisper and doors slam as ushers and witnesses move in and out of the courtroom; stimuli which might cause over-responsivity for autistic defendants with hyper-aurality, potentially compounded by hyper-tactility from wearing a suit or tie for the first time or other unfamiliar clothes lent to the defendant by prison or hospital stores. Expressing his anxiety about wearing borrowed clothes while remanded in custody, William remarked that from December 2013 he was 'no-longer' able to have his 'own clothes sent in on visits'; he could 'only wear prison clothes', which had 'holes in them' and were 'not suitable for wearing' (Letter Correspondence).

Amplified over-responsivity to stimuli in the court environment risks diminishing defendants' comprehension of proceedings. Research field notes of Claire, Robert and William's cases record how these defendants and their families struggled to follow proceedings and establish what had been decided by the court. William's barrister, 'Mr Minelli', described his 'dislike' of courtrooms where 'the defendant is walled off by glass because it does create a barrier' and the 'defendant is always, inevitably, behind you' so, 'unless someone attracts your attention' … you don't have the opportunity to observe the defendant all the time' (Research Interview). Thus:

> When you represent anyone, you need eyes not just in the back of your head, but all [a]round … [you]. Your main focus is inevitably the judge, or if it's a trial, the judge and the jury. You're also trying to make sure the prosecution … don't surprise you with anything that hasn't previously been disclosed … (ibid).

Coupled with other sensory barriers, the physical barriers, therefore, potentially disconnect autistic defendants from their legal representative impacting upon 'questions of understanding', which undermine comprehension of court proceedings for defendants more generally (see Jacobson et al, 2016). The *Revised Statutory Guidance* acknowledges the sensory differences that can affect autistic people as well as the impact of over-responsivity on communication, socialising and independent living for autistic people (DOH, 2015: 42). It also states that all public sector organisations, under the Equality Act 2010, including service providers such as HMCTS, are 'required to make reasonable adjustments' to ensure they are 'accessible to disabled people, including people with autism' (DOH, 2015: 42). Yet, in the cases observed in both the modern and 'historic' courts, reasonable adjustments for the over-responsivity of autistic defendants had not been considered at all.

ii. Video, Virtual and Remote Courts

On the surface, utilising virtual or remote courts or video links for evidence may appear to overcome this inaccessibility of the physical courtroom. However, this shift, expedited by the COVID-19 pandemic, may not be entirely beneficial for disabled defendants. Proceedings were conducted via video link from the prison for one Crown Court session in William's case and one of Robert's later bail hearings while they were remanded in custody. This created tension and signalled, inappropriately, to the defendant that the outcome of their bail and Plea and Case Management Hearings were a forgone conclusion: they would remain in custody on remand until sentence and this would likely involve incarceration. William had to instruct Mr Minelli from a video link room prior to the hearing and described this 'remote' court experience:

> … as you walk into the room itself … to the right … was a curtain and to the left … was a large television with a camera on top … I sat facing the television. The Officer that took me over to video link sat with me while my court case took place. I wasn't told why this was … the Clerk introduced me to who everybody was by using the web-cam (Letter Correspondence).

The camera was directed at counsel, and so he could not see his mother sitting in the public gallery. It is standard practice around the world for bail applications and remand renewal applications to be performed remotely to save costs (Diamond et al, 2010) and they may be specifically requested by defendants as a Special Measure (Plotnikoff and Wilson, 2004). However, researching its use in Australia, McKay found that such video links framed 'the prisoner in the context of their detention, intruding on legal process, and affecting prisoners' comprehension and participation' (2016: 21).

Neither William nor Robert had an intermediary or appropriate adult present. Thus, attending via video link further atrophied their ability to participate with Robert's mother commenting during proceedings: 'look at him, he's not listening. I know he doesn't know what's going on' (Court Observation). In William's case, he recounted that:

> After being introduced to everybody the Clerk of the Court then read out my offence and asked me how I … [wished] … to plead … I told the Clerk … I wished to plead guilty … the judge apologised that I had to remain in custody so that the Probation Service and this Doctor … [could] see me [and] … said that when … [they do he] … wanted me to co-operate with both … I told the Judge that I would. My court hearing lasted at the very most ten minutes, I have to say … [it] was a lot shorter than I thought [it would be (Letter Correspondence).

Many commentators have argued that the trial (and all pre-trial stages) should be viewed as a 'communicative process, whereby the State tries to let the convicted defendant know, in terms which he can understand, why he is to be subjected to censure of the criminal sanction' (Ashworth and Redmayne, 2014: 25–6; Duff et al, 2007; Redmayne, 2009). In doing so, however, 'the state must also establish the legitimacy of its own claim to hold the defendant to account' (Ashworth and Redmayne, 2014: 25–6). This must be done by observing 'norms that require the defendant to be treated as a citizen of a liberal polity' (Duff et al, 2007: 288). While for some disabled defendants video link may form a reasonable adjustment which minimises anxiety and facilitates comprehension, where live transcription is available, the use of a video link for such important stages in the pre-trial process risks disconnecting the defendant from the communicative *space* of the courtroom. This in turn can undermine their ability to relate to the expressive effect of the communicative *process*. For autistic defendants, this experience is likely to be exacerbated by specific aspects of their impairment. Research on theory of mind demonstrates how difficult it can be for autistic people to transfer experience and knowledge from one context to another and to predict the behaviour of others and determine the most appropriate behaviour in response (Baron-Cohen, 1997). Although more research is needed, remote court appearances via video link may create additional barriers to the autistic defendant being able to relate the alleged wrongdoing of their criminal actions to the administration of justice in the processing of their case. Importantly, this is also likely to reduce the expressive effect of the sanctioning of the wrongful conduct. Such physical barriers lead disabled defendants to be excluded from the participative aspects of the pre-trial stages of the criminal process; with the state failing to treat such defendants as 'citizens of a liberal polity' (Duff et al, 2007: 288) and reducing the state's legitimacy in their claim to hold the defendant to account.

Such issues are pertinent now, more than ever. The Coronavirus Act 2020 was passed after these cases were heard in court and accelerated the use of live audio or video links in place of in-person hearings (HMCTS, 2020). A range of different technological products were adopted to enable remote hearings during the COVID-19 pandemic with a shift from video conferencing or audio-visual link (AVL), or 'video enabled' hearings, to virtual hearings. Although the shift facilitated dealing with some of the backlog of cases during the pandemic, commentators raised key concerns about open justice during virtual hearings – centred on 'sotto voice' conversations between the judge and counsel – procedural fairness, impartiality, and diminution of 'the ritualist aspects of courts' (Rossner et al, 2021). The latter was inhibited by the design and layout arrangements on screen in 'displaying' the judge and other parties, as well as the 'journey into the courtroom' (see Rossner et al, 2021). Systematic research is needed to understand trends in the assistive technology used for remote hearings, across the range of technological products during this time and the availability of Special Measures and reasonable adjustments for those defendants who need them; for example, whether virtual courts are utilising increased text-size for chat messaging, Otter.Ai transcription software to support those with SPLD and hearing impairment or whether BSL interpreters pinned on screen were used for deaf defendants.

It has been recognised by judges as well as numerous legal practitioners that the technology behind remote video links often fails or internet connection is lost (Transform Justice, 2017; Mulcahy, 2021). Courtroom dynamics are disrupted by online hearings; increasing barriers to disclosing disability (Transform Justice, 2017), making it harder for defence lawyers to carry out their 'tacit functions' in supporting their clients to navigate the 'daunting court experience and comply with courtroom customs' (Long, 2021: 77), and to achieve personal and accessible interaction with the judge (Hilborne, 2020). This amounts to a greater need for research into digital exclusion, social-capital and embodiment on screen and the impact of any physical separation from legal counsel (Long, 2021) and intermediaries or appropriate adults.

Mulcahy makes a strong case that 'critics of the use of technology are in danger of romanticising physical courthouses as places which are better at dignifying lay users of the justice system or encouraging their participation' (2021: 43). From a disability perspective, it is important we identify and remove barriers to participation and access to justice in both the physical and virtual courtrooms, as well as hybrid models. We need clearer understanding of the groups who could be most affected by any future developments, shared concepts and understanding. Strengthening the position of the UNCRPD in UK Law and ensuring law and policy around digital justice and digital courts is reformed to reflect this would be a significant first step. Better integration of Web Content Accessibility Guidelines (Web Accessibility Initiative, 2018) into the regulation of digital justice would also help drive improvements in technology used for remote justice and virtual courts. Additionally, Rossner et al have highlighted the need to support defendants, victims and witnesses to feel 'present' and 'journey' into the virtual courtroom, along with 'virtual family visits' pre-court and formalising the virtual space with layout, framing and symbols of state (2021).

B. Barriers to Negotiating Information and Communication

The inaccessibility of the courtroom space is exacerbated by barriers to understanding information and materials used in court. Navigating the CJS can be a significant challenge 'for any offender who may have difficulties with reading and/or writing' (Parsons and Sherwood, 2015: 5). Compared to '14.9% of the general population, 50% of prisoners' have literacy below the L1 skill level – considered the appropriate level for 'succeeding in most types of employment' (Crease, 2015: 5). No equivalent data exists for defendants in court but similar literacy patterns could be expected. Indeed, in Patrick's trial for racially aggravated assault in the youth court, he was unable to read the oath and so repeated it after the usher. Several charities (Betts, 2011) have worked closely with criminal justice professionals to produce Easy Read versions of documentation, including the police 'Notice of Rights and Entitlements' document (PCC Bedfordshire et al, 2016). However, no such materials were used for defendants in the case study cohort. More should be done to disseminate accessible materials and train staff to use them with defendants.

Special Measures and intermediaries were not used in any of the cases observed; amounting to significant barriers to negotiating information and communication for the cohort of case studies. Six of the eight autistic defendants ultimately entered a guilty plea (see below). One solicitor perceived intermediaries as irrelevant where the defendant was 'always going to plead guilty to the charge' but thought it would have been 'interesting' to look at their 'role' if the defendant 'had denied the case there' (Mr Griffiths, Solicitor, Interview). This solicitor made a distinction for the type of autism diagnosis. He was 'not sure' that intermediaries 'would have been necessary' for his defendant because 'he does have Asperger's, he is very bright …' (ibid). There was also a differentiation made between Crown Courts, where 'people appreciate [such conditions] more', and Magistrates courts in determining the need for intermediaries and Special Measures (ibid). Other solicitors, representing clients in the cohort, demonstrated a surprising lack of knowledge about the role and purpose of intermediaries; asking what was meant by 'intermediaries' and how they would 'get one appointed by the court'? When the role was explained, they responded that whilst they 'certainly involved outside experts [they hadn't] used an intermediary' (Mr Arkwright, Solicitor, Interview). Indeed, other solicitors admitted that, before acting for the client in the cohort they 'didn't know … the first thing about autism' until a solicitor colleague 'brought [them] up to speed with it' (Mr McKinnery, Solicitor, Interview).

This is surprising given how long a number of autism-specific materials have been available on the *Advocate's Gateway*, in practice directions and online training for solicitors (see ATC, 2013). Such a paucity of awareness indicates that further training is required on access to these resources. However, there was evidence of solicitors operationalising professional empathy in their practice to rectify their lack of knowledge about the defendant's condition. For example, by visiting the defendant's parents' home so that they could 'fill [them] in on the sort of different things autistic people face … and how they get into trouble like this' (Mr McKinnery, Solicitor, Interview). Rather than using Special Measures, solicitors asked for other 'more simplistic things to be done' such as Noah's father being allowed to sit 'with his father' and not 'in the dock' (Mr Grundy). Both of these things were acceded to' by the judge (Mr Grundy, Solicitor, Interview). It is interesting that instead of describing these solutions as reasonable adjustments and relating them to their defendant's legal status accorded by the Equality Act 2010, solicitors described such measures as common-sense problem-solving techniques. These empathetic strategies also involved the solicitor going in to court and explaining to the clerk 'any specific behaviour' or 'difficulties and why they may occur, for instance, the inability to look at the clerk, or look at the court' (Mr Arkwright, Solicitor). Talking about why sitting outside the dock was an important adjustment for Noah, his Solicitor said:

> … this lad clearly found the court process difficult … to deal with and he was very anxious during the court case and after. His dad would tell me that after each court case, they had a terrible few days, so clearly all of these appearances had an impact on him (Mr Grundy Interview).

Henry was also allowed to sit next to his parents, behind his legal representative, rather than standing in the dock and his solicitor 'had seen the District Judge beforehand' and 'explained' Henry's autism (Mr McKinnery, Solicitor, Interview).

Although Claire was allowed to sit near her Offender Manager in the public gallery for her Plea and Case Management Hearing, the Usher had not arranged this at her sentencing proceedings. Instead, they followed procedure and placed Claire in the dock at this court appearance; doing so left her 'in shock' and Claire was unable to concentrate on what was said to her as she did not 'like going in there' because she 'struggle[s] with [her] hearing … [and] freaked' (Interview). Claire 'couldn't make eye contact with [her] solicitor or anyone that [she] knew in the court' and she 'didn't know what was going on' which meant that she thought she 'was going to jail … [and] was very scared' (ibid). Thus, despite the judge explaining her sentence to her, Claire perceived the symbolism of being placed in the glass-panelled, segregated dock as signifying that she would be given a prison sentence and not the community order her Offender Manager and solicitor had indicated. This meant that she was confused about the outcome of her case and burst into tears as we left the courtroom. Conversely, Claire described being allowed to sit in the main courtroom as being 'alright' because '… you can hear a lot better than when you are in the box; [where she] … sometimes just agree[d]' with what people said to her (ibid). This had implications for her participation in the case against her. Claire said that 'to put your case properly' it would be better for autistic people if there were not 'too many people in there' as she found that 'easier to cope with … when the court was not full … because she didn't like to hear their arguments' (Interview).

Solicitors also highlighted the impact of delays in court listings on the anxiety of their clients. In Miles' case, his solicitor 'stressed to the usher and … the court clerk that this was a young man who would become increasingly frustrated, increasingly anxious the longer he had to wait' (Mr Griffiths, Solicitor Interview). While 'there was a degree of sympathy for the situation … it became secondary to the normal court business' (ibid). Other solicitors also commented on the significance of their seniority and the type of court on the expediency of court administration: 'they will tend to listen to me … [rather] than [a] younger advocate' (Mr Jason, Solicitor, Interview). However, there was a frustration amongst other defence solicitors that other actors in court 'didn't believe [the defendant] had a diagnosis of Asperger's syndrome' (Mr Grundy, Solicitor). As this solicitor recounted that there 'was a reluctance to accept' the defendant's autism 'like he was trying it on' and 'they didn't really try to put his case on any earlier, or deal with him any differently than any other defendant' (ibid). Such incredulity about the defendants' autism and differential treatment based on the seniority of the advocate is contrary to the *Equal Treatment Bench Book* editions applicable at the time and currently (Judicial College, 2013: 14; 2022). Indeed, judges 'should be able to identify situations in which a person may be at a disadvantage owing to some personal attribute' and 'take steps to remedy the disadvantage' quickly, where possible, obtaining information 'in advance of a hearing about any disability or medical or other circumstance affecting a person so that individual needs can be accommodated' (Judicial College, 2014: 14; 2022: 7). In reality, court observations indicated there was an endemic problem of early and effective identification of the defendant's autism and a failure of the court in exercising their duty to provide reasonable adjustments to disabled people under section 20 of the Equality Act 2010.

However, obstructive attitudes towards the solicitors' requests in court were not universal. Another solicitor commented that if the defendant is 'feeling a little uncomfortable and wants someone with him' then it 'wasn't a problem' because the District Judge was 'perfectly happy to allow that' in order to 'try and achieve fairness for the defendant' (Mr McKinnery, Solicitor Interview). However, what did emerge was the 'distinct difference between the Magistrates' Court' in dealing with autistic people and 'the Crown Court' (Mr Griffiths, Solicitor Interview). As the solicitor in Miles' case explained:

> The magistrates' court is very much 'let's get on and deal with this case as quickly as possible', allowing no real opportunity to get further details such as a psychiatrist's assessment, yet in the Crown Court there is a far greater willingness to appreciate the background to offending (ibid).

Mr Griffiths went on to explain the impact that this has on the processing of the case and the engagement of his client in the process:

> The Crown Courts proceed pretty well, they are far more formal; there is less business in each court. It's just a calmer environment … [so] it was easier for [Miles] to concentrate on the matter in hand. [In contrast] … the Magistrates' court has lots of papers listed, solicitors going to and fro, in and out of court (Mr Griffiths, Solicitor, Interview).

These interviews and court observations reveal that much more needs to be done to entrench the 'concept of barrier-free spaces for the administration of justice' (Flynn, 2015). Especially given the 'paternalistic history and legacy of the medical model of disability which has dominated the legal system' (ibid) amongst those who administer justice – ushers, court clerks, magistrates, judges, the CPS and defence solicitors. Also, to ensure inclusive and accessible infrastructure and design of the courtroom where justice is administered. This should be done not only because of its important symbolism and state legitimacy but because of its substantive impact on access to justice for autistic defendants.

2. Who Governs What? Remand and Adjournment for Expert Witness Evidence

A. Remand

The decision about whether to remand a defendant on bail or in custody arises at five different stages of the court process (see Redmayne and Ashworth, 2010: 228–9). The power of the arresting officer to release an arrestee on bail, 'street bail', to report to a police station, at a specified time, is the first of such stages. The second is the bail decision by the police at the police station while the defendant awaits their first appearance in court. Whether to remand the defendant between the first and last appearance in court is the third stage – a decision determined by the court, rather than the police. At the fourth stage, remand is considered post-conviction and prior to sentence while, for example, expert witness evidence reports are prepared. Finally, the question of remand is determined whilst awaiting an appeal against the verdict or sentence (ibid). According to MOJ figures, 1.53 million defendants were directed by the police to appear at Magistrates' courts in the 14 months[1] ending June 2015 and 11 per cent were remanded in custody by the police (2015: 13). In 2015, 48,330 defendants were remanded in custody to await trial, spending an average of nine weeks there, with 15 per cent of those people subsequently receiving a non-custodial sentence (MOJ, 2015). By the year ending September 2022, the proportion remanded in custody by the Magistrates' Court was 4 per cent at Crown Court, the percentage increased on previous years to 40 per cent (34,200 defendants) and the proportion remanded in custody by police to 9 per cent (MOJ, 2023). However, these figures do not accurately portray the differential rates of remands in custody across different courts. Studies argue that this is influenced by court culture; differential recommendations are made by the CPS and defence lawyers in different courts, with the latter sometimes 'placing their credibility and status with the court above the interests of their clients' (Hucklesby, 1997: 276) rather than being 'full and fearless' in their defence (Ashworth and Redmayne, 2014: 255).

With regards to the cases in the present cohort, William and Robert were remanded in custody. Ollie's case was concluded in the Magistrates' court and he was not remanded. Patrick and Miles were given conditional bail, and Patrick was also electronically tagged. Noah and Claire were given unconditional bail. This section will focus specifically on decision-making by the courts about remand at the third and fourth stages of the court process in William's case. Applicable to each of the decision-making stages where remand can be ordered, Article 5(1) of the European Convention on Human Rights (ECHR) sets out the general presumption of liberty and the circumstances in which it can be deprived in accordance with the law (see Article 5(1)(a)–(f)). Article 5(1)(c) deems it lawful to arrest a person for the purpose of bringing them before 'the competent legal authority on reasonable suspicion of having committed an offence or when it is reasonably considered necessary to prevent his committing an offence or fleeing after having done so'. Article 5(1)(a) provides that the general right can also be deprived for the lawful detention of a person after conviction by a competent court. Deprivation of liberty requires a strong justification given its 'profound implications for the human rights of defendants' (Player, 2007: 245). Although the ECHR was incorporated into domestic legislation in the Human Rights Act 1998, the general right to bail of accused persons is covered by section 4 of the Bail Act 1976 as amended. As shown later in this Section, the statutory compatibility of this domestic legislation and the right to liberty under Article 5 is a vexed question. Its application, in decisions made by the courts, is especially problematic for disabled defendants where it risks disproportionately negative effects on their rights and liberties.

Under the 1976 Act, the courts have four options at their disposal: unconditional bail; conditional bail; bail subject to surety or security or, alternatively, they can remand the accused in custody (see section 3(2), (4), (6) and Schedule 1,

[1] Spanning the period these case studies were observed. In the year ending September 2022, the figure was 1.2 million defendants.

Part 1 (paragraph 2) respectively). The general presumption in favour of granting bail in section 4 is qualified by the exceptions provided in Schedule 1 of the 1976 Act (section 4(1)). Paragraph 2 of this Schedule sets out three exceptions that may justify the court's refusal to grant bail. First, if they are satisfied that there are *substantial grounds* for believing that the defendant, if released on bail, would fail to surrender to custody and therefore present a risk of absconding. Second, there are substantial grounds to believe the defendant would commit an offence while on bail prior to sentencing or, third 'interfere with witnesses or otherwise obstruct the course of justice, whether in relation to himself or any other person'. These grounds broadly correspond to those 'approved by the European Court of Human Rights in its development of Article 5(3)' (Campbell, Ashworth and Redmayne, 2019: 245).

The court should have regard to four further considerations for decisions to deny the right to bail under paragraph 2 (Bail Act 1976, Schedule 1: para 9). These are: the defendant's fulfilment of their prior bail obligations; the 'nature and seriousness of the offence or default (and the probable method of dealing with the defendant for it)'; the 'character, antecedents, associations and community ties of the defendant' and 'the strength of the evidence of his having committed the offence or having defaulted'. 'Community ties' are considered relevant to the probability of the defendant's attendance at court; however, a lack of fixed residence does not justify imposing pre-trial detention (*Sulaoja v Estonoa* (2006) 43 EHRR 36, para 64). A further exception to the right to grant bail, is applicable to defendants whose case is adjourned for inquiries or a report, where 'it appears to the court that it would be impracticable to complete the inquiries or make the report without keeping the defendant in custody' (Bail Act 1976, Schedule 1: para 7). This exception is particularly relevant in relation to the cohort of case studies considered here, with the assumption being those with temporary or unstable domiciliary arrangements are more likely to abscond (Ashworth and Redmayne, 2014: 252). The Mental Health Act 1983 introduced the power to remand defendants to psychiatric hospital for reports to be prepared, but this has not been widely used and such defendants have been given custodial remands in large numbers (Ashworth and Redmayne, 2014: 252).

In William's case, the court had initially been willing to grant him unconditional bail but his mother, Alice, did not feel that she could 'have him at home with her again' (Interview). Alice made this decision because she could no longer deal with the restrictive requirements of his SOPO which required him to travel on public transport accompanied by an adult who had full knowledge of his previous convictions. William's shame about his previous convictions meant that he did not want anybody else to know about them and, consequently, Alice was the only person with whom he could travel. It is worth noting that 'homelessness should not lead to a custodial remand without thorough exploration of other alternatives' (see Ashworth and Redmayne 2014; *sic* Home Office Circular, 155/1975). No attempt was made by William's defence solicitor or the court to make alternative community arrangements for William so that he could be bailed to a different address, such as a hostel or independent living placement nor to utilise the provision in the Mental Health Act 1983 to remand him to psychiatric hospital. This evinces the criminal law operating in a silo, without cognisance of guidance on disabled defendants under adult social care and mental health law. If William's social care needs had been assessed properly in these circumstances he may have met the threshold for a support package from his local authority and bail granted; preventing the nine months he was remanded in custody.

The 'bail/custody decision' raises one of the criminal justice process's most 'acute conflicts' – with the defendant's right to liberty on the one hand and public interest in protection of crime on the other. Nevertheless, Ashworth and Redmayne argue, the fallibility of predictions of dangerousness means that there are no persuasive reasons for the state to take power over defendants in the pre-trial period, especially for non-serious offences (2014). The concept of 'balancing' is 'manifestly inadequate' in this context where more cogent appreciation of the rights of the defendant at each of these stages is needed and the evidential basis for the calculations of risk must be given (ibid). Imprisonment on remand can be 'immensely stressful and upsetting', particularly given the 'inherent uncertainty of the situation … for many prisoners it can be as damaging to their social, domestic, and financial circumstances as a period of imprisonment under sentence' (Player et al, 2010: 231–2). Research has long documented the higher proportion of defendants from certain racial backgrounds remanded in custody pending trial (Hood, 1992) and the higher proportion of female than male defendants held on remand (Player et al, 2010).

There is, however, limited research on the 'pains of imprisonment' (Sykes, 1958; Crewe, 2011) and the failure to make reasonable adjustments for disabled defendants who are held on remand (see Gormley, 2019; 2022). A joint report of the HM Prison and Probation Inspectorate on the treatment of defendants with Learning Disabilities, including autistic people, serving a sentence in prison or on remand, only identified one such prisoner on remand out of a cohort of 26 (2015). Inspectors found that 'many prisons and probation trusts' were either unaware or unwilling to implement the Equality Act 2010', overlooking their 'statutory duty to make reasonable adjustments' to their services and to make them accessible to disabled offenders, including those with a learning disability (ibid: 11). Although, the inspectors attributed this to prison and probation service failure to screen populations properly, they were emphatic that that it did 'not remove' their obligations under the Act (ibid). This failure was certainly evident in William's case and was exacerbated by factors related to his autism. Consequently, the pains of his imprisonment on remand were severely felt. William was remanded in custody in July 2013 for approximately 270 days, more than four-times the 63-day average (see Hansard HC, 21 January 2013, c51W).

When William was first moved to prison on remand, he was placed in a holding wing, and was then moved to the high security wing; describing the latter as not 'easy by any means' (Letter Correspondence). He recorded the conditions of his cell as 'awful'. There were 'two beds one either side of the cell' and the 'bed was extremely uncomfortable', near 'the door, there was a toilet which was not private by any means … the sink was on the verge of coming off the wall' and he 'even had cockroaches in [his] cell which is just about as disgusting as it comes' (Letter Correspondence). In addition to these conditions, William had to 'share the cell with someone who self-harm[ed]' and William felt 'responsible for this individual' (ibid). William's letters frequently mentioned the pains he experienced in his back and ankles, which were caused by a small curvature of his spine and early onset arthritis which were diagnosed by prison healthcare staff. This was made worse by the prison beds, one of which he described as being 'made up of two hospital beds' on top of each other, with 'an exercise mat' as a mattress (ibid). When his cell door was closed, some of the inmates came up to the door of his cell 'and started to shout abuse' at him (ibid). After over two weeks, he was moved to a wing for vulnerable persons, which he described as 'an absolute blessing' until the same 'self-harmer' was moved into his cell with him. Following another court adjournment in late December 2013, William had to return to the prison to await the psychiatrist's expert witness report. When he arrived 'spaces were so limited, the only space that there was available' for him was back on the high security wing and 'even the Senior Officer said he didn't want to put me back [there]' (ibid). Instead, he was put into a suicide cell. This made William 'feel that [he was being] punished for something that [he hadn't done]' and that this was 'disability discrimination'.

In March 2014, William was still on remand but was transferred to a prison further away from his home, after another adjournment for the second medical report. It is troubling that a case such as his should have led to his incarceration for nine months before the court meted out a non-custodial sentence in the form of detention in a psychiatric hospital. The seriousness of his offence and low risk of absconding and re-offending should have inclined the court to give him unconditional bail. As discussed above, that the decision fell on the absence of alternative accommodation for him in the community, without any alternatives being made available by the probation service. William's case provides a further example of invasive governance, which did not properly consider his protected characteristic under the Equality Act 2010.

Campbell, Ashworth and Redmayne provide a principled call to action to overhaul the decision on types of remand, with these decisions 'governed by a statutory framework or by guidelines similar to those for sentencing' (2019: 265). Unconditional bail is the preferred starting level of disposal, followed by conditional bail and then progressive levels of departure; with each level accompanied by reasons for departure. Remand in custody should only be used where conviction is likely on the strength of evidence for the charge and the court is satisfied that if proven at trial, would be likely to result in the imposition of a custodial sentence, and where the 'evidence for the chosen ground for refusing bail is clear and convincing' (Ashworth and Redmayne, 2014: 245; 255). The likelihood of custodial sentence, in the second part of this formulation, is particularly germane for disabled defendants where they are likely to be given a community sentence or a Hospital Order under the Mental Health Act 1983. In line with the principles they establish, remand in custody should not be used 'unless there is a substantial risk of *serious* offences being committed if the defendant were left at liberty' and where it is unavoidable, 'must be for the shortest period possible'; ensuring that the existing time limits are circumscribed (*cf* Ashworth and Redmayne, 2014: 245). In addition to these recommendations, it is necessary to build in better checks for sequential and repeat renewal and a flagging system which alerts the prosecution and defence, along with the bench who presides over the case at each court stage, when consecutive renewals have passed a three-month period. There are clearly decency issues documented in William's account of his time on remand and his 'pains of imprisonment' during this period are blatant (see Crewe, 2011). In the context of Scottish prisons, Gormley writes movingly of prison being 'disproportionately difficult to navigate for people with learning disabilities' because of the 'inherent structural, procedural, and communicative barriers' and 'hidden harms' which are exponential to established pains of imprisonment, (re)producing 'disability inequalities and immeasurable injustice' (2022: 275). Campbell, Ashworth and Redmayne are careful to point out remand 'is not a prisons problem' but a 'justice problem' and 'efforts to develop non-custodial facilities for holding defendants in the community must be redoubled' (2019: 266). Nonetheless, the 'disabling effects' (Ben-Moshe 2020: 17; Gormley, 2022) of imprisonment on remand for autistic defendants and those with learning disabilities underlines the urgency of achieving this outcome.

B. Expert Witness Evidence

The variable quality of expert evidence and the slow-moving process of seeking it for the court, was a theme throughout the cases observed. In five of the eight cases, medical reports were sought either prior to the entry of the plea, when the defendant was remanded on bail or in custody or before the sentencing hearing. Procedural rules dictate that a magistrates' court may exercise its power to adjourn the case for the 'purpose of enabling inquiries to be made or of determining the most suitable method of dealing with the case … after convicting the accused and before sentencing him or otherwise dealing with him' (Magistrates' Courts Act 1980, s 10(3)A). The court has the power to remand the defendant in custody or on bail for medical examination and the preparation of medical reports if they are satisfied that the defendant: (a) 'did the act or made the omission charged' and are (b) 'of the opinion that an inquiry ought to be made into his physical or mental condition before the method of dealing with him is determined' (Powers of Criminal Courts (Sentencing) Act 2000, s 11(1)). However, there was some evidence of reluctance to use this power of adjournment.

Describing changes in access to obtaining expert witnesses over the period 2009–2013, one solicitor noted that there had been changes in 'the Magistrates' court, without question':

> There is far less willingness to allow adjournment for reports to be prepared. It's seen as delaying tactics … [they say]: 'oh the probation service can deal with this issue; you don't need a psychiatric report'. Or … you're given unrealistic timetables [for] … psychiatrists to produce a report … and if you haven't got the report in that timeline … they [won't give] … any more time' (Mr Griffiths, Solicitor).

The solicitor accepted that 'years ago, cases used to last … months unnecessarily' in the Magistrates' court and there had to be 'more intense case supervision' but that the 'pendulum had swung too far to the fact that cases are driven more by cost rather than by justice' (ibid). His view was that this was 'particularly' the case 'when you've got … vulnerable offenders' but that 'was less likely in Crown Court' where there is 'a greater willingness to allow adjournments for reports' (ibid). Another solicitor corroborated this difficulty with getting an adjournment as '… nowadays speed is of the essence' but when there was a good reason for solicitors to ask 'for an expert's report, the courts will accommodate that' (Mr McKinnery, Solicitor, Interview).

The quality of such reports was also raised. William's barrister commented on the necessity to be 'fairly careful about who you choose to give the report; there is the good, bad and the ugly in any profession'. Therefore, he would 'make a recommendation based on previous experience' but acknowledged that it was 'difficult to assess somebody's clinical judgement if you are not a clinician' (Mr Manson, Interview). Under Article 25 of the UNCRPD, States Parties should recognise that disabled people have the 'right to the enjoyment of the highest attainable standard of health without discrimination on the basis of disability' and provide them with 'the same range, quality and standard of free or affordable health care' as provided to other persons. It further emphasises that those specific health services needed by disabled people 'because of their disabilities', including intervention and 'services designed to minimize and prevent further disabilities' (UNCRPD, Article 25(b)). Ordering reports on the defendant's mental health by the courts can be seen as such interventions and expert witness statements can amount to 'services designed to minimize and prevent further disabilities'. However, court observations and interviews with the defendants' solicitors revealed varying quality of expert evidence and difficulties in 'identifying the expert', were factors which led to delay but once the expert was secured it 'was a relatively simple process in getting that final authority [from the Crown Court]' (Mr Griffiths, Solicitor).

There is no directory of professionals with specific expertise that can be accessed by defence solicitors. In Robert's case, no medical report was requested. He was not registered with a GP and as his mother, Nicola, pointed out, the onus was 'on him to make the appointment' but he did 'not want to go to the doctors on his own' (Mother, Interview). Nicola said that he was 'hard to deal with' and should have had 'a specialist worker' but she had been told by social services that 'because he has Aspergers [as opposed to autism or learning disability diagnosis] they won't deal with him … and probation [kept] passing the buck' (ibid). Unsurprisingly, the cost of obtaining a report was also an important consideration, as was the social capital of the defendant and their support network. This impacted on their ability to request and scrutinise the expert report, along with the expediency with which they could obtain a second opinion. Written reports from two registered medical practitioners are necessary for a defendant to be sectioned by the court, as in William's case. New reports may also be necessary to update the case file of an individual whose case has taken a long time to be listed, as was the situation for Noah, or to counteract reports made by experts with vested interests in recommending the sort of clinical placement their own service provided. This raises clear issues around health inequality for autistic defendants from certain socio-economic groups; augmenting structural barriers facing such individuals' access to justice. General disparities in access to expertise as a form of social capital has been documented in the context of race and class (Cornwell and Cornwell, 2008), as well the impact of free marketisation on forensic science services (Roberts, 1996). There remains, however, a paucity of material on barriers to obtaining Expert Reports and Testimonies for disabled defendants and the impact this has on inhibiting equitable access to justice.

3. The Context of Plea: The Dominant Skew Towards 'Guilty'

The statutory, judicial and prosecutorial policy legitimation of the professional pressures on defendants to plead guilty generates a 'guilty plea culture' which, in turn, drives the practices of defence lawyers who trail 'the prosecution in adopting a strategy of case disposals through guilty pleas' (McConville, 1998). This occupational culture and resultant trial avoidance emerged as an important theme underpinning the rationalities and strategies of governance, which influenced the prosecution and defence professional practices, in relation to what plea was entered by the cohort of autistic adults. Over two-thirds of cases in the Crown Court, and 90 per cent of cases in the Magistrates' Courts, proceeded on a plea of guilty 'which means that no trial of guilt ever takes place' (Ashworth and Redmayne, 2014: 418) during the period present case studies were heard. More recently, since summer 2021, the guilty plea rate among defendants dealt with in 'for trial' cases at the Crown Court, fell back to pre-COVID levels, remaining at 67 per cent in 2022; in contrast to peaks in late 2020 at 79 per cent[2] (MOJ, 2023). Indeed, guilty pleas often 'reflect a contingent and highly contested version of events' where 'the truth' is 'just as elusive' as in cases that have gone to trial (Ashworth and Redmayne, 2014: 418). Far from being inevitable, the guilty plea outcome results because of 'strong structural incentives to plead guilty and to enter that plea at the first stage of proceedings' (Campbell, Ashworth and Redmayne, 2019: 342). For the defendant, the incentives are expediency and, more compellingly, sentence discounts for a guilty plea of up to one third.

[2] Attributed to the restricted ability of courts to progress jury trials (see MOJ, 2023: 9).

Bridges identifies that the most important step in 'formalising and systematising the sentence discount for guilty pleas' was the Sentencing Guidelines Council's[3] *Guideline on Reduction in Sentence for a Guilty Plea*[4] (2006; 2004; *cf* 2007). It was borne out of the Blairite 're-balancing' of the CJS in favour of the victim, which was not, according to Blair, designed to dispense with 'human rights … [but in] deciding whose [rights] come first' (2005).[5] It marked a shift from 'the classical justification in English jurisprudence for the reduction in sentence being based on the defendant's remorse, as shown through the fact of guilty plea, and instead gives precedence to various administrative rationales around expeditious disposal, cost effectiveness and saving 'victims and witnesses from the concern about having to give evidence' (Bridges, 2006: 84). The plea 'in itself qualifies the defendant for a reduced sentence' and can have a 'significant bearing' on 'personal mitigation' considered at sentencing (Jacobson et al, 2016: 60–1).

Advice by defence lawyers to defendants to enter a guilty plea becomes an 'achieved outcome' in their intervention 'and the way they handle clients'; contributing to a culture in which the views of clients are given 'little weight' and their accounts are not investigated' (McConville, 1998: 572). Consequently, the 'case proceeds on the basis that the lawyer knows best' incentivising the guilty plea (ibid). Thus, what 'ought to be different ethical orientations may' become 'submerged beneath the working practices and occupational cultures of the local groups of professionals' (Ashworth and Remayne, 2014: 418). In the present research, the 'guilty plea culture' – affecting the working practices of the prosecution, defence and wider circle of court actors – had an instrumental influence on the plea which was ultimately entered by the defendants in the cohort. One interesting theme was around the use of a guilty plea to 'get help' for the autistic defendant (William, Robert and Claire). There was a sense that determining culpability for the offence – even whether the defendant could form the requisite *mens rea* – would delay the inevitable. Instead, it was seen as expeditious to plead guilty, by both the prosecution and defence, not just to maximise the opportunity for sentence reduction but also to ensure the 'right' outcome was secured for the defendant by pleading guilty. The pressures on prosecutors to achieve early guilty pleas and for the courts to improve efficiency created a context in which defence lawyers did not always focus on determining whether their client was fit to plead or to allow the court to establish that they were not guilty. There was also a protective dimension to this approach: an early guilty plea would reduce the distress caused to the autistic person and their family. Instead, trailing the pressures of the prosecution to enter an early guilty plea, there was evidence that some defence solicitors shifted their professional energies from the processual decision about plea to working with the

[3] Now the 'Sentencing Council'.

[4] The Sentencing Council introduced a revised guideline for plea-based sentence reductions in 2017. Roberts and Pina-Sánchez found that the overall guilty plea remained stable between 2014–2019, with the guideline appearing to 'have had no effect on the timing of guilty pleas entered, and in fact the percentage of "cracked" trials rose' after it was published (2022: 327).

[5] Full transcript of Tony Blair's speech available at news.bbc.co.uk/1/hi/uk_politics/4287370.stm.

individual, family and probation to secure the most appropriate dispositive decision for their client.

Five of the eight autistic defendants ultimately entered a guilty plea (Claire, Robert, Ollie, William, Miles). Henry was the only participant in the cohort to plead not guilty at any stage for the offences alleged against him. Robert entered a late guilty plea, after his mother Nicola had been encouraged to be a witness for the prosecution. Miles elected not to enter a plea at the Magistrates' court and instead chose to enter a guilty plea at the Crown Court Plea and Case Management Hearing. Patrick entered not guilty on the first count of racially aggravated assault but guilty on the other counts with which he was charged. Noah initially pleaded guilty at the Magistrates' Court but then vacated his plea at the Crown Court. This was followed by a trial of the facts after the judge found he was unfit to plead. The timing and decision on plea were utilised to achieve 'better' outcomes for the autistic defendant. Whether through the negligence of solicitors to recognise the need to enter a plea of unfitness to plead, in Noah's case, or as a result of more competent defence solicitors adopting the strategy of entering a late plea to obtain better expert evidence, as in Miles' and Henry's cases. This had an important consequential impact on their governance in relation to the dispositive decisions made by the court in their sentencing.

Henry pleaded not guilty at the Plea and Case Management Hearing. The case went to trial in the Magistrates' Court in front of a District Judge. In the intervening period, Henry's defence solicitor had instructed a psychiatrist to produce an expert witness report. In it, the consultant psychiatrist said that Henry was not fit to stand trial. As described in the previous chapter, the CPS did not 'seem terribly satisfied about his autism up until the very end in court'; even though they approved this psychiatric report which confirmed that he was unfit to plead (Mr McKinnery, Solicitor, Interview). Nevertheless, the CPS pursued the early entry of a guilty plea, saying: 'no, he can plead guilty and we'll even put his autism in his litigation' (ibid); implying that the strategies of governance, embedded in the CPS Business Plan, were driving the prosecutorial culture.

The dominance of this prosecutorial culture towards pleading guilty can also be seen in Noah's case, where the first solicitor, Mr Jenkins, entered a guilty plea at the first appearance at the Magistrates' Court. This was *despite* the joint expert witness report between his consultant psychiatrist and lead psychologist, which said:

> … [Noah] does not have the capacity to understand the nature of the forthcoming proceedings. He will not be able to fully understand the information given to him about the hearing and, therefore, would not be able to retain information … to make the decision [about plea]. … [H]e will [not]be able to weigh up the information or communicate any meaningful information to his solicitor. There is no guarantee that what [Noah] does communicate is in reality his own thoughts or beliefs and is not a response designed to appease others (Psychiatrist, Expert Witness Report).

The second solicitor, Mr Grundy, who later acted for Noah, recalled that there was 'only one conclusion that you can come to [after reading the report] because that screams out to you "not fit to plead"' (Interview). However, when represented by his first solicitor, Mr Jenkins, told Noah's father, Leo, that he was going to do 'a deal with the prosecution' to 'drop the assault [and] we'll plead guilty for the primary offence and to criminal damage' (Interview). Leo recalled thinking: 'well that's fine … if they drop the assault … [which] was really worrying me and [my wife]' because it made Noah 'sound extremely dangerous' and 'like it's a five-year prison sentence' (ibid).

The advice of the first defence solicitor and his 'deal' with the CPS was contrary to the current and previous *Codes for Crown Prosecutors*, applicable at the time, which say that prosecutors should never proceed with:

> more charges than are necessary just to encourage a defendant to plead guilty to a few. In the same way, they should never go ahead with a more serious charge just to encourage a defendant to plead guilty to a less serious one (2013: 13; 2018: 14).

Noah's parents did not know about this Code, nor the seriousness of pleading guilty to knife crime. Instead, they agreed with Mr Jenkins' plea bargain because 'most importantly' they thought it would 'get the case dealt with' that day (Mr Grundy, Solicitor, Interview). That is not what happened. Noah pleaded guilty to possession of a knife, the Magistrates' Court 'committed [his case] for sentence to the Crown Court. Shock horror! Best laid plans and all this has gone to tatters!' (ibid).

Noah's father, Leo, described the stark realisation of what had happened in the Magistrates' Court when Mr Jenkins entered the plea:

> … the prosecution … were making quite clear the use of the knife … [was dangerous and Noah's behaviour] was very threatening. … [A]fter this occurred, I couldn't believe it … [our solicitor was] saying: 'yes I've listened to the [interview] tape and [Noah] did say he'd raised a knife above his head and threatened to kill Mr [Coyle]' … So, I'm thinking: 'you're meant to be our guide, what are you doing?' And he didn't raise anything about the psychiatric report. … I'm listening to our own solicitor agreeing with the prosecution … [and] he's not defending him properly … (Interview).

Consequently, Noah's father intervened in the proceedings and spoke directly to the Chair of the Magistrates:

> I said: 'if you read the psychiatric report … you will see that it says [Noah] is not fit to plead, and I think that's really important'.
>
> [T]hen the [court clerk] said: 'excuse me Mr [Herbert], you are raising a legal issue here'.
>
> I don't know if it's a legal issue or not but I think 'it's something you need to know about here!'
>
> The Clerk then says to the Magistrates: 'you might want to take some time to consider this, as this is a legal point to be made' (ibid).

After an adjournment to read the psychiatric report, the Magistrates informed Noah's father that they agreed with him but that they were 'not able to deal with the case' and it would have to be transferred to the Crown Court. As Leo recalled, it became 'a legal mess' because Noah had already been 'prompted' to plead guilty 'but the psychiatric report is saying [he's] not fit to plead' (ibid).

The decision of Noah's first solicitor to enter a plea in this way had a massive impact on the processual decisions about his case and caused great distress for him and his family. So concerned were Noah's parents with the prospect that Noah might go to prison, they sought a second opinion from defence solicitor, Mr Grundy, who took over his case. Legal Aid was not transmutable from the first solicitor, so Noah's parents had to pay for him privately. Mr Grundy applied to vacate the plea. This was 'done reasonably quickly and … [the case was] listed … for September 2011' (Interview). However, the first appearance at the Crown Court did not happen until August 2012 and the case was not listed for trial until July 2013, over two years after the alleged offences occurred. Mr Grundy believed that Mr Jenkins had 'dealt with this case dreadfully simplistically' given that the medical report 'made it abundantly clear that [Noah] was not capable of understanding the proceedings or … capable of giving instructions' which 'are the tests for any lawyer that's taken a degree in the last 120 years for fitness to plead' (Interview). Mr Grundy went further than criticising the duty solicitor, however, and emphasised the point that the legal question of fitness to plead may be raised by 'the [court] clerk who is a qualified solicitor sitting in front of the magistrate' the prosecution, defence, or Judge. He spelled out that 'the Magistrates' Court got this wrong' but all 'three [solicitors] are officers of the court and under criminal procedure rules they are required to assist the courts'. The magistrates, therefore, are 'entitled to rely upon [them]' (Mr Grundy, Interview).

The failure of the Crown Prosecutor to pay regard to the question of unfitness to plead is also contrary to the *Prosecution Policy and Guidance* which stated that if during proceedings 'the CPS is provided with a medical report which states that the strain of criminal proceedings may lead to a considerable worsening of the defendant's mental health, the implications of the report should be considered very carefully' (2012). Such consideration was not made. Equivalent language has been softened slightly in subsequent guidance, nevertheless, prosecutors should still consider the 'impact of a prosecution where there is evidence of its likely interaction with a suspect's mental health, particularly in a case where there is evidence that it can be exacerbated, or it is degenerating' (CPS, 2019). Noah's case instead reflects subversion of the 'ethics of client representation' (Bridges, 2006) by the first solicitor. Indeed, so immersed were Mr Jenkins, the duty solicitor acting for the defence, the CPS solicitor and the Court Clerk in the occupational culture towards early guilty plea, that it obfuscated the need to even consider Noah's fitness to plead. Amounting to what Peay and Player describe as 'an *inducement* to plead guilty' which places 'uneven burdens on defendants and fails to pay due regard to the duties owed by public authorities under the Equality Act 2010' (2018: 929)

Once the question of unfitness to plead was raised before the Crown Court and Mr Grundy 'notified both the prosecution and the defence [barristers] that Noah was not fit to plead, [things] changed completely' (Interview). The 'prosecution took a completely neutral stance in relation to [first] our application [to vacate] the guilty plea' which 'they didn't oppose' and, secondly, the 'CPS lawyers had agreed … that they would not oppose [our other requests]' (ibid). The barrister, who the CPS had instructed for the Crown Court proceedings, took this different approach, to the CPS solicitor in the Magistrates' Court, because they viewed the psychiatrists' expert witness evidence as 'so simple, straightforward and forceful' that they would 'not instruct [their] own psychiatrist' (Mr Grundy, Interview). They accepted Noah was 'not fit to go through proceedings' (ibid). They went further and worked collaboratively with the defence counsel and said: 'let's look at what we can do to make these proceedings as simple and as short as possible' (Mr Grundy, Interview). Consequently, they agreed in advance 'that they wouldn't call any factual testimony' and that the 'facts that the prosecution read out' in court were an attempt 'to try and shortcut the case as much as possible' (ibid).

This change in the decision-making approach from the CPS solicitors at the Magistrates' Court, to the barristers at the Crown Court, also indicates how different working practices amongst prosecutorial professionals can impact on the programmes of governance which are applied to a defendant's case. When the Crown Court heard the case, the Judge made an order that Noah was unfit to plead. There followed proceedings for a jury to determine whether Noah committed the act or made the omission charged against him for the offence under section 4A(2) of the Criminal Procedure (Insanity) Act 1964. The proceedings were simplified: the judge agreed that the counts of possession of a knife and damage to the two vehicles could be heard together on a summary indictment in three counts. He also determined that 'the summary of the evidence [should be given by the prosecution] instead of extracts of the witness statements' (Court Observation).

Further, the defence barrister advised the judge 'to direct the jury to make an appropriate special verdict that doing the act [was his] use of a knife' and recommended that there was no 'need for the jury to retire' (Court Observation). When the jury entered court, the judge instructed them accordingly that the defendant:

> … suffers from such disability that he is not able to take part in the trial and therefore is not fit to plead. That's the decision I have made (Court Observation).

The jury examined the photographs of the knife and car damage and the judge directed them as follows:

> … there is no controversy of the evidence [in this case], the defendant has admitted to it and this is not challenged in effect. What you have to say is whether he did the act, not that he was guilty of the offences just that he did the act: he had a knife for an offensive purpose and damaged the car. … Foreman, there is no necessity to adjourn this case for you to make your findings (ibid).

A highly unusual approach, but streamlining proceedings in this way minimised Noah's distress. The jury conferred quietly in the courtroom and the foreman told the judge that he committed all the acts on the indictment and remained in court whilst the judge determined whether to dispose of the case through a Hospital Order, a supervision order or an absolute discharge. Therefore, this shift in the processual decision about plea, directly impacted upon the disposal of Noah's case and the strategies of governance that were applied to him.

In Robert's case, the victim of his assault was his mother, Nicola, and the CPS, together with his defence solicitor, treated his case straightforwardly as one of domestic violence. Prior to his case being heard in the Magistrates' Court, Nicola had told the police and the CPS that she wished to retract the witness statement which had been taken in hospital immediately after the incident: 'but the CPS would not accept my retraction' (Interview). A summons was ordered for her to attend court as a witness for the prosecution and she was told that 'she would get arrested if not because the police wanted to pursue the case, because [Robert] was aggressive and abusive towards the police when they had arrested him at the scene' (Interview). Robert's solicitor told her that he was not able to 'speak to [her] until after the case' (ibid). Nicola, therefore, described the difficult position she was in: she did not want Robert 'to be locked up' and thought retracting her statement would be enough for them to drop the case 'but now [the police] are bringing things in that [happened after the assault and were] nothing to do with [her]'. In these circumstances, Nicola was both victim and primary carer, and so this required a more nuanced understanding than a straightforward domestic violence case. Before Robert's trial at the Magistrates' Court, Nicola had numerous meetings with the CPS and Victim Support, along with other MAPPA agencies. These professionals placed pressure on her to testify against Robert in order to persuade him to make an early guilty plea. In the exchange between Nicola and the Senior Prosecutor, which took place at court just before Roberts's trial, she emphasised that she did not 'want [her] son locked up' but the Senior Prosecutor was steadfast in persuading her to testify. This is evidenced in the following exchange observed in a meeting room at court, just before proceedings began:

> **Crown Prosecutor**: Aspergers, OCD and semantic pragmatic literal understanding, that's a heady cocktail. I know that he is a nuisance to you. [The violence], [i]t's frequent isn't it?
>
> **Nicola**: I just want [him] settled in his own flat and to get outside agencies involved [such as support to live independently] … He's not got the mentality of a 22-year-old; I don't think he can cope with his flat without support. …
>
> **Crown Prosecutor:** It's not easy to give evidence against any family member but we don't want you to keep getting assaulted; he needs to understand that.
>
> **Nicola:** As his main carer, I do his washing, taking him to appointments, supporting him in his house and if he wants to go to the doctor or the dentist.

This dialogue reveals much about the responsibility Nicola felt towards Robert as his main carer. On the one hand, Nicola's response reflects the technique of an 'appeal to higher loyalties' (Sykes and Matza, 1957) in justifying a continuing relationship with someone who has committed a serious offence by 'holding up family bonds … to counter real or perceived criticism of their support' (Condry, 2007). On the other hand, this interpretation overlooks the pragmatic need for Nicola to be Robert's main carer because other services had failed to help support him. The Senior Crown Prosecutor continued to persuade her to testify:

> … if you [say you will] give evidence, [his] defence will collapse and he will get an easy bonus for his guilty plea. [He's in front of a] reasonable district judge who is not known to be too harsh. Probably because this is a different type of offence [to what Robert had previously been convicted of] it would be unlikely to activate his suspended sentence because of [his] mitigating factors (Pre-Court Meeting Observation).

In that context, the Senior Crown Prosecutor gave Nicola a choice:

> [But the] [o]nly way to guarantee that he won't do this again is to [threaten] prison. Which is better? Not going to prison or getting treatment? … I'm not sure what probation would do in this situation. Do you want to give evidence or not? … If you say at this stage that you are happy to testify, I can go to speak to the defence solicitor … (ibid).

Nicola nodded her head in consent, saying: 'this is the most difficult decision I've ever made'. The Senior Crown Prosecutor returned and informed Nicola that Robert was going to 'change his plea to admit that he is guilty' and 'is going to get a probation order and an alcohol awareness course'. He reassured Nicola that he would put: 'his views across forcefully to the court that [she] did not want him to be sentenced [to prison]' (Pre-Court Meeting Observation).

These passages demonstrate the determination to obtain an early guilty plea; deferring consideration of Robert's autism until it could be included as a mitigating factor at sentencing. According to guidelines issued by the Sentencing Guidelines Council, the justification for the reduction for a guilty plea 'derives from the need for effective administration of justice and not as an aspect of mitigation' (2007: 4). However, such a fine distinction is not so clear in reality. The Senior Crown Prosecutor reassured Nicola that 'he will get an easy bonus for his guilty plea' and his 'heady mix' of Aspergers, OCD and semantic pragmatic disorders could be used as mitigating factors to prevent the suspended sentence from being triggered. This echoes the approach of the police and the CPS in Henry's case (above). The guarantee of reduction for a guilty plea was used to persuade her to testify because this will create the opportunity for his disability to be properly considered later in the process at mitigation.

In Claire's case, the Detective Constable, DC Kim, from the Integrated Offender Management Service worked closely with the CPS and Claire's defence solicitor. In relation to plea, DC Kim said:

> She always pleads guilty to [possession of a] bladed article but nothing else; at the advice of her solicitor, they feel, quite rightly, very strongly about her trying to get help (Interview).

Again, evincing the use the guilty plea to obtain 'help' for autistic defendants. Thus, augmenting the use of the 'guilty plea culture' with another layer, relating specifically to certain disabled defendants. Justiciable issues are examined by the defence, prosecution and Magistrates' or Crown Court judges from the perspective of wrongdoing from the criminal justice paradigm, rather than perceiving the parallel legal rights which arise in relation to the person's disability in the context of the social care system.

Bridges regards the reality of the current sentence discount to be that a 'guilty plea (whether honest or dishonest) is to be treated *per se* as a mitigating factor and rewarded by a lesser sentence' (2006: 89). These cases also show that there is a tendency for the culture towards the guilty plea to shift material consideration of the person's autism from fitness to plead to its relevance to mitigation at sentencing. These aspects of the 'guilty plea culture' represent the kind of 'politics and policies of criminalisation and crime control which are grounded on an ideology of difference, rather than on an acknowledgement of diversity' (Hudson, 2007).

Conclusion

Chapters seven and eight contribute to an understanding of the 'disablement' (see chapters one and three) faced by the cohort of eight defendants. Chapter seven has demonstrated that the inequitable experiences of autistic defendants arise out of the failure of decision-makers to conceptualise them as 'disabled' at the processual and temporising decision-making stages. We have seen that in the organisational culture of attaining an early guilty plea for administrative expediency and re-balancing the system towards the victim, consideration of the defendant's autism is shifted further down the criminal justice pathway, becoming relevant in the context of mitigation at sentencing. This is not an argument in favour of increased use of fitness to plead proceedings. Others have already set out the difficulties around current legislation and The Law Commission's proposed reforms (2016) to this legislation in relation to compatibility with the UNCRPD (see Gooding and O'Mahony, 2015). Gooding and O'Mahony give the example of those who are deemed unfit to plead, and who routinely face extended periods of detention in secure settings, for longer periods of time than if they received the maximum sentence for the alleged crime (ibid: 2; see ALRC, 2014). Rather, the aim is to highlight that the specific impact of the guilty plea culture on autistic defendants means that this strategy of government fails to ensure that these defendants receive access to justice.

8

Dividing Practices in Case Disposal: Aggravating and Mitigating Factors and Sentencing

Introduction

The disparate actions and siloed working practices of criminal justice decision-makers in arriving at 'processual' and 'temporising' decisions (see chapter seven above) become evident when these actors come together in the courtroom and are brought under the scrutiny of the court. Section 1 gives an overview of considerations of 'mental disorders' in aggravating and mitigating factors in sentencing. It then moves on to analyse how the autism of defendants', in the case study cohort, was used by their defence solicitor or barrister as a mitigating factor and the extent to which sentencers took this into account in adjusting the level and type of sentence. Section 1 also explicates whether the person's autism was associated with rationalities such as dangerousness, increasing the prospect of and length of incapacitation (see Manson, 2011).

Only four studies, found in a systematic literature review, and all based in the US, were identified which investigated jurors' and/or judges' evaluations of a defendant with an autism diagnosis and the impact this had on sentencing decisions (Alley and Cooper, 2017). Section 2 looks at the technologies and programmes of governance which were applied to autistic defendants at sentencing. It examines the court observation and other qualitative data to ascertain what logics were applied by the courts in determining the sentence for the defendants in the cohort through: (i) actual or suspended sentence; (ii) Community Orders, and (iii) Hospital Orders under the Mental Health Act 1983. The cases of Claire, William and Noah are illustrative of the ways in which 'civil and administrative processes are increasingly being repurposed so as to accommodate the goals of criminal law' (Spivakovsky, 2014a: 3). In the absence of 'disabled justice' there may be principled reasons for using measures within health and social care, however, there is some evidence of invasive governance of autistic adult defendants as these measures are re-purposed and integrated into SOPOs, Community Orders and Supervision Orders.

1. Aggravating and Mitigating Factors

In six of the eight case studies, Ollie, Robert, Patrick, Miles, Claire and William, the autistic defendants were convicted of the offences alleged against them. Noah was unfit to plead but found by the jury to have committed the acts alleged in his unfitness to plead proceedings. Henry was the only defendant to be acquitted unreservedly. Research shows that judicial recognition of personal mitigation still plays the largest role in tipping the balance away from a custodial term (Hough et al, 2003); changing what otherwise would have been a period in custody to a community-based sentence in one third of cases (see Hough and Jacobson, 2007). The present Section examines the relevance of the defendant's autism in personal mitigation. The legislature creates statutory sentencing factors which allow for judicial discretion to consider mitigation at sentencing (Roberts, 2011). At the time the defendants in this cohort went through court, section 142(1) of the Criminal Justice Act (CJA) 2003 placed five such factors on a statutory footing in England and Wales, to which the court had to have regard in respect of sentencing for the defendant's offence. The Sentencing Act 2020 repeals this section, consolidating existing sentencing procedure into this single Act and introducing the Sentencing Code in Parts 2 to 13 of this Act (see section 1(1)).[1] Section 57(2) of this Act replaces the CJA provision but uses identical aims and language of section 142(1) CJA, such that the court must have regard to the following purposes of sentencing adults:

(a) the punishment of offenders,
(b) the reduction of crime (including its reduction by deterrence),
(c) the reform and rehabilitation of offenders,
(d) the protection of the public, and
(e) the making of reparation by offenders to persons affected by their offences.

Section 58 of the Sentencing Act 2020 sets out that nothing within the Sentencing Code, in relation to offenders aged under 18, affects the duties of the court to have regard to the principal aim of the youth justice system – which is to prevent offending (or re-offending) by persons aged under 18 (see section 37 of the Crime and Disorder Act 1998). Nor does it affect the duties of the court to have regard to their welfare and, in certain cases, to take steps in relation to surroundings and provision of education (see section 44 of the Children and Young Persons Act 1933).

The Coroners and Justice Act 2009 created a single Sentencing Council, replacing the former Sentencing Guidelines Council and Sentencing Advisory Panel. Unless it would be contrary to the interests of justice, Guidelines issued by the Council 'must' be followed by the court. These guidelines, which supplemented

[1] Throughout this chapter, applicable sections of the CJA and new provisions are noted. Differences or meaningful differences are explained where relevant to understanding changes in governance to autistic defendants but detailed comparison between the two Acts is not made.

statute and statutory interpretation by the judiciary (Coroners and Justice Act 2009), were designed to assist judges and magistrates in deciding 'the appropriate sentence for a criminal offence' (Sentencing Council, 2009). The 2004 version of the definitive guideline, *Overarching Principles*, which was in place when the eight case studies went to court, has now been superseded by the Sentencing Council's 2019 *General guideline: overarching principles*. The former version explained that the seriousness of an offence is determined by two main parameters 'the culpability of the offender and the harm caused or risked being caused by the offence' (2004), the new edition replicates this language but removes the phrase 'or risked being caused' (2019). Interestingly, Ashworth notes that the 2004 edition of *Overarching Principles*, listed the aggravating and mitigating factors, dividing the former into 'factors indicating higher culpability' such as 'previous convictions' and 'factors indicating more than [a] usually serious degree of harm' such as vulnerability of the victim (Ashworth, 2011; c.f. Sentencing Guidelines Council, 2004: 10). In the current edition of the *Overarching Principles*, there is no such division in aggravating factors, and they are listed as 'Factors increasing seriousness', with subsets for statutory and 'other aggravating factors'. There are five statutory factors in the new Sentencing Code, including 'Hostility' where an offence demonstrates or is motivated by hostility based to a 'protected characteristic' (Sentencing Act 2020, s 66), such as disability. Notable in the non-statutory list, is where an offender targets a vulnerable victim – this 'betokens greater culpability' (Ashworth and Kelly, 2021) and 'greater harm' in such cases (Wasik, 1998). There is also an 'enormous' list of aggravating factors in separate offence specific guidelines (see Ashworth and Kelly, 2021: 157).

Roberts criticised the original *Overarching Principles: Seriousness* guideline in England and Wales for providing only a 'limited rationale for the invocation of any specific factor' and for making 'no distinctions among the thirty-one aggravating circumstances related to harm and culpability' (2011: 11; 14; *cf* Sentencing Guidelines Council, 2004). Most individual offences are now covered by the offence specific guidelines, which incorporate 'extended explanations' of some aggravating and mitigating factors related to offence-seriousness. There is also now a guideline on *Sentencing offenders with mental disorders, developmental disorders, or neurological impairments* (Sentencing Council, 2020; see below). It demonstrates some progress in recognising that disability is often dynamic (Burchardt, 2000; see chapter three above), acknowledging 'some mental disorders can fluctuate and an offender's state during proceedings may not be representative of their condition at the time the offence was committed' (Sentencing Council, 2020). Further, it engages sentencers to think intersectionally in being 'aware of relevant cultural, ethnicity and gender considerations of offenders within a mental health context' and emphasises that these groups 'may be more likely' to enter mental health services 'via the courts or the police rather than primary care' (Sentencing Council, 2020). This guideline on *Sentencing offenders with mental disorders* also emphasises that where the offender is or appears to have a 'mental disorder' at the date of sentencing, the court must obtain and consider a medical report before passing a custodial sentence other than one fixed by law (Sentencing Act 2020, s 232). However, nothing in section 232 on such offenders should limit any requirement for a court to take into account all information that is available to it about the circumstances of any offence, including any aggravating or mitigating factors.

The shorter list of mitigating factors, in place when the defendants in the case studies went to court, only indicated a lower level of culpability, and not harm (see Roberts, 2011). Section 166 of the CJA 2003 gave powers to judges to mitigate sentences and deal appropriately with mentally disordered offenders. It stated that nothing in previous sections relating to imposing custodial and community sentences 'prevents a court from mitigating an offender's sentence by taking into account any such matters as, in the opinion of the court, are relevant in mitigation of sentence' (Shapland, 2011: 66–7). 'Mental illness or disability' was one of the four mitigating factors set out in the 2004 *Overarching Principles* which indicates that an offender's culpability was 'significantly lower'. However, '[m]itigating factors that lower culpability' could be assigned 'much less weight if they do not diminish the estimated need for public protection from the offender' (Ashworth, 2011: 25). On the other hand, 'reduced culpability and matters of personal mitigation may be highly important if the purpose of sentencing is reform or rehabilitation' (ibid). There are two statutory mitigating factors listed in the new Sentencing Code: the guilty plea (section 73) and reduction in sentence for assistance to prosecution (section 74). In the present *General Guideline*, the longer list of a further 17 mitigating factors includes 'Physical disability or serious medical condition requiring urgent, intensive or long-term treatment' and 'Mental disorder or learning disability' (Sentencing Council, 2019). In addition to these general mitigating factors, there are specific factors pertaining only to guidance on sentencing certain offences (mirroring the approach to specific aggravating factors by offence type).

In following the guideline on *Sentencing offenders with mental disorders*, the sentencer should make an initial assessment of culpability, in accordance with any relevant offence-specific guideline, and then they should 'consider whether culpability was reduced by reason of the impairment or disorder' (Sentencing Council, 2020). Autism is included as such a disorder and listed in Annex A of the guideline. This two-step process is characterised by Roberts and Rafferty as 'shaping the provisional sentence' and then fine tuning 'the calibration of harm and culpability' (2011: 684). Ashworth and Kelly (2021: 392) chart how the last two decades have seen a shift from the language of rehabilitation and treatment through more repressive policy in terms of public protection and risk (*cf* Peay, 2017), and an increased emphasis on punishment of offenders with mental disorder according to the degree of their responsibility for the offence (see Sentencing Council's 2020 Guidelines). The former fails to properly assess the empirical foundations and normative implications of dangerousness and the latter reflects a shift, following *Vowles* (2015), that means the 'court should assess the extent to which the offender is culpable for the offence, rather than the offence being attributable to the mental disorder' (Ashworth and Kelly, 2021: 399).

The impact of the sentence on the individual offender is a factor identified by Ashworth as one of a group of mitigating factors which are extraneous to harm and culpability and have no bearing on proportionality. As Ashworth explains, once the judge has set the 'appropriate provisional punishment', it should then be adjusted 'to reflect the degree of "sensibility" of the individual offender', such as health, bodily imperfection and pecuniary circumstances (2011: 26). The underlying principle is that of equality of impact: 'sentences should be adjusted downwards or upwards where that is necessary to ensure the delivery of the same amount of punishment' to the individual before the court (ibid). These 'circumstances influencing sensibility' (Bentham, 1948 [1789]) should, Ashworth argues, be taken into account in proportionality theory in relation to the principle of 'equal impact' (2011). Ashworth describes the incorporation of 'wider social policies' into sentencing law and practice such as was incorporated into section 146 of the CJA 2003 through the 'statutory requirement to aggravate sentence where an offence has been motivated by … discrimination on grounds of disability or sexual orientation' (Ashworth, 2011: 29). This is now covered by section 66 of the Sentencing Act 2020, where the seriousness of an offence is aggravated by hostility towards, for example, disability. English and Welsh guidelines adopt a 'sensibilities' approach by progressively lowering the sentencing starting point where the age 'of the young offender is lower' (Sentencing Guidelines Council, 2009: 24; *cf* Ashworth, 2011: 27). Recommendations by the Sentencing Advisory Panel extend this to women, because of 'the multiple harms that are likely to result from incarceration' (2010: 75). Citing the example of the 'demonstrably greater negative impact on women' of imprisonment because of such harms, Ashworth argues that 'mitigation of sentence must be the correct approach until the negative impacts are removed' (ibid: 30). This equality of impact approach is not meted out in relation to the impact of sentence on defendants with mental health problems or disability in the *Overarching Principles*.

So how was the law and sentencing guidance applied to the cohort of autistic defendants in considering aggravating and mitigating factors? Neither the 2004 nor 2019 *Overarching Principles* include mental ill-health or disability as a potential aggravating factor. Nevertheless, the present research attended to whether other aggravating factors were linked, by court actors, to the symptomatology of a person's autism and whether the shift towards 'repressive policy in terms of public protection and risk', described above, was evinced in the case studies. For example, whether sentencers connected certain behaviour associated to the person's autism to factors such as a defendant's 'failure to respond to warnings or concerns expressed by others about the offender's behaviour', or 'failure to respond to previous sentences' (Sentencing Guidelines Council, 2004: 6). In the interviews with the cohort's defence solicitors and barristers, Mr McKinnery, Henry's solicitor, was adamant that autism would not be treated as an aggravating factor in the sentencing of a defendant with this condition '[u]nless someone was seen to be extremely dangerous' (Interview). Whilst sentencers 'may take steps to protect others from' the defendant or give 'some sort of sentence which … wouldn't be deserved',

Henry's solicitor did not 'think' it would ever be 'seen as an aggravating feature' (ibid). William's barrister echoed this. Despite him observing judges disregarding autism as a mitigating factor and dismissing 'the suggestion [that the] behaviour is rooted in autism', even the most 'cynical judges' had never 'suggested that the autism [was] an aggravating feature' (Mr Manson, Interview).

Other defence solicitors acknowledged that they were not so convinced about a bright line shielding conditions like autism from being considered as an aggravating factor at sentencing. Despite refuting its role as an aggravating factor (see above), William's defence barrister conceded that it could become a sentencing problem 'if the medical opinion was that because of the autism the defendant would be unlikely to change his behaviour, then you have a problem in dealing with future risk' (Mr Manson, Interview). In Miles' case, his defence solicitor, Mr Griffiths, believed that '... even without any previous convictions ... he was looking at a custodial sentence according to the Guidelines' because there were significant aggravating features (Interview). Miles had previous convictions for offences of downloading indecent images of children and was subject at the time to both a community order and a SOPO. Although the latter had been 'removed because the police felt that [Miles] was no longer a risk', his defence solicitor knew that 'there were significant aggravating features' and he was:

> ... anxious not to just jump in and say plead guilty and ... get your credit for an early guilty plea because ... unless the court had the fullest possible information about his disability and how it impacted on the case and, more importantly, how he could be treated in the future, as part of a community order then he would inevitably receive a custodial sentence (Mr Griffiths, Interview).

Thus, these considerations affected how he advised Miles about entering his plea and the relevance of Miles' autism to his mitigation:

> ... [I]n terms of mitigation ... it was important to get a detailed report from an expert; to assess what his condition meant to him; how it impacted on the offences and how his risk could be managed in the future (ibid).

The imperative to get a good quality expert witness report was created by the 'woeful' supervision Miles received from the Probation service as 'he effectively didn't receive any proper intervention to address his offending behaviour' (*op cit.*). Although Miles' defence solicitor conceded that this was not an 'excuse' for the repeat offending, his view was that 'if he had had that proper intervention' there would have been 'a greater likelihood ... [of him] complying with the prior SOPO' (Mr Griffiths, Interview).

Sentencers are 'required to hear any speech in mitigation that the offender or his legal representative wishes to make' when sentencing an offender in England and Wales (Shapland, 1981; 2011). However, in the court observation of the cohort of autistic defendants, the defence solicitor or barristers' speech in mitigation were not quite the standalone, all-encompassing monologues that one might assume. Instead, the defence solicitor or counsel presented the mitigating factors to the court as part of a disparate and fragmented process of providing the sentencer with information about offence mitigation. In her work on personal mitigation, Shapland contends that this process of providing information to sentencers on personal mitigation is not well-developed and can be unreliable. Consequently, although the probation service's pre-sentence reports are a source of information on personal mitigation, they are not always requested (2011). Miles' original solicitor, Mr Arkwright, reflected on the cynicism of sentencers in discounting defendants' autism as a mitigating factor in relation to disability or mental ill-health:

> You have to explain [the autism] to the magistrates [in mitigation] … how this [criminal] behaviour is predicated by the autism … [S]ome magistrates are ready to listen and be sympathetic. Others … have no great interest in this … [and they say]: you've done it … [even though you have a probation] report to that effect. And, of course, the more previous convictions you have got … it undermines your position, and [the District Judges] just say: 'well yes, he is just a n'ere do well, isn't he?!' (Interview).

The description of this solicitor's approach to deploying a defendant's autism as a mitigating factor, 'clothing' the criminal behaviour, reveals a focus on its relevance to the culpability of the defendant. However, attitudes of magistrates and District Judges, relayed by defence solicitors and barristers, evince inconsistency and unpreparedness by sentencers to consider the defendant's disability or mental health problems as mitigating culpability. In some cases, without paying regard to the probation reports that were produced. Henry's solicitor corroborated this view. Where 'the probation report' gives evidence of 'a mitigating factor where someone has pleaded guilty', and it states that the autistic defendant is '"not a person who views the world in the same way as we do"', the magistrates, nevertheless 'will have judged them by our standards but you know his view of the world is completely different' (Mr McKinnery, Interview). Here, the defence solicitor's account moves beyond the relevance of a condition like autism to culpability, and acknowledged different norms of behaviour which highlight the 'sensibilities' of the defendant.

In the court observations, defence solicitors and barristers placed greater emphasis on these personal 'sensibilities' of the defendant in making their case for mitigation to avoid the impact of a custodial sentence, rather than focusing on its relevance to culpability. For example, when Miles returned to court to be sentenced after he had re-offended, his barrister 'Mr Parkinson' relayed how Miles' psychiatrist had set out 'the deleterious effects' of a short immediate custodial sentence, submitting that this 'may lead to the occurrence of further offences'. Thus, in court, he recommended that the judge utilise a 'firestorm' effect of putting a suspended custodial sentence in place, rather than immediate custody, in order to prevent Miles from re-offending (Court Observation). He explained to the judge that Miles' 'Asperger Syndrome means the "firestorm" is useless unless there is a temporal aspect' of a suspended sentence because, although Miles 'sympathises with' the victims 'in the images', unless there is an immediate response to downloading the images, he just 'looks at images and then feels guilty' (Mr Parkinson, Court Observation). The defence barrister's speech in mitigation emphasised that Miles was 'aware of those difficulties and is coming to realise that he needs to deal with those difficulties' but that their expert witness, Dr Toale, had said in their report that 'the lack of good psychiatric support has been part of the downfall' (*op cit.*).

The next main point in his barrister's speech in mitigation focused upon the probation and community support that Miles had received following his earlier offending. When Miles was discharged from a section 3 Order in June 2014, 'despite the good work he was doing, this rendered him isolated and his computer became his life … [and] he only had a low level of support from the probation service' (Mr Parkinson, Court Observation). His barrister argued that the 'situation [had] now changed' as he was 'undertaking privately funded support to deal with these difficulties' which involved writing 'person-centred essays that deal with the effects of downloading of images' and was 'continuing to deal with and to face problems with empathy' (ibid). What emerges here is that the impact that the defendant's autism had on personal mitigation depended on the quality of the expert witness reports and pre-sentence reports made by the probation service. This brings us back to Shapland's concern about consistency among magistrates and the judiciary in finding information about offender mitigation. A lack of consistency in obtaining such information for defendants with a known diagnosis of autism makes it paramount to have a diligent defence counsel who is capable of accessing good quality expert evidence.

In making his speech in mitigation at the Magistrates' Court, Robert's solicitor, Mr Morecombe, took a highly paternalistic approach in referring to Robert's autism:

> My client's long-suffering mother expresses grave concern for his well-being and hers. … [He] has one conviction for violence against the mother who is very forgiving in the past and let the prosecution pass. This is the first time she has wisely stood her ground so my client accepts that he was abusive and violent to her. He does not fully appreciate the effect of his behaviour on his mother. For all of his life, he has always had her support but he is no longer a small child [who can] have tantrums. He requires a great deal of care but he probably does not help himself because he does not take his medication. So, the doctors have stopped prescribing it. The probation service can perhaps impress upon him to take medication (Court Observation).

There is a clear attribution of Robert's offending behaviour to his autism but Mr Morecombe's argument was not structured around the underlying unmet mental health needs and the absence of social care support to enable him to live more independently without the intensive care and support of his mother.

The social model of disability would prove helpful in developing a coherent principle of equality of impact for disabled defendants, especially if disability (including autism) and mental illness are considered in guidelines such as the *Overarching Principles* through this lens. Instead, at present, we can see the current inclusion of disability in the list of mitigating factors, which impact on culpability as representing the 'impairment' branch of the distinction. For autistic defendants, this relates to the discussion in the 'psy' disciplines on the link between the committal of an alleged offence and the symptomatology of autism. However, the impairment branch of the distinction also requires sentencers to be alert to 'the degree of "sensibility" of the individual offender' and how the individual experiential aspect of their condition impacts on them because of the harms which are likely to result from incarceration.

These factors must be squarely and purposively considered by sentencers and determined more explicitly in the *Overarching Principles*. The disablement branch of the social model's distinction would also require a direct evaluation of the structural factors impacting on the disadvantage or restriction of activity, caused by the failure to take account of impairment. Akin to Ashworth's example of the 'demonstrably greater negative impact on women' (see above). For example, the failure of local authorities to support the needs of autistic adults in the community or the greater risk to longer-term institutionalisation because of delayed discharge from a court-ordered Hospital Order under the Mental Health Act 1983. Embedding the consideration of disability as a mitigating factor in the underlying principle of equality of impact, and not just culpability, would assist the courts in doing justice to difference for disabled defendants, including autistic defendants. Developing more detailed guidance on the provision of information to sentencers on personal mitigation related to the defendant's disability, which integrates the social model and an Equality rights-based approach, would be a positive step forward. Ensuring this is directly related to a revised set of *Overarching Principles* would also improve consistency in considering disability in mitigation, and would be transformative to the treatment and decision-making process about disabled defendants at sentencing.

2. Dividing Practices in Case Disposal: Conviction and Sentence

Drawing on Foucault, Seddon focuses on the 'dividing practices' that channel individuals into prisons, rather than on the field of 'mentally disordered offenders' as a whole. This section analyses the technologies and programmes of governance applied in the dispositive decisions at sentencing for the cohort of autistic defendants included in the case studies.[2] Whilst the range of options available at sentencing are determined in part by 'the offence and the characteristics of the offender', the 'sentencer has a fairly wide range of possibilities in disposing of the case' (Sprack, 2012: 394), subject to the legislative framework that was laid down

[2] It should be noted that none of the seven defendants in the cohort who were convicted were given an absolute or conditional discharge. Ollie was the only defendant who was given a fine and is not discussed further in this section. The fine was deducted from his disability-related benefits, Employment Support Allowance and Disability Living Allowance, of which he was in receipt.

by the CJA 2003 at the time these cases went to court, and now set out in the Sentencing Act 2020.

A. Actual or Suspended Sentence

In determining whether to impose a community (see Section 2B below) or custodial sentence, the Sentencing Code, and previously the CJA 2003, set out the criteria which the sentencer must consider in order to establish if the offender has crossed the threshold for a custodial sentence. Under section 230(2), previously section 152(2) of the CJA 2003, the threshold is reached if the court is of the opinion that 'the offence, or the combination of the offence and one or more offences associated with it, was so serious that neither a fine alone nor a community sentence can be justified for the offence'. If the court decides on custody, that sentence should be for the shortest term 'commensurate with the seriousness of the offence' (Sentencing Act 2020, s 231). Nothing in subsection 230(2) prevents the court from passing a custodial sentence on the offender if the offender fails to express willingness to comply with a requirement 'which the court proposes to include in a community order, but which may be included only if the offender expresses willingness to comply with it (CJA 2003, s 230(4); previously s 152 (3)(a)). Subsection 230(5) of the Sentencing Code also gives the court power to deal with an offender who does not express willingness to comply with a number of other requirements, in schedules to the Sentencing Act, including the amended drug rehabilitation requirement.

The seriousness of the offence is one factor in determining whether a custodial or community sentence is passed. The test for assessing seriousness is included section 63 of the Sentencing Code (previously CJA 2003, s 143(1)), whereby the court must consider 'the offender's culpability in committing the offence and any harm which the offence caused, was intended to cause or might foreseeably have caused'. In forming an opinion on whether the court can justify the passing of a custodial sentence, the court is obligated, if the offender is aged 18 or over, to 'obtain and consider a pre-sentence report' (formerly CJA 2003, s 156) before forming the opinion 'unless, in the circumstances of the case, it considers that it is unnecessary to obtain' such a report (Sentencing Act 2020, s 30(2)). Under section 232 of the Sentencing Code, where the offender is or appears to have a mental disorder, the court must 'obtain and consider a medical report unless, in the circumstances of the case, it considers that it is unnecessary to obtain a medical report'. In making the latter deliberations, before passing the sentence, the court must consider 'any information before it which relates to the offender's mental condition (whether given in a medical report, a pre-sentence report or otherwise)' and 'the likely effect of such a sentence on that condition and on any treatment which may be available for it' (Sentencing Act 2020, s 232(3); formerly of CJA 2003, s 157(3)).

None of the defendants in this cohort received an immediate custodial sentence, though it was considered in Robert and Miles' cases. Miles and Robert were both given suspended sentences with Suspended Sentence Orders during their 'supervision period'. The power of the court to suspend certain sentences of imprisonment for persons aged 21 or over[3] is legislated for in section 277 of the Sentencing Act 2020 (previously CJA 2003, s 189). At the same time as exercising its power to suspend a sentence, the court may impose specific additional requirements by a Suspended Sentence Order with which the offender must comply during 'the supervision period'. These requirements are listed in section 286 of the Sentencing Act (formerly CJA 2003, s 190).

In Robert's case, the lead magistrate, the chairman, considered it to be a threat: 'We could say we have had enough and send you to prison today to make you accept and apologise. Yes?!' (Court Observation). Robert, at the time of sentencing for the assault on his mother, was already on a suspended sentence 'because he was involved in cultivating cannabis plants in his flat … [but] he rarely lived in the flat as he was abused by local thugs' (Mr Morecombe, Solicitor, Court Observation). The Court Clerk, therefore, advised the three magistrates, as the breach was 'dissimilar and less serious', than the previous offence, under Sentencing Council Guidelines at the time, it was 'unjust to activate the suspended sentence in this case' (Court Observation). Consequently, instead of activating his existing suspended sentence or imposing a new term of custody, the magistrates decided to extend his 'suspended sentenced for 18 months', telling him: '[y]ou are not going to prison today' (Court Observation). They also gave him an 18-month community order but decided not to give him a restraint requirement to stay away from his mother's house, as they thought it would 'aggravate' the situation with her.

Whilst the chairman said they were 'not going to go through' the detail of the community order, after passing the sentence this lead magistrate spoke directly to Robert: 'I am not being rude but you can read and write can't you? Do you understand everything today?' (Magistrate, Court Observation) In the context of telling his mother that she did not 'deserve' any more abuse, the magistrate admonished Robert further:

> you are going to end up in prison or a mental institution … [Robert], before you leave today you can learn to stand up straight. You don't need to lean on anything. We don't need to see you in court again and be nice to your mother (Court Observation).

This excerpt reflects what Beresford et al describe as a 'deficit deviant model' (2010) in professionals' understanding of disability. The Magistrate perceived Robert's autism as biologically determined without any perception of the social barriers leading to disablement, including the lack of available social care support to minimise his reliance on Nicola, his mother.

[3] The availability of suspended sentence orders for offenders under 21 is covered by section 264 of the Sentencing Act 2020.

When Miles was sentenced the second time for downloading indecent images of children, his solicitor was 'fairly certain' that Miles 'would have ended up getting a custodial sentence' if they had not delayed the entry of plea (see above) to get expert witness reports, 'because the sentencing court wouldn't have been aware of his special needs' (Mr Griffiths, Interview). The due diligence on the part of this defence solicitor made the difference between 'the judgement' of 'possibly, a suspended sentence and a community order'. Mr Griffiths believed that:

> there is no doubt he did cross the custody threshold, but the judge again, quite rightly … felt that a community order was better because it would give a longer period of supervision (ibid).

In court, the judge who sentenced Miles, for the second set of offences of downloading indecent images of children, stated that his offending took him to the 'bottom range of the guidance for a period of 18 months in custody' but recognised that 'unfortunately, the young man before him … clearly falls in the Asperger range of the autism spectrum and has difficulties' (Court Observation). It was his 'judgement that he would receive full support and guidance in the community … it was unlikely that he would get this support in prison because he would get a shorter sentence due to his vulnerabilities' (Judge, Court Observation). Therefore, the judge in this case imposed a community order and extended his SOPO and Community Order. The latter included a requirement for him to undergo psychiatric support from a specialist, in the town where he was studying at university.

In 2014, however, Miles reoffended again. He was sentenced in the Crown Court to a 12-month sentence, which was suspended for two years. The judge suspended it 'with understandable hesitation' as he saw the most recent offence as:

> a deliberate and cynical breach which would meet the threshold for incarceration. Against this background, a sentence of prison for 18 months would be justified (District Judge, Court Observation).

The reference to the 'cynical breach' was because of Miles' 'quite deliberate download of software to hide [his] web history' (ibid). The implications were 'that [he knew] the material that [he was] going to download was illegal' (ibid). However, it appeared that the judge was persuaded by the submissions made by Miles' defence barrister described above that the suspended sentence would have a 'furnace effect' and the medical report 'sets out the deleterious effects' of 'a short immediate custodial sentence' and that 'it may lead to the occurrence of further offences' (Mr Parkinson, Court Observation).

Consequently, the judge also imposed 200 hours of unpaid work as a requirement and modified Miles' SOPO, making it indefinite and added a further prohibition not to use any device capable of accessing the internet including, but not limited to, a personal computer, laptop, 'unless internet capability is disabled and unless [he] make[s] the device available to the police when requested' (District Judge, Court Observation). Under this Order, Miles was prohibited until further notice from:

1) using any device capable of accessing the internet unless internet capability has been disabled;
2) from deleting any internet history;
3) from possessing any device capable of accessing the internet unless you disable that device;
4) prohibited from any contact with children under the age of 18, whether inadvertent or unavoidable, without the consent of the child's parent or guardian who [themselves] know about your offending history (ibid).

Speaking directly to Miles, the judge stated that failure to 'fulfil' these requirements and committing 'any offence that breaches the SOPO then the overwhelming likelihood is [he would] serve 12-month[s] in addition to any other sentence given by any other court' (ibid). Thus, when Miles was sentenced for a second and third time for charges of downloading indecent images of children, the respective judges were sympathetic to Miles' vulnerability deriving from his autism, were persuaded that custody would have had a deleterious effect on him, and were reassured by the fact that he was receiving psychiatric care. They saw short prison sentences as failing to facilitate long-term psychiatric treatment. At sentencing, it was evident that the rigour and consistency of the medical reports was a pivotal factor in determining the outcome.

B. Community Sentence

A 'community sentence' consists of or includes a community order or a youth rehabilitation order.[4] For persons over the age of 18 and convicted of an offence, a community order can impose one or more community order requirements in section 206 and Schedule 9 of the Sentencing Act 2020 (previously section 177 of the CJA Act). Such requirements include those relating to unpaid work, a prohibited activity, curfew, residency, mental health treatment, drug rehabilitation and alcohol treatment. Section 204 of the Sentencing Code provides the threshold that a court 'must not make a community order unless it is of the opinion that the offence, or the combination of the offence and one or more offences associated with it, was serious enough to warrant the making of such an order' (see section 148 of the CJA 2003 for the analogous provision). Once it has decided that the offence has passed this threshold, the court has to be of the opinion, under section 208(3) and (5) of the Sentencing Act 2020, that the particular requirement(s) which form part of the community order are 'the most suitable for the offender' and the restrictions on liberty imposed by the order must be 'commensurate with the seriousness of the offence' or the combination of the offences associated with it (analogous to section 148(2)(a) and (b) of the CJA 2003 respectively).

[4] See sections 173 and 174 of the Sentencing Act 2020.

Patrick, Claire and Noah were all given Community Orders. In Patrick's case, the District Judge sentenced him for the racially aggravated assault as a youth court matter and, during the same sentencing proceedings at the youth court, dealt with the theft of copper and damage to a vehicle under sentencing provisions for adult offenders. For the racially aggravated assault, he was given a 12-week Community Order with supervision and a 11pm to 6am curfew requirement for this period under section 177(1)(e) of the CJA 2003. He was also ordered to pay a £150 fine 'not because of what it is worth – you can't put a figure on it – but because it is an appropriate starting point for what [he] did to that man' (District Judge, Court Observation) and a £250 contribution towards prosecution costs. With regards to those offences dealt with in the adult court, Patrick received a 12-month Community Order and was ordered to pay £60. This was to be paid out of his disability living allowance and employment support allowance over a 14-week period. The Community Orders given were commensurate with the offence, however, the underlying logic informing the attitude towards decision-making is revealed in the District Judge's statement to Patrick, in passing his sentence. Here, she told him to 'grow up a bit: take responsibility for yourself and behave better to others' and that if he breached 'his supervision order', he would find her 'in a different mood and lock him up!' This response echoes the attitudes of the judges and magistrates in Robert and Miles' cases cited above. These paternalistic admonishments denoting a simplistic understanding of self-control and reflect the performative aspect of passing sentence, rather than the specific logics applied to the case at hand.

Claire's case reflects how the dividing practices in her local authority and local mental health and learning disability services left her without support because 'there is a gap and [Claire] does not fit into their services' (DC Kim, Court Observation). Indeed, the court proceedings themselves revealed how the criminal law sentencing options were re-purposed to obtain social care support for Claire. In interview, DC Kim, from the IOMS, was quick to say that she did not want Claire to go to prison because of 'how vulnerable' she was. However, they had to 'use "bad"', getting the court to sentence Claire to a community order, 'to do some "good"', to get a mental health requirement for psychological support and a residency requirement (DC Kim, Interview). At Claire's court appearance before her sentencing, DC Kim explained to the judge why an adjournment of the sentencing decision was requested to 'better understand why the defendant does what she does', because the 'forensic psychologist says that her autism is linked to her offending; dealing with this is linked to her treatment' (Court Observation). The District Judge regarded this as 'an unusual situation' in that 'an agency [the police], other than the probation service, are providing assistance' by trying to ascertain 'how and whether that could be combined in Mental Health Services' (Court Observation). Nevertheless, the District Judge was sympathetic and he explained directly, to Claire, that he thought it was:

very important that the court is able to consider some sort of way forward for you rather than just considering a Community Order where you may only see the probation officer for 15 minutes once a week … You don't fall into one box but a little bit in lots of boxes. It seems to me that the court is more aware of what might be possible through this psychologist … so I'm going to adjourn your case … (Court Observation).

This exchange is insightful. As we saw in chapter five, the *raison d'être* for the development of the Autism Act 2009 and accompanying policy was to prevent autistic people, like Claire, '"falling through the gap" between mental health or learning disability support' and increasing the likelihood of 'complex mental health interventions or coming into contact with the CJS' (DOH, 2010c: 26–7). In particular, the umbrella term 'autism' was used to prevent exclusion from such support because of having an IQ >70 (*op cit.*: 10). However, despite Claire's low assessed IQ, the 'learning disability services just didn't want to know' and she failed 'various tests and assessments social services [did] … of her needs' and, therefore, the local social worker found her not to be eligible under the *Fair Access to Care Criteria* (see DOH, 2010f; Offender Manager, Interview). Even though the Autism Act 2009 and accompanying 2010 Autism Statutory Guidance had already been enacted by the time Claire's case went to court and provided guidance for local authorities and the NHS to adjust service delivery 'to include adults with autism' ((DOH, 2010c: 2). Further, at that time, the 'Standard Contract for Mental Health and Learning Disabilities' explicitly required service providers, 'to demonstrate how reasonable adjustments for adults with autism are made' (ibid; see DOH, 2010f). It was because Claire's local authority did not do this that DC Kim, her Offender Manager, had to work closely with the Police and Crime Commissioner to put pressure on senior decision-makers in local social services to put together a funded package of support for her in the Community. The view of these services was that Claire needed to be compelled by the court to be resident in the supported living placement, arranged by her Offender Manager, for it to work. In addition, if a Mental Health Treatment Requirement was ordered for her to have sessions of CBT with a psychologist.

These recommendations were included in Claire's pre-sentence report, after extensive input from DC Kim. At the final sentencing, Claire was before a different District Judge who addressed her directly:

[Claire], other people have been doing lots of work around you to stop you getting into a situation where you are at serious risk of doing harm, not because you mean to but sometimes it's the way you behave. I'm being asked to give you a Community Order for 12-months, this is a special order. Given all the bad things you have had to deal with this is a good opportunity. I don't get invited to make these orders very often. You'll do your bit to make it work won't you?

Claire: 'Yes' (Court Observation).

Thus, for Claire to finally receive funded social care support and mental health intervention, she was subject to a 12-month Community Order. Along with a

12-month Supervision Order, a six-month Mental Health Treatment Requirement to engage with a named psychologist, to undergo Cognitive Behaviour Therapy, and a six-month residency requirement for her to be domiciled at the supported living placement that would be paid for by the Police and Crime Commissioner's budget. Under the Sentencing Guideline, when determining the seriousness of the offence (culpability and harm) of possessing a knife, the court must identify the appropriate starting point. Where the weapon was not used to threaten or cause fear, as in Claire's case, the appropriate starting point is a high-level community order (Sentencing Council, 2008; 2018). The court must then consider the effect of aggravating and mitigating factors, with Mental disorder or learning disability being factors which lower culpability.

On the one hand, the problem-solving approach used in Claire's case seems progressive. The Offender Manager and Police and Crime Commissioner re-purposed the criminal law to achieve a care package that social services had failed to put in place. On the other hand, utilising these criminal justice orders, and attendant requirements, to obtain the social care support and mental health intervention she was already eligible for, flies in the face of the paradigm to which the Autism Statutory Guidance subscribes. This guidance emphasises that 'all health and social care organisations need to understand the principle of least restrictive care – which means identifying a range of interventions and seeking the least restrictive ones for people with autism' (DOH, 2015b: 46). Re-purposing the criminal law in this way, even with the intention to achieve an 'opportunity' for Claire to be better supported, is achieved through mechanisms which are not required to take account of this principle.

Therefore, Claire's preferences – which should have been central to the personalisation model of social care in autism specific policies discussed in chapter five – were not a material consideration. Claire was given a residency requirement which meant that she had to leave her family home to live in a new city in supported living accommodation, procured by her Offender Manager and social services. Conversely, the Autism Statutory Guidance states that people 'should live in their own homes with support to live independently if that is the right model of care for them' (ibid). There was only limited consideration of whether Claire should remain in or near to her family's home:

> She lives with her parents; she wants to leave but the difficulty we're having is that she tells them what they want to hear: 'I don't want to leave'. [So], it's hard to gauge what she actually genuinely wants (DC Kim, Interview).

A seemingly insufficient attempt to attain Claire's preferences in the circumstances of guidance which states that '[b]ehaviour others may find challenging lessens with the right support and individuals benefit from personalised care' (DOH, 2015b: 46). Further, the approach of the judge, although willing to sentence Claire to these measures, also displays 'the lingering precedence given to a narrow, medical view of mental disorder', with a resultant 'focus on biological cure or management of the condition or person' (Clough, 2014: 2). Like the rebukes used for Patrick and Robert, the District Judge perceived the 'diagnosis and classification functioning as ends' (ibid: 3) with 'consequences and limitations stemming from the disability … seen as regrettable but inherent to the condition' (ibid).

In Noah's case, after the jury agreed that the defendant had committed the acts alleged, the judge had to decide whether to give 'a Hospital Order, a supervision order [or] an absolute discharge' (Judge, Court Observation). Following advice from the defence barrister (see below), who explained that Noah had now been given 'an increase from 35 hours' social service support to 67 hours from social services to keep him in as much as possible' (Mr Reilly, Court Observation), the judge gave Noah a two-year Supervision Order. In his case, Noah's social worker was the named person, rather than the probation officer, for the purposes of that Order. His defence barrister emphasised to the judge that, whilst in the past 'there have been unreliable resources allocated to help him and the public', the increase in social service support meant that he would 'live entirely independently' with the additional help of 'the care and fortitude of his father' (Mr Reilly, Court Observation). Like Claire's case, the availability of intensive social care provision and the additional support of his parents were decisive in influencing the decision about the disposal of his case. After making the supervision order, the Judge told Noah 'you don't have to come to court again' and 'the court is pleased to know that Mum and Dad give lots of support to help you. You can go home now' (Court Observation). Indeed, as acknowledged by the presiding judge, that 'quality foundation of love … must be a great burden.' The symbiotic harms of such a 'burden' of intensive support by his parents is discussed below in chapter nine.

C. Hospital Orders under the Mental Health Act 1983

Part III Patients Concerned in Criminal Proceedings or Under Sentence of the Mental Health Act 1983 sets out four Hospital Orders which can be made for 'mentally disordered offenders' by the court at the point of sentencing. First, there is a section 37 order which gives the power to the Crown Court or the Magistrates' Court on conviction, or once they are satisfied that the defendant has committed the act or omission, to order hospital admission or guardianship for up to six months in the first instance. With this order, there is the option to renew for a further six months, and then a year at a time after that. Second, where the court wants to test the appropriateness of a full Hospital Order, a section 38 interim Hospital Order may be made initially for up to 12 weeks. Third, a section 41 order provides for the power of higher courts to restrict discharge from hospital when a section 37 has been used. Finally, the section 45A power of higher courts to direct hospital admission is a 'Hybrid Order' as it is 'a prison sentence together with a requirement for hospital treatment with limitation directions' (Barber et al, 2009: 53). In the eight cases in the cohort for this book, only a section 37 Order and the use of this section, in conjunction with the section 41 Power of the courts to restrict discharge, were either considered or ordered by the courts. The present part of the chapter will, therefore, focus on the use of a section 37 Order for autistic defendants. The use of a section 37 Order was proposed by the CPS but was quickly dismissed by the District Judge in Henry's case. It was also considered by the Judge but ultimately dismissed in Noah's and Miles' cases. William was the only defendant for whom the court made a section 37 Hospital Order but, after some deliberation, the Crown Court judge decided not make an accompanying restriction order under section 41. The court also put in place a SOPO, for seven years, and William was placed immediately in a forensic hospital. At that point, William had already been on remand for nine months. Unlike Claire and Noah's cases, there was no interaction with social services or consideration of social care support for William. Before examining these cases in more detail, it is necessary to analyse the logics which are applied to autistic defendants more generally in the schema of applying section 37 and the Mental Health Act 1983.

Once the defendant is convicted by the Crown Court or has been convicted or found to have committed the act or omission by the Magistrates' Court, the conditions in section 37(2) must be satisfied before a Hospital Order is made. Section 37(2) can be split into four grounds, which the court must be satisfied the offender fulfils, based on medical evidence, to meet the conditions of compulsory detention. First, in the view of two registered mental practitioners, the offender is 'suffering from' a mental disorder. Second, the mental disorder must be of the 'nature or degree which makes it appropriate for him to be detained in a hospital for medical treatment' (section 37(2)(i); emphasis added). Third, there is a requirement that 'appropriate medical treatment is available' (ibid). Fourth, once these prior conditions are met, that it is the opinion of the court that 'the most suitable method of disposing of the case is by means of an order under this section', determining this by 'having regard' to circumstances including the nature of the offence and the character and antecedents of the offender, as well as 'other available methods of dealing with him' (section 37(2)(ii)). It is important to understand how statutory guidance considers autism in relation to these grounds and how the courts applied them in Henry's and William's cases.

Section 1(2) of the 1983 Act defines 'mental disorder' as 'any disorder or disability of the mind'. The Code sets out a qualified and non-exhaustive list of clinically recognised conditions which could fall within the Act's definition of mental disorder; including '[l]earning disabilities' and '[a]utistic spectrum disorders (including Asperger's syndrome)' (DOH, 2015: 26). Notably, amendments made to the 1983 Act, by section 1(2A(a) and (b)) of the Mental Health Act 2007, inserted what is termed the 'learning disability qualification'. This provides a higher threshold for detention and treatment of persons with learning disabilities under the Act than for those with an 'autistic spectrum disorder'. Thus 'a person with a learning disability **shall not** be considered by reason of that disability' to be 'suffering from' a mental disorder or requiring treatment in hospital for a mental disorder unless that disability is associated with their '**abnormally aggressive** or **seriously irresponsible** conduct' (section 1(2A(a) emphasis added).

The 2015 *Mental Health Act 1983: Code of Practice* ('the Code') provides statutory guidance to registered medical practitioners, approved clinicians and mental health professionals to carry out their functions under the Act (ibid). People with learning disabilities or 'autistic spectrum disorders', along with patients concerned with criminal proceeding are given additional special consideration in the Code, elaborating upon the general guidance, suggesting a similar policy approach towards both groups. The *Code of Practice* clarifies that '**abnormally aggressive** or **seriously irresponsible** conduct' must be 'abnormally aggressive', not 'simply aggressive', and lists the relevant factors which must be considered when assessing such behaviour (see DOH, 2015: 208). 'Irresponsible' is best interpreted 'in the sense of liable to cause injury to herself or himself or another, rather than simply being rowdy or disruptive' (Herring, 2010: 556) and the Code stresses that the conduct associated with the person's learning disabilities must be 'seriously irresponsible', setting out relevant factors for this criterion (DOH, 2015: 22). Further, unless such conduct is present, this learning disability qualification also applies so that they may not be detained for treatment or made subject to guardianship or a community treatment order (CTO) (ibid). The intention behind the qualification was 'probably that such patients should be managed for preference under the Mental Capacity Act' via deprivation of Liberty Safeguards (Barber et al 2009: 23–4). However, the 2015 Code states that this so-called 'learning disability qualification' does not 'apply to detention for assessment under section 2 of the Act'.

Significantly, for our purposes, an analogous qualification 'does not apply to autistic spectrum disorders (including Asperger's syndrome)' (DOH, 2015: 28). This means, therefore, that even if the person's autism is not associated with abnormally aggressive or seriously irresponsible behaviour, it is 'possible for someone with an autistic spectrum disorder to meet the criteria for compulsory measures under the Act without having any other form of mental disorder' (ibid). The drafting here is problematic as the Code goes on to qualify it, saying that whilst 'experience suggests that this is likely to be **necessary only very rarely**, the possibility should never automatically be discounted' (ibid), even though the Code later emphasises that autism is *not* a mental illness and is 'developmental in nature' (DOH, 2015: 28; 210). Thus, despite the caveat in the guidance that the use of compulsory measures for autistic people will 'be necessary only very rarely', this group do not need to have met the threshold of 'abnormally aggressive or seriously irresponsible' behaviour before a Hospital Order is used (ibid). This caveat is irrelevant in terms of the legal test to determine mental disorder: autistic spectrum disorder is one of the clinically recognised conditions which could fall within the Act's definition (see DOH, 2015: 209).

However, the caveat does suggest a policy attempt to differentiate this clinically recognised condition without going so far as to introduce an autism qualification to raise the threshold for this group. The rationality of policymakers drafting the

Code is to avoid compulsory hospitalisation for people with learning disabilities unless a higher threshold can be met. Conversely, having a diagnosis of autism takes the person over the threshold of inclusion in the category of mental disorder but the Code attempts to be of more limited application to autistic people. The differentiation of people with 'autistic spectrum disorders' from people with learning disabilities in the application of the 'learning disability qualification', without any explicit justification for differential treatment, makes the policy approach confused. It also sits awkwardly with the discussion of autistic people presenting with behaviour that challenges services in *Think Autism* (DOH, 2014; see chapter five).

Under the second ground of meeting the conditions for a Section 37 Hospital Order, it is 'insufficient simply to show that a person has a mental disorder: the disorder must be such that it cannot be treated in the community, and hospital treatment is required' (Herring, 2010: 558). Although the 'caveat' discussed above does not amount to an analogous 'autism qualification', it could be argued that it acts to emphasise the second ground in subsection 2(i) of section 37 of the Mental Health Act 1983 by focusing on ensuring that the offender's mental disorder 'is of a nature **or** degree which makes it appropriate for him to be detained in a hospital ...' (emphasis added). The discussion in chapter seven showed how the District Judge rejected the prosecution's approach in Henry's case and said the prosecution was not in the public interest. This ultimately led to the case collapsing. However, the prosecution's attempt, at the behest of the police, to advise the court to subject Henry to a section 37 Order as an alternative disposal if he was not convicted appears opportunistic. If the judge had found him unfit to plead and decided to allow the case to proceed as a trial on the facts, a section 37 would only have been available as a disposal option for the judge in these circumstances where there was written or oral evidence of two registered medical practitioners recommending such an order. The prosecution and the police would have known of this evidentiary requirement but had already accepted the defence's expert witness evidence report, without instructing their own report, which said that a Hospital Order was not appropriate for Henry (see above).

Not only did the District Judge reject the prosecution's blithe attempt to argue for this Hospital Order, contrary to the medical evidence that they had approved, he rejected an application of the second ground and the use of the section 37 Order more broadly for autistic defendants. He told the court that 'no doctor would say that [Henry] needs a Hospital Order' and went on to say that '[Henry] suffers from a form of autism and therefore **it can't be right that all people with Aspergers' end up in hospital**' (Case Observation, emphasis added). The District Judge's mentality reflected in this statement is stronger than the caveat contained in the Code that 'compulsory measures' will 'be necessary only very rarely.' Instead, he evinces a rationality which proceeds on the understanding that the compulsory hospitalisation of autistic people is something that should be limited. The normative language in his statement would seem to imply that there is a justification for differentiating autism from other clinical conditions which fall into the Act's definition of mental disorder, and applies something akin to the 'learning disability qualification.'

However, by contrast, this was not the approach taken by the judge to William's case. At sentencing, the Crown Court judge told the court that he shared the view in the report that 'a Hospital Order of Section 37 without a Section 41 restraint' was 'necessary' pending the availability of a forensic hospital place for him (Court Observation). The approach taken was to treat the decision of the court to give a Hospital Order as a matter of public protection because 'although it [was] not the most serious offence of this type', he had 'touched the victim in a sexual manner' and this was 'viewed seriously by the court' (ibid). The judge emphasised that William's 'antecedent history and conduct of the type' meant that William's interests and 'the interests of the public' were 'concurrent' in the judge's decision to give 'a Section 37', and that he was 'detained there [and placed on] the [hospital's] sex offenders programme for people with learning disabilities' (ibid). His statement to the court indicated that the focus of his decision-making was around the public interest, rather than dissecting the second grounds as to whether William's autism was of the 'nature or degree … which makes it appropriate for him to be detained in a hospital for medical treatment'. This implies that he saw the *actus reus* of the offence as evincing that the mental disorder was of a sufficient nature or degree to make it appropriate for William to be detained in hospital.

The meaning of the third ground is that 'appropriate medical treatment is available'. As supplemented by section 145(4) MHA, such 'treatment' means 'treatment the purpose of which is to alleviate, or prevent a worsening of, the disorder or one or more of its symptoms or manifestations'. Herring argues that this condition appears to 'indicate that if no medical treatment is available to the patient, then he cannot be detained under the Act' (2010: 559). He explains that the 'reasoning behind this is that if there is nothing the doctors can do to assist the patient, they should not be required to simply detain him or her, acting as a "warehouse" for the untreatable' (ibid). The Code is more nuanced in its guidance on autistic persons stating that for them compulsory 'treatment in a hospital setting is rarely likely to be helpful' because they may 'be very distressed by even minor changes in routine' and are 'likely to find detention in hospital anxiety provoking' (DOH, 2015b: 209). Instead, sensitive, 'person-centred support in a familiar setting will usually be more helpful' and, wherever possible, 'less restrictive alternative' treatment or support should be found (*op cit.*).

In William's case, the judge took the existence of the hospital's 'sex offenders' programme for people with learning disabilities' as being the appropriate medical treatment for William (Court Observation). Indeed, the judge's statement to the court gives limited focus to the second and third ground of section 37(2). Instead, he concentrated on the specific aspects of the fourth ground, telling William that considering his 'antecedent history and conduct of [this] type seems to me that the interests of the public and of you are concurrent' (Court Observation). Even though the Judge deemed these antecedent offences to be 'minor' sexual assaults, he did not have regard to 'the other available methods of dealing with him'

(Court Observation). There was no consideration of 'less restrictive' community alternatives and whether, under the fourth ground, 'the most suitable method of disposing of the case is by means of an order under this section' (section 37(2)(ii)(b)). Conversely, the Code's specific chapter on autism shows, through evidence-based good practice, 'that most' autistic people's needs can best be met at home or in community settings' (DOH, 2015: 206). Further, it spells out that detention under the Act, where there is no treatment in the community, is 'not a substitute for appropriate commissioning of care' (ibid: 214).

In court, William's defence barrister told the judge that William and his family would 'welcome' the 'disposal' under a Hospital Order (Court Observation). William and his family did think that this was the best option but it was the only option presented to them by the medical practitioners who had given expert witness statements to the court. At the point of sentencing, William had already been on remand in prison for nine months; this was partly due to adjournments whilst the court awaited these reports. In William's words, his experience on remand was 'awful to say the very least' (Written Correspondence) and Alice, his mother saw his time on remand in prison as:

> a complete miscarriage of justice and prison is not the right place nor will it help [William] to address his offending behaviour. He realises what he did and has done in the past is wrong and inappropriate and says that he wants and needs help (Letter Correspondence).

His mother was in her seventies and the terms of his SOPO were a 'restraint on [her] liberty' (District Judge, Court Observation) such that she 'could not cope' to have him back home on bail (Alice, Interview). Alice had repeatedly tried to get social care support for William to live independently but he had always been assessed as not meeting the social care criteria by his local authority (Interview). He was not offered any community sex offenders treatment programme after the committal of any of the offences. It is not surprising, therefore, that when it was presented as a binary option between prison and a Hospital Order, a hospital placement would be deemed the preferred option. There was no consideration of an alternative Community Order with a Mental Health Treatment Requirement. Further, the mentality of the District Judge in this case was contrary to the *Code of Practice*, which recommends the 'least restrictive option' and emphasises the importance of 'maximising independence, and respect and dignity', as cited above (DOH, 2015b: 46).

Restrictions imposed on the patient under the MHA 1984 must be 'proportionate and kept to a minimum needed to meet the purpose and aim of the restriction' (DOH, 2015b: 224). So, it is useful to compare the use of the section 37 Order for William to what actual or suspended sentence he might have received. The Sentencing Council's *Sexual Offences Definitive Guideline* which was in force when William was finally sentenced, the first step for the court is to determine which categories of harm and culpability the offence falls into (2014: 18). There were no category 1 harm factors in William's case. He touched the girl's breast over the top of her bra which means it probably should not have fallen into category 2, 'the touching of naked genitalia or naked breasts' but category 3 as 'factors within categories 1 and 2 were not present' (ibid). His case comes within culpability band B as no factors in category A were present (ibid). In Step 2, 'the court should use the corresponding starting points to reach a sentence within the category range'. Where there is a 'sufficient prospect of rehabilitation', under section 202 of the CJA 2003, a 'proper alternative to a short or moderate length custodial sentence' would be 'a community order with a sex offender treatment programme requirement' (ibid). For category 3 harm in band B culpability, the starting point is a high-level community order, with a category range of a medium-level community order to 26 weeks of custody. The sentencer should then consider the aggravating and mitigating factors.

William's failure to comply with his prior court orders, and the fact that his offence type was similar to his antecedent history, meant that the statutory aggravating factors did apply to him and would have resulted in an upward adjustment of sentence. However, his autism was clearly a relevant mitigating factor amounting to 'mental disorder or learning disability, particularly where linked to the commission of the offence' (*Sentencing Council*, 2014: 11). William was also remorseful and pleaded guilty at the Plea and Case Management Hearing. There was no evidence of 'dangerousness' of the kind which would meet the criteria in chapter five (Part 12) of the CJA 2003 and, therefore, it would not have been appropriate to award an extended sentence. Finally, the court must consider whether to give credit for time spent on bail in accordance with section 240A of the CJA 2003.

When he was finally sentenced, after the extensive delays for adjournment and court listing, William had been on remand for nine months. Even when the aggravating features of William's case are considered, which may have put him at the top end of the Category, and bearing in mind his early guilty plea, it is likely that he would have been sentenced, at most, to 20 weeks of custody. This amounts to over half the time he had already served in custody on remand. This time on bail was not considered by the judge. By 2016, William had been detained in an institution for nearly three years, serving eight months on remand and two years on the Section 37 Order. That is the equivalent of 128 weeks' detention. That length of time, if given as a prison sentence, is one which would be ordered for an offence which meets a category 1 level of harm and band A level of culpability, where, for example, the defendant has planned the forced entry into their victim's home. This is startling post-Winterbourne, and does not appear to meet the *Code of Practice* guidance[5] that the restrictions imposed are 'proportionate and kept to a minimum needed to meet the purpose and aim of the restriction' (DOH, 2015b: 214).

This outcome is unsurprising given the court's peripheral consideration of defendants like William being regarded as disabled citizens with attendant rights. Unfortunately, the Code of Practice embeds this issue. Chapter two of the Code

[5] The 2008 Code, applicable when William was sentenced, is identical on this point.

focuses on human rights, equality and the duty to reduce inequalities. It specifically references the Equality Act 2010 and the UNCRPD and explicates that the 'protected characteristic of disability includes a mental impairment …' (ibid: 31). However, while this material is presented as a preface to the Code it is not paradigmatically central to it or harmonised throughout. Further, Peay argues that the location of 'mentally disordered offenders' in Part III of the 1983 Mental Health Act 'is a logical one, coming as it does after the sections dealing with compulsory admission of civil patients' but has 'the consequence of relegating them to a form of secondary status' (2013: 105). She goes on to reason that this affected the time given to deliberations about this material during the drafting of the MHA 1983 and other reform committees on which she sat, including the Joint Committee on Human Rights. Accordingly, the 'profile of mentally disordered offenders, and the problems they raised' were 'relatively low' on the agenda 'throughout that reform process' (ibid). Even though the Bradley review and the subsequent Liaison and Diversion Agenda has led to a more concerted consideration of this group, they remained peripheral in the statutory provisions of the Equality Act 2010.

Forty years on from the inception of the legislators continue to grapple with these complexities as they work to reform the MHA 1983. The Draft Mental Health Bill 2022 (DOHSC and MOJ), aims to address the inappropriate detention of autistic people and people with learning disabilities whilst trying to guard against the risk that complete removal of powers of these groups to be detained under section 3 of the MHA may actually increase entry to the criminal justice system.[6] This is because the draft Bill 'does not introduce the new "harm-based" detention criterion for those under Part III of the MHA, nor remove autistic people or those with learning disabilities from the definition of "mental disorder" under this Part' (2023: 42). Consequently, the Joint Committee on the Draft Mental Health Bill have recommended that 'the changes in detention criteria should be consistent for individuals under either Part II or Part III of the MHA' (2023: 42). Further, it emphasises, as this book does, that proper 'implementation of community care improvements and stronger safeguards against inappropriate detention will be vital' (2023: 6). Finally, as discussed in chapter five, where autistic adult defendants are at the legal intersection of the category of 'Mentally Disordered Offenders', the statutory coverage of the Autism Act 2009 fails to extend to bodies within the CJS. This also explains the divided practices in the governance of autistic defendants and why their status as disabled citizens tend to be overlooked.

Conclusion

Chapters six, seven and eight have sought to shift the understanding of the governance of autistic adults from macro-level strategies and rationalities to

[6] Consequently, this policy paper emphasises the need to properly implement improvements in community care and stronger safeguards against inappropriate detention (2022: 6).

the micro-level mentalities of governance in the technologies applied to autistic defendants at the different stages of decision-making, as their case moved through the court to their disposal at sentence. We have seen how the combination of professional culture and policy pressures for defendants to make early pleas shifted consideration of the appropriateness of prosecution and determination of culpability from plea to decisions relating to mitigation and the type of sentence given to the defendants in this cohort. Here, the extent to which the defendant's autism was relevant to culpability in deliberations about sentence depended on the quality and availability of expert witness evidence and other information available to the court. 'Dividing practices' emerged in the type of sentence given to the defendant and the nexus between health, social care and criminal justice systems. There was also evidence of shifting epistemologies, with the civil and administrative processes being 're-purposed' (see Spivakovsky, 2014a) so as to 'accommodate the goals of criminal law' and criminal justice decision-makers re-purposing the criminal law to try to 'seek help' for the autistic person and attain social care services. Although the intentions of criminal justice professionals may well demonstrate a 'best interests' approach towards the defendant, there was not a rights-focused approach which placed the person's disability at the forefront of decision-making. In turn, this overlooked equality law protection and led to more invasive governance of autistic defendants and their families through increased net-widening and symbiotic harms for their parents and their wider family. It is the latter we explore next.

9

Governance Through the Family: Collateral Impact and 'Symbiotic Harm' for Defendants' Families

Introduction

In seven out of the eight cases, the autistic adult defendant was supported by one or more family members. The role and experiences of these family members became an important theme in understanding the governance of the defendants. Indeed, there was evidence of 'governing through the family' (Donzelot, 1979). Consequently, the present chapter examines the difficulties encountered by the autistic defendant when negotiating the CJS and how this type of governance had a collateral impact or caused 'symbiotic harm' to the defendant's family. In understanding the governance of autistic defendants through the nature and impact of sentencing, it is also important to analyse the consequences of punishment for third parties. This is a 'part of the powerful impact of deprivation of liberty' on the incarceration of the offender (Ashworth, 2011: 32). The consequential effects of the sentence on third parties emerged through the fieldwork as an important theme in understanding the governance of the defendants in this cohort. However, this was not the only stage in the court process which had deleterious effects on the parents of autistic defendants. Consequences for family members, in parallel to the defendant, arose throughout the criminal process because 'relatives are involved with each stage of the investigation, which in some cases can take years to process from discovery to sentencing' (Condry, 2007: 52). Condry's book *Families Shamed* details how relatives of offenders are embroiled in the 'shaming process' which follows the discovery of a serious crime (2007). She suggests that the families' stigma 'is more than just a shadow of the offender's stigma, and that it has roots in notions of kin contamination and kin culpability' (ibid: 6). The emotional response to the crime itself and the 'shadow of stigma' emerged as only part of the collateral impact upon the parents of autistic defendants in the present research.

Such consequential effects have been conceptualised in the literature variously as 'secondary punishment' (see Mauer and Chesney-Lind, 2002; Comfort, 2008), 'collateral' consequences or effects (Foster and Hagan, 2007; Condry et al, 2016) and, 'symbiotic harms' (Condry and Minson, 2021). Our understanding of the concept of the 'collateral' or consequential effects of the criminal justice process on family members is situated in the etymological origins of the word, with earlier literature utilising its late Middle English meaning 'situated side by side' or 'in parallel' rather than using the more common adjectival meaning of 'collateral' of 'additional but subordinate; secondary'. This connotation is via the medieval Latin *collateralis*, from the prefix *col-* 'together with' plus *lateralis* (from latus, later- 'side') (see OED, 2016; Condry, 2016, unpublished; Condry and Minson, 2021). However, the concept of 'collateral' effects or consequences has recently been critiqued for its lack of precision and sufficiency, along with its association with the description of the secondary effects of punishment on the *offender*, at worst, subordinating and marginalising the families' experiences (Condry and Minson, 2021). Condry and Minson also dismiss the utility of the notion of secondary punishment because family members have not committed an offence and the harms 'are not "punishment" in the legal sense but a punishing experience' (2021). Instead, they posit the concept of 'symbiotic harms' for families of those who have been imprisoned, which encapsulates the 'negative effects that flow both ways through the interdependencies of intimate associations such as kin relationships' (2021). 'Symbiotic harms' is the preferred term because it more fully characterises these harms by encompassing their 'relational, mutual, non-linear, agentic, and heterogeneous properties' (ibid).

Condry and Minson do not consider harms which arise from criminal justice contact more generally but do think that the analysis they propose, in relation to 'symbiotic harm' for families of prisoners, could be extended to the harms linked to arrest, trial, and community sanctions. Building on this, the present research finds the concept of 'symbiotic harms' especially helpful in understanding the effects of governance through the family and impacts that were evident throughout the criminal justice process upon parents of autistic defendants. Such harms were varied in acuteness and did not merely follow imprisonment. Further, the concept aligns well with work on the 'sociology of disablement' which recognises the interdependency of disabled people (Reindal, 1999; see chapter three above and chapter ten below) and reflects the webs of relationships and trust which focus 'on both the receiver and the giver of care within an interdependent relationship' for mothers of disabled offenders (Rogers, 2020: 929).

The concept of symbiotic harm includes relational and agentic dimensions, enabling us to perceive both the complex family relationships between autistic defendants and their kin, and how those relationships are embodied through displays of care and commitment (*cf* Condry and Minson, 2021; Jardine, 2017). Life after discovery for the family of serious offenders has negative consequences on 'women in the middle' (Brody, 2004) because of the considerable caring responsibilities they face around 'dealing with the various stages of the criminal process' (Condry, 2007: 52). In the present research, these caring responsibilities were even more acute for the parents of the autistic defendants. Parents were repeatedly called upon throughout the criminal justice process to share their specialist knowledge about their son and daughter with various professionals who lacked sufficient knowledge of autism. In seven out of the eight cases, the autistic defendant was supported through the court process by one or more family members. The only exception was Claire, whose family never attended court with her (Court Observation; Interview). The 'core' family supporters were mainly either one or both parents of the defendant. Female family members did predominate this 'core' of support but in the cases of Henry, Noah and Miles, both parents were involved at each stage of proceedings but only Noah's father attended his court appearances. In Patrick, William and Robert's cases the defendant's mother was the main supporter; their father having either died or been estranged from the family. Ollie lived with his grandmother and she attended court with him. Henry, Noah, Patrick and William had a wider group of supporters who came to attend court. In the cases of Henry and Patrick, this included their sisters.

In the cases of Henry, William and Patrick, their mother's sister – the defendant's aunt – also attended court with them. Beyond this outer family circle, at the sentencing and trial appearances, William, Robert and Noah also had professional supporters who attended court with the core family members. These 'champions' of the defendant included: former teachers, Independent Mental Health Advocates, autism-specific social workers and retired criminal justice professionals with specialist knowledge of autism. Close friends of the defendant also attended court in the cases of Ollie, Patrick and Henry. Space precludes discussion of the role of this outer circle of support and the impact of proceedings on them. This chapter focuses instead on two factors which produced the significant 'symbiotic harm' for the defendants' parents: Section 1 covers the role of the parent as advocate and primary care-giver, and Section 2 on the responsibilisation of parents for their adult child's behaviour, and the consequential restrictions to their own liberty. The deleterious effects arising from these factors included stress and health problems; a threat or change to their employment, and a restriction upon their lifestyle, such as the need to move home or change their daily routines in order to accommodate the requirements of Community Orders.

1. The Parent as Carer-Advocate

This first factor arose where the state had failed to provide adequate support to the autistic person. Wider literature about parents of 'chronically mentally ill' adults has long characterised them as '*de facto* therapists' (Thompson and Doll, 1982: 379). Parents were charged not only with the role of initiating psychiatric hospitalisations (Horwitz, 1978) but also 'providing aftercare in their attempts to reintegrate the ill member back into the community' (Cook, 1988: 42). When treatment programmes and attempts at reintegration into the community fail repeatedly, the family becomes the 'only advocate willing and committed to help the increasingly chronic patient secure effective services' (ibid; *cf* Eckholm, 1986). Thirty years after these earlier findings on people with mental health problems, the first Autism Strategy found that 'too many' autistic adults are still 'reliant on the care and support of their parents both financially and for practical help' (DOH, 2010a: 2). Consequently, family members of autistic defendants experience 'symbiotic harm' through their role in what Condry and Minson describe as 'agentic actors who make decisions, manage problems, negotiate relationships, and choose to act in particular way' (2021). The revised Autism Statutory Guidance recognised that it is the parents and carers who are left to 'pick up the pieces' when 'people with autism do not have the right preventative support' and they 'spiral into mental health crises' which can result in 'expensive and inappropriate inpatient admissions or even contact with the CJS' (DOH, 2015a: 36). The role of being an advocate for an autistic adult child is an important theme in the qualitative literature (Graetz, 2010; Krauss et al, 2005; Ryan, 2010), which was reviewed in the meta-analysis carried out for the NICE Guideline for Autism (2012). However, NICE's review of evidence found that there was scant qualitative research on the experience that parents had of public services for either themselves, or for their son or daughter, reflecting 'the limited availability of services for adults [with autism]' (ibid).

In the present research, the allied relationship of advocate and care-giver 'left to pick up the pieces', as the defendant moved through the criminal process, resulted from this lack of the 'right preventative support' (DOH, 2015a: 36). Interviews, correspondence and court observations demonstrated the relentless demands of this carer-advocate role. Amanda, Miles' mother, described being cast as a 'pushy parent' and the need for her to 'just step back' so that this 'box they were putting her in' did not impede her ability to be an effective advocate for Miles (Interview) To illustrate this point, Amanda recounted her words to one of the detectives who 'literally had tears in his eyes' when he came to their home to arrest Miles for re-offending:

> I've been the parent/carer [but] I've been dismissed by probation [as a 'pushy mother']; probation have done absolutely nothing; they haven't been trained in autism and have got no idea how to deal with him. We warned them … that would be the case (Amanda, Interview).

The excerpt expresses the constancy of her advice to criminal justice professionals and the tendency to feel ignored even when professional expertise about autism appeared to be inadequate.

The relentlessness of the parents' advocacy role is also reflected in William's description of his mother, Alice, 'work[ing] so hard getting together' people to 'give a character reference' but he was told that 'none of the people' that she had found could give a reference (Letter Correspondence). Alice's letter described that she 'felt so helpless and at a loss to know what to do or who to contact' after visiting William in prison when the court had cancelled his court appearance whilst he was on remand:

> … [William] should not have been put through all that. It seems to me that the system lets [people] down enormously and causes unnecessary worry, anxiety, distress, solitude, isolation … to these very vulnerable people (Letter Correspondence).

William and Alice's correspondence eloquently expresses the 'mutuality' of symbiotic harms families experience; where 'harms can be intensified when families worry about prisoners and this in turn affects their well-being' (Condry and Minson, 2021).

In Robert and Noah's cases, one of their parents was also a witness to the offences with which they were charged. In chapter seven above, we saw the difficulty this created for Robert's mother, Nicola, in deciding whether or not to be a witness for the prosecution as the victim of his assault. She repeatedly described the situation this had left her in as his main carer:

> I don't feel that I have the right support, I feel that I'm the vulnerable adult – I feel the CJS has failed me – I don't want him locked up. I just want programmes that are going to support him, like anger management … [or] a mentor … that will listen that's not part of probation … [but] someone who could support and explain things … (Interview).

The difficulty of her dual position as care-giver and victim was evident in the dialogue in court following Robert's sentence:

> **Defence Solicitor**: [My client's mother] has great regret that he is not able to live at home with her. Nevertheless, she steps in as his carer to assist with his finances, washing and meals but cannot have him live with her at her home. This has led to resentment on my client's behalf whether he appreciates it or not this is part of my client's condition.
>
> **Magistrate** [to Nicola]: I think you are very good but just be careful.
>
> **Nicola** [to Magistrate]: He won't go to the doctor. I am there to support him but I cannot take anymore.
>
> **Magistrate** [to Nicola]: … Any more abuse, can you report it to the police please? Because you don't deserve it (Court Observation).

As a parent-victim, this poignant exchange demonstrates the 'parental proximity' Nicola experienced, being subjected to the 'double bind' of 'responsibilization and marginalization in the care' of her autistic child (Miles et al, 2023). Although utilised previously in matricide cases, 'parental proximity' is useful for the parent-carer victim in such domestic violence cases too, capturing as it does tension for a mother overburdened with the extensive caring responsibilities, and her advocacy role in obtaining services for him, and becoming increasingly isolated by the intensity of this relationship.

Being both carer-advocate *and* witness to the offence placed Nicola and Leo, Noah's father, in very difficult positions both legally and in terms of their ability to support their adult child through the proceedings. In Noah's case, Leo arrived at the scene to pick Noah up and saw some of what had happened. When Noah's first solicitor discovered this, he told Leo that he could not proceed to talk to him, as he may be 'a potential witness for the prosecution', and Leo panicked as he described being 'stuck in this kind of legal nightmare' where no solicitor who is supposed to be advising him 'will talk to [me]' and 'the person they're defending can't give instructions' (Interview).

The deleterious effect of proceedings on the physical and mental health of the parents was a common theme. During the period after Robert's conviction, Nicola had a heart attack and several other acute health problems. The emotional challenges encountered by parents supporting their adult child through the criminal justice process is summed up by Miles' mother, Amanda:

> I think the whole thing is just really desperately sad … the repercussions of something like this … [mean our daughter is] now costing the NHS money because she's on anti-depressants; I'm on anti-depressants … I've had … loads of time off [work]. … So, apart from the emotional fall-out these tragedies bring to families there [is] a cost: … I feel desperate for my son … he didn't … want to be this sex offender which is [what] he's been now labelled for the rest of this life (Interview).

Noah's father also described the emotional impact of waiting 'two-and-a-half years from the incident to [the] court trial' as 'outrageous' because it 'caused a huge amount of stress [for Noah], which in turn caused stress' for them (Interview). In Leo's view, Noah 'would have been better on a supervision order two-and-a-half years ago rather than waiting' until the trial of the facts to be given one (Interview). Like Amanda (Miles' mother), Noah's father, Leo, also explained the impact of the case on his own livelihood. He was a foster carer and Noah lived in their home so Noah 'had to have an enhanced CRB' which could have affected their employability, and although Noah did not have a 'criminal conviction … this [incident] is always going to be on a police database and it appears shocking' (Interview).

In addition to the symbiotic harms of proceedings which filtered through into the parents' health and employment, supporting their adult child through this process led to changes to housing and accommodation. Miles' family felt let down by the lack of specialist provision given by the probation service and social services in their domiciliary local authority (Amanda, Interview). Consequently, they instructed their solicitor to work with the court, police, probation and health service to move all of his support from the local authority where their family home was located, to the local authority where Miles was at university. In order to achieve this shift in provision, she was emphatic with his social worker that the university is 'his permanent address now … he doesn't live with us anymore … I don't want him back … you will have to put him in a hostel, a police station or put him on the street' (ibid). The family even considered moving house to be within Miles' university's local authority, so concerned were they about the mental health provision at their local psychiatric hospital and probation service.

Although living in a different domiciliary local authority to Miles' parents, this was exactly the step taken by Noah's parents, who 'moved house' elsewhere in the country after Noah was arrested, partly, because it was 'difficult' for Noah to live in their home town as 'his bail condition' stated that he 'mustn't go near the [alleged victims] or their road' (Leo, Interview). This made Noah 'scared of going out anywhere' as he was thinking: 'what if I see them in the shop?' (ibid).

Noah's father explained that this meant they 'never allowed [him] to be alone' and one of his parents or carers was always with him, so they were 'in a lockdown situation' which meant they could not 'go out because you might accidentally meet' the alleged victims, so it became 'really difficult living in that situation' (Leo, Interview). Like Miles' experience, this move to a different local authority also had a positive impact on Noah's care and the new local authority was the 'best thing that happened' to them because 'social services and others' were 'phenomenal ... in terms of support' (ibid). The package of social care support increased to '53 hours support a week', an average of 'about 9 hours a day'; which Leo described as 'huge' compared to their original local authority where they had 'nothing like it' (ibid).

As we saw above, the availability of this intensive social care provision informed the decision made by the judge about the disposal of Noah's case. Not all the defendants' parents were present or able to provide this carer-advocate role, but the community order by the courts affected domiciliary arrangements in Claire's case too. Her parents did not attend court or play an active role through the court process but, until her sentencing, she lived with them. Claire's Offender Manager, DC Kim, said this was a dilemma for Claire because although 'she wants to leave them ... she tells them what they want to hear: "I don't want to leave"' but because 'her parents have never really known what's wrong with her' and were 'very proud, well-off people ... that has been difficult' (Interview). The stipulation in Claire's Community Order to move into supported living accommodation in a different local authority would have marked a significant change in Claire's parents' domiciliary arrangements; affecting the regularity with which they would see her. The experiences of Robert, Miles, Claire and Noah's families reflect the 'non-linear' messiness of the symbiotic harms experienced by families, described by Condry and Minson (2021), and borne outside the criminal justice process.

In recognition of the important role that family plays for autistic people, the NICE Guideline, applicable while the case study cohort went to court, recommended that if 'the person with autism wants their family, partner or carer(s) to be involved' professionals should 'encourage this involvement and negotiate between the person with autism and their family, partner or carer(s) about confidentiality and sharing of information on an ongoing basis' (2013: 85). As discussed in chapter five above, this is for professionals who have direct contact with, and make decisions concerning the care of, autistic adults and would have best practice application for those working in the CJS. Importantly, the guideline also recommends that professionals should 'make sure that no services are withdrawn because of involvement of the family, partner or carer(s), unless this has been clearly agreed with ... the person with autism and their family, partner or carer(s)' (ibid). Clearly, these steps were not taken in cases like Claire's, where the criminal law sentencing options were re-purposed to obtain social care support and Miles' Hospital Order was withdrawn (see above). Recent NICE guidance emphasises that health and social care organisations should encourage adult carers to recognise their role and rights as carers and that carers' assessments should be offered to those providing care, including through transition between inpatient mental health and community settings (2020; 2016). Neither guidance, however, mentions the supporting role of family carers of defendants (or victims and witnesses) through the court process. It is troubling that when parents did play an active role as carer-advocate for autistic defendants, they became subject to greater incursions on their own liberty. Further, where parents were unable to offer sustained support, this led to more restrictive deprivations of liberty for the autistic person. It is to this we now turn.

2. Responsibilisation and Governing Through the Family

Early theories which linked unemotional parenting styles with the causes of autism (see Bettelheim, 1967) have been emphatically disproved (see Abrahams and Geschwind, 2008). However, in the realm of public discourse about crime and its control, 'individualistic explanations for crime have held sway, firmly placing responsibility for crime with offenders and their families, while down-playing structural factors (such as material conditions or unemployment) and the complex processes that might lead to crime' (Condry, 2007: 4; Hill and McMahon, 2001). In the 1980s, the New Right blamed the breakdown of the family for the rising crime rates (Abbott and Wallace, 1992). By the 1990s, this discourse was utilised in debates about disorder where families and mothers, in particular, were blamed for the actions of their young sons (Hunter and Nixon, 2001). The Anti-Social Behaviour Act 2003 entrenched the penalisation of parents for their children's behaviour (see Arthur, 2005). New Labour's criminal justice agenda centred on 'the responsibilisation of young people and their families' with a 'focus on "problem families" and a "parenting deficit" as a cause of youth offending' (Condry and Miles, 2012: 243). In the end, this criminalised 'inadequate parenting' (Muncie, 1999) and produced 'an individualised analysis which failed to take account of structural inequalities' (Condry and Miles, 2012: 243). No parenting orders were given to the parents of defendants in this cohort and all were over the age of 18 at the time of sentence. Nevertheless, analogies can be drawn between these measures and the restrictions imposed through Community Sentences placed on the defendant, which led to the responsibilisation of parents for their adult child's behaviour through net-widening. This responsibilisation of parents generally, and mothers specifically, for the conduct and care of their children has been further entrenched by a 'retraction of state welfare burdening women' expected to pick up the slack of diminishing state health and social care services (Condry & Miles, 2012; Bakker, 2007; Miles et al, 2023).

William's case is particularly illustrative here. The effect of the 'draconian' prohibition in the terms of William's SOPO effectively barred him 'from any public transport unless accompanied by an appropriate adult' and that 'must have been his long-suffering mother' (defence barrister, Interview). William's mother, Alice, confirmed this as she recalled how William 'would not tell other people about his offending' due to his 'embarrassment about what he had done', and this meant that he was 'not able to travel anywhere without [her]' (Interview), thus also restricting her own liberty. The symbiotic harm, in terms of the SOPO responsibilised Alice for William's behaviour on public transport. This 'governance through the family' was entrenched by the reliance of the state on William's mother to have him reside with her during bail (see above). When she refused because she 'could not cope with this situation any longer', bail was refused and no other alternative was sought. In the lead up to Noah's trial, Leo and his wife were 'finding it hard' to support Noah as he became 'more and more stressed' about the court appearance [Leo, Interview]. On a trip to see the GP, for example, Noah 'shout[ed] out in the street: "kill all Muslims!"' (Leo, Interview). After the protracted 'two-and-a-half years' of waiting for his case to be listed, so frightened were his parents that an 'incident in the community' like this might increase the likelihood of him being imprisoned, they 'had him sectioned … for the two weeks immediately prior to the court [appearance]; effectively just to keep him safe' (ibid).

Conclusion

These cases show how parents are embroiled in the modes of governance where the state has failed to put in place the appropriate support for the defendant, whether provided by social care, criminal justice professionals or mental health teams. These approaches also, inadvertently, led to more restrictive deprivation of liberty for the autistic defendant within the community. Their rights as disabled citizens were not a focal point in decision-making. Instead, a more paternalistic set of strategies were employed to manage behaviour due to a distrust of the CJS achieving the 'right' outcome. Many autistic defendants may not be in contact with parents; they may be deceased or unable take on the role of carer-advocate (see Bates and Tully, 2022). However, the case studies show the important role that parents of autistic adults can play in filling the gaps in local authority social care support, and the limited autism-specific knowledge amongst criminal justice practitioners. Indeed, when they are present, parents appear to plug a significant gap when social care services have failed, and provide an intense resource of support throughout the court process. The parents' carer-advocate role increased the deleterious effects of the 'physical and emotional labours of parenting' (Holt, 2009). Furthermore, assisting their child in the CJS as their carer-advocate resulted in increased stress and disruption to employment. Somewhat ironically, the more central the role that parents play in supporting their autistic adult child, the more likely it is that punitive techniques of governance are deployed to 'responsibilise' parents in the management of their child's behaviour. The experiences of families are not only the by-product of the criminal justice process but, if society is to claim to be just, it is important to address the inequities they experience in their own right (Condry et al, 2016).

Not only do these techniques fail to take account of structural inequalities, like those which directly criminalise 'inadequate parenting' (Muncie, 1999; Condry and Miles, 2012), they infantilise the defendant and fail to recognise their rights to live independently and be included in the community under the Care Act 2014 (see below) and Article 19 of the UNCRPD. They also ignore the duty and power of local authorities to meet a carer's needs for support under the Care Act 2014 (see below).

PART IV

'The Creation of Other Possible Ways of Living'

10

Conclusion: The Normative Case for Disabling Criminal Justice

Introduction

This book has investigated how autistic adult defendants are governed through English criminal justice policy and criminal court practice. The research has connected analysis of the more abstract technologies and broader political rationalities of governance, in Parts I and II of the book, with everyday practices and techniques of governance in the collection of case studies in Part III. Analysis of the broader rationalities of government in chapter four revealed the dominance of vulnerability: a conceptualisation, it is argued, which masks the status of autistic people, and those with mental health ill health and learning disabilities, as disabled citizens with rights. Chapter five explored the specific programmes of government developed through the Autism Act 2009 and related policy and the extent to which its programmes apply to autistic people who enter the CJS. It found that the imperative to get the Autism Act 2009 passed in Parliament before the uncertainty of the looming 2010 election, along with a reticent MOJ, meant that its statutory ambit did not cover public bodies within the CJS in a way which reflected the purview of the Equality Act 2010.

The cohort of case studies discussed in chapters six to nine incorporated 'the real' into this book's analysis. Chapter six illuminated the importance of the pre-trial process. Chapters seven and eight moved from an analysis of consideration of autism in dispositive pre-trial decisions through to mitigation and sentencing, demonstrating a failure of agencies to adapt techniques of governance to consider the defendant's autism and conceptualise them in terms of the protected characteristic of disability and the social model. Instead, the discussion of the defendant in court showed the dominance of a functionalist (*cf* Parsons, 1951) conceptualisation of their autism. Such an approach, focusing on bodily normality and abnormality, 'foregrounds the ways in which disorder and deficiency cause a functional limitation or incapacity on the part of the individual' (Dowse et al, 2009: 35). The case studies also revealed a reluctance of criminal justice decision-makers to use strategies of diversion early in the criminal justice process, shifting consideration and differential disposal to the mitigation and sentencing stages of the court process (see chapters seven and eight). Chapter nine examined the symbiotic harm to the autistic defendant's family, arising from their responsibilisation for the defendant and attendant issues arising out of the barriers faced by the autistic defendant negotiating the CJS. This is in direct contrast to the contemporaneous statutory developments in the Care Act 2014. Section 1(A) of the present chapter, therefore, looks at the relationship between adult social care and criminal justice and its relevance to the changing epistemologies for criminology and the urgent need for a more robust disability perspective within our discipline.

The present research found that a significant barrier to autistic defendants being considered as 'disabled' under the Equality Act 2010 is the dominant rationality of vulnerability. Section 1(B) argues that the critique of this rationality assists in 'the creation of other possible ways of living' (*cf* Foucault, 1984; O'Malley et al, 1997: 506–7). Section 2 looks at the normative case for reimagining autistic defendants through the social model of disability.

1. Dividing Practices Applied to Autistic Defendants

A. The Relationship between Social Care and Criminal Justice

Chapter seven discussed how the 'guilty plea culture' led to criminal justice decision-makers justifying their decision to pursue the prosecution of the case to 'get help' for the individual. Yet in parallel to this strategy of government, in the cases of Noah, Miles, William, Ollie, Robert and Claire, family members and supporting professionals reported repeated failed attempts to get appropriate adult social care support for these defendants prior to the offending or throughout the criminal justice process. Chapter eight provided evidence of shifting epistemologies in dispositive decision-making at sentencing, with the civil and administrative processes being 're-purposed' so as to 'accommodate the goals of criminal law' (Spivakovsky, 2014a), and criminal justice decision-makers re-purposing the criminal law to try to 'seek help' for the autistic person and secure social care services. These are examples of the CJS stepping in to fill gaps left by the welfare state and local authority care provision. This is in direct contrast to statutory developments in adult social care law over the last decade. The Coalition government expressly implemented the Care Act 2014 to make:

> the most substantial reform of the care and support system in England for over 65 years, enshrining individual rights and clarifying the roles and responsibilities of local authorities and other partners (Norman Lamb MP, HC Deb 23 October 2014, Vol: 586, c80WH).

This Act synthesised the disparate pieces of legislation and statutory guidance which had proliferated in relation to the regulation of adult social care law. Although many of its duties did not come into force until 1 April 2016, after many of the cases in this cohort went through the courts, the previous statutory provision did place a duty on local authorities such that 'once a person has been identified [by them] as having an eligible need, councils should take steps to ensure that those needs are met, regardless of the person's ability to contribute to the cost of these services' (section 29 of the National Assistance Act 1948 and LAC(93)10; section 2 of the Chronically Sick and Disabled Persons Act 1970). Further, *Prioritising need in the context of Putting People First* was the statutory guidance on eligibility criteria for adult social care, when the cohort of case studies in this research were heard in courts, and reinforced this statutory duty at that time (DOH, 2010f: 25).

Section 13 of the Care Act now sets out the regulatory framework to assess the eligibility of care and support needs arising from or relating to a physical or mental impairment or illness. The Care and Support (Eligibility Criteria) Regulations 2015 ('The Regulations') and the accompanying DOH Statutory Guidance provide the detail of the eligibility criteria. The Regulations clearly state that adults who need care and support meet the eligibility criteria under the Care Act 2014 if:

(a) the adult's needs arise from or are related to a physical or mental impairment or illness;
(b) as a result of the adult's needs the adult is unable to achieve two or more of the outcomes specified in paragraph (2) (section 2(1)).

For the purposes of this section, such 'mental impairment' comprises autistic adults (DOH, 2015a). Importantly, the outcomes specified in section 2(2) include developing and maintaining family or other personal relationships, accessing and engaging in work, training, education or volunteering and making use of necessary facilities or services in the local community including public transport, and recreational facilities or services (DOH, 2015a).

These outcomes are not hierarchical and local authorities cannot give priority to any one outcome; nor are they allowed to confine themselves to only providing care and support to people who are unable to achieve one specified outcome, such as managing personal hygiene (section 2(2)(a)). The *Revised Autism Statutory Guidance* explicates the relevance of the Care Act 2014 with regards to adults with care and support needs arising from their autism (DOH, 2015b: 36). Section 2 of the Act places a duty on local authorities to 'provide or arrange preventative services for people within their communities' (DOH, 2015b: 36). Local authorities, in discharging their duties on prevention, should 'ensure they are considering the needs of their local adult population who have autism, including those who do not meet the eligibility threshold for care and support' (ibid). Under the Care Act 2014, 'prevention' or 'preventative' support covers 'wide-scale whole-population' public health measures to more 'targeted, individual interventions aimed at improving skills or functioning for one person' or 'the impact of caring on a carer's health and wellbeing' (ibid). This objective of lessening the impact of caring on a carer's health and wellbeing is important in light of the 'symbiotic harm' on parents of the autistic defendants recorded in chapters seven, eight and nine. Further, in considering how to give effect to their responsibilities, the *Revised Statutory Guidance* stated that 'local authorities should consider the range of options available, and how those different approaches could support the needs of people with autism' (ibid). However, for defendants in the present cohort such cognisance and preventative intervention, by their local authority, was largely absent despite these statutory requirements.

Even under the statutory regime which pre-dated the Care Act 2014, local authorities were already 'required to assess people who are about to be discharged from hospital and may need community care services under the delayed discharges legislation' (ibid: 20). The DOH Guidance also set out the pragmatic approach of the Courts to the meaning of a person who 'may need community care services'. The case of *R (on the application of B) v Camden LBC and Camden and Islington Mental Health and Social Care Trust* [2005] 1366 (Admin) concerned a 'detained patient whose conditional discharge had been deferred until suitable hostel accommodation could be found'. It was held that 'the words "a person … may be in need of such services" refer to a person who may be in need at the time, or who may be about to be in need' (DOH, 2010: 20). The guidance elucidates that 'a prisoner who will not be given parole until suitable care arrangements are in place' would also be in a similar position.

Despite this ruling, as the *Care and Support Statutory Guidance* highlights, 'in the past, the responsibilities for meeting the needs of prisoners have been unclear, and this has led to confusion between local authorities, prisons and other organisations' (DOH, 2016a: para 17: 1). So, section 76 of the 2014 Care Act deals specifically with prisoners and 'the responsibilities for provision of care and support for adult prisoners and people residing in approved premises'[1] (LGA, 2014: 9). Chapter seventeen of the aforementioned guidance, issued under the Act, is dedicated to the application of the Act to prisons, approved premises and bail accommodation and emphasises that '[a]ccess to good integrated health and care support will be particularly important for' prisoners and that they should have access to the 'same level of care and support as the rest of the population' (DOH, 2016a, para: 17.2). Thus, under section 76 of the Act, where 'it appears that adults in prison or approved premises have needs for care and support, they should have their needs assessed by local authorities and where they meet eligibility criteria, have services provided by the local authority in question' (LGA, 2014: 9). The section makes it clear that most 'duties on councils under the act – including [providing] information and advice and preventive services …' apply to prisoners (Donovan, 2015) and the 'threshold for the provision of care and support does not change in custodial settings' (DOH, 2016a: para 17.23). From April 2015, 'all local authorities with a prison in their area received an additional non-ringfenced funding allocation to support these new responsibilities' (Anderson/ADASS, 2015). Importantly, for the purpose of cases like that of William discussed above, the *Care and Support Statutory Guidance* states that under section 76, people bailed to a particular address in

[1] Approved premises are 'Premises approved as accommodation under Section 13 of the Offender Management Act 2007 for the supervision and rehabilitation of offenders, and for people on bail' (ibid).

criminal proceedings are, like those in prison or approved premises, 'treated for the purposes of the Care Act as ordinarily resident in the local authority where they are required to reside and the provisions in the Care Act apply accordingly' (DOH, 2016: para 17: 3). Had this been properly applied to his case, William may not have spent nine months in custody.

When someone arrives in prison or approved premises, the prison or approved premises 'should inform local authorities if they believe that person has care and support needs' and where 'a local authority is made aware that an adult in a custodial setting may have care and support needs, they must carry out an assessment as they would for someone in the community' (DOH, 2016: 325). In cases like William's, the transparency of the *Care and Support Statutory Guidance* in this area could transform the care they receive as it stipulates that 'people in a custodial setting have a right to self-refer for an assessment' and local authorities 'should work with the managers of the custodial setting to consider how to facilitate and respond to self-referrals' (ibid).

However, despite these positive changes, according to the Association of Directors of Adult Social Services (ADASS), implementation of Care Act provisions for councils to assess and respond to the social care needs of prisoners had a 'slow start' (Anderson/ADASS, 2015). Of 59 local authorities, only 33 responded to the ADASS survey; providing data for 79 of the 115 prisons in England. These authorities received 542 referrals from prisons during the first three months of the Act's implementation and in 60 prisons, only 10 referrals were generated; with even fewer, five or less, in 41 of the prisons. The ADASS survey revealed that only two referrals were made for prisoners with an autistic spectrum condition. Representing 0.4 per cent of the total number of referrals, there was 'under identification of such individuals' and this evidenced, therefore, that identification of prisoners with 'autistic spectrum condition is lower than one would reasonably expect within this population' and that they are 'often not recognised as having specific needs within the prison system' (Anderson/ADASS, 2015: 3; 10). Robinson et al explored the early arrangements put in place following the Care Act for prisoners on release through a national survey of local authorities, undertaken in 2016 (2022). Although they found provision for those already known to local authorities generally worked well, the surveys, with 88 of 158 local authorities, revealed that for those individuals who were not already known to them, there were difficulties with the identification of cases, with a reliance on referrals from other agencies, problems with care planning and co-ordination with other agencies and difficulties in sharing assessments and information between local authorities (2022). Indeed, many local authorities were 'still developing care and support arrangements for people discharged from custody' Robinson et al (2022: 998).

The *2021–26 Autism Strategy* commits to building the 'right support in the community and supporting people in inpatient' settings by improving the suitability and availability of housing support and social care through 'increasing the provision of supported housing, enabling more people to access adaptations to their homes and reforming the social care system so it is fit for purpose' (DOHSC & DfE, 2021a: 31). It also emphasises that the government will drive better access to health and social care services for those in 'contact with the criminal and youth justice systems, including the support they may need as they leave custody' (DOHSC & DfE, 2021a: 36). Time will tell whether this is realised in practice. There is growing literature on provision of social care for older prisoners in incarceration and following release from prison (Lee et al, 2019; Ridley, 2022; Robinson et al, 2022; Stewart, 2020; 2022; Walton et al, 2023). Certainly, more longitudinal research is needed on working aged disabled defendants, including autistic defendants, to track the use of social care support earlier on in the criminal justice process, effectiveness of interventions in prison, provision on release into the community (see Tucker et al, 2019) and implications for their governance.

Conceptualising the person's status as a citizen with a disability, with the attendant equality law protection and rights to social care and support, will be an important step towards closing this lacuna in implementation. Understanding the shifting epistemologies between health, social care and criminal justice will become even more important. Crucially, that the 'principle of equivalence of care forms the basis of the policy intent for the Act' and its statutory guidance guarantees that 'those in need of care and support achieve the outcomes that matter to them, and that will support them to live as independently as possible at the end of their detention' (DOH, 2016: 322). What is striking is that the *Care and Support Statutory Guidance* goes further than this, adding that not only will this principle be necessary in ensuring that individual needs are met but that 'this will contribute to the effectiveness of rehabilitation and improve community safety' (ibid).

Although many positives may flow from such an approach, it will become all the more pertinent for criminologists to be alert to the re-purposing of social care to achieve criminal justice goals. What is writ large in the case studies analysed in chapters six to eight is that the individual experiences of impairment and social disadvantage are powerfully amplified when they come into contact with exclusionary techniques of governance at the intersection between social care, health and criminal justice. The issue of interconnecting pathways – criminal justice, clinical and adult social care – along with the diversionary agenda for adult offenders with mental health problems and learning disabilities, present clears challenges to the epistemological framework within which criminology has developed, making the need for the disability perspective explored throughout this book especially pertinent. Undoubtedly, there is a tension between failure of adequate access to timely and high-quality social care in the community for working age disabled people, this resulting in, therefore, them falling between the gaps of public services and then some of them ending up in the criminal justice system on the one hand. On the other, relying on the criminal courts to secure social care provision where local authorities have failed, as in the cases of Claire and Noah, and social care being re-purposed to achieve criminal justice aims is concerning. Steele's analysis enables us to better perceive these tensions and epistemological challenges through her nuancing of the net-widening critique (see Cohen, 1985) by explicating the:

> continuous control dispersed across spaces and mediated by different institutions as 'care', 'punishment', and 'protection' and, ultimately, have shown that on a larger scale criminalized people designated as disabled are exposed to an ongoing continuum of practices of detention, intervention, and surveillance across material and legal spaces because the possibility for control rests in the carceral space of their body by reason of medico-legal designation as disabled (2017: 340).

She suggests that 'it is not so much that the "net" is enlarged' expanding spaces of control, but 'rather that disabled bodies make space punitive by stretching the net as they move through space because of the control that attaches to their bodies … by reason of legal orders', for example, through guardianship and civil mental health orders (2017: 341). Chapter four drew attention to problems with broader rationales and strategies of governance of disabled citizens; this may further challenge criminology's existing epistemological boundaries. It is to this issue that we now turn.

B. Strategies of Governance in National Policy: Vulnerability not Disability

Chapter four analysed findings from the policy texts relating to Liaison and Diversion, along with the data gathered in the research interviews. This material evinced the attraction of using the concept of vulnerability. In developing criminal justice and clinical governance strategies for policymaking around offenders with mental health problems and learning disabilities, it is possible to benefit from the expansive and flexible nature of the concept. There is an important divergence between the conceptualisation of the groups as vulnerable versus being disabled. The etymological origin of vulnerability derives from *vulner/vulnous*; denoting the person being 'a risk' and 'at risk' (Stanford, 2012). The former connotation derives from the Latin root 'wrong', implying that people deemed to be 'vulnerable' have an impaired ability to defend themselves within the judicial process or pursue their own best interests (Bartkowiak-Théron and Corbo-Crehan, 2012: 39).

The related connotation derives from the Latin route *vulnous*, meaning 'injury', associated with disadvantage and the vulnerable being susceptible to discrimination, misunderstanding and miscommunication (ibid). Therefore, Stanford argues people conceptualised as 'vulnerable' have 'constructed moral identities' which reflect both their innocence (vulnerable/at risk) and culpability (as being dangerous/a risk). Bartkowiak-Théron and Corbo-Crehan contend that such use of 'vulnerability' is a labelling exercise, taking into account the complex nature of individuality, fractured across several categories. The intent behind such labelling is to 'provide vulnerable people with a series of services intended to address the inequalities they would otherwise encounter in their dealings with the CJS' (2012: 44). This intent may be laudable but the objectives should be carried out through an equalities and not vulnerabilities framework in order to escape the problems associated with these constructed moral identities. Policies that use the categorisation of 'vulnerability' 'do not directly engage with disability as a protected characteristic; instead, they rely on ambiguous definitions of "vulnerability" and 'individual capacity' (Gormley and Watson, 2021: 493). Moving away from this concept and giving better prominence to an equalities framework would illuminate the individual's intrinsic rights associated with a protected characteristic.

In some ways, the category of vulnerability has natural appeal as a dividing practice, utilised in the governance of certain populations in the CJS; reducing the complex problems of the populations designated as vulnerable, by the rationalities now evident in criminal justice policy, into simple caricatures of the individual connoting weakness and vulnerability to abuse. Such caricatures elicit public sympathy more easily perhaps than a purposive rights-based framework. Over the last decade academics have written on the utility of the *concept* of vulnerability (Fineman, 2008; 2010; 2017) and its challenges and implications for law, including in social care and mental capacity law (Herring, 2016a; 2016b; Bedford and Herring, 2020), along with disability and criminal justice (Rogers, 2019; McNamara, 2023; Fairclough and Greenwood, 2023; Fairclough et al, 2023). Fineman's (2008, 2010) 'universal vulnerability approach' nuances the understanding of vulnerability beyond its etymological roots by making the case that everyone is vulnerable due to unpredictable external circumstances, environment and access to resources, which impacts resilience (Fineman, 2017). Herring examines vulnerability in the context of mental capacity, challenging the boundaries of utilising the concept for disparate categories of groups such as disabled people and 'the elderly' and instead situates it as central to the human condition (2016). Herring uses this notion that we are all, in fact, 'vulnerable', to draw on feminist and disability perspectives to replace the competent, able-bodied, independent person as the norm upon which the law is based with an approach which recognises our intrinsic interdependence and mutuality. Indeed, he advocates we should 'embrace' 'universal beneficial vulnerability' as a 'desirable attribute of all humankind' (2020: 63).

The attraction of universal vulnerability as a *concept* and the pragmatism vulnerability allows for in decision-making as a *strategy of governance* in the CJS context is clear. However, its appeal as a concept and strategy of governance are outweighed by the operation of the vulnerability status as a dividing practice; in seriously undermining the individual's autonomy to formulate preferences, plans and values and his or her ability to act in pursuit of those preferences, plans and values (Bartkowiak-Théron and Corbo-Crehan, 2012: 44). Vulnerability as a dividing practice in the governance of disabled people brings the individual within the sphere of control and surveillance of the state. This is because conferring the status of vulnerability through legal instruments fails to connect this categorisation with an individual's actual capacities. Thus, the individual is considered as belonging to a group of people pre-determined as 'lacking capacity' (Williams, 2002: 303). Furthermore, it was evident from the research discussed above that the fluid category of 'vulnerability' is used as a strategy of government designed to ration services and opaque in its ability to achieve substantive equality; establishing a 'problematic discourse' and a cycle of inequality (Williams, 2002: 303). As Stanford argues, the fluidity from vulnerability's connotations of being 'at risk' to being seen as 'a risk' have negative implications: disabled people are invited to see themselves and others 'in terms of a deficit model of self which they alone are charged with the responsibility of resolving' (2012: 25). This is antithetical to identity first approaches to disability, especially as it is too entrenched with notions of powerlessness and susceptibility to harm (Brown 2011).

Disabled defendants, including autistic defendants, are not only human rights holders, but hold specific rights as recognised in the UNCRPD (Articles 12, 13, 14 and 15). They also have anti-discrimination protection under the Equality Act 2010 by virtue of having the protected characteristic of disability. However, as Dowse et al argue in relation to the Australian jurisdiction, these 'umbrella protections' 'appear to have had limited impact' on defendants with mental health disorders and cognitive disabilities (2009: 30). This idea was evinced in this books' analysis of the broader rationalities of government which are applied to autistic defendants in chapters four and five and in the techniques of government applied to them in the courts (chapters six to eight). Dowse et al argue that addressing 'current obstructions to the achievement of human rights protections' for such groups involves addressing 'the ways social structures and people in relevant agencies have positioned [these groups] in theory and in practice' (2009: 30). The positioning of autistic defendants, in the locale of policy on offenders with mental health problems, as 'vulnerable' amounts to such an obstruction in theory and practice. As such, there is both descriptive and normative value in repositioning these groups as disabled under the social model.

Whilst there is not the space here to offer a full-scale rebuttal of the literature in the growing cannon on vulnerability, there is room to posit a challenge to the supposed pragmatic benefits of this apparently benign concept when used as a dividing practice. Accordingly, to shine a light on what barriers it creates for disabled people in a criminal justice context, as a rationality of governance; a dividing practice which acts to mask the protected characteristic of disability for disabled defendants – further heightening the exclusion of disabled people. Also we can pose the question, following the research in this book: do we need vulnerability to recognise that disabled people are interdependent, to recognise the mutuality of all human interaction? There is a case to be made that disabled people's interdependency is better expressed and advocated for, without the attendant baggage of the concept of vulnerability, through a more developed sociology of disablism (Reindal, 1999) based on the social model of disability. Reindel argues that to move beyond 'personal autonomy that is not caught in the independence–dependence dichotomy the subject must be founded in a philosophical tradition that sees the human condition as one of interdependence' (1999). He acknowledges 'the human condition is viewed as one of interdependency and vulnerability', leading to an understanding of independence as 'partnership' (1999: 364). Thus, in the social model the disabled subject is embodied and embedded (Relational) and interdependence means 'independence as partnership' (1999: 365). It is argued that it is more helpful to transpose language of 'vulnerability' in Reindal's formulation with the disablement branch of the social model; in other words, barriers to participation in mainstream social activities and inclusion.

In a criminal justice context, as found through the present research, vulnerability is conflated with impairment (MacDonald, 2015), in turn the CJS locates the 'problem' within the individual rather than the structures that create it which shapes definitions of 'vulnerability' (Roulstone and Sadique, 2013). The complexities of vulnerability are reduced to the question of fit within constructions of 'normalcy' (Dowse, 2017); increasing exclusion of disabled defendants. Baldry and others have thrown into sharp relief the ongoing cycling of disabled people through the CJS as a result of lifelong dimensions of marginalisation, institutional failure and lack of appropriate supports to (Baldry et al, 2012, 2015). Thus, even if we disrupt or 'refigure' (Bedford, 2020) the concept of vulnerability, and such normalcy, in the way Fineman, Herring, Bedford and others suggest to perceive 'we are all vulnerable', we lose the impairment-disablement distinction of the social model. In doing so we lose sight of the recognition that disabled people, in society in general and within the CJS in particular, are systemically excluded. It is argued that recognising the heterogeneity and intrinsic value of human life and overcoming the 'cultural fantasy of the body as a neutral, compliant instrument of some transcendent will' (Garland Thomson, 2011: 592) is better achieved by the social model of disability, augmented by the human rights model (Degener, 2016) with the models of disability having complementary and supportive roles (see Lawson and Beckett, 2021), rather than the concept of vulnerability.

2. Normative Implications

Thus, the normative case for moving away from the rationality of 'vulnerability' and reimagining autistic people, and indeed those with mental health problems and learning disabilities, as disabled people from a social model perspective enables 'an iterative process of identifying, understanding and removing obstacles to resources combined with a deeper analysis of the dynamics of both impairment and disability' (Baldry et al, 2008: 32–33). Delimiting diagnostic categories and identifying those who fall within them 'is a complex process characterised by ambiguous relationships to the theoretical paradigms that shape our thinking about such people' (Dowse et al, 2009: 31). As we saw in chapter eight and Section 1(A) above, the interconnecting pathways between health, social care and criminal justice require the consistent categorisation of autistic defendants as disabled people from a social model perspective. This will assist in promoting their status as rights holders with the protected characteristic of disability, which flows from the Equality Act 2010, as they move between the competing and fluid dividing practices of the health, social care and criminal justice systems. Focusing attention on the inequitable composition of the prison population and the role of imprisonment, Scott has argued that legitimacy's normative 'face' requires us, as a society, to be clearer about the core of offenders for whom prison is appropriate by taking a 'moral approach' that recognises that the sanction of imprisonment is entirely misapplied for certain categories of harm, and wrongdoers such as the 'mentally ill' (2007: 49; 68). Diverting categories of offenders, such as autistic people, into health or social care placements may better recognise and meet their needs but boundaries need to be drawn to prevent oppressive control by alternative modes of regulation, as seen in some of the case studies above. Where a coercive measure or detention regime 'is for prevention or regulation or administrative convenience' states have been quick to claim 'it is not, by definition, punishment' but 'this privileging of purpose does not mitigate the pains imposed by coercive measures' (Zedner, 2016: 4). Therefore, to merely 're-label measures as non-punitive' is often nothing less than 'a cynical subversion of the criminal process and its human rights protections' (ibid).

Thus, there is a normative imperative to develop the intellectual agenda outlined here; 'one about the nature of state authority and its power to punish' (Zedner, 2016: 4). Re-conceptualising autistic people, as well as those with mental health problems and learning disabilities by bringing together critical criminology and critical disability studies, brings disability to the centre of analysis in what Dowse et al call 'disabling critical criminology' (2009). In doing so, it provides a new perspective to 'make visible material structures, ideological discourses and experiences of impairment that fundamentally and differentially structure an individual's pathway into, around and often back into the CJS' (Dowse et al, 2009: 39). This analysis situates disabled defendants, including autistic defendants, in 'individual and social systemic contexts, opening up new ways to identify conceptualisations, structure and interventions that enable the development of new individual, systemic and political engagement' (ibid). In doing so, it highlights appropriate social support for the particular individual and 'enables thinking around ways that can make it possible for individuals to more frequently take non-offending pathways' (Dowse et al, 2009: 39). This incorporates an interdisciplinary, 'life course perspective' into criminological research with the potential to highlight the ways in which, for example, impairment, gender and socio-economic status interact with each other (ibid). This better reflects the protected characteristic model, used across disability, age, gender reassignment, marriage and civil partnership, pregnancy and maternity, race, religion or belief and sex in the Equality Act 2010, rather than the ambiguous concept of vulnerability, for which the latter can be used as a dividing practice by the State to circumvent participation in justice proceedings for disabled people and remove the rights of individuals (Spivakovsky, 2014).

McNamara uses Ireland as a case study to explore the barriers disabled people face in equally exercising their rights in criminal proceedings. Although she writes in an edited collection on *Vulnerability, the Accused, and the Criminal Justice System*, her arguments on the transformative power of human rights laws are not based on the utility of the concept of 'vulnerability' per se but the role of UNCRPD in providing a robust normative framework to enhance the rights of access to justice for all disabled people getting involved in the criminal justice system. This follows a series of pieces examining the UNCRPD in relation to criminal justice (Weller, 2014; Gormley and Watson, 2021) and legal capacity and equal recognition before the law (Minkowitz, 2014), unfitness to stand trial (Gooding and O'Mahoney, 2015) and the marginalisation of disability domestic violence (Harpur and Douglas, 2014). In parallel there are exciting discussions within disability law and disability studies in developing a complementary thesis which brings together the social and human rights models, each with a distinctive role to play in the furtherance of human rights for disabled people, in ways that are 'complementary and symbiotic' (Lawson and Beckett, 2021). While the present book has focused on the social model, because this was embedded in the Equality Act 2010, and there was scant research on its role in influencing the conceptualisation of disabled defendants in general and autistic defendants in particular, such intellectual resources provide fertile ground to continue to 'disable' the criminological mainstream. As such, the UNCRPD offers exciting lines of enquiry into the role of the human rights model of disability in criminal justice theory and practice in future.

Conclusion

This chapter has connected the need to understand implications of the relationship between adult social care and Criminal Justice and the potential for disabled people moving between these systems of 'continuous control' with unpacking the potential barriers and exclusions created by 'vulnerability' as a dividing practice. One of the main findings of this book has been the paucity of understanding amongst criminal justice decision-makers of the Equality Act 2010, Autism Act 2009 and accompanying statutory guidance, and their implications for autistic defendants. This amplifies the need for future research to analyse the awareness of such decision-makers of the UNCRPD and the extent of its harmonisation. Building on the intellectual resources garnered from the development of a disability perspective in chapter three and its discussion of the entrenchment of the social model of disability in the Equality Act 2010, it posits that it is necessary to move away from the reductive mad-bad binary and the rationality of 'vulnerability' to the recognition of autistic people, along with those with learning disabilities and mental health problems, as disabled citizens.

In doing so, the book has drawn on critical disability studies and literature which 'disables' criminology to analyse the governance of autistic adult defendants.

It argues that there is descriptive and normative value in proactively categorising these groups as 'disabled' under the 'social model' of 'disability'; enabling an enquiry into other conditions of possibility. Much more purposive work needs to be done to proactively embed the Equality Act 2010 and the protected characteristic of disability into criminal justice policies and broader rationalities of governance. This Act, along with the UNCRPD, are too often treated as adjuncts to legislation and guidance on disabled defendants, including those with mental health problems and learning disabilities: the locale of policy-making under which autism is included. To correct this would require systematic harmonisation of the UNCRPD across numerous legislative instruments. Criminology and criminal justice studies must support this law-making venture by positioning disabled people centrally within theoretical approaches, empirical research and by 'disabling' our own discipline to critique concepts, rationalities and strategies of governance which are inherently ableist and disablist.

BIBLIOGRAPHY

Abbott, P, and C Wallace, (1992) *The Family and the New Right* (Pluto Press).

Abrahams, BS, and DH Geschwind, (2008) 'Advances in autism genetics: on the threshold of a new neurobiology, Nature reviews' *Genetics* 9, 341.

Abu-Akel, A, (2003) 'A neurobiological mapping of theory of mind' *Brain Research Reviews* 43, 29.

Adebowale, VO, (2013) *Independent Commission on Mental Health and Policing Report*, news.bbc.co.uk/1/shared/bsp/hi/pdfs/10_05_13_report.pdf.

Advocacy Training Council, (2013) *Advocates Gateway: Planning to Question Someone with an Autism Spectrum Disorder, including Asperger Syndrome Toolkit 3*, www.theadvocatesgateway.org.

All-Party Parliamentary Group on Autism and National Autistic Society, (2019) *The Autism Act, 10 Years On: A report from the All-Party Parliamentary Group on Autism on understanding, services and support for autistic people and their families in England*, pearsfoundation.org.uk/wp-content/uploads/2019/09/APPGA-Autism-Act-Inquiry-Report.pdf.

Allely, CS, (2016) 'Sexual offending and autism spectrum disorders' *Journal Of Intellectual Disabilities and Offending Behaviour* 7, 35.

Allely, CS, (2022) *Autism spectrum disorder in the criminal justice System: A guide to understanding suspects, defendants and offenders with autism* (Routledge).

Allely, CS, E Chaplin, J Salter, J McCarthy, and F Gerry, (2023) 'Autistic Defendants in Court: Perceptions and Support for Accessing Justice' in T Smith (ed), *Autism and Criminal Justice* (Routledge).

Allely, CS, and P Cooper, (2017) 'Jurors' and judges' evaluation of defendants with autism and the impact on sentencing: A systematic preferred reporting items for systematic reviews and meta-analyses (PRISMA) review of autism spectrum disorder in the courtroom' *Journal of Law and Medicine* 25, 105.

Allely, CS, and T Wood, (2022) '"Cardboard gangsters", "in crowd" and "no control": A case study of autism spectrum disorder in the prison environment' *Journal of Intellectual Disabilities and Offending Behaviour* 13, 57.

Allen, D, C Evan, A Hider, S Hawkins, H Peckett, and H Morgan, (2008) 'Offending Behaviour in Adults with Asperger Syndrome' *Autism Developmental Disorder* 38, 748.

American Psychiatric Association (APA), (1994) *Diagnostic and Statistical Manual of Mental Disorders Third Edition* (American Psychiatric Association).

American Psychiatric Association (APA), (2000) *Diagnostic and Statistical Manual of Mental Disorders Fourth Edition*, (American Psychiatric Association).

American Psychiatric Association (APA), (2013) *Diagnostic and Statistical Manual of Mental Disorders Fifth Edition* (American Psychiatric Association).

Anderson, I/ADASS, (2015) *A report on the findings of the ADASS survey of social care activity in prisons and approved premises – Quarter 1 2015/16*, www.adass.org.uk/media/4231/an-analysis-of-social-care-activity-in-prisons-and-approved-premises.pdf.

Annison H, and R Condry, (2022) 'The Pains of Hope: Families of Indeterminate Sentenced Prisoners and Political Campaigning by Lay Citizens' *British Journal of Criminology* 62, 1252.

Archer, N, and EA Hurley, (2013) 'A justice system failing the autistic community' *Journal of Intellectual Disabilities and Offending Behaviour* 4, 53.

Arthur, R, (2005) 'Punishing parents for the crimes of their children' *The Howard Journal of Criminal Justice* 44, 233.

Ashtiany, S, (2011) 'The Equality Act 2010: Main Concepts' *International Journal of Discrimination and the Law* 11, 29.

Ashworth, A, E Genders, G Mansfield, J Peay, and E Player, (1984) *Oxford Pilot Study – Sentencing in the Crown Court: Report of an Exploratory Study* (Oxford University Centre for Criminology).

Ashworth, A, (2011a) 'Re-evaluating the justifications for aggravation and mitigation in sentencing' in JV Roberts (ed), *Mitigation and Aggravation at Sentencing* (Cambridge University Press).

Ashworth, A, (2011b) 'Criminal Justice, Not Criminology?' in M Bosworth and C Hoyle (eds), *What is Criminology?* (Oxford University Press).

Ashworth, A, and M Redmayne, (2014) *The Criminal Process, Fourth Edition* (Oxford University Press).

Asperger, H, (1944) 'Die "Autistischen Psychopathen" im Kindesalter' ['The "autistic psychopaths" in childhood'], *Archiv für Psychiatrie und Nervenkrankheiten* 117, 76.

Association of Chief Police Officers and National Policing Improvement Agency, (2010) *Guidance on responding to people with mental ill health or learning disabilities*, www.scie-socialcareonline.org.uk/guidance-on-responding-to-people-with-mental-ill-health-or-learning-disabilities/r/a11G00000017zUkIAI.

Asquith, NL, and I Bartkowiak-Théron, (2012) 'Vulnerability and Diversity in Policing' in I Bartkowiak-Théron, and NL Asquith (eds), *Policing Vulnerability* (The Federation Press).

Attwood, T, (2007) *The Complete Guide to Asperger's Syndrome* (Jessica Kingsley Publishers).

Autism West Midlands/Tidball, M., (2010a) *Response to Birmingham City Council's Learning Disability Strategy* www.autismwestmidlands.org.uk.

Autism West Midlands/Tidball, M, (2010b) *Response to the Department of Health Autism Strategy guidance*, www.autismwestmidlands.org.uk.

Autism West Midlands/Tidball, M, (2011) *Response to Birmingham City Council's Vision for Adult Social Care – 24 February 2011*, www.autismwestmidlands.org.uk.

Bahdi, R, (2007) 'Background Paper on Women's Access to Justice in the MENA Region (International Development Research Centre (IDRC)' *Women's Rights and Citizenship Program (WRC) and the Middle East Regional Office (MERO), Middle East and North African (MENA) Regional Consultation Conference* 9–11 December 2007, Cairo, Egypt.

Baldry, E, (2014) 'Disability at the margins: limits of the law' *Griffith Law Review* 23, 370.

Baldry, E, L Dowse, P Snoyman, M Clarence, and I Webster, (2008) 'A critical perspective on Mental Health Disorders and Cognitive Disability in the Criminal Justice System' *Proceedings of the 2nd Australian & New Zealand Critical Criminology Conference* 19–20 June 2008.

Baldry, E, D Brown, M Brown, C Cunneen, M Schwartz, and A Steel, (2011) 'Imprisoning rationalities' *Australian & New Zealand Journal of Criminology* 44, 24.

Baldry, E, L Dowse, and M Clarence, (2012) 'People with mental and cognitive disabilities: pathways into prison' in *Background Paper for Outlaws to Inclusion Conference*, Kensington, Sydney: University of New South Wales, www.mhdcd.unsw.edu.au/sites/www.mhdcd.unsw.edu.au/files/u18/pdf/MHDCDbackgroundOutlaws%20Conf1.pdf.

Baldwin, J (2007) 'Research on the Criminal Courts' in R King and E Wincup (eds), *Doing Research on Crime and Justice* (Oxford University Press).

Baldwin, J, and M McConville, (1977) *Negotiated justice: Pressures to plead guilty* (Martin Robertson).

Barber, P, R Brown, and D Martin, (2009) *Mental Health Law in England and Wales – A Guide for Mental Health Professionals* (Learning Matters).

Barnes, C, (1991) *Disabled People in Britain and Discrimination: A case for anti-discrimination legislation* (Hurst & Co).

Barnes, C, (1998) 'The Social Model of Disability: a sociological phenomenon ignored by sociologists' in T Shakespeare (ed), *The Disability Studies Reader* (Cassell).

Barnes, C, (2012) 'Understanding the Social Model of Disability: Past, Present and Future' in N Watson, A Roulstone, and C Thomas (eds), *Routledge Handbook of Disability Studies* (Routledge).

Barnes, C, G Mercer, and T Shakespeare (eds), (1999) *Exploring Disability: a sociological introduction* (Polity).

Baron-Cohen, S, (1988) 'An assessment of violence in a young man with Asperger's Syndrome' *Journal of Child Psychology and Psychiatry and Allied Disciplines* 29, 351.

Baron-Cohen, S, (1997) *Mindblindness: An essay on autism and theory of mind* (MIT Press).

Baron-Cohen, S, (2008) *Autism and Asperger Syndrome* (Oxford University Press).

Barry-Walsh, JB, and PE Mullen, (2004) Forensic aspects of Asperger's Syndrome, *Journal of Forensic Psychiatry and Psychology* 15, 96.
Bartkowiak-Théron, I, and A Corbo-Crehan, (2012) '"For when equality is given to unequals, the result is inequality": The Socio-legal Ethics of Vulnerable People' in I Bartkowiak-Théron, and NL Asquith (eds), *Policing Vulnerability* (The Federation Press).
Bates, Y, and RJ Tully, (2022) 'Supporting autistic people in prisons' in *Working with Autistic People in the Criminal Justice and Forensic Mental Health Systems* (Routledge) 67–78.
Beardon, L, (2008) 'Asperger Syndrome and Perceived Offending Conduct: A Qualitative Study', *Doctorate of Education Thesis* (Sheffield Hallam University) shura.shu.ac.uk/7155/1/Beardon_aspergers_-_full.pdf.
Beardon, L, (2017) *Perspectives on Autism* (Online Blog) blogs.shu.ac.uk/autism/?doing_wp_cron=1490259625.4494929313659667968750.
Becker, H, (1967) 'Whose Side Are We On?' *Social Problems* 14, 234.
Bedford, D, (2020) 'Introduction: Vulnerability refigured' in D Bedford and J Herring (eds), *Embracing Vulnerability* (Routledge).
Bedford, D, and J Herring, (2020) *Embracing Vulnerability* (Routledge).
Ben-Moshe, L, (2013) 'Disabling incarceration: Connecting disability to divergent confinements in the USA' *Critical Sociology* 39, 385.
Ben-Moshe, L, (2020) *Decarcerating Disability: Deinstitutionalisation and Prison Abolition* (University of Minnesota Press).
Beresford, P, (2010) *Towards a Social Model of Madness and Distress? Exploring What Service Users Say* (Joseph Rowntree Foundation).
Berthoz, S, and EL Hill, (2005) 'The validity of using self-reports to assess emotion regulation abilities in adults with autism spectrum disorder' *European Psychiatry* 20, 291.
Berryessa, CM, (2014) 'Judiciary views on criminal behaviour and intention of offenders with high-functioning autism' *Journal of Intellectual Disabilities and Offending Behaviour* 5, 97.
Berryessa, CM, (2016) 'Brief report: Judicial attitudes regarding the sentencing of offenders with high functioning autism' *Journal of Autism and Developmental Disorders* 46, 2770.
Berryessa, CM, (2017) 'Educator of the court: The role of the expert witness in cases involving autism spectrum disorder' *Psychology, Crime and Law* 23, 575.
Berryessa, C, (2021) *Defendants with autism spectrum disorder in criminal court: A judges' toolkit*, papers.ssrn.com/sol3/papers.cfm?abstract_id=3730822.
Bettelheim, (1967) *The Empty Fortress: Infantile Autism and the Birth of the Self* (Simon & Schuster Incorporated).
Betts, N, and KeyRing, (2011) *'Easy Read' in the Criminal Justice System*, www.keyring.org/cjs-easyread.
Betts, N, and NHS England (Health and Justice team), (2015) *Equal Access, Equal Care; Guidance for Prison Healthcare Staff treating Patients with Learning Disabilities*, www.england.nhs.uk/commissioning/wp-content/uploads/sites/12/2015/08/equal-access-equal-care-guidance-patients-ld.pdf.
Bigham, S, J Boucher, A Mayes and S Anns, (2010) 'Assessing recollection and familiarity in autistic spectrum disorders: Methods and findings' *Journal of Autism and Developmental Disorders* 40, 878.
Birmingham City Council (BCC), (2010) *A Vision for Adult Social Care in Birmingham* (Birmingham City Council).
Birmingham City Council (BCC), (2010) *Adults with autism and the criminal justice system – Report of the Health & Social Care Overview and Scrutiny Committee* (Birmingham City Council).
Blackman, L, (2009) *Autism Bill*, HC Deb 27 February 2009, vol 488, cols 481–548.
Blair, ACL, (2005) *Keynote speech to the 2005 Labour Party Conference in Brighton*, news.bbc.co.uk/1/hi/uk_politics/4287370.stm.
Blackmore, CE, EL Woodhouse, N Gillan, E Wilson, KL Ashwood, V Stoencheva, and E Daly, (2022) 'Adults with autism spectrum disorder and the criminal justice system: An investigation of prevalence of contact with the criminal justice system, risk factors and sex differences in a specialist assessment service' *Autism* 26, 2098.

Bradley, K, (2009) 'The Bradley Report: Lord Bradley's review of people with mental health problems or learning disabilities in the criminal justice system' (produced by COI for the Department of Health) webarchive.nationalarchives.gov.uk/20130107105354/http://www.dh.gov.uk/prod_consum_dh/groups/dh_digitalassets/documents/digitalasset/dh_098698.pdf.

Bradley, K, Westminster Policy Forum, (2009) *Reducing re-offending: mental health and value for money in the criminal justice system,* Transcript for Westminster Legal Policy Forum Keynote Seminar: 3rd November 2009.

Brereton, B, (1997) 'How Different Are Rape Trials? A Comparison of the Cross-Examination of Complainants in Rape and Assault Trials' *British Journal of Criminology* 37, 242.

Bryen, DN and CH Wickman, (2011) 'Ending the Silence of People with Little or No Functional Speech: Testifying in Court' *Disability Studies Quarterly* 31.

Bosworth, M, D Campbell, B Demby, SM Ferranti, and M Santos, (2005) 'Doing prison research: Views from inside' *Qualitative inquiry* 11, 249.

Bosworth, M, and C Hoyle (eds), (2011) *What is Criminology?* (Oxford University Press).

Botha, M, J Hanlon, and GL Williams, (2023) 'Does Language Matter? Identity-First Versus Person-First Language Use in Autism Research: A Response to Vivanti' *Journal of Autism Developmental Disorders* 53, 870.

Bottema-Beutel, K, SK Kapp, JN Lester, NJ Sasson, and BN Hand, (2021) 'Avoiding ableist language: Suggestions for autism researchers' *Autism in adulthood* 3, 18.

Bottoms, A, (1995) 'The philosophy and politics of punishment and sentencing' in C Clarkson and R Morgan (eds), *The politics of sentencing reform* (Clarendon Press).

Bottoms, AE, JD McClean, and I Todd, (1976) *Defendants in the Criminal Process* (Routledge).

Bridges, L, (2006) 'Ethics of Representation on Guilty Pleas' *Legal Ethics* 9, 80.

Brody, EM, (2004) *Women in the Middle* (Springer).

Brown, K, (2011) 'Vulnerability: handle with care' *Ethics and Social Welfare* 5, 313.

Brown-Lavoie, SM, MA Viecili, and JA Weiss, (2014) 'Sexual knowledge and victimization in adults with autism spectrum disorders' *Journal of Autism and Developmental Disorders* 44, 2185.

Browning, A, (2008) *Adults with Autism Bill 2008 Hansard* HC Deb 20 May 2008, col 163.

Browning, A, (2009) *Autism Bill Hansard* HC Deb 19 Jun 2009, cols 540–583.

Browning, A, and L Caulfield, (2011) 'The prevalence and treatment of people with Asperger's Syndrome in the criminal justice system' *Criminology and Criminal Justice* 11, 165.

Brugha, T, S McManus, H Meltzer, J Smith, FJ Scott, S Purdon, J Harris, and J Bankart, (2009) *Autism spectrum disorders in adults living in households throughout England: Report from the adult psychiatric morbidity survey 2007* (The NHS Information Centre for Health and Social Care).

Brugha, TS, S McManus, J Bankart, F Scott, S Purdon, J Smith, P Bebbington, R Jenkins and H Meltzer, (2011) 'Epidemiology of autism spectrum disorders in adults in the community in England' *Archives of general psychiatry* 68, 459.

Brugha, TS, Spiers, N Bankart, J Cooper, SA McManus, S Scott, J Smith, and F Tyrer, (2016) 'Epidemiology of autism in adults across age groups and ability levels' *The British Journal of Psychiatry* 209, 498.

Bullock, K, (2011) 'The Construction and Interpretation of Risk Management Technologies in Contemporary Probation Practice' *British Journal of Criminology* 51, 120.

Bullock, K, and R Condry, (2013) 'Responding to denial, minimization and blame in correctional settings: The "real world" implications of offender neutralizations' *European Journal of Criminology* 10, 572.

Burawoy, M, A Burton, A Arnett Ferguson, KJ Fox, J Gamson, N Gartrell, L Hurst, C Kurzman, L Salzinger, J Schiffman, and S Ui, (1991) *Ethnography Unbound* (University of California Press).

Burch, E, and J Rose, (2020) 'The subjective experiences of liaison and diversion staff who encounter individuals with autism' *Journal of Criminological Research, Policy and Practice* 6, 137.

Burchardt, T, (2000) 'The Dynamics of Being Disabled' *Journal of Social Policy* 29, 645.

Burney, E, and L Gelsthorpe, (2008) 'Do we need a "naughty step"? Rethinking the parenting order after ten years' *The Howard Journal of Criminal Justice* 47, 470.

Butlin, SF, (2011) 'The UN Convention on the Rights of Persons with Disabilities: Does the Equality Act 2010 Measure up to UK International Commitments?' *Industrial Law Journal* 40, 428.

Cameron, D, (2010) Transcript of a speech by the Prime Minister on the Big Society (19 July 2010) www.gov.uk/government/speeches/big-society-speech.

Cameron, D, (2011) Transcript of a speech by the Prime Minister on the Big Society (14 February 2011) www.gov.uk/government/speeches/pms-speech-on-big-society.

Campbell FAK, (2001) 'Inciting legal fictions: "Disability's" date with ontology and the ableist body of the law' *Griffith Law Review* 10, 42.

Campbell, F, (2008) 'Exploring Internalized Ableism Using Critical Race Theory' *Disability and Society* 23, 151.

Campbell, FK, (2005) 'Legislating Disability – Negative Ontologies and the Government of Legal Identities' in S Tremain (ed), *Foucault and the Government of Disability* (University of Michigan Press).

Campbell, FK, (2009a) *The contours of ableism: The production of disability and abledness*, (Palgrave MacMillan).

Campbell, FK, (2009c) 'Disability harms: Exploring internalized ableism' in CA Marshall, E Kendall, and ME Banks *et al* (eds), *Disabilities: Insights from across Fields and around the World, vol 1, The Experience: Definitions, Causes, and Consequences* (Praeger Publishers).

Campbell, L, A Ashworth and M Redmayne, (2019) *The Criminal Process* (Oxford University Press).

Cape, E, (1994) 'Defence services: what should defence lawyers do at police stations?' in M McConville and L Bridges (eds), *Criminal Justice in Crisis* (Edward Elgar).

Cape, E, (2004) '50th anniversary article: The rise (and fall?) of a criminal defence profession' *The Criminal Law Review* 401.

Carlen, P, (1976a) *Magistrates' Justice* (Martin Robertson).

Carlen, P, (1976b) 'The Staging of Magistrates' Justice' *British Journal of Criminology* 16, 48.

Cashin, A, (2006) 'Two terms – one meaning: The conundrum of contemporary nomenclature in autism' *Journal of Child and Adolescent Psychiatric Nursing* 19, 137.

Cashin, ARN, C Newman, (2009) 'Autism in the Criminal Justice Detention System: A Review of the Literature' *Journal of Forensic Nursing* 5, 70.

Cavadino, M, (1997) 'Pre-sentence reports: The effects of legislation and national standards' *British Journal of Criminology* 37, 529.

Central University Research Ethics Committee (CUREC), (2012) *Guidelines MSD/GUIDE/4.1 – Best practice guidance on nonymization and identifiers*, researchsupport.admin.ox.ac.uk/governance/ethics/resources/bpg.

Centre for Mental Health, (2014) *The Bradley Report five years on: An independent review of progress to date and priorities for further development*, cdn.basw.co.uk/upload/basw_15825-2.pdf.

Chadwick, DD, and C Wesson, (2020) '"Blocked at every level": criminal justice system professionals' experiences of including people with intellectual disabilities within a targeted magistrates' court' *Journal of Intellectual Disabilities and Offending Behaviour* 11, 133.

Chakraborti, N and J Garland, (2012) 'Reconceptualizing hate crime victimization through the lens of vulnerability' *Theoretical Criminology* 16, 499.

Change, (2012) *Change Pictures*, www.changepeople.org/projects/easy-read-in-the-criminal-justice-system.

Chaplin, E, and J McCarthy, (2022) 'Autism and offending behaviour' in *Working with Autistic People in the Criminal Justice and Forensic Mental Health Systems* (Routledge).

Chaplin, E, J McCarthy, and A Forrester, (2017) 'Defendants with autism spectrum disorders: What is the role of court liaison and diversion?' *Advances in Autism* 3, 220.

Chaplin, E, J McCarthy, CS Allely, A Forrester, L Underwood, H Hayward, J Sabet, S Young, R Mills, P Asherson, and D Murphy, (2021a) 'Self-harm and mental health characteristics of prisoners with elevated rates of autistic traits' *Research in Developmental Disabilities*, 114, 103987.

Chaplin, E, J McCarthy, K Marshall-Tate, S Ali, K Xenitidis, J Childs, D Harvey, I McKinnon, L Robinson, S Hardy, A Forrester, and S Srivastava, (2021b) 'Evaluation of a liaison and diversion Court Mental Health Service for defendants with neurodevelopmental disorders' *Research in Developmental Disabilities* 119, 104103.

Chaplin, E, J McCarthy, and L Underwood, (2013) 'Autism spectrum conditions and offending: An introduction to the special edition' *Journal of Intellectual Disabilities and Offending Behaviour* 4, 5.

Charman, T, CRG Jones, A Pickles, E Simonoff, G Baird, and F Happé, (2011) 'Defining the cognitive phenotype of autism' *Brain Research* 1380, 10.

Chen, PS, SJ Chen, YK Yang, TL Yeh, CC Chen, and HY Lo, (2003) 'Asperger's disorder: A case report of repeated stealing and the collecting behaviours of an adolescent patient' *Acta Psychiatrica Scandinavica* 107, 73.

Chester, V, K Bunning, S Tromans, R Alexander, and P Langdon, (2022) 'The Prevalence of Autism in the Criminal Justice System: A Systematic Review' *British Journal of Psychiatry Open* 8, S45.

Chesterman P, and SC Rutter, (1993) 'Case report: Asperger's Syndrome and sexual offending' *Journal of Forensic Psychiatry* 4, 555.

Clarke, K, (2010) 'Prison Does Not Work', Key *Speech made to judges at Mansion House, London*, www.crimlinks.com/News2010/July142010.html.

Clarke, DJ, CJ Littlejohns, JA, and S Joseph, (1989) 'Pervasive developmental disorders and psychoses in adult life' *British Journal of Psychiatry* 155, 692.

Clough, B, (2014) '"People like that": Realising the Social Model in Mental Capacity Jurisprudence' *Medical Law Review* 23, 53.

Corcoran, MS, (2005) 'Researching Women Political Prisoners in Northern Ireland: Ethnographic Problems and Negotiations', in T Skinner, M Hester, and E Malos (eds), *Researching Gender Violence: Feminist Methodology in Action* (Willan Publishing).

Collins, J, K Horton, E Gale-St. Ives, G Murphy, and M Barnoux, (2023) 'A Systematic Review of Autistic People and the Criminal Justice System: An Update of King and Murphy (2014)' *Journal of Autism and Developmental Disorders* 53, 3151.

Condry, R, (2007) *Families shamed: The consequences of crime for relatives of serious offenders* (Willan Publishing).

Condry, R, (2016, unpublished) 'Understanding the notion of "collateral effects" on families' *Centre for Criminology Seminar Series* (Centre for Criminology).

Condry, R, A Kotova, and S Minson, (2016) 'Social Injustice and Collateral Damage: The Families and Children of Prisoners' in Y Jewkes, J Bennett, and B Crewe (eds), *Handbook on Prisons*, revised 2nd edn (Routledge).

Condry, R and C Miles, (2012) 'Adolescent to Parent Violence and Youth Justice in England and Wales', *Social Policy and Society* 11, 241.

Condry, R, and C Miles, (2014) 'Adolescent to Parent Violence: Framing and Mapping a Hidden Problem' *Criminology and Criminal Justice* 0, 1–19.

Condry, R, and S Minson, (2021) 'Conceptualizing the effects of imprisonment on families: Collateral consequences, secondary punishment, or symbiotic harms?' *Theoretical Criminology* 25, 540.

Cook, JA, (1988) 'Who "Mothers" the Chronically Mentally Ill?' *Family Relations* 37, 42–49.

Cooper, SA, WN Mohamed, and RA Collacott, (1993) 'Possible Asperger's Syndrome in a mentally handicapped transvestite offender' *Journal of Intellectual Disability Research* 37(2): 189–194.

Cooper, DS, D Uppal, KS Railey, A Blank Wilson, K Maras, E Zimmerman, J Bornman, and LL Shea, (2022) 'Policy gaps and opportunities: A systematic review of autism spectrum disorder and criminal justice intersections' *Autism* 26, 1014.

Copeland, A, J McLean, and G Glover, (2012) *Local Authority self-assessment of services for people with autism in 2010/2011 – Ratings atlas*, www.improvinghealthandlives.org.uk.

Cornwell, EY, and B Cornwell, (2008) 'Access to Expertise as a Form of Social Capital: An Examination of Race- and Class-Based Disparities in Network Ties to Experts' *Sociological Perspectives* 51, 853.

Crane, L, and L Goddard, (2008) 'Episodic and semantic autobiographical memory in adults with autism spectrum disorders' *Journal of Autism and Developmental Disorders*, 38(3), 498–506.

Crane, L, and K Maras, (2018) 'General memory abilities for autobiographical events in adults with autism spectrum disorder' in JL Johnson, GS Goodman, and PC Mundy (eds), *The Wiley handbook of memory, autism spectrum disorder, and the law* (Wiley Blackwell).

Crane, L, KL Maras, T Hawken, S Mulcahy, and A Memon, (2016) 'Experiences of autism spectrum disorder and policing in England and Wales: Surveying police and the autism community', *Journal of Autism and Developmental Disorders* 46, 2028.

Crease, B, (2015) *An assessment of the English and maths skills levels of prisoners in England*, www.nrdc.org.uk/wp-content/uploads/2015/11/An-assessment-of-the-English-and-maths-skills-levels-of-prisoners-in-England1.pdf.

Crewe, B, (2011) 'Depth, weight, tightness: Revisiting the pains of imprisonment' *Punishment & Society* 13, 509.

Crow, L, (1996) 'Including all of our lives: renewing the social model of disability' in C Barnes, and G Mercer (eds), *Exploring the Divide* (The Disability Press).

Crow, I, and J Cove, (1984) 'Ethnic Minorities and the Courts' *The Criminal Law Review* 413.

Crown Prosecution Service, (2012) *Prosecution Policy and Guidance: Mentally disordered offenders*, www.cps.gov.uk/.

Crown Prosecution Service, (2013) *The Code for Crown Prosecutors*, www.cps.gov.uk/.

Crown Prosecution Service, (2013) *Crown Prosecution Service Business Plan 2012–13*, www.cps.gov.uk/.

Crown Prosecution Service, (2014) *Crown Prosecution Service Business Plan 2014–15*, www.cps.gov.uk/.

Crown Prosecution Service, (2015) *Crown Prosecution Service Business Plan 2015–16*, www.cps.gov.uk/sites/default/files/documents/publications/cps_business_plan_2015_-_16_v2.pdf.

Crown Prosecution Service, (2015) *Autism: Checklist for Prosecutors*, www.cps.gov.uk/.

Crown Prosecution Service, (2019) *Legal Guidance, Mental Health: Suspects and Defendants with Mental Health Conditions or Disorders*, www.cps.gov.uk/legal-guidance/mental-health-suspects-and-defendants-mental-health-conditions-or-disorders.

Crown Prosecution Service, (2018) *The Code for Crown Prosecutors*, www.cps.gov.uk/publication/code-crown-prosecutors.

Crowther, N, and L Sayce OBE, (2020) 'Was Ratification of the CRPD the High Watermark for United Kingdom Disability Rights? Ten Years of Monitoring Implementation of the CRPD' in EJ Kakoullis, and K Johnson, (eds), *Recognising Human Rights in Different Cultural Contexts* (Palgrave Macmillan).

Daly, K, (1989) 'Rethinking Judicial Paternalism: Gender, Work-Family Relations, and Sentencing' *Gender and Society* 3, 9.

Davies, K, J Lewis, J Byatt, E Purvis and B Cole, (2004) 'An evaluation of the literacy demands of general offending behaviour programmes' *Home Office Findings 233* (Home Office).

Davis, W, (2011) 'Big society', Discussant Big Society Workshop, Paper presented at *The Big Society: One Day Workshop, June 6, in Centre for Research on Socio-Cultural Change*, University of Manchester.

De Coster, S, and K Heimer, (2006) 'Crime at the Intersections: Race, Class, Gender and Violent Offending' in RD Peterson, LJ Krivo, and J Hagan, *The Many Colours of Crime: Inequalities of Race, Ethnicity and Crime in America* (New York Press).

Degener, T, (2016) 'Disability in a Human Rights Context' *Laws* 35.

Dean, M, (1999) *Governmentality: Power and Rule in Modern Society* (Sage).

Department of Health, (2009) *The Mental Capacity Fact Sheet for Social Scientists*, webarchive.nationalarchives.gov.uk/20130107105354/http://www.dh.gov.uk/prod_consum_dh/groups/dh_digitalassets/@dh/@en/@pg/documents/digitalasset/dh_106217.pdf.

Department of Health, (2009) *Improving Health, Supporting Justice The National Delivery Plan of the Health and Criminal Justice Programme Board*, webarchive.nationalarchives.gov.uk/20130107105354/http://www.dh.gov.uk/prod_consum_dh/groups/dh_digitalassets/documents/digitalasset/dh_109155.pdf.

Department of Health, (2010a) *Fulfilling and rewarding lives: The strategy for adults with autism in England (2010)*, webarchive.nationalarchives.gov.uk/20130107105354/http://www.dh.gov.uk/prod_consum_dh/groups/dh_digitalassets/@dh/@en/@ps/documents/digitalasset/dh_113405.pdf.

Department of Health, (2010b) *Towards 'Fulfilling and rewarding lives': The first year delivery plan for adults with autism in England*, webarchive.nationalarchives.gov.uk/20130107105354/http:/www.dh.gov.uk/prod_consum_dh/groups/dh_digitalassets/@dh/@en/@ps/documents/digitalasset/dh_115121.pdf.

Department of Health, (2010c) *Implementing Fulfilling and rewarding lives*, first published 17 December 2010, www.gov.uk/government/uploads/system/uploads/attachment_data/file/216129/dh_122908.pdf.

Department of Health, (2010d) *Transparency in Outcomes: a framework for Adult Social Care*, www.cpa.org.uk/cpa_documents/Transparency%20_in_Outcomes_for_adult_social_care.pdf.

Department of Health, (2010e) *A Vision for Adult Social Care: Capable Communities and Active Citizens*, webarchive.nationalarchives.gov.uk/ukgwa/+/http://www.dh.gov.uk/en/Publicationsandstatistics/Publications/PublicationsPolicyandGuidance/DH_121508.

Department of Health, (2010f) *Prioritising need in the context of Putting People First: A whole system approach to eligibility for social care Guidance on Eligibility Criteria for Adult Social Care, England 2010*, webarchive.nationalarchives.gov.uk/20130107105354/http:/www.dh.gov.uk/prod_consum_dh/groups/dh_digitalassets/@dh/@en/@ps/documents/digitalasset/dh_113155.pdf.

Department of Health, (2010g) *Making written information easier to understand for people with learning disabilities Guidance for people who commission or produce Easy Read information – Revised Edition 2010*, www.gov.uk/government/publications/making-written-information-easier-to-understand-for-people-with-learning-disabilities-guidance-for-people-who-commission-or-produce-easy-read-information-revised-edition-2010.

Department of Health, (2012a) *Risks and Issues Log: Adult Autism Strategy*, available on request: Michael.Swaffield@dh.gsi.gov.uk.

Department of Health, (2012b) *Adult Autism Strategy Programme Plan 2012/13*, available on request: Michael.Swaffield@dh.gsi.gov.uk.

Department of Health, (2012c) *Caring for our future: reforming care and support White Paper*, www.gov.uk/government/uploads/system/uploads/attachment_data/file/136422/White-Paper-Caring-for-our-future-reforming-care-and-support-PDF-1580K.pdf

Department of Health, (2013) *The Mandate: A mandate from the Government to NHS England: April 2014 to March 2015*, www.gov.uk/government/uploads/system/uploads/attachment_data/file/383495/2902896_DoH_Mandate_Accessible_v0.2.pdf.

Department of Health, (2014) *Think Autism Fulfilling and Rewarding Lives, the strategy for adults with autism in England: an update*, www.gov.uk/government/uploads/system/uploads/attachment_data/file/299866/Autism_Strategy.pdf.

Department of Health, (2015a) *Statutory guidance for Local Authorities and NHS organisations to support implementation of the Adult Autism Strategy*, www.gov.uk/government/uploads/system/uploads/attachment_data/file/422338/autism-guidance.pdf.

Department of Health, (2015b) *Mental Health Act 1983: Code of Practice*, www.gov.uk/government/uploads/system/uploads/attachment_data/file/435512/MHA_Code_of_Practice.PDF.

Department of Health, (2016a) *Care and Support Statutory Guidance*, www.gov.uk/government/publications/care-act-statutory-guidance/care-and-support-statutory-guidance.

Department of Health, (2016b) *Progress Report on Think Autism: the updated strategy for adults with autism in England*, www.gov.uk/government/uploads/system/uploads/attachment_data/file/492011/autism-progress-report.pdf.

Department of Health and Concordat Signatories, (2014) *Mental Health Crisis Care Concordat: Improving outcomes for people experiencing mental health crisis*, www.gov.uk/government/uploads/system/uploads/attachment_data/file/281242/36353_Mental_Health_Crisis_accessible.pdf.

Department of Health and Social Care and the Department for Education, (2021a) *The national strategy for autistic children, young people and adults: 2021 to 2026*, www.gov.uk/government/publications/national-strategy-for-autistic-children-young-people-and-adults-2021-to-2026.

Department of Health and Social Care and the Department for Education, (2021b) *Autism strategy implementation plan: 2021 to 2022 (Annex A)*, www.gov.uk/government/publications/national-strategy-for-autistic-children-young-people-and-adults-2021-to-2026.

Department of Health and the Home Office, (2000), *No Secrets: Guidance on developing and implementing multi-agency policies and procedures to protect vulnerable adults from abuse*, www.gov.uk/government/uploads/system/uploads/attachment_data/file/194272/No_secrets__guidance_on_developing_and_implementing_multiagency_policies_and_procedures_to_protect_vulnerable_adults_from_abuse.pdf.

Department of Health and Social Care and Ministry of Justice, (2022) *Policy paper: Draft Mental Health Bill 2022*, www.gov.uk/government/publications/draft-mental-health-bill-2022.
Diamond, SS, LE Bowman, M Wong, and MM Patton, (2010) 'Efficiency and Cost: the Impact of Video-conferenced Hearings on Bail Decisions' *The Journal of Criminal Law & Criminology* 100, 869.
Disability Rights Commission (DRC), (2006) *The Disability Equality Duty: Guidance on gathering and analysing evidence to inform action* (Disability Rights Commission).
Disability Rights UK (DRUK), (2022) *Social Model of Disability: Language*, www.disabilityrightsuk.org/social-model-disability-language?fbclid=IwAR0vRXHbahWOnDByb3wfG_Rg_SEmhMC7_UbKb9dbBSfxxme1_glvLXqd0-A.
Disley, E, E Gkousis, S Hulme, KI Morley, J Pollard, CL Saunders, J Sussex, and A Sutherland, (2021) *Outcome Evaluation of the National Model for Liaison and Diversion*, Santa Monica, CA: RAND Corporation, www.rand.org/pubs/research_reports/RRA1271-1.html.
Doak, J, (2008) *Victims' rights, human rights and criminal justice: reconceiving the role of third parties* (Bloomsbury Publishing).
Donovan, T, (2015) '"Slow start" to implementation of Care Act duty to support prisoners with care needs' *Community Care*, www.communitycare.co.uk/2015/09/23/slow-start-implementation-care-act-duty-support-prisoners-care-needs/.
Dodd, S, (2013) 'Personalisation, individualism and the politics of disablement' *Disability & Society* 28, 260.
Dodd, S, C Doyle, H Dickinson, F Buick, and S Yates, (2022) 'The forgotten prisoners: Exploring the impact of imprisonment on people with disability in Australia' *Criminology & Criminal Justice*.
Donzelot, J, (1979) *Policing the family* (Pantheon).
Dowse, L, (2017) 'Disruptive, dangerous and disturbing: the "challenge" of behaviour in the construction of normalcy and vulnerability' *Continuum* 31, 447.
Dowse, L, E Baldry, and P Snoyman, (2009) 'Disabling Criminology: Conceptualising the Intersections of Critical Disability Studies and Critical Criminology for People with Mental Health and Cognitive Disabilities in the Criminal Justice System' *Australian Journal of Human Rights* 15, 29.
Duff, A, L Farmer and S Marshall, (2007) *The Trial on Trial (vol 3): Towards a Normative Theory of the Criminal Trial: Towards a Normative Theory of the Criminal Trial* (Hart Publishing).
Dupont, I, (2008) 'Beyond Doing No Harm: A Call for Participatory Action Research with Marginalized Populations in Criminological Research' *Critical Criminology* 16, 197.
Dunn, DS, and EE Andrews, (2015) 'Person-first and identity-first language: Developing psychologists' cultural competence using disability language' *American Psychologist* 70, 255.
Eckholm, E, (1986) 'Schizophrenia's victims include strained families' *The New York Times* 45.
Edwards, SS, (1984) *Women on trial: a study of the female suspect, defendant, and offender in the criminal law and criminal justice system* (Manchester University Press).
Ehlers, S, and C Gillberg, (1993) 'The epidemiology of Asperger Syndrome, A total population study' *Journal of Child Psychology and Psychiatry* 34, 1327.
Eisenmajer, R, M Prior, S Leekam, L Wing, J Gould, M Welham, and B Ong, (1996) 'Comparison of clinical symptoms in autism and Asperger's disorder' *Journal of the American Academy of Child and Adolescent Psychiatry* 35, 1523.
Ellison, L, and VE Munro, (2009) 'Reacting to rape exploring mock jurors' assessments of complainant credibility' *British Journal of Criminology* 49, 202.
Evans, K, (2011) '"Big Society" in the UK: A Policy Review' *Children & Society* 25, 164.
Everall, IP, and A LeCouteur, (1990) 'Firesetting in an adolescent boy with Asperger's Syndrome' *British Journal of Psychiatry* 157, 284.
Equality and Human Rights Commission, (2010) *Guidance: Using a Service: reasonable adjustments for disabled people*, www.equalityhumanrights.com/en/multipage-guide/using-service-reasonable-adjustments-disabled-people.
Equality and Human Rights Commission, (2011) *Guidance: Your rights to equality from the criminal and civil justice systems and national security*, www.bl.uk/collection-items/your-rights-to-equality-from-the-criminal-and-civil-justice-systems-and-national-security.

Equality and Human Rights Commission, (2012a) *The essential guide to the public sector equality duty*, www.equalityhumanrights.com/en/publication-download/essential-guide-public-sector-equality-duty.

Equality and Human Rights Commission, (2012b) *Meeting the equality duty in policy and decision-making*, www.equalityhumanrights.com.

Equality and Human Rights Commission, (2015) *Your rights to equality from the criminal and civil justice systems and national security (vol 3 of 7)*, www.bl.uk/collection-items/your-rights-to-equality-from-the-criminal-and-civil-justice-systems-and-national-security.

Equality and Human Rights Commission, (2020) *Inclusive Justice: A System Designed for All – Findings and Recommendations*, www.equalityhumanrights.com/sites/default/files/ehrc_inclusive_justice_a_system_designed_for_all_june_2020.pdf.

Ericson, RV, (1982) *Reproducing order: A study of police patrol work* (vol 5) (University of Toronto Press).

Fairclough, S, L Mergaerts, and R Dehaghani, (2023) 'Introduction: The vulnerable accused in the criminal justice system' in *Vulnerability, the Accused, and the Criminal Justice System* (Routledge).

Fairclough, S, and H Greenwood, (2023) 'Vulnerable Defendants, Special Measures and Miscarriages of Justice in England and Wales' in R Dehaghani, S Fairclough and L Mergaerts (eds), *Vulnerability, the Accused, and the Criminal Justice System* (Routledge).

Farrington, DP, and A Morris, (1983) 'Sex, sentencing and reconviction' *British Journal of Criminology* 23, 229.

Ferguson, I, (2012) 'Personalisation, social justice and social work: a reply to Simon Duffy' *Journal of Social Work Practice: Psychotherapeutic Approaches in Health, Welfare and the Community* 26, 55.

Fielding, N, (1994) 'Cop Canteen Culture' in T Newburn, and EA Stanko (eds), *Just Boys Doing Business? Men, Masculinities and Crime* (Routledge)

Fineman, MA, (2008) 'The vulnerable subject: anchoring equality in the human condition' *Yale Journal of Law & Feminism* 20, 1.

Fineman, MA, (2010) 'The vulnerable subject and the responsive state' *Emory Law Journal* 60, 251.

Fineman, MA, (2017) 'Vulnerability and inevitable inequality' *Oslo Law Review* 4, 133.

Flesch, R, (1948) *The Flesch Reading Ease Readability Formula*, www.readabilityformulas.com/flesch-reading-ease-readability-formula.php.

Flint, J, (2003) 'Housing and ethopolitics: constructing identities of active consumption and responsible communities' *Economy and Society* 32, 611.

Flint, J, (2006) *Housing and Anti-social Behaviour: Perspectives, Policy and Practice* (Policy Press).

Flynn, E, (2013) 'Making Human Rights Meaningful for People with Disabilities: Advocacy, Access to Justice and Equality before the Law' *International Journal of Human Rights* 17.

Flynn, E, (2015) *Disabled Justice? Access to Justice and the UN Convention on the Rights of Persons with Disabilities* (Routledge).

Ford, JD, JD Elhai, DF Connor, and BC Frueh, (2010) 'Poly-victimization and risk of posttraumatic, depressive, and substance use disorders and involvement in delinquency in a national sample of adolescents' *Journal of Adolescent Health* 46, 545.

Foster, R, (2014) 'Does the Equality Act 2010 ensure equality for individuals with Asperger syndrome in the legal arena?: A survey of recent UK case law' *Autism Policy & Practice* 1, 58.

Foucault, M, (1967) *Madness and Civilisation: a History of Insanity in the Age of Reason* (Routledge).

Foucault, M, (1977) *Discipline and Punish: the Birth of the Prison* (Allen Lane).

Foucault, M, (1984) 'What is enlightenment?' in P Rabinow (ed), *Foucault Reader* (Penguin).

Foucault, M, (1991) 'Governmentality' in G Burchell, C Gordon, and P Miller (eds), *The Foucault Effect: Studies in Governmentality* (Harvester Wheatsheaf).

Freckelton, I, and D List, (2009) 'Asperger's disorder, criminal responsibility and criminal culpability. Psychiatry' *Psychology and Law* 16, 16.

Fredman, S, (2005) 'Disability Equality: A Challenge to the Existing Anti-Discrimination Paradigm' in A Lawson, and C Gooding (eds), *Disability Rights in Europe: From Theory to Practice* (Hart Publishing).

Fredman, S, (2011a) *Discrimination Law* (Oxford University Press).

Fredman, S, (2011b) 'The Public Sector Equality Duty' *Industrial Law Journal* 40, 405.
French, S, (1993) 'Disability, impairment or something in between?' in J Swain, V Finkelstein, S French, and M Oliver (eds), *Disabling Barriers, Enabling Environments* (Sage).
Fujikawa, Y, S Umeshita, and H Mutura, (2002) 'Sexual crimes committed by adolescents with Asperger's disorder: Problems of management by the viewpoint of probation officers at a family Court' *Japanese Journal of Child and Adolescent Psychiatry* 43, 280.
Fyson, R, (2007) 'Young people with learning disabilities who sexually harm others: the role of criminal justice within a multi-agency response' *British Journal of Learning Disabilities* 35, 181.
Galligan, DJ, (1987) 'Regulating Pre-Trial Decisions' in IH Dennis (ed), *Criminal Law and Justice*, (Sweet & Maxwell).
Galligan, DJ, (2010) 'Legal Theory and Empirical Research' in P Cane, and HM Kritzer (eds), *The Oxford Handbook of Empirical Legal Research*, (Oxford University Press).
Garland, D, (2001) *The Culture of Control* (Oxford University Press).
Garland, D, and R Sparks, (2000) *Criminology and Social Theory* (Clarendon).
Gelsthorpe, L, and P Raynor, (1995) 'Quality and Effectiveness in Probation Officers' Reports to Sentencers' *British Journal of Criminology* 35, 188.
Genn, H, (1999) *Paths to Justice* (Hart Publishing).
Gerring, J, (2004) 'What is a Case Study and What is it Good For?' *American Political Science Review* 98, 341.
Gernsbacher, MA, (2017) 'Editorial perspective: The use of person-first language in scholarly writing may accentuate stigma' *Journal of Child Psychology and Psychiatry* 58, 859.
Ghaziuddin, M, L Tsai, and N Ghazziuddin, (1991) 'Violence in Asperger's Syndrome: A Critique' *Journal of Autism and Developmental Disorders* 21, 349.
Gillan, C, (2009) *Autism Bill, Hansard* HC Deb, 21 Jan 2009, col 754.
Gillan, C, (2009) *Autism Bill, Hansard* HC Deb 27 February 2009, vol 488, cols 481–548.
Gillan, C., (2009) *Autism Bill, Hansard* HC Deb 29 April 2009, col 5.
Gillan, C, (2009) *Autism Bill, Hansard* HC Deb 19 Jun 2009, cols 540–583.
Gillan, C, (2009) *Autism Bill (Money), Hansard* HC Deb 5 May 2009, cols 140–142.
Gillberg, IC, and C Gillberg, (1989) 'Asperger syndrome – some epidemiological considerations: a research note' *Journal of Child Psychology and Psychiatry* 30, 631.
Gillberg, C, (1991) 'Clinical and neurobiological aspects of Asperger's syndrome in six family studies' in U Frith (ed), *Autism and Asperger's Syndrome* (Cambridge University Press).
Gillberg, C, (1998) 'Asperger's syndrome and high functioning autism' *British Journal of Psychiatry* 172, 200.
Gilling, D, (2010) 'Crime Control and Due Process in Confidence-Building Strategies: A Governmentality Perspective' *British Journal of Criminology* 50, 1136.
Glaser, W, and K Deane, (1999) 'Normalisation in an abnormal world: A study of prisoners with intellectual disability' *International Journal of Offender Therapy and Comparative Criminology* 43, 338.
Glover, G, and I Brown, (2015) 'People with intellectual disabilities hospitalised by courts in England' *Tizard Learning Disability Review* 20, 41.
Goddard, L, P Howlin, B Dritschel, and T Patel, (2007) 'Autobiographical memory and social problem-solving in Asperger syndrome' *Journal of Autism Developmental Disorders* 37, 291.
Goldberg, WA, KL Jarvis, K Osann, TM Laulhere, C Straub, E Thomas, P Filipek, and MA Spence, (2005) 'Brief report: Early social communication behaviors in the younger siblings of children with autism' *Journal of Autism and Developmental Disorders* 35, 657.
Goldson, B, and J Jamieson, (2002) 'Youth crime, the "parenting deficit" and state intervention: a contextual critique' *Youth Justice* 2, 82.
Gooding, P, and C O'Mahony, (2016) 'Laws on unfitness to stand trial and the UN Convention on the Rights of Persons with Disabilities: Comparing reform in England, Wales, Northern Ireland and Australia' *International Journal of Law, Crime and Justice* 44, 122.
Goodley, D, (2000) *Self-Advocacy in the Lives of People with Learning Disabilities* (Open University Press).

Goodley, D, (2011) *Disability studies: An interdisciplinary introduction* (Sage).
Goodley, D, (in press) *Disability studies* 3rd edn (Sage).
Gordon, C, (1991) 'Governmental Rationality: An Introduction' in G Burchell, C Gordon, and P Miller (eds), *The Foucault Effect: Studies in Governmentality* (University of Chicago Press).
Gormley, C, (2019) 'The prison experiences of people with learning disabilities' *The Howard League for Penal Reform ECAN Bulletin* 41, 32.
Gormley, C, (2022) 'The hidden harms of prison life for people with learning disabilities' *The British Journal of Criminology* 62, 261.
Gormley, C, and N Watson, (2021) 'Inaccessible justice: Exploring the barriers to justice and fairness for disabled people accused of a crime' *The Howard Journal of Crime and Justice* 60, 493.
Graby, S, (2016) 'Unworkable Conditions: Work, Benefits and Disabled People's Resistance to Capitalism' *Paper presented to Association for Social and Political Philosophy conference* London, 29 June, www.academia.edu/28495623/Unworkable_Conditions_work_benefits_and_disabled_peoples_resistance_to_capitalism_2016_.
Graetz, JE, (2010) 'Autism grows up: opportunities for adults with autism' *Disability and Society* 25, 33.
Granello, DH, and TA Gibbs, (2016) 'The power of language and labels: "the mentally ill" versus "people with mental illnesses"' *Journal of Counselling and Development* 94, 31.
Gudjonsson, GH, and L Henry, (2003) 'Child and adult witnesses with intellectual disability: The importance of suggestibility' *Legal and Criminological Psychology*, 8, 241.
Handley, P, (2003) 'Theorising Disability: Beyond "Common Sense"' *Politics* 23, 109.
Happé, FG, (1993) 'Communicative competence and theory of mind in autism: A test of relevance theory' *Cognition* 48, 101.
Hare, DJ, J Gould, R Mills, and L Wing, (1999) *A preliminary study of individuals with autistic spectrum disorders in three special hospitals in England* (The National Autistic Society at the Centre for Social and Communication Disorders).
Hare, DJ, C Pratt, M Burton, J Bromley, and E Emerson, (2004) 'The health and social care needs of family carers supporting adults with autistic spectrum disorders' *Autism* 8, 425.
Harris, J, (2003) 'Time to make up your mind: why choosing is difficult' *British Journal of Learning Disabilities* 31, 3.
Haskins, BG, and AS Silva, (2006) 'Asperger's disorder and criminal behaviour: Forensic-Psychiatric considerations' *Journal of the American Academy of Psychiatry and the Law* 34, 374.
Hay, C, and MM Evans, (2006) 'Violent victimization and involvement in delinquency: Examining predictions from general strain theory' *Journal of Criminal Justice* 34, 261.
Hayes, SC, P Shackell, P Mottram, and R Lancaster, (2007) 'Prevalence of intellectual disability in a major UK prison' *British Journal of Learning Disabilities* 35, 162.
Hayes, S, (2007a) 'Missing Out: offenders with learning disabilities and the criminal justice system' *British Journal of Learning Disabilities* 35, 146.
Hayes, S, (2007b) 'Women with Learning Disabilities who Offend: what do we know?' *British Journal of Learning Disabilities* 35, 187.
Hennessy, P, M Kite, and M Howie, (2011) 'Cameron relaunches Big Society "with moral purpose"' *The Telegraph*, 12 February 2011.
Hepple, B, (2010) 'The new single Equality Act in Britain' *The Equal Rights Review* 5, 11.
Hepworth, D, (2017) 'A critical review of current police training and policy for autism spectrum disorder' *Journal of Intellectual Disability and Offending Behaviour* 8, 212.
Herring, J, (2010) *Medical Law and Ethics Third Edition* (Oxford University Press).
Herring, J, (2016a) *Vulnerable Adults and the Law* (Oxford University Press).
Herring J, (2016b) 'Health As Vulnerability; Interdependence and Relationality' *The New bioethics: a multidisciplinary journal of biotechnology and the body* 22, 18.
Herring, J, (2020) 'Ageing and universal beneficial vulnerability' in D Bedford, and J Herring (eds), *Embracing Vulnerability: The Challenges and Implications for Law* (Routledge).
Higham, L, A Girardi, and HV Edwards, (2021) 'Clinical and criminal profile of internet offenders with ASD' *Journal of Intellectual Disabilities and Offending Behaviour* 12, 61.

Hill, E, S Berthoz, and U Frith, (2004) 'Brief report: Cognitive processing of own emotions in individuals with autistic spectrum disorder and in their relatives' *Journal of Autism and Developmental Disorders* 34, 229.

Hill, R, and A McMahon, (2001) *Families, Crime and Juvenile Justice* (Peter Lang Publishing).

HM Government, (2010) *Equality Act 2010: Explanatory Notes*, www.legislation.gov.uk/ukpga/2010/15/notes/contents.

HM Government, (2015) *The Care and Support (Eligibility Criteria) Regulations*, www.legislation.gov.uk/uksi/2015/313/pdfs/uksi_20150313_en.pdf.

HM Government, (2018), *Crown Court Digital Case System Guidance*, www.gov.uk/guidance/crown-court-digital-case-system-guidance.

HMI Probation, HMI Constabulary, HM Crown Prosecution Inspectorate and the Care Quality Commission, (2014) *A joint inspection of the treatment of offenders with learning disabilities within the criminal justice system – phase 1 from arrest to sentence*, webarchive.nationalarchives.gov.uk/20130128112038/http://www.justice.gov.uk/downloads/publications/inspectorate-reports/hmiprobation/learning-disabilities-thematic-report.pdf.

HMI Probation and HMI Prisons, (2015) *A joint inspection of the treatment of offenders with learning disabilities within the criminal justice system – phase two in custody and the community*, </a>www.justiceinspectorates.gov.uk/cjji/wp-content/uploads/sites/2/2015/03/Learning-Disabilities-phase-two-report.pdf.

Holdaway, S, (2013) 'Police race relations in the Big Society: Continuity and change' *Criminology and Criminal Justice* 13, 215.

Hollist, DR, LA Hughes, and LM Schaible, (2009) 'Adolescent maltreatment, negative emotion, and delinquency: An assessment of general strain theory and family-based strain' *Journal of Criminal Justice* 37, 379.

Holt, A, (2009) '(En)gendering responsibilities: experiences of parenting a "young offender"' *The Howard Journal of Criminal Justice* 48, 344.

Home Office, (1975) *Home Office Circular (155/1975): Bail Procedures* (Home Office).

Home Office, (2014) *Revised Code of Practice for the Detention, Treatment and Questioning of Persons by Police Officers Police and Criminal Evidence Act 1984 (PACE) – Code C*, www.gov.uk/government/publications/pace-code-c-2014.

Home Office, (2019) *CODE C Revised Code of Practice for the detention, treatment and questioning of persons by Police Officers*, assets.publishing.service.gov.uk/government/uploads/system/uploads/attachment_data/file/903473/pace-code-c-2019.pdf.

Home Office and Department of Health, (2000) *No secrets: Guidance on developing and implementing multi-agency policies and procedures to protect vulnerable adults from abuse*, www.gov.uk/government/publications/no-secrets-guidance-on-protecting-vulnerable-adults-in-care.

Home Secretary, the Lord Chancellor and the Attorney General, (2002) *White Paper: Justice for All*, The Stationery Office, brdo.com.ua/wp-content/uploads/2016/01/Justice-for-All-WPUK.pdf.

Hood, R, (1992) *Race and Sentencing* (Oxford University Press).

Hope, P, (2009) *Autism Bill, Hansard* HC Deb 27 February 2009, vol 488, cols 481–548.

Horwitz, A, (1978) 'Family, kin and friendship network in psychiatric help-seeking' *Social Science and Medicine* 12, 297.

Hough, M, J Jacobson, and A Millie, (2003) *The Decision to Imprison: Sentencing and the Prison Population*, (Prison Reform Trust).

Hoyano, LCH, (2010) 'Coroners and Justice Act 2009: (3) Special Measures Directions Take Two: Entrenching Unequal Access to Justice?' *The Criminal Law Review* 5, 345.

Hoyano, LCH, (2015) 'Reforming the adversarial trial for vulnerable witnesses and defendants' *The Criminal Law Review* 2, 107.

Hoyle, C, (2000) 'Being "a nosy bloody cow": ethical and methodological issues in researching domestic violence' in R King and E Wincup (eds), *Doing Research on Crime and Justice* (Oxford University Press).

Howard, H, (2021) 'Effective Participation of Mentally Vulnerable Defendants in the Magistrates' Courts in England and Wales – The "Front Line" from a Legal Perspective' *The Journal of Criminal Law* 85, 3.

Howlin, P, (2004) *Autism and Asperger Syndrome. Preparing for Adulthood*, 2nd edn (Routledge).

Hucklesby, A, (1996) 'Bail or Jail? The Practical Operations of the Bail Act 1976' *Journal of Legal Studies* 23, 213.

Hucklesby, A, (1997a) 'Court Culture: an explanation of Variations in the Use of Bail by Magistrates' Courts' *Howard Journal of Criminal Justice* 36, 129.

Hucklesby, A, (1997b) 'Remand Decision Makers' *The Criminal Law Review* 269.

Hudson, B, (1989) 'Discrimination and disparity: the influence of race on sentencing' *Journal of Ethnic and Migration Studies* 16, 23.

Hudson, B, (1998a) 'Mitigation for Socially Deprived Offenders' in A von Hirsch, and A Ashworth (eds), *Principled Sentencing: Readings on Theory and Policy*, (Northwestern University Press).

Hudson, B, (1998b) 'Doing Justice to Difference' in A Ashworth, and M Wasik (eds), *Fundamentals of Sentencing Theory* (Oxford University Press).

Hudson, B, (2001) 'Punishment, Rights, and Difference: Defending Justice in the Risk Society' in K Stenson, and R Sullivan (eds), *Crime, Risk and Justice: the Politics of Crime Control in Liberal Democracies* (Willan).

Hudson, B, (2004) *Justice in the Risk Society* (Sage).

Hudson, B, (2006) 'Beyond White Man's Justice: Race, Gender and Justice in Late Modernity' *Theoretical Criminology* 10, 29.

Hudson, B, (2007) 'Diversity, Crime and Criminal Justice' in M Maguire, R Morgan, and R Reiner (eds), *The Oxford Handbook of Criminology*, 4th edn (Oxford University Press).

Hudson, B, (2008) 'Difference, diversity and criminology: The cosmopolitan vision' *Theoretical Criminology* 12, 275.

Hudson, B, and G Bramhall, (2005) 'Assessing the "Other"' *British Journal of Criminology* 45, 721.

Hughes, B, (2002) 'Invalidated strangers: impairment and the cultures of modernity and postmodernity' *Disability and Society* 17, 571.

Hughes, B, and K Paterson, (1997) 'The social model of disability and the disappearing body: Towards a sociology of impairment' *Disability & Society* 12, 325.

Hughes, C, (2016) *Developing autism accreditation for prison services* (National Autistic Society).

Hughes, C, (2019) *Supporting autistic people in prison and probation services* (National Autistic Society).

Hughes C, J Russell, and TW Robbins, (1994) 'Evidence for executive function in autism' *Neuropsychologia* 32, 477.

Huitt, RK, and RL Peabody, (1969) *Congress: Two Decades of Analysis* (Harper and Row).

Hunter, C, N Hodge, J Nixon, and S Parr, (2007) 'Anti-social behaviour and disability – the response of social landlords' *People, Place & Policy Online* 1, 149.

Hunter, C, and J Nixon, (2001) 'Taking the blame and losing the home: women and anti-social behaviour' *Journal of Social Welfare and Family Law* 23, 395.

Inclusion London, (2015) *Factsheet: The Social Model of Disability*, www.inclusionlondon.org.uk/disability-in-london/social-model/the-social-model-of-disability-and-the-cultural-model-of-deafness/.

Jacobson, J, and M Hough, (2007) *Mitigation: The Role of Personal Factors in Sentencing* (Prison Reform Trust).

Jacobson, J, G Hunter, and A Kirby, (2016) *Inside Crown Court*, (Policy Press).

Jacobson, J, and J Talbot, (2009) *Vulnerable Defendants in the Criminal Courts: a review of provision for adults and children* (Prison Reform Trust).

James, IA, E Mukaetova-Ladinska, and K Reichelt, (2006) 'Diagnosing Aspergers syndrome in the elderly: a series of case presentations' *International Journal of Geriatric Psychiatry* 21, 951.

Johns, D, (2018) 'Confronting the disabling effects of imprisonment' *Social Justice* 45, 27.

Judicial College, (2013) *The Equal Treatment Bench Book*, see specifically the sections on *Physical Disability* and *Mental Disability, including mental illness*, www.sentencingcouncil.org.uk/wp-content/uploads/equal-treatment-bench-book-2013-with-2015-amendment.pdf.

Judicial College, (2022) *Equal Treatment Bench Book*, www.judiciary.uk/about-the-judiciary/diversity/equal-treatment-bench-book/.

Jupp, V, (2000) 'Formulating Research Problems' (in research) P Davies, P Francis, and V Jupp, *Doing Criminological Research* (Sage).

Kalunta-Crumpton, A, (1998) 'The Prosecution and Defence of Black Defendants in Drug Trials: Evidence of Claims-Making' *The British Journal of Criminology* 38, 561.

Kanner, L, (1943) 'Autistic disturbance of affective contact' *Nervous Child* 2, 217.

Katz, N, and Z Zemishlany, (2006) 'Criminal responsibility in Asperger's syndrome' *Israel Journal of Psychiatry and Related Science* 43, 166.

Keen, A., (2009) *Autism Bill, Hansard* HC Deb 19 Jun 2009, cols 540–583.

King, C, and GH Murphy, (2014) 'A systematic review of people with autism spectrum disorder and the criminal justice system' *Journal of Autism and Developmental Disorders* 44, 2717.

Kinnealey, M, and M Fuiek, (1999) 'The relationship between sensory defensiveness, anxiety, depression and perception of pain in adults' *Occupational Therapy International* 6, 195.

Kinnealey M, KP Koenig, and S Smith, (2011) 'Relationships between sensory modulation and social supports and health related quality of life' *American Journal of Occupational Therapy* 65, 320.

Knapp, M, R Romeo, and J Beecham, (2009) 'Economic cost of autism in the UK' *Autism* 13, 317.

Kohn, Y, T Fahum, G, Ratzoni, and A Apter, (1998) 'Aggression and sexual offence in Asperger's Syndrome' *Israel Journal of Psychiatry and Related Sciences* 35, 293.

Krauss MW, and MM Seltzer, (1999) 'An unanticipated life: the impact of lifelong caregiving', in JH Bersani (ed), *Responding to the Challenge: Current Trends and International Issues in Developmental Disabilities* (Brookline Books).

Krauss, MW, MM Seltzer, and HT Jacobson, (2005) 'Adults with autism living at home or in non-family settings: positive and negative aspects of residential status' *Journal of Intellectual Disability Research* 49, 111.

Kupfer, DJ, and DA Regier, (2008) *Current Activities: Report of the DSM-5 Task Force (September 2008)*, DSM-5 Task Force and Work group Update APA Division of Research Report to the APA BOT, dxrevisionwatch.files.wordpress.com/2009/12/item-11-a-dsm-task-force-report.pdf.

Ladyman, S, (2009) *Autism Bill, Hansard* HC Deb 27 February 2009, vol 488, cols 481–548.

Landa, RJ, and MC Goldberg, (2005) 'Language, social, and executive functions in high functioning autism: A continuum of performance' *Journal of autism and developmental disorders* 35, 557.

Lent, A, (2011) 'Big Society overview paper', Presented at *The Big Society: One Day Workshop*, June 6, in Centre for Research on Socio-Cultural Change, University of Manchester.

Lawless, CJ, (2011) 'Policing Markets: The Contested Shaping of Neo-Liberal Forensic Science' *The British Journal of Criminology* 51, 671.

Lawson, A, and M Priestley, (2017) 'The Social Model of Disability: Questions for Law and Legal Scholarship' in E Flynn, and P Blanck (eds), *Routledge Handbook of Disability Law and Human Rights* (Routledge).

Lewis, D, (2011) 'There is no crisis of civic participation: the Big Society risks undermining the integrity of both state and civil society' *British Politics and Policy at LSE* (26 Jan 2011), Blog Entry, blogs.lse.ac.uk/politicsandpolicy/big-society-risks-undermining-state-and-civil-society/.

Lippert, R, (2010) 'Mundane and Mutant Devices of Power' *European Journal of Cultural Studies* 13, 477.

Lippert, R, (2016) 'Governmentality analytics and human rights in criminology' in L Weber, E Fishwick, and M Marmo (eds), *The Routledge international handbook of criminology and human rights* (Routledge).

Lippert, R, and K Stenson, (2010) 'Advancing governmentality studies: Lessons from social constructionism' *Theoretical Criminology* 14, 473.

Loader, I, (1998) 'Criminology and the Public Sphere: Arguments for Utopian Realism' in P Walton, and J Young (eds), *The New Criminology Revisited* (Macmillan).

Loader, I, (2006) 'Fall of the "Platonic Guardians": Liberalism, Criminology and Political Responses to Crime in England and Wales' *British Journal of Criminology* 46, 561.

Loader, I, (2009) 'Ice cream and incarceration: On appetites for security and punishment' *Punishment & Society* 11, 241.

Local Government Group *et al*, (2010) *Think Local, Act Personal: Next Steps for Transforming Adult Social Care*, www.thinklocalactpersonal.org.uk/Browse/ThinkLocalActPersonal/.

Local Government Association, (2014) *Under pressure: How councils are planning for future cuts*, www.local.gov.uk/publications/under-pressure-how-councils-are-planning-future-cuts.

Local Government Association, (2014) *Get in on the Act: The Care Act 2014*, www.local.gov.uk/sites/default/files/documents/get-act-care-act-2014-pdf-006.pdf.

Long, V, (2021) 'Online Courts: Re-Assessing Inequality in the "Remote" Courtroom' *Excursions Journal* 11, 77.

Lord, C, M Rutter, and PC DiLavore, (2001) *Autism Diagnostic Observation Schedule* (Western Psychological Services).

Lord Chancellor's Department, (1997) *Who decides: making decisions on behalf of mentally incapacitated adults*, Cm 3803 (Stationery Office).

Loucks, N, (2006) *No One Knows: offenders with learning difficulties and learning disabilities review of prevalence and associated needs* (Prison Reform Trust).

Loucks, N, (2007) *Prisoners with learning difficulties and learning disabilities – review of prevalence and associated needs* (Prison Reform Trust).

Luke, L, IC Clare, H Ring, M Redley, and P Watson, (2012) 'Decision-making difficulties experienced by adults with autism spectrum conditions' *Autism* 16 612.

MacDonald, SJ, (2015) '"Community fear and harassment": learning difficulties and hate crime incidents in north-east England' *Disability & Society* 30, 353.

MacDonald, SK, (2006) 'The Principle of Composite Sentencing: Its Centrality to, and Implications for, the ASBO' *SSRN Working Paper Series*.

Mackay, RD, (2002) 'Mentally Disordered Offenders: Disposal and criminal responsibility issues' in M McConville, and G Wilson (eds), *The Handbook of the Criminal Justice System* (Oxford University Press).

Mackenzie, R, and J Watts, (2010) 'Injustice and disabilities: the case against the extradition of Gary McKinnon to the USA' *Tizard Learning Disability Review* 15, 45.

McNamara, D, (2023) 'Access to Justice for Persons with Disabilities as Suspects of Crime: The Transformative Power of Human Rights Laws' in R Dehaghani, S Fairclough, and L Mergaerts *Vulnerability, the Accused, and the Criminal Justice System* (Routledge).

Magill, C, and V Rivers/Crown Prosecution Service, (2010) *Prosecution of offenders with mental health problems or learning disabilities*, www.scie-socialcareonline.org.uk/prosecution-of-offenders-with-mental-health-problems-or-learning-disabilities/r/a11G00000017z20IAA.

Mair, G, (1986) 'Ethnic Minorities, Probation and Magistrates' Court' *British Journal of Criminology* 26, 147.

Manasse, ME, and NM Ganem, (2009) 'Victimization as a cause of delinquency: The role of depression and gender' *Journal of Criminal Justice* 37, 371.

Maras, K, I Marshall, and C Sands, (2019) 'Mock juror perceptions of credibility and culpability in an autistic defendant' *Journal of Autism and Developmental Disorders* 49, 996.

Maras, KL, L Crane, S Mulcahy, T Hawken, P Cooper, D Wurtzel, and A Memon, (2017) 'Brief report: Autism in the courtroom: Experiences of legal professionals and the autism community' *Journal of Autism and Developmental Disorders* 47, 2610–2620.

Marshall, G, (1975) 'The Judgement of One's Peers: Some Aims and Ideals of Jury Trials' in N Walker (ed), *The British Jury System* (Institute of Criminology).

Marshall-Tate, K, (2019) 'Autism Legislation and Policy' *A Clinician's Guide to Mental Health Conditions in Adults with Autism Spectrum Disorders: Assessment and Interventions* 40–51.

Mattison, M, and CS Allely, (2022) 'Questioning autistic people: Police and courts' in N Tyler, and A Sheeran *Working with Autistic People in the Criminal Justice and Forensic Mental Health Systems* (Routledge).

Mawson, D, A Grounds, and D Tantam, (1985) 'Violence and Asperger's Syndrome: A Case Study' *British Journal of Psychiatry* 147, 566.

Mayes, TA, (2003) 'Persons with Autism and Criminal Justice core concepts and leading cases' *Journal of Positive Behavior Interventions* 5, 92.

Mays, JM, (2006) 'Feminist disability theory: domestic violence against women with a disability' *Disability & Society* 21,147.

Mazurek, MO, (2014) 'Loneliness, friendship, and well-being in adults with autism spectrum disorders' *Autism* 18, 223.

McAdam, P, (2012) 'Knowledge and understanding of the autism spectrum amongst prison staff' *Prison Service Journal* 202, 26.

McBarnet, D, (1981) 'Magistrates' courts and the ideology of justice' *British Journal of Law and Society* 8, 181.

McCallum, D, (2001) *Personality and Dangerousness: Genealogies of Anti-social Personality Disorder* (Cambridge University Press).

McConville, M, (1998) 'Plea Bargaining: Ethics and Politics' *Journal of Law and Society* 25, 572.

McConville, M, (2000) 'Plea Bargaining: Ethics and Politics' in S Doran, and J Jackson (eds), *The Judicial Role in Criminal Proceedings* (Hart Publishing).

McConville, M, and J Baldwin, (1981) *Courts, Prosecution, and Conviction* (Clarendon Press).

McConville, M, and J Baldwin, (1982) 'The influence of race on sentencing in England' *The Criminal Law Review* 652.

McConville, M, A Sanders, and R Leng, (1991) *The Case for the Prosecution* (Routledge).

McConville, M, and J Hodgson, (1993) *Custodial legal advice and the right to silence* (HM Stationery Office).

McConville, M, J Hodgson, L Bridges, and A Pavlovic, (1994) *Standing Accused: The Organization and Practices of Criminal Defence Lawyers in Britain* (Clarendon Press).

McEwan, J, (2013) 'Vulnerable defendants and the fairness of trials' *Criminal Law Review* 2, 100.

McKay, C, (2016) 'Video Links from Prison: Permeability and the Carceral World' *International Journal for Crime, Justice & Social Democracy* 5, 21.

Mclaren, S (ed), (2011) *Transcripts of Judicial Proceedings in England and Wales: a Guide to Sources* (Inner Temple).

McLaughlin, P, (2021) 'Diversion and liaison services in England and Wales for mentally disorder offenders – a narrative review' *British Journal of Psychology Open* 7, S271.

Medland, A, for the Office for National Statistics (ONS), (2011) *Regional Trends: Portrait of the West Midlands* (Office for National Statistics).

Mencap, (2009) *Mencap's Make it clear: A guide to making easy read information*, inclusionireland.ie/wp-content/uploads/2020/10/makeitclearapr09.pdf.

Mercer, JE, and CS Allely, (2020) 'Autism spectrum disorders and stalking' *Journal of Criminal Psychology* 10, 201.

Miles C, R Condry, and E Windsor, (2023) 'Parricide, Mental Illness, and Parental Proximity: The Gendered Contexts of Parricide in England and Wales' *Violence against women* 29, 87.

Miller, P, and N Rose, (1990) 'Governing Economic Life' *Economy and Society* 19, 1.

Millie, A, J Jacobson and M Hough, (2003) 'Understanding the growth in the prison population in England and Wales' *Criminology and Criminal Justice* 3, 369.

Milton, D, (2012) 'On the ontological status of autism: The "double empathy problem"' *Disability and Society* 27, 1.

Milton, D, (2018) *The double empathy problem* (National Autistic Society).

Mind, (2023) *Mental health language*, www.mind.org.uk/media/7582/mental-health-language.pdf.

Ministry of Justice, (2008) *Disability Equality Scheme 2008–2011* (Ministry of Justice).

Ministry of Justice, (2010a) Green Paper *Breaking the Cycle: Effective Punishment Rehabilitation and Sentencing of Offenders*, webarchive.nationalarchives.gov.uk/20120119200607/http:/www.justice.gov.uk/consultations/docs/breaking-the-cycle.pdf.

Ministry of Justice, (2010b) 'Breaking the Cycle: Effective Punishment, Rehabilitation and Sentencing of Offenders' *Green Paper Evidence Report*, www.gov.uk/government/uploads/system/uploads/attachment_data/file/185947/green-paper-evidence-a.pdf.

Ministry of Justice, (2010c) *Good practice guidance: commissioning, administering and producing psychiatric reports for sentencing Prepared for: Her Majesty's Court Service*, pdf4pro.com/view/good-practice-guidance-commissioning-1a05f3.html.

Ministry of Justice, (2012a) *Estimating the prevalence of disability amongst prisoners: results from the Surveying Prisoner Crime Reduction (SPCR) survey*, www.gov.uk/government/publications/estimating-the-prevalence-of-disability-amongst-prisoners.

Ministry of Justice, (2012b) *Swift and Sure Justice: The Government's Plans for Reform of the Criminal Justice System*, assets.publishing.service.gov.uk/government/uploads/system/uploads/attachment_data/file/217328/swift-and-sure-justice.pdf.

Ministry of Justice, (2013a) *Results from the Offender Management Community Cohort Study (OMCCS): Assessment and sentence planning*, assets.publishing.service.gov.uk/government/uploads/system/uploads/attachment_data/file/309959/results-omccs pdf.

Ministry of Justice, (2013b) *Transforming Rehabilitation: A Strategy for Reform*, consult.justice.gov.uk/digital-communications/transforming-rehabilitation/results/transforming-rehabilitation-response.pdf.

Ministry of Justice, (2013c) *Consolidated Criminal Practice Direction:* Practice Direction III.30 (Ministry of Justice).

Ministry of Justice, (2015) *Criminal Justice Statistics Quarterly Update to June 2015: England and Wales Ministry of Justice Statistics bulletin*, www.gov.uk/government/uploads/system/uploads/attachment_data/file/478037/criminal-justice-statistics-quarterly-june-2015.pdf.

Ministry of Justice, (2023) *Criminal Justice Statistics quarterly, England and Wales, year ending September 2022 (quarterly)*, assets.publishing.service.gov.uk/government/uploads/system/uploads/attachment_data/file/1136825/criminal-justice-statistics-september-2022.pdf.

Minkowitz, T, (2014) 'Rethinking criminal responsibility from a critical disability perspective: The abolition of insanity/incapacity acquittals and unfitness to plead, and beyond' *Griffith Law Review* 23, 434.

Morris, J, (1991) *Pride Against Prejudice* (Women's Press).

Mouridsen, S, B Rich, T Isager and N Nedergaard, (2007) 'Pervasive developmental disorders and criminal behaviour – A case control study' *International Journal of Offender Therapy and Comparative Criminology* 7, 1.

Mulcahy, L, (2007) 'Architects of Justice: The Politics of Courtroom Design' *Social and Legal Studies* 16, 383.

Mulcahy, L, (2021) 'Virtual Poverty? What Happens When Criminal Trials Go Online?' in D Cowan, and A Mumford (eds), *Pandemic Legalities: Legal Responses to COVID-19 – Justice and Social Responsibility* (Bristol University Press).

Mulgan, G, N Bacon, P Griffith, and S Tucker, (2010) *Investing in Social Growth: Can the Big Society be more than a slogan?* (The Young Foundation).

Muncie, J, (1999) 'Institutionalised Intolerance: youth justice and the 1998 Crime and Disorder Act' *Critical Social Policy* 19, 147.

Mundy P, (2009) 'Lessons learned from autism: An information processing model of joint attention and social cognition' *Minnesota Symposium on Child Psychology: Meeting the Challenge of Translational Research in Child Psychology* 35, 59.

Murphy, D, (2002) 'Asperger's Syndrome: Forensic Considerations' *Forensic Update* 68: 10–16

Murphy, D, (2010) 'Understanding offenders with autism-spectrum disorders: what can forensic services do?' *Advances in Psychiatric Treatment* 16, 44.

Murphy, D, (2018) 'Interviewing individuals with an autism spectrum disorder in forensic settings' *International Journal of Forensic Mental Health* 17, 310.

Murrie, DC, JI Warren, M Kristiansson, and PE Dietz, (2002) 'Asperger's Syndrome in forensic settings' *International Journal of Forensic Mental Health* 1, 59.

NACRO, (2006) *Liaison and diversion for mentally disordered offenders*, www.yumpu.com/en/document/view/24222498/criminal-justice-liaison-and-diversion-schemes-a-focus-on-nacro.

National Audit Office, (2009) *Report: Supporting people with autism through adulthood* TSO (The Stationery Office), www.nao.org.uk/wp-content/uploads/2009/06/0809556.pdf.

National Audit Office, (2012) *Progress in implementing the 2010 Adult Autism Strategy*, www.nao.org.uk/briefings/memorandum-progress-in-implementing-the-2010-adult-autism-strategy/.

National Audit Office, (2015) *Care services for people with learning disabilities and challenging behaviour*, www.nao.org.uk/wp-content/uploads/2015/02/Care-services-for-people-with-learning-disabilities-and-challenging-behaviour.pdf.

National Autistic Society, (2005) *Autism: A Guide for Criminal Justice Professionals* (National Autistic Society).

National Autistic Society, (2008) *I Exist: The message from adults with autism in England* (National Autistic Society).

National Autistic Society, (2020) *Left Stranded*, www.autism.org.uk/what-we-do/news/coronavirus-report.

National Autistic Society, (2020) *Criminal justice*, www.autism.org.uk/advice-and-guidance/topics/criminal-justice/criminal-justice.

National Autistic Society, (2021) *Autism accreditation*.

National Autistic Society, (2022) '"My life could be so different": Experiences of autistic young people in the youth justice system' www.autism.org.uk/what-we-do/news/youth-justice-report.

National Development Team for inclusion (NDTi), (2013) *The Green Light Toolkit 2013: A guide to auditing and improving your mental health service so that it is effective in supporting people with autism and people with learning disabilities*, surveys.ndti.org.uk/site/assets/files/1290/green-light-toolkit-2013.pdf.

National Institute for Health and Clinical Excellence (NICE), (2012a) *Full Guideline – Autism spectrum disorder in adults: diagnosis and management Clinical guideline*, www.nice.org.uk/guidance/cg142.

National Institute for Health and Clinical Excellence (NICE), (2012b) 'Autism: The NICE Guideline on recognition, referral, diagnosis and management of adults on the autism spectrum', *National Clinical Guideline Number 142* https://www.nice.org.uk/guidance/cg142/evidence/full-guideline-186587677.

National Institute for Health and Clinical Excellence (NICE), (January 2014) *Autism Quality standard*, www.nice.org.uk/guidance/qs51.

National Institute for Health and Clinical Excellence (NICE), (2021) *2021 surveillance of autism (NICE guidelines CG128, CG142 and CG170)*, www.nice.org.uk/guidance/cg142/resources/2021-surveillance-of-autism-nice-guidelines-cg128-cg142-and-cg170-pdf-11846121650629.

National Police Autistic Association, (2022) *Alert card schemes*, www.npaa.org.uk/alert-card-schemes/.

National Police Improvement Agency (NPIA), (2009) *Guidance on Personal Safety*, library.college.police.uk/docs/college-of-policing/PSM_2020/MOD_01_INTRODUCTION.pdf.

Newman, C, A Cashin, and I Graham, (2019) 'Identification of service development needs for incarcerated adults with autism spectrum disorders in an Australian prison system' *International Journal of Prisoner Health*, 15, 24.

NHS England, (2010) *Guidance on the NHS Standard Contract for Mental Health and Learning Disability Services 2010/11*, www.gov.uk/government/publications/leave-for-will-pls-nhs-standard-contracts-for-2012-13.

NHS England, (2014b) *Liaison and Diversion Standard Service Specification 2013/14*, www.england.nhs.uk/wp-content/uploads/2014/04/ld-op-mod-1314.pdf.

NHS England, (2019a) *Liaison and Diversion Standard Service Specification 2019*, www.england.nhs.uk/wp-content/uploads/2019/12/national-liaison-and-diversion-service-specification-2019.pdf.

NHS England, (2019b) People with a learning disability, autism or both Liaison and Diversion Managers and Practitioner resources, www.england.nhs.uk/wp-content/uploads/2020/01/Learning-disability-and-autism.pdf.

NHS England, (2019c) Police and Courts: Liaison and Diversion Manager and Practitioner Resources, www.england.nhs.uk/wp-content/uploads/2020/01/Police-and-courts-briefing.pdf.

Nicholson, G, (2011) *Vanguard local views*, Paper presented at The Big Society: One Day Workshop, 6 June, in Centre for Research on Socio-Cultural Change, University of Manchester, United Kingdom.

Nind, M, (2008) 'Conducting qualitative research with people with learning, communication and other disabilities: Methodological challenges' *ESRC National Centre for Research Methods Review Paper*, eprints.ncrm.ac.uk/491/1/MethodsReviewPaperNCRM-012.pdf.

Nirje, B, (1985) 'The basis and logic of the normalisation principle' *Australian and New Zealand Journal of Developmental Disabilities* 11, 65.

North, AS, AJ Russell, and GH Gudjonsson, (2008) 'High functioning autism spectrum disorders: an investigation of psychological vulnerabilities during interrogative interview' *Journal of Forensic Psychiatry & Psychology* 19, 323.

Nussbaum, MC, (2006) 'Frontiers of Justice: Disability, Nationality, Species Membership' *Tanner Lectures on Human Values* (Harvard University Press).

Office for Disability Issues, (2012) *Equality Act 2010 Guidance: Guidance on matters to be taken into account in determining questions relating to the definition of disability*, www.gov.uk/government/uploads/system/uploads/attachment_data/file/85038/disability-definition.pdf.

O'Grady, A, P Pleasence, N Balmer, A Duck, and H Genn, (2004), 'Disability, social exclusion and the consequential experience of justiciable problems' *Disability and Society* 19, 259.

Oliver, M, (1990) *The Politics of Disablement* (Macmillan).

Oliver, M, (1996) *Understanding Disability: From Theory to Practice* (Macmillan).

Oliver, M, and C Barnes, (1998) *Disabled people and social policy: from exclusion to inclusion* (Longman).

O'Malley, P, (1992) 'Risk, Power, and Crime Prevention' *Economy and Society* 21, 252.

O'Malley, P, L Weir, and C Shearing, (1997) 'Governmentality, Criticism, Politics' *Economy and Society* 26, 501.

O'Mahony, C, (2015) 'The Implications of the United Nations Convention in the Rights of Persons with Disabilities on Criminal Responsibility' in C O'Mahony and G Quinn (eds), *The United Nations Convention on the Rights of Persons with Disabilities: Comparative, Regional and Thematic Perspectives* (Intersentia).

O'Mahony, C, and C Hackett, (2015) 'The CRPD and the Fusion of Mental Health and Legal Capacity Legislation' in C O'Mahony, and G Quinn (eds), *The United Nations Convention on the Rights of Persons with Disabilities: Comparative, Regional and Thematic Perspectives* (Intersentia).

O'Nions, E, I Petersen, JE Buckman, R Charlton, C Cooper, A Corbett, and J Stott, (2023) 'Autism in England: assessing underdiagnosis in a population-based cohort study of prospectively collected primary care data' *The Lancet Regional Health – Europe* 29.

Ortoleva, S, (2011) 'Inaccessible Justice: Human Rights, Persons with Disabilities and the Legal System' *ILSA Journal of International and Comparative Law* 17, 281.

O'Sullivan, C, and D McNamara, (2021) 'The "necessity" of austerity and its relationship with the UN Convention on the Rights of Persons with Disabilities: A case study of Ireland and the United Kingdom' *Human Rights Law Review* 21, 157.

Pais, S and M Knapp, (2021) *The Impact of COVID-19 on Autistic People in the United Kingdom Final report*, piru.ac.uk/assets/files/The_Impact_of_COVID-19_on_Autistic_People_in_the_United_Kingdom_Final_Report.pdf.

Parsons, S and G Sherwood, (2015) *The Widgit Symbol Custody Sheet Pilot Project – Final Report* The University of Southampton, www.widgit.com.

Parsons, S, and G Sherwood, (2015) 'A pilot evaluation of using symbol-based information in police custody' *British Journal of Learning Disabilities*.

Parsons, T, (1951) *The Social System* (Free Press).

Payne, KL, KL Maras, AJ Russell, and MJ Brosnan, (2020) 'Are mental health, family and childhood adversity, substance use and conduct problems risk factors for offending in autism?' *Journal of Autism and Developmental Disorders*.

Payne, KL, A Russell, R Mills, K Maras, D Rai, and M Brosnan, (2019) 'Is there a relationship between cyber-dependent crime, autistic-like traits and autism?' *Journal of Autism and Developmental Disorders*, 49, 4159.

Peabody, RL, SW Hammond, J Torcom, LP Brown, C Thompson, and R Kolodny, (1990) 'Interviewing Political Elites' *Political Science and Politics* 23, 451.

Peay, J, (2007) 'Mentally Disordered Offenders, Mental Health, and Crime, in M Maguire, R Morgan, and R Reiner (eds), *The Oxford Handbook of Criminology* (Oxford University Press).

Peay, J, (2013) *Mental Health and Crime* (Routledge).

Peay, J, (2014) 'Imprisoning the mentally disordered: a manifest injustice?' *Law Society and Economy Working Paper Series*, WP7/2014, (London School of Economics and Political Science).

Peay, J, and E Player, (2018) 'Pleading Guilty: Why Vulnerability Matters' *The Modern Law Review* 81, 929.

Pellicano, E, (2013) 'Sensory symptoms in autism: A blooming, buzzing confusion?' *Child Development Perspectives* 7, 143.

Pennington, L, (2015) 'A case study approach to procedural justice: Parents' views in two juvenile delinquency courts in the United States' *British Journal of Criminology* 55, 901.

Perham, L, (2002) *Autism* 377, col 226-47WH

Phillips, C, D Brown, Z James, and P Goodrich, (1998) *Entry into the criminal justice system: a survey of police arrests and their outcomes – Home Office Research Study 185* (Home Office).

Player, E, (2007) 'Remanding Women in Custody: Concerns for Human Rights' *Modern Law Review* 70, 402.

Player, E, J Roberts, J Jacobson, M Hough, and J Robottom, (2010) 'Remanded in Custody: An Analysis of Recent Trends in England and Wales' *The Howard Journal* 49, 231.

Plotnikoff, J, and R Woolfson, (2004) *In Their Own Words: The Experiences of 50 Young Witnesses in Criminal Proceedings* (NSPCC).

Plotnikoff, J, and R Woolfson, (2009) *Measuring Up? Evaluating implementation of Government commitments to young witnesses in Criminal Proceedings* (NSPCC).

Plotnikoff, J, and R Woolfson, (2014) 'Coming soon to a Court Room Near You' *Law in Practice*, 11.

Police and Crime Commissioners of Bedfordshire, Cambridgeshire and Hertfordshire (2016), *Notice of Rights and Entitlements: easy read*, www.herts.police.uk/SysSiteAssets/media/downloads/hertfordshire/rights-and-entitlements-easy-read-booklet/rights-and-entitlements-easy-read-booklet.pdf.

Priestley, M, (1998) 'Constructions and Creations: Idealism, Materialism and Disability Theory' (1998) *Disability & Society* 13, 75.

Prison Reform Trust, (2012) *Making the Difference: the role of adult social care services in supporting vulnerable offenders*, www.prisonreformtrust.org.uk/Portals/0/Documents/Making%20the%20difference.pdf.

Prison Reform Trust (PRT) and Rethink, (2013) *Mental Health and Learning Disabilities in the Criminal Courts: Information for magistrates, district judges and court staff*, www.mhldcc.org.uk/media/493/rmi_prt_mhldcc_sept2013.pdf.

Prison Reform Trust, (2014) *Prison: the facts Bromley Briefings Summer 2014*, www.thebromleytrust.org.uk/files/prisonfactsmay2014.pdf.

Prison Reform Trust, (2015) *Prison: the facts Bromley Briefings Summer 2015*, prisonreformtrust.org.uk/publication/bromley-briefings-prison-factfile-autumn-2015/.

Public Bill Committee, (2009) *Autism Bill* 29 April 2009 HC Deb col 3.

Public Bill Committee, (2009) *Autism Bill*, 6 May 2009 HC Deb col 19.

Public Bill Committee, (2009) *Autism Bill*, 13 May 2009 HC Deb cols 23–27.

Quarmby, K, (2013) *Scapegoat: Why We are Failing Disabled People* (Portobello Books Ltd).

Quirk, H, T Seddon, and G Smith, (2010) *Regulation and Criminal Justice: Innovations in Policy and Research* (Cambridge University Press).

Redmayne, M, (2009) 'Theorizing the Criminal Trial' *New Criminal Law Review* 12, 287.

Reid, JA, and CJ Sullivan, (2012) 'Unravelling Victim-Offender Overlap: Exploring Profiles and Constellations of Risk *Victims & Offenders: An International Journal of Evidence-based Research, Policy, and Practice* 7, 327.

Reindal, SM, (1999) 'Independence, dependence, interdependence: Some reflections on the subject and personal autonomy' *Disability and Society* 14, 353.

Reiner, R, (2013) 'Who governs? Democracy, plutocracy, science and prophecy in policing' *Criminology and criminal justice* 13, 161.

Reveley, S, and I Dickie, (2023) '"Street" policing and autism: perceptions and preconceptions of police officers when interacting with autistic suspects in the community' in *Autism and Criminal Justice* (Routledge).

Richards, D, (1996) 'Elite Interviewing: Approaches and Pitfalls' *Politics* 16, 199.

Ridley, L, (2022) 'No place for old men? Meeting the needs of an ageing male prison population in England and Wales' *Social Policy and Society* 21, 597.

Rioux, MH, L Basser, and M Jones, (2011) *Critical Perspectives on Human Rights and Disability Law* (Martinus Nijhoff).

Rioux, M, and CA Riddle, (2011) 'Values in Disability Policy and Law: Equality' in MH Rioux, L Basser, and M Jones (eds), *Critical Perspectives on Human Rights and Disability Law* (Martinus Nijhoff).

Ritchie, J, J Lewis, and G Elam, (2003) 'Designing and selecting samples' in J Ritchie, and J Lewis (eds), *Qualitative research practice: A guide for social science students and researchers* (Sage).

Roberts, JV, (2011) 'Punishing, more or less: exploring aggravation and mitigation in sentencing' in JV Roberts (ed), *Mitigation and Aggravation at Sentencing* (Cambridge University Press).

Roberts, JV, and J Pina-Sánchez, (2022) 'Sentence reductions for a guilty plea: The impact of the revised guideline on rates of pleas and "cracked trials"' *The Journal of Criminal Law* 86, 327.

Roberts, P, (1996) 'What Price A Free Market in Forensic Science Services? The Organization and Regulation of Science in the Criminal Process' *The British Journal of Criminology* 36, 37.

Robertson, B, S Dell, A Grounds, and K James, (1992) 'Mentally Disordered Remand Prisoners' *Home Office Research Bulletin* 32, 1.

Robinson, L, S Tucker, C Hargreaves, A Roberts, J Shaw, and D Challis, (2022) 'Providing social care following release from prison: Emerging practice arrangements further to the introduction of the 2014 Care Act' *The British Journal of Social Work* 52, 982.

Rocha, P, and S Hean, (2021) 'Tracing the historical development of a service model for interagency collaboration: contradictions as barriers and potential drivers for change' in S Hean, B Johnsen, A Kajamaa, and L Kloetzer (eds), *Improving Interagency Collaboration, Innovation and Learning in Criminal Justice Systems* (Palgrave Macmillan).

Rodger, JJ, (2012) '"Regulating the Poor': Observations on the "Structural Coupling" of Welfare, Criminal Justice and the Voluntary Sector in a "Big Society"' *Social Policy & Administration* 46, 413.

Rodriguez, SM, L Ben-Moshe, and H Rakes, (2020) 'Carceral protectionism and the perpetually (in)vulnerable' *Criminology and Criminal Justice* 20, 537–50.

Rogers, J, (2006) 'Restructuring the Exercise of Prosecutorial Discretion in England' *Oxford Journal of Legal Studies* 26, 775.

Rogers, C, (2020) 'Just mothers: criminal justice, care ethics and 'disabled' offenders' *Disability & Society* 35, 926.

Rose, N, (1996) 'The Death of the Social? Re-Figuring the Territory of Government' *Economy and Society* 25, 327.

Rose, N, (1999) *Powers of Freedom: Reframing Political Thought* (Cambridge University Press).

Rose, N, P O'Malley, and M Valverde, (2006) 'Governmentality' *Annual Review of Law and Social Science* 2, 83.

Rossner, M, D Tait, and M McCurdy, (2021) 'Justice reimagined: challenges and opportunities with implementing virtual courts' *Current Issues in Criminal Justice* 33, 94.

Roulstone, A, P Thomas, and S Balderston, (2011) 'Between hate and vulnerability: unpacking the British criminal justice system's construction of disablist hate crime' *Disability & Society* 26, 351.

Roulstone, A, and K Sadique, (2013) 'Vulnerable to misinterpretation: disabled people, "vulnerability", hate crime and the fight for legal recognition' in A Roulstone, and H Mason-Bish (eds), *Disability, Hate Crime and Violence* (Routledge).

Runswick-Cole, K, and D Goodley, (2011) 'Big Society: a dismodernist critique' *Disability & Society* 26, 881.

Ryan, S, (2010) '"Meltdowns", surveillance and managing emotions; going out with children with autism' *Health and Place* 16, 868.

Ryan, A, and HR Bernard, (2003) 'Techniques to identify themes' *Field Methods* 15, 85.

Ryan, S, and KR Cole, (2009) 'From advocate to activist? Mapping the experiences of mothers of children on the autism spectrum' *Journal of Applied Research in Intellectual Disabilities* 22, 43.

Sandahl, C, (2003) 'Queering the crip or cripping the queer? Intersections of queer and crip identities in solo autobiographical performance' *GLQ: A Journal of Lesbian and Gay Studies* 9, 25.

Sanders, A, (1989) *Advice and assistance at police stations and the 24 hour duty solicitor scheme*, (Lord Chancellor's Department).

Schwartz-Watts, DM, (2005) 'Asperger's disorder and murder' *Journal of the American Academy of Psychiatry and the Law* 33, 390.

Schoen, SA, LJ Miller, and KE Green, (2008) 'Pilot study of the Sensory Over-Responsivity Scales: assessment and inventory' *American Journal of Occupational Therapy* 62, 393.

Scott, D, (2007) 'The changing face of the English Prison: a critical review of imprisonment' in Y Jewkes (ed), *Handbook On Prisons 2007*.

Schulze, M, (2010) 'Understanding The UN Convention On The Rights Of Persons With Disabilities: A Handbook on the Human Rights of Persons with Disabilities', www.internationaldisabilityalliance.org/sites/default/files/documents/hi_crpd_manual2010.pdf.

Scragg, P, and A Shah, (1994) 'Prevalence of Asperger Syndrome in a secure hospital' *British Journal of Psychiatry* 165, 679.

Seddon, T, (2007) *Punishment and Madness: Governing Prisoners with Mental Health Problems* (Routledge-Cavendish).

Seddon, T, (2008) 'Dangerous Liaisons: Personality disorder and the politics of risk' *Punishment and Society* 10, 301.

Seltzer, MM, and MW Krauss, (1994) 'Aging parents with co-resident adult children: the impact of lifelong caregiving' in MM Seltzer, MW Krauss, and MP Janicki (eds), *Life Course Perspectives on Adulthood and Old Age* (The American Association on Mental Retardation Monograph Series).

Seltzer, MM, MW Krauss, GI Orsmond, and C Vestal, (2001) 'Families of adolescents and adults with autism: uncharted territory' *International Review of Research in Mental Retardation* 23, 267.

Seltzer, MM, MW Krauss, PT Shattuck, G Orsmond, A Swe, and C Lord, (2003) 'The symptoms of autism spectrum disorders in adolescence and adulthood' *Journal of Autism and Developmental Disorders* 33, 565.

Sentencing Guidelines Council, (2004) *Overarching Principles: Seriousness* (Sentencing Guidelines Council), www.sentencingcouncil.org.uk/wp-content/uploads/web_seriousness_guideline.pdf.

Sentencing Guidelines Council, (2004) *Guideline on Reduction in Sentence for a Guilty Plea*, (Sentencing Guidelines Council).

Sentencing Guidelines Council, (2007) *Guideline on Reduction in Sentence for a Guilty Plea: Definitive Guideline (Revised 2007)* Sentencing Guidelines Council, www.sentencingcouncil.org.uk/wp-content/uploads/Reduction-in-Sentence-for-Guilty-Plea-definitive-guideline-SC-Web.pdf.

Sentencing Guidelines Council, (2009) *Overarching Principles: Sentencing Youths* (Sentencing Guidelines Council), www.sentencingcouncil.org.uk.

Sentencing Council, (2014) *Sexual Offences Definitive Guideline* (Sentencing Council), www.sentencingcouncil.org.uk/wp-content/uploads/Final_Sexual_Offences_Definitive_Guideline_content_web1.pdf.

Sentencing Council, (2017) *Reduction in Sentence for a Guilty Plea, Definitive Guideline* (Sentencing Council), www.sentencingcouncil.org.uk/overarching-guides/magistrates-court/item/reduction-in-sentence-for-a-guilty-plea-first-hearing-on-or-after-1-june-2017/#B.%20Key%20principles.

Sentencing Council, (2018) *Bladed Articles and Offensive Weapons, Definitive Guideline*, www.sentencingcouncil.org.uk/wp-content/uploads/Bladed-Article-Definitive-guideline_WEB-1.pdf.

Sentencing Council, (2019) *General guideline: overarching principles* (Sentencing Council), www.sentencingcouncil.org.uk/overarching-guides/crown-court/item/general-guideline-overarching-principles/.

Sentencing Council, (2020) *Sentencing offenders with mental disorders, developmental disorders, or neurological impairments*, London: Sentencing Council, www.sentencingcouncil.org.uk/overarching-guides/crown-court/item/sentencing-offenders-with-mental-disorders-developmental-disorders-or-neurological-impairments/.

Sevlever, M, ME Roth, and JM Gillis, (2013) 'Sexual abuse and offending in autism spectrum disorders' *Sexuality and Disability*, 31, 189.

Shakespeare, T, (2006a) 'The social model of disability' *The disability studies reader* 2, 197.

Shakespeare, T, (2006b) *Disability Rights and Wrongs* (Routledge).
Shakespeare, T, and N Watson, (2001) 'The social model of disability: an outdated ideology? Exploring theories and expanding methodologies' *Research in Social Science and Disability* 2, 9.
Shapland, J, (1981) *Between Conviction and Sentence* (Routledge).
Shapland, J, (2011) 'Personal mitigation and assumptions about offending and desistence' in JV Roberts (ed), *Mitigation and Aggravation at Sentencing* (Cambridge University Press).
Shute, S, R Hood, and F Seemungal, (2005) *A Fair Hearing? Ethnic Minorities in the Criminal Courts* (Willan Publishing).
Sinclair, J, (1999) *Why I dislike "person-first" language*, web.archive.org/web/20090210190652/http://web.syr.edu/~jisincla/person_first.htm.
Simon, J, (2001) 'Governing through Crime Metaphors' *Brooklyn Law Review* 67, 1035.
Simon, J, (2007) *Governing through crime: How the war on crime transformed American democracy and created a culture of fear* (Oxford University Press).
Siponmaa, L, M Kristiansson, C Jonson, A Nyden, and C Gillberg, (2001) 'Juvenile and young adult mentally disordered offenders: The role of child neuropsychiatric disorders' *Journal of the American Academy of Psychiatry and the Law* 29, 420.
Slavny-Cross, R, C Allison, S Griffiths, and S Baron-Cohen, (2022) 'Autism and the criminal justice system: An analysis of 93 cases' *Autism Research* 15, 904.
Smith, T (ed), (2023) *Autism and Criminal Justice: The Experience of Suspects, Defendants and Offenders in England and Wales* (Taylor & Francis).
Social Exclusion Unit, (2001) *Preventing Social Exclusion* (The Cabinet Office), www.bris.ac.uk/poverty/downloads/keyofficialdocuments/Preventing%20Social%20Exclusion.pdf.
Social Sciences & Humanities Inter-divisional Research Ethics Committee (IDREC), (2008) *Protocol for Elite Interviews: PROTOCOL NO. SSD/IDREC/2008/P 14.1: 4* (University of Oxford Central University Research Ethics Committee (CUREC)).
Sokoloff, NJ, and I Dupont, (2005) 'Domestic violence at the intersections of race, class, and gender challenges and contributions to understanding violence against marginalized women in diverse communities' *Violence against women* 11, 38.
Spectrum Centre for Independent Living, (2018) Sticks and Stones: the Language of Disability, spectrumcil.co.uk/wp-content/uploads/2018/02/ULO19-The-Language-of-Disability.pdf.
Spivakovsky, C, (2014a) 'From punishment to protection: Containing and controlling the lives of people with disabilities in human rights' *Punishment & Society* 16, 560.
Spivakovsky, C, (2014b) 'Making risk and dangerousness intelligible in intellectual disability' *Griffith Law Review* 23, 389.
Spivakovsky, C, and LR Steele, (2022) 'Disability law in a pandemic: the temporal folds of medico-legal violence' *Social and Legal Studies* 31, 175.
Sprack, J, (2012) *A Practical Approach to Criminal Procedure, Fourteenth Edition* (Oxford University Press).
Squires, P, and DE Stephen, (2005) Rougher *Justice: Young People and Anti-social Behaviour*, (Willan Publishing).
Stanford, S, 'Critically Reflecting on Being "at Risk" and "a risk" in vulnerable people policing' in I Bartkowiak-Théron, and NL, Asquith (eds), (2012) *Policing Vulnerability* (The Federation Press).
Steele, L, (2017) 'Disabling forensic mental health detention: The carcerality of the disabled body' *Punishment & Society* 19, 327.
Steele, L, (2020) Disability, *Criminal Justice and Law* (Routledge).
Steele, S, and S Thomas, (2014) 'Disability at the periphery: legal theory, disability and criminal law' *Griffith Law Review* 23, 357.
Stern, V.H./Westminster Policy Forum, (2009) 'Reducing re-offending: mental health and value for money in the criminal justice system', *Transcript for Westminster Legal Policy Forum Keynote Seminar: 3rd November 2009*, www.westminsterforumprojects.co.uk/legalpolicyforum/publications.html.
Stewart, W, (2020) 'Intrapersonal and Inter-subjective Challenges of Researching Older and Vulnerable Males Convicted of Sexual Offences' *Ethics and Social Welfare* 14, 384.

Stewart, W, (2022) '"Helping Not Hurting": Horizontal Care and Learning to Peer Care in Prison' *Ethics and Social Welfare* 16, 90.

Stone, DA, (1985) *The Disabled State* (Macmillan).

Sykes, GM, (1958) *The Society of Captives: A Study of a Maximum-Security Prison* (Princeton University Press).

Sykes, GM, and D Matza, (1957) 'Techniques of neutralization: A theory of delinquency' *American Sociological Review* 22, 664.

Talbot, J./Prison Reform Trust, (2008) *No-one Knows: Report and Final Recommendations, Prisoners' Voices: Experiences of the criminal justice system by prisoners with learning disabilities and difficulties* (Prison Reform Trust).

Talbot, J, (2010) 'Prisoners' voices: experiences of the criminal justice system by prisoners with learning disabilities' *Tizard Learning Disability Review* 15, 33.

Talbot, J./PRT, (2010) *Fair Access to Justice? Support for vulnerable defendants in the criminal courts*, prisonreformtrust.org.uk/publication/fair-access-to-justice-support-for-vulnerable-defendants-in-the-criminal-courts/.

Talbot, J, (2012) *Fair Access to Justice? Support for vulnerable defendants in the criminal courts*, www.ojp.gov/ncjrs/virtual-library/abstracts/fair-access-justice-support-vulnerable-defendants-criminal-courts/.

Talbot, J, and C Riley, (2007) 'No One Knows: Offenders with learning difficulties and learning disabilities' *British Journal of Learning Disabilities* 35, 154.

Tavassoli, T, LJ Miller, SA Schoen, DM Nielsen, and S Baron-Cohen, (2014) 'Sensory over-responsivity in adults with autism spectrum conditions' *Autism* 18, 428.

The Advocate's Gateway, (2015) *Witnesses and Defendants with Autism: Memory and Sensory Issues*, www.theadvocatesgateway.org/.

The British Society of Criminology, (2006) *Code of Ethics for Researchers in the Field of Criminology*, www.britsoccrim.org/ethics/.

The Central and Western Sector of the West Midlands CPS, (2014), *CPS West Midlands Crown Court Unit Webpage*, www.cps.gov.uk/westmidlands/about/.

The Law Commission, (2016) 'Unfitness to Plead Volume 1: Report', *LAW COM No 364*, www.lawcom.gov.uk/project/unfitness-to-plead/.

The Rt Hon Theresa May MP and Home Office, (2014) *Care Not Custody speech*, www.gov.uk/government/speeches/care-not-custody-speech.

Thomas, C, (2007) *Sociologies of Disability and Illness. Contested ideas in Disability Studies and Medical Sociology* (Palgrave).

Thompson, EH, and W Doll, (1982) 'The burden of families coping with the mentally ill: An invisible crisis' *Family Relations* 31, 379.

Thorneycroft, R, and NL Asquith, (2021) 'Cripping criminology' *Theoretical Criminology* 25, 187.

Tonge, J, (2009) *Autism Bill* HL Deb 10 July 2009, col 894.

Tonry, M, (2010) '"Rebalancing the Criminal Justice System in favour of the victim": the costly consequences of populist rhetoric' in A Bottoms, and J Roberts *Hearing the Victim: Adversarial Justice, Crime Victims and the State* (Willan).

Transform Justice, (2017) *Transform Justice Briefing on the Prisons and Courts Bill*, files.justice.org.uk/wp-content/uploads/2017/04/06170657/JUSTICE-briefing-Prison-and-Courts-Bill.pdf.

Tremain, S, (2001) 'On the Government of Disability' *Social Theory and Practice* 27, 617.

Tremain, S, (2002) 'On the Subject of Impairment' in M Corker, and T Shakespeare (eds), *Disability/Postmodernity: Embodying Political Theory* (Continuum Press).

Tremain, S, (2005) 'Foucault, Governmentality, and Critical Disability Theory: An Introduction', in S Tremain (ed), *Foucault and the Government of Disability* (University of Michigan Press).

Tyler, N, and A Sheeran (eds), (2022) *Working with Autistic People in the Criminal Justice and Forensic Mental Health Systems: A Handbook for Practitioners* (Routledge).

UK Parliament, *The Autism Bill, Hansard* Bill 10, HC 2008-9.

Underwood, L, A Forrester, E Chaplin, and J McCarthy, (2013) 'Prisoners with neurodevelopmental disorders' *Journal of Intellectual Disabilities and Offending Behaviour* 4, 17.

Union of the Physically Impaired Against Segregation (UPIAS), (1976) *Fundamental Principles of Disability* (Union of the Physically Impaired Against Segregation), disability-studies.leeds.ac.uk/wp-content/uploads/sites/40/library/UPIAS-UPIAS.pdf.

United Nations General Assembly, (1993), *Standard Rules on the Equalization of Opportunities for Persons with Disabilities*, annexed to General Assembly resolution 48/96 of 20 December 1993, www.un.org/development/desa/disabilities/standard-rules-on-the-equalization-of-opportunities-for-persons-with-disabilities.html.

United Nations Committee on Economic, Social and Cultural Rights, (1994) *General Comment No. 5: Persons with Disabilities Adopted at the Eleventh Session of the Committee on Economic, Social and Cultural Rights* on 9 December 1994 (Contained in Document E/1995/22), www.refworld.org/pdfid/4538838f0.pdf.

US Access Board Courthouse Advisory Committee, (2006) *Justice for All: Designing Accessible Courthouses*, www.access-board.gov/ada/additional-resources/designing-accessible-courthouses.html.

Vinter, LP, (2020) *Working with autistic individuals in prison-based interventions to address sexual offending*, PhD thesis, Nottingham Trent University, Nottingham.

Vinter, LP, G Dillon, and B Winder, (2020) '"People don't like you when you're different": Exploring the prison experiences of autistic individuals' *Psychology, Crime and Law* 1.

Vivanti, G, (2019), 'Ask the Editor: What is the Most Appropriate Way to Talk About Individuals with a Diagnosis of Autism?' *Journal of Autism Developmental Disorders* 50, 691.

Walsh, T, (2018) 'Keeping vulnerable offenders out of the courts: lessons from the United Kingdom' *Criminal Law Journal* 42, 160.

Walton, H, SM Tomini, C Sherlaw-Johnson, PL Ng, and NJ Fulop, (2023) 'How is Social Care Provided in Adult Prisons in England and Wales?' *The British Journal of Social Work*, 53, 718.

Webb, EJ, DT Campbell, RD Schwartz, and L Sechrest, (1966) *Unobtrusive Measures: Non-reactive Research in the Social Sciences* (Rand McNally)

Web Accessibility Initiative, (2018) *Web Content Accessibility Guidelines* (WCAG), www.w3.org/WAI/standards-guidelines/wcag/.

Weller, P, (2014) 'Reconsidering legal capacity: radical critiques, governmentality and dividing practice' *Griffith Law Review*, 23, 498.

Wheat, K, E Brohan, C Henderson, and G Thorncroft, (2010) 'Mental illness and the workplace: conceal or reveal?' *Journal of the Royal Society of Medicine* 103, 83.

Wilczynski, A, (1997) 'Mad or bad? Child-killers, gender and the courts' *British Journal of Criminology* 37, 419.

Williams, J, (2002) 'Public Law Protection to Vulnerable Adults: the Debate Continues, So Does the Abuse' *Journal of Social Work* 2, 23.

Wing, L, (1971) *Autistic Children: A Guide for Parents* (Constable & Co).

Wing, L, (1981) 'Asperger's Syndrome: A clinical account' *Psychological Medicine* 11, 115.

Wing, L, (1995) *Autistic Spectrum Disorders: An Aid to Diagnosis* (National Autistic Society).

Woodbury-Smith, MR, ICH Clarea, AJ Hollanda and A Kearns, (2006) 'High functioning autistic spectrum disorders, offending and other law-breaking: findings from a community sample' *The Journal of Forensic Psychiatry & Psychology* 17, 108.

Woodbury-Smith, M, and K Dein, (2014) 'Autism spectrum disorder (ASD) and unlawful behaviour: Where do we go from here?' *Journal of Autism and Developmental Disorders*, 44, 2734.

Woods, R, (2017) 'Exploring how the social model of disability can be re-invigorated for autism: In response to Jonathan Levitt' *Disability and Society* 32, 1090.

World Health Organization (WHO), (1992) *The ICD-10 classification of mental and behavioural disorders: Clinical descriptions and diagnostic guidelines* (World Health Organization).

Worrall, A, (1981) 'Out of place: Female offenders in court' *Probation Journal* 28, 90.

Worthington, R, (2022) 'What support interventions are helpful for families and carers of autistic people in the criminal justice system?' in N Tyler, and A Sheeran (eds), *Working with Autistic People in the Criminal Justice and Forensic Mental Health Systems* (Routledge).

Young, S, RA González, H Mullens, L Mutch, I Malet-Lambert, and GH Gudjonsson, (2018) 'Neurodevelopmental disorders in prison inmates: Comorbidity and combined associations with psychiatric symptoms and behavioural disturbance' *Psychiatry Research* 261, 109.

Zedner, L, (2004) *Criminal Justice*, (Oxford University Press).

Zedner, L, (2007) 'Pre-crime and post-criminology?' *Theoretical Criminology* 11, 261.

Zedner, L, (2010) 'Reflections on Criminal Justice as a Social Institution' in T Newburn (ed), *The Eternal Recurrence of Crime and Control* (Oxford University Press).

Zedner, L, (2011) 'Putting Crime Back on the Agenda' in M Bosworth, and C Hoyle (eds), *What is Criminology?* (Oxford University Press).

Zedner, L, (2016) 'Penal subversions: When is a punishment not punishment, who decides and on what grounds?' *Theoretical Criminology* 20, 3.

INDEX

www.ingramcontent.com/pod-product-compliance
Ingram Content Group UK Ltd.
Pitfield, Milton Keynes, MK11 3LW, UK
UKHW020247290926
15470UKWH00002B/778

9 781509 956944